54507

MT
6
.R278
P7

Regelski, Thomas
A. 1941-

Principles and
problems of music
education

| DATE | | | |
|---|---|---|---|
| | | | |
| | | | |
| | | | |
| | | | |
| | | | |
| | | | |
| | | | |
| | | | |
| | | | |
| | | | |
| | | | |
| | | | |
| | | | |

WITHDRAWN

THOMAS A. REGELSKI

*State University College*
*Fredonia, New York*

# *principles*
# *and*
# *problems*
# *of*
# *music education*

Prentice-Hall, Inc., Englewood Cliffs, New Jersey

*Library of Congress Cataloging in Publication Data*

REGELSKI, THOMAS A, date
   Principles and problems of music education.

   Bibliography: p.
   1. Music—Instruction and study—Programmed instruc-
tion.   I. Title.
MT6.R278P7        372.8′7′044        74-14967
ISBN  0-13-709840-5
ISBN  0-13-709832-4 (pbk.)

© 1975 by PRENTICE-HALL, INC.
Englewood Cliffs, New Jersey

Printed in the United States of America

10  9  8  7  6  5  4  3  2  1

PRENTICE-HALL INTERNATIONAL, INC., *London*
PRENTICE-HALL OF AUSTRALIA, PTY. LTD., *Sydney*
PRENTICE-HALL OF CANADA, LTD., *Toronto*
PRENTICE-HALL OF INDIA PRIVATE LIMITED, *New Delhi*
PRENTICE-HALL OF JAPAN, INC., *Tokyo*

To

MISS VIRGINIA MEIERHOFFER

who inspired me to seek the best for
Music Education, and who started me off
on the right foot as a teacher

# contents

preface, ix

introduction, xv

CHAPTER ONE

## learning and music, 1

A Philosophy of Learning, 2    Evidences of Learning, 4
Transfer of Learning, 6    Teaching for Meaning, 8
Perception and Conception in Music, 10    Summary, 15
Frames, 18

CHAPTER TWO

## teaching music, 40

Structuring Learning, 41    Listening, 42    Performance, 43
Why Teach Performance?, 46    Summary, 49    Frames 51

CHAPTER THREE

## music education for the individual, 62

Readiness, 64    The Activity, 65
Student Attitude and Interest (Motivation), 67
Decision Making and Problem Solving, 70
Observable Behavior, 72    The Consequences of an Action, 74
Adaptive or Nonadaptive Behavior, 74    Summary, 77    Frames, 79

CHAPTER FOUR

## understanding and guiding
## student behavior, 93

A Good Offense Is Your Best Defense, 94    Discipline Redefined, 97
Growth-typical Behavior, 99
Curricular Organization: Three Styles, 102    Adolescent Traits, 103
Guidelines for Dealing with Behavior Problems, 107
Classroom Teaching Styles, 113    Permissipline Reconsidered, 115
The Problem of Grades, 119
Other Sources of Problem Behavior, 121    Summary, 127
Frames, 128


CHAPTER FIVE

## a point of view
## on music and behaviorism, 157

The Dilemma, 159    Behaviorism, 159
Criticism of Behaviorism, 160    Purposes and Nature of Art, 163
Purposes and Nature of Arts Education, 164
Criticism of Some Past Educational Practices, 166
Conditions of Synthesis, 168
Operant Conditioning and Behavior, 174    Summary, 177
One Additional Consideration: An Editorial, 180    Frames, 184


CHAPTER SIX

## types of musical behavior, 205

Cognitive Behaviors, 207    Affective Behaviors, 210
Psychomotor Behavior, 213    Summary of Covert Behaviors, 219
Overt Behaviors, 220    Summary, 226    Frames, 230


CHAPTER SEVEN

## the design of behavioral objectives
## for music learning, 244

Precautions, 245    Elements of an Objective, 246
Analyses of Sample Objectives, 248
Example of Relating Objectives, 250
Example of a Cognitive Objective for General Music Classes, 252
Example of an Affective Objective for Performance Classes, 254
Examples of Skill Objectives for Performance Groups, 255
A Recommended Form for Objectives, 256    Exceptions, 259
Summary and Conclusion, 261    Frames, 265

CHAPTER EIGHT

## *the use of behavioral objectives, 279*

*Behavioral Objectives as a Teaching Medium, 280*
*Interpreting the Results of Behavioral Objectives, 281*
*Evaluation, 284   Revision, 284   Reapplication, 286*
*Systematic Evaluation: Summary, 287*
*Behavioral Objectives as Aids in Implementing Activities, 288*
*Behavioral Objectives as Long-range Curricular Goals, 290*
*Behavioral Objectives and Short-term Planning, 294*
*Behavioral Objectives as Personal Research, 295*
*Behavioral Objectives as Student "Contracts," 299*
*Behavioral Objectives as Bases for Grading, 301*
*Grading Skilled Learning, 304   Codetta, 305   Frames, 307*

## **a bibliography for teachers, 319**

## *index, 323*

# *preface*

Writing a book of this kind at times seems like a very unnatural act. It is unnatural to the degree that it must represent a temporary stopping-off point of a thinking process that is ongoing and resistant to any single once-and-for-all formulation. It is also unnatural in that it can only represent the writer's own thoughts—as they are impressed by discoveries and developments of other writers and researchers—on the issues at hand. These developments and discoveries march ever on, while the ideas considered in these pages come to a stop—for the time being at least—in their formulation as written words.

Unnatural as this may be, it is seemingly unavoidable. Sometimes it is necessary for one to stop and look where he is before he can continue on his way. Sometimes what seemed like a promising route turns out to be a dead end, or involves detours and U-turns. Such events seldom have an air of inviolable authenticity or absolute truth, and for these reasons the current work can best be regarded as an attempt to enable the reader to travel the same roads, to consider many of the same problems, and to discover for himself some of the most promising paths. Absolutes in the way of total certainty are seldom, if ever, encountered along the way. This is the kind of venture that never reaches a definitive conclusion: you never arrive! You can merely reach a point where certain new problems and challenges await your attention and efforts.

For these reasons this book may be unique in several ways, in my opinion, in that it attempts to bring to the awareness of the readers those factors that condition or influence music learning of all kinds. It is not a methods text that presents formulas and prescriptions for mindless action. It is instead, among other things, an attempt to highlight the need for an application of principles of learning and philosophical points of view to typical problems of music learning in all areas of music education. It recognizes that a gulf can often separate what is learned in aesthetics and psychology courses from the practices and procedures of teaching music; and that all music teachers can profit from a thoughtful consideration of the factors that such disciplines bring to bear on frequently encountered musical and pedagogical problems.

The points considered here should provide the foundations for concepts, principles, and theories of a pedagogy of music. They are related—insofar as it is possible in a book—to actual and typical classroom problems in all the various types of music education: instrumental music, choral and vocal music, and general music. They call upon readers *to think* seriously in order to invent and apply ideas of their own. Little of value will result if the reader does not make an active attempt to transform these concepts into teaching techniques that suit the circumstances and idiosyncracies of the variety of teaching situations he is likely to encounter.

Not only is education in general *not* a singular thing, but music education and the practices it must adopt is perhaps even more diverse. Given this infinite variety of teaching problems, it seems unlikely that a single "method," as mastered by the incipient, beginning, or in-service teacher, is likely to serve equally well in all teaching circumstances. Thus, the teacher is called upon to analyze the situation and to draw upon a framework of general principles that can allow the formulation of a teaching approach suited to the contingencies of the situation at hand. This book seeks to establish such a framework, while at the same time suggesting *general* teaching techniques that can, with appropriate alteration and adjustment, be applied fruitfully in a wide range of particular instances. It also presents examples of teaching practices that should, at the very least, be reconsidered in light of currently understood principles of learning.

The conceptual framework sought here not only can serve to assist the teacher in understanding and dealing with daily and long-range teaching efforts, but also can enable each teacher to understand the nature of a total music program and its application. Though "subject matter" teachers are usually able to place their efforts within the total context of instruction in their area, music teachers often seem unaware of what other music specialists are doing, why they are doing it, and how. General music teachers, choral and vocal teachers, and instrumental teachers can often be unaware of the problems and practices of one another, and can have difficulty in understanding the role and place of their efforts in the total scheme of music instruction in general.

This text seeks to overcome some of the seeming inertia of this condition by considering the problems of musical instruction as somewhat common to all music teachers. Most of the principles to be considered are dealt with generally, from each teacher's particular point of view. This can enable each teacher to understand the efforts of other teachers, and at the same time to appreciate the fact that most of the bases and goals of music learning are the same. It is only the means that are unique.

What some readers might consider a lack of definite methodology, practices, and materials should be considered, therefore, as an opportunity for specifics to be filled in by the reader, in conjunction with the college teacher.

Here, each music education specialty can be dealt with in terms that are unique to the class, geographic area, state policy, or school system. In-service teachers are encouraged to derive specifics that suit their unique contingencies.

Though it is probably true that a person cannot be taught to be a good teacher, it is also true that a person can learn to be a good teacher. College-level instruction or in-service education can greatly assist the teacher to learn how to teach well. When combined with psychological understanding designed to allow the teacher to analyze the learning situation before acting, such instruction can help avoid much of the trial and error that would otherwise be necessary. It can also provide a broad enough foundation for each teacher to develop his or her own strengths and potential in ways that are unique to each teacher, and to each teaching position. To this end, a consideration of the learning theories, philosophies, and traits of human development that are being applied today in virtually all other segments of the public school have particular merit in the learning process of becoming a successful teacher of music.

Psychology and philosophy have not always been separate disciplines, nor are they in every case today. Psychology as we know it today grew out of the philosophical concerns of the previous century; in its early years, it often took the form of the psychology of aesthetics. William James, the philosopher-psychologist who is among the earliest noted American thinkers in this area, undertook in 1892 a series of *Talks to Teachers*. As with much of his thought, his advice on the relationship between psychology and teaching is still relevant today, and it reinforces the basic premises of this book. After warning that, "It is only the fundamental conceptions of psychology which are of real value to the teacher . . . ," he clearly states how teaching methods should evolve:

> . . . you make a great, a very great mistake, if you think that psychology, being the science of the mind's laws, is something from which you can deduce definite programmes and schemes and methods of instruction for immediate classroom use. Psychology is a science, and teaching is an art; and sciences never generate arts directly out of themselves. An intermediary inventive mind must make the application by using its originality.
> . . . A science only lays down lines within which the rules of the art must fall, laws which the follower of the art must not transgress; but what particular thing he shall positively do within these lines is left exclusively to his own genius. One genius will do his work well and succeed in one way, while another succeeds as well quite differently; yet neither will transgress the lines.
> . . . And so everywhere the teaching must *agree* with the psychology, but need not necessarily be the only kind of teaching that would so agree for many diverse methods of teaching may equally well agree with psychological laws.[1]

It is in this spirit that this book is offered. Its intent is to assist the reader in learning these major "psychological laws" insofar as they are understood and regarded today, and to suggest a general application of these laws to the

[1] William James, *Talks to Teachers* (New York: Norton, 1958), pp. 23–24.

various aspects and kinds of musical instruction. The inventive mind and genius of each reader will need to be called into play to invent other applications, as well as to modify the many general suggestions provided here from all areas of musical instruction to suit the particular circumstances of an instructional problem. Thus, the major attempt of this work is to assist the reader in acquiring the principles with which *to think* about instructional problems and the encouragement *to apply* this thinking by suitable modification of pedagogical ideas—as presented in this book, or as invented by the teacher—to real instructional problems.

You will note throughout this book that it is often necessary to evaluate a particular instructional problem in qualitative terms. Certain practices or alternatives are qualified as more or less successful, stronger or weaker in potential. The inability of a writer to conduct a true dialogue with the reader seems inevitable in a work designed to encourage individual thinking. However, the reader is encouraged to attempt such a dialogue with the writer, challenging certain assumptions, resisting certain conclusions. Comments and observations based on such an interior dialogue might be noted in the margins or in a separate location; certainly, they should form the basis of ongoing discussions and debates among the readers and between the readers and the college teacher.

Finally, the awareness has always existed that not even the psychological laws referred to by James are susceptible to objective or impartial application. A subjective side exists as well:

> We know in advance, if we are psychologists, that certain methods will be wrong, so our psychology saves us from mistakes. It makes us, moreover, more clear as to what we are about. We gain confidence in respect to any method which we are using as soon as we believe that it has theory as well as practice at its back. Most of all, it fructifies our independence and it reanimates our interest, to see our subject at two different angles, . . . Such a complete knowledge as this of the pupil, at once intuitive and analytic, is surely the knowledge at which every teacher ought to aim.[2]

Thus, there is a certain inevitability that our personalities, experiences, and musical backgrounds—and our resulting unique philosophical points of view —will color our application of these concepts. For this reason, it is necessary to adopt an inquiring attitude and a tolerance for diverse applications, as long as each is supported by an updated understanding of these psychological laws.

Therefore, the present book is at best a useful analysis and appreciation of some of the major principles and problems of music learning, in terms of some major psychological laws. At worst, it inevitably presents a point of view colored by the unique experiences, learnings, and applications of the writer. Yet even this is equally useful if it stimulates a deep consideration of each principle and problem, as well as a curiosity nurtured by the issues analyzed.

It is anticipated that the college teacher will supplement this book with

2 *Ibid.,* pp. 25–26.

whatever complementary or contrasting ideas are suitable to the purposes for which the course is being offered. As usual, the synthesis alluded to as "meaning" or "relevance" must be forged by each reader: no author or teacher can do that for anyone. How you teach will indicate the nature and extent of your synthesis. How well you are able to seize upon, analyze, and apply all the principles to be considered will determine the success of your learning within the context of this book.

T.A.R.

# introduction

During the early years of school music, music educators had but one objective for instruction in music: for students to learn to read music and to sing well. With these criteria in mind, it was very easy to determine whether or not instruction was successful; the students in the singing classes could either read music and sing well, or they could not.

As the profession matured, instrumental music was added to the school music programs. Here again, there was but one major objective: to teach youngsters to play musical instruments. The operative principle was that performance and contact with music developed musical understanding, but learning was assessed in terms of performance behavior rather than in terms of understanding. Either the student read music and played his instrument, or he did not.

Once these two major goals of school music had become firmly established, another objective was added: to teach performance skills of a high caliber, that is, to develop bands, choruses, and orchestras of significant musical merit. With the institution of this objective came the development of the Contest, the Competition Festival, and the process of adjudication. By grading the difficulty of the available repertory for school groups, and by adjudicating the performance of groups and individuals, a serious attempt was made to improve the level of musical performance. This amounted to a more organized attempt to define learning in music in terms of performance, for now the *criteria* of acceptable musical behavior were codified and specified in advance.

This procedure worked well, perhaps too well. Some music educators became increasingly aware of several potential difficulties. First, the procedure tended to encourage a very small repertory, since music for competition was often over-rehearsed. Second, it became increasingly clear that the performance of music, while necessary and helpful for the talented few, did not provide an understanding or appreciation of music as an art for the population at large. In other words, performance requires *overt behavior,* and understanding and appreciation generally involve *covert behavior.*[1]

Hence, a third objective came into being, that of directly teaching musical understanding and the appreciation of music. Unfortunately, this objective was neither well understood nor well implemented because this kind of instruction tended to the study of *facts about music,* which have little to do with the aural perception of music. Initial approaches attempted to render certain assumed covert conditions—such as understanding—by overt means. The direct result of this new emphasis was a plethora of workbooks dealing with musical information and bearing little or no direct relation to listening skills or the cognition of music. Implicit here was the assumption that understanding and appreciation were the result of acquiring musical information.

Finally, the idea that musical instruction should be the study of *music itself*—of concepts of music rather than information about music—became a major objective of music educators, at least at the theoretical level. Professional writings were concerned almost exclusively with the conceptual approach to music. Teaching materials intended to develop musical concepts were designed by both educators and commercial concerns. The only problem was that the older objectives of teaching youngsters to sing and play instruments and to play and sing well remained ascendant among most of the teachers in the field. School music often continued to emphasize the performance of music by the talented few and tended to overlook the vast majority of the students, who had little talent or inclination toward the performance of music, but who had the ability to understand and respond to music at the conceptual level. Recently, this trend has shown signs of weakening. A younger generation of teachers, well taught by the educational theorists who comprise music education faculties in the teacher training programs, attempted to implement the conceptual approach to the teaching of music.

But even with the advent of conceptual teaching in the general music arena, the problem of learning theory and instructional objectives has not been solved. Indeed, it may have been complicated, for conceptual learning is not as obvious in terms of overt indications of effective learning as are performance skills. Even with the latter, when the student either can or cannot show overt evidence of performing the desired skilled behavior, it is difficult to tell how much true understanding or rote imitation is involved. Conceptual learning—whether involved in consuming, composing, or performing music—is very subtle and therefore more difficult to evaluate because so much covert behavior is involved. This book will attempt to clarify some of the current misconceptions about music learning and its manifestations by providing a more viable means for the teacher to understand, prepare, and use valid instructional objectives according to established learning theory.

The use of learning theory and the development and use of instructional

---

[1] *Overt behavior* involves actions that are outwardly apparent and thus open to view. *Covert behavior* involves actions that are purely mental or intraorganic, and thus not readily observable as such.

objectives by the music teacher is dependent on a working understanding of several important aspects of the learning process:

1. What is music learning and how is it identified?
2. What different kinds of learning are possible in musical situations?
3. Which kinds of learning are most suitable in specific kinds of situations?
4. What are musical concepts?
5. How are they learned?
6. How will the teacher know when or to what degree concepts have been learned?
7. What methods and materials seem most effective in specific kinds of situations?

Once the nature of learning in music is clarified in your mind it remains to be seen:

1. How instructional objectives can be devised to meet the needs of the learning situation at hand.
2. How instructional objectives specified in terms of overt behavior assist in defining the musical concepts to be learned.
3. How these behavioral objectives assist the learner in the acquisition and identification of learning.
4. How behavioral objectives permit the teacher *and* the student to identify and evaluate learning.
5. How behavioral objectives clearly indicate the general kinds of methods and materials likely to be most suitable.
6. How behavioral objectives and supporting learning theory can help clarify the issues of discipline and problem behavior.
7. How behavioral objectives are indispensable to an understanding of current thought on the aesthetics of music, and aesthetic education in general.

Therefore, the instructional objectives for this book can now be stated in general and long-range behavioral terms.

Given specific learning situations and concepts or skills to be learned, the teacher will be able to create suitable teaching objectives that:

1. Are conducive to learning in the specific learning situation.
2. Clearly specify the concepts or skills to be learned.
3. Indicate who will be affected by the instruction.
4. Provide means for observing or evaluating covert learning in terms of overt behavior.
5. Assist the learner in the identification of his own progress.
6. Provide the teacher with a valid means of identifying and assessing the learning of *each student*.
7. Clearly indicate the possible methods, strategies, and materials to be used.

8. Properly accord with recognized learning theory.
9. Properly provide for "feeling" and aesthetic responses to music.

This may seem like a large and overwhelming assignment, but the responsibilities of teaching and guiding youngsters through musical instruction to the rewards of music are equally severe. Because many collegiate music faculties resist the notion that teaching is based upon a firm discipline, which is separate from the discipline being taught, it often happens that many prospective or experienced music teachers are somewhat deficient in the skills and learnings that constitute the act of teaching.

Even though this study seeks to make the act of teaching music a more empirical, controlled process, the essence of what is contained in these pages is often philosophic. In sorting and examining the many basic issues facing current music educators, resource is made of the empirical investigations of learning theorists and psychologists. As will be abundantly clear, however, the "scientific truths" or "facts" developed by psychologists in the sterility of the testing laboratory, or in experiments with typing classes, are not capable of strict or pure implementation where the issues of arts education are at stake. Teachers of the arts, as well as artists, have always been able to perceive in the aesthetic or artistic experience a fundamental quality that is unique to it. Therefore, the main task here has been to conceive of new meanings and implications of currently accepted research in learning, as they may apply to the act of teaching music.

Therefore, it will not be the facts as such that are important. These you could find in any good educational psychology text. What is important is *an application, and even alteration where necessary, of the facts to the problems of teaching music.* New meaning is thus given to these facts, and many of the traditional criteria and goals of music education are called into question.

The American philosopher Susanne Langer, whose writings on aesthetics and Mind have influenced the present work, has written about this problem of philosophically manipulating established "facts." In complaining about the banality and sterility of purely factual research in psychology, she writes:

> We have reached a point at which a sounder substructure is required, and the philosophical work of construing the facts in logically negotiable, intellectually fertile ways is imperative.
> If a science is to come into existence at all, it will do so as more and more powerful concepts are introduced. Their formulation is often the work of empirical investigators, but it is philosophical, nonetheless, because it is concerned with meanings rather than facts, and the systematic construction of meanings is philosophy. Wherever a new way of thinking may originate, its effect is apt to be revolutionary because it transforms questions and criteria, and therewith the appearance and value of facts.[2]

This, in sum, is the major purpose of this work: to transform the "questions and criteria, and therewith the appearance and value of facts" of both

---

[2] Susanne K. Langer, *Mind: An Essay on Human Feeling,* Vol. 1 (Baltimore: Johns Hopkins University Press, 1967), p. 52.

the psychology of learning (which has steadfastly avoided learning in the arts because they are considered subjective and mystical) and the "science" of teaching music (which has steadfastly maintained that because the arts are dealing with subjective realities and truths teaching music must therefore be totally subjective and personal in its approach and methodology).

Music teachers must realize that their responsibilities are dual. They must master their own discipline and they must become competent musician-scholars. Those who in the formal sense wish to be teachers of music—music educators—must go one step beyond their musical capabilities and master the science of teaching music. Though there will always be much leeway for purely human decisions and functioning in any aspect of teaching, fewer decisions about the specific nature of the instruction to be undertaken can be left solely to the caprices of individual teachers.

This book makes no pretense about leading to a mastery of the skills necessary to teach, but it can provide the important conceptual bases necessary for the teacher to develop these skills and cognitions independently. In order to perform this challenging task, this book itself attempts to accord with the learning theory and teaching skills it will deal with—as much as the medium of a printed book can do, that is.

For this reason, this book is not quite like an ordinary textbook. Periodically, you will be asked questions or given certain tasks to perform before going on. On the basis of your answers you will be directed to other specific places in the text, or given other tasks to do. In order to profit most from this kind of teaching, you must follow directions explicitly rather than reading along a page at a time as in ordinary texts. This format has been devised to help you meet your needs and to avoid unnecessary reading. If you approach this text with the correct spirit and follow directions, you will become increasingly aware of your growing competence with the learnings involved.

Because you will find yourself skipping back and forth throughout the book, you will probably find two bookmarks useful. At this time, if you haven't already, you should also furnish yourself with a pencil and some scrap paper. Then, hopefully, you will be ready to work.

# learning and music

Knowledge grows with exploration, adding new facts, correcting old beliefs. It grows like a tree, at every tip, so that the crown seems to spread out an ever-growing fringe.

. . . in the growth of culture, as in the growth of a high organism, there is something that does not increase by addition of elements, but by modification and stretching that is mentality itself, which comprises much more than knowledge. Pure factual knowledge, however wide, would not constitute a mental life.

Susanne K. Langer, Philosophical Sketches (New York: New American Library, 1964), pp. 123, 124.

Learning has been defined in various ways by various psychologists representing various schools of psychology. For several hundred years it has also occupied much of the thinking of philosophers whose theories of the sources, structure, methods, and validity of knowledge have often formed the cornerstone of their composite philosophical theories.

A recent and important philosopher, Susanne K. Langer, has recently taken an entirely new approach to knowledge in her book *Mind: An Essay on Human Feeling* (Baltimore: Johns Hopkins University Press, 1967) and in writings that led to this culminating work. *Mind* and most of the previous writings are especially important to the music educator, for they frequently refer to the nature of musical art in explaining and arriving at a concept of all art. In *Mind,* however, it becomes apparent that in all of her writings, Langer has not been developing an esthetic philosophy at all; rather, she has been developing a theory of mind.

One reviewer has very concisely summarized the relevance of her recent work for those involved in arts education:

> . . . Langer approaches the theory of mind from the esthetic rather than from the cognitive angle. . . . Mind in its most elementary form is not *res cognitans* [i.e., a thing which knows] but rather feeling. Feeling is an aspect of evolving reality which emerges gradually within the system of nature, becomes progressively differentiated and articulated, and achieves its fullest expression in the rhythms, patterns, and symbols of art. If we are to find the key to the understanding of mind we must consequently look first at artistic expression in all its forms.[1]

This brilliant new conception of mind brings new light and relevance to the arts. It also should foster some new thinking as to the processes and goals of arts education.

> Mind has traditionally been regarded as that which thinks, and above all as that which thinks rationally; and esthetics has consequently tended to become a luxury item, if not a downright nuisance. If, however, mind in its elemental form is feeling rather than knowing, then not only does esthetics become central in a philosophy of mind but the sciences which purport to study mind, the so-called behavioral sciences, must undergo a drastic reorientation. This promises to be healthy.[2]

It might be added, parenthetically, that the so-called science of teaching in the area of esthetic education could also undergo a "drastic reorientation." Clearly, factual teaching as it has been known and practiced in esthetic edu-

---

[1] Robert B. MacLeod, "The Arts as Phenomena of the Life Process," review of *Mind: An Essay on Human Feeling,* by Susanne K. Langer, in *Science,* 157 (September 1967), 1544.
[2] *Ibid.*

cation will have no significance if it does not enhance the ability of the individual to feel, to have feelings. In this sense, art, and in the specific case at hand, music, becomes a kind of mental process that is as important, if not more so, as the factual, object-oriented, discursive thinking ascribed to intellect by science. It becomes a logic of another kind, one that increases intuitive knowledge of things and ourselves by providing a new and direct contact with our feelings. In this way too, so-called appreciation courses in the arts should be separated from the more scientific and fact-oriented disciplines of musicology, art history, and the like.

Before reading any further, use your bookmark to identify this page, since you will be returning to it in a few minutes. Then go to Frame 1 on page 18.

---

It should be noted at this point that the "symbols of art" referred to in the quote on page 2 do not refer to the notational symbols of music, or even musical "symbolism" (in the sense that triple rhythms in medieval music symbolized the Holy Trinity). Instead, the symbols are what Langer has called "the art symbol" or "expressive form," by which she means the work of art as perceived and the manner in which it seems to embody or reflect feelings or felt life. It is a kind of artistic equivalent for inner feelings, inner experiences. The artist makes an object or event of his feelings and offers it to others for their contemplation. As such, the art object

> . . . seems, indeed, to have a sort of life, or be imbued with feeling, or somehow, without being a genuine practical object, yet present the beholder with more than an arrangement of sense data. It carries with it something that people have sometimes called a quality, . . . sometimes an emotional content, or the emotional tone of the work, or simply its life. This is what I mean by *artistic import*.[3]

Ideally, then, it is the realization of "expressive form" leading to the apprehension of "felt life" or "artistic import" that should be the major goal of esthetic education in general, and music education in particular. As a result, it should be the guiding principle as you begin to formulate your own instructional objectives. With this line of thought, "the art symbol," "expressive form," "felt life," or "artistic import" take precedence over pure facts and information, as the student learns to apprehend these qualities as realized in the work of art.

*GO TO FRAME 2, PAGE 18.*

[3] Susanne K. Langer, *Problems of Art* (New York: Charles Scribner's Sons, 1957), p. 129. For more information, see all of Chapter 9 of this volume, "The Art Symbol and the Symbol in Art," pp. 124–39.

## EVIDENCES OF LEARNING

Thus far we have covered some of the philosophical and logical premises to be considered in structuring learning situations in music classes. It is now time to consider learning as psychologists view it.

First, it is useful to describe how learning is identified by describing the *results* of learning in general terms.

1. Learning results when behavior is changed as a result of experience.

This description requires that the teacher make two important provisions in the formulation of instructional objectives. There should be (a) much actual experience with the object(s) and behavior(s) to be learned, and (b) various means for observing such change(s) of behavior; in music classes this often means finding ways of externalizing responses that are inherently covert or internal.

2. Learning is also shown when the *frequency of a behavior increases*. It is not, as is too often thought, simply the acquisition of knowledge or skill by means of rote training or the like. It is the kind of comprehension or mastery that results in observable changes in the frequency of a behavior.

Not *any* new response indicates the kind of learning sought by the teacher; learning can also result from incorrect responses. If the teacher assists the student in assessing the incorrect responses and provides other opportunities for the correct response, then other positive learning can take place.

This definition of learning also aptly describes a less desirable kind of learning. This occurs when the learner literally "learns" the *wrong* response or when the frequency of this wrong behavior increases. This too is learning, of course, but not usually the kind for which teachers plan. Therefore, since wrong responses are inevitable—even among the best students (and professionals)—the reasons for increasing experience with the learning at hand become even more evident.

The more experience with the learning at hand, the more opportunity and likelihood there is for the correct behavioral response to occur. Multiple experiences with the learning also insures against those situations where the correct response occurs *accidentally*. A second or third opportunity will soon bring to light whether the behavior has in fact signaled learning or luck.

*GO TO FRAME 3, PAGE 18*

To put it another way, a behavioral objective indicates and clarifies many of the elements in a structured learning situation:

1. *Given.* This provision specifies what material or means will be used. In the lesson just considered, this would entail specifying the name of the composition, and possibly the specific passage in question.

2. *Who.* This part of the objective clearly designates who will be affected by the instruction; in this instance it would be each individual in the chorus.

3. *Covert behavior.* At this point, the kind of mental activity involved in the completion of the lesson is emphasized; in the example being considered here, that mental activity would involve attention to the notation of the passage.

4. *What.* This section outlines the content, instruction, knowledge, skill, and so forth, that will be the basis for the lesson. Thus, in the example given, pitch, rhythm, and phrasing are the important areas under consideration.

5. *Overt behavior.* Here, the activity, device, technique, or means of making the covert behavior observable, or measurable, is indicated. This section is of considerable importance. It insures that the teacher thinks of student learning in terms of overt behavior, rather than in terms of teacher activity. In the example given, the teacher would observe the ability of the chorus to deal with the notation in terms of pitch, rhythm, and phrasing, by performing it (not by passing a test, or by writing an essay on the passage).

6. *Proficiency.* Where applicable or useful, the degree of behavioral success may be indicated. In the given lesson, the qualification "accurately and with consistency thereafter" would indicate the degree of mastery sought by the teacher and could serve as a criterion for both teacher and student evaluation of the performance on this and subsequent occasions. Some teachers feel that criteria should be more specific, and might expect "approximately ninty-five percent accuracy."

One further factor could have been indicated, and should be in situations where it is relevant:

7. *Time allowed.* Often the amount of time necessary for, or the amount of time allotted to, the acquisition of the desired behavior should be indicated. This is more than a practical detail. The amount of time necessary to complete a given task can often have great bearing on how much has been learned, or how well it was learned.

a. In the objective at hand, a teacher preparing for a concert might specify the amount of time he can afford to spend learning the passage in question. If it cannot be learned as specified within that time period, he may then (1) take his chances in concert; (2) give in and use more time; or (3) discard the piece as beyond the competency of the chorus (or of the director?).

b. There are many situations where time need not be a factor; in the lesson at hand, a lack of time specification would indicate that the teacher attaches enough importance to the activity to devote whatever time is necessary—hopefully, though, spreading such rehearsing over several rehearsals.

c. Often, when the time factor is long-range or on-going, it can be best located at the end of an objective: "by the end of the term" and "improving to ninety-five percent accuracy by the next marking period" are typical long-range time references.

d. More specific or daily time allocations are often included in the "given" factor that usually begins an objective: "Given their choice of materials, and twenty minutes," "Given an unfamiliar composition, and ten minutes of practice" are typical ways of doing this.

In sum, then, a behavioral objective can greatly assist the teacher in organizing the learning situation, and in evaluating the effect of the teaching undertaken in terms of student learning. When the students are advised of the objectives at hand, it is more possible for the students to evaluate their own performance. In a way this may be of even more importance, for often a major responsibility of teachers in performance classes is to develop musical independence on the part of the students. Students must be able to practice and perform independently. To do so, they must be able to evaluate their own performance.

## TRANSFER OF LEARNING

Here is a description of another aspect of learning that is useful to the music teacher.

> Learning is shown when the learner displays the ability to respond to a new situation (stimulus) in terms of successful behavior(s) used previously under different conditions or in a different context.

Some psychologists call this *transfer of learning*. One writes, "Transfer of a behavior is likely whenever the person recognizes a new situation as similar to other situations where the behavior has been appropriate."[4]

Applying this to a performance situation, transfer of learning will have occurred when a group is consistently able to cope successfully with a musical problem that occurs—in similar form—in many musical contexts. For example, many young performers have not learned the concept of simple and compound meters effectively, and thus invariably confuse $\frac{6}{8}$ ♩ ♪♩ ♪ and

$\frac{4}{4}$ ♩. ♪♩. ♪ in their performances. In a given composition, at a given time, the teacher may think the problem has been solved. In another composition sometime later when the same metric problem recurs, if the group is able to perform it correctly without undue coaxing, transfer of learning has occurred. If they are unable to perform it accurately, no transfer of learning has occurred, and some psychologists would be inclined to argue that no

[4] Lee J. Cronbach, *Educational Psychology* (New York: Harcourt Brace Jovanovich, Inc., 1963), p. 346.

learning had ever occurred. They would not even consider the temporary mastery of the problem on the first occasion as learning since it had no continuous connection to subsequent applications.

So often, it seems, teachers overlook these important distinctions and find themselves repeating the same information, giving the same explanations and demonstrations, rehearsing the same general problems. This is often a sign that the teacher (1) has no behavioral objective with its criteria in mind; and (2) has been using rote methods of instruction (correction) where students imitate the correct behavior in a given situation but never comprehend the basic musical concept at hand.

Thus, students are unable to transfer this learning to new yet similar situations and contexts. They require the direct assistance of the teacher on each subsequent occasion. When this happens outside of school as well as in the lesson or rehearsal, it is easy to see how inefficient the process is, and how little is contributed to the possibility of a student functioning musically on his own after graduation from school. It can be assumed that this is the reason that many school musicians cease performing upon graduation.

Another way of approaching this aspect of learning—the ability to respond to a new situation or stimulus in terms of behavior previously used under different conditions or with different stimuli—is to apply Jean Piaget's principle of *conservation* to musical situations at various levels. Conservation ". . . refers to an individual's ability to retain the invariant qualities of a particular stimulus when the stimulus field has been changed."[5]

The sonata principle and the fugue principle are examples of a type of "invariant quality" very likely to be found in compositions bearing those titles (as well as elsewhere). The apprehension of these principles in operation in any given composition indicates that the learner has learned them to be characteristics of that particular composition. Play the same work for him again, and he is likely to respond with the same learned behavior by identifying the form correctly. But play another sonata or another fugue for him? This changes the stimulus field and if the learner is able to recognize the "invariant qualities" of the sonata or fugue principle in these new situations, then he has demonstrated *conservation*.

If he cannot deal with the change of stimulus field, then more experiences with the invariant qualities of these two principles are needed, and more opportunity is needed to apply these learnings.

Thus, frequent and varied opportunities with these invariant qualities serve two purposes: (1) they help in the cognition and recognition of the invariant features; and (2) they provide opportunities for the learner to apply his learning to a variety of new and increasingly refined situations.

*GO TO FRAME 4, PAGE 19.*

[5] Marilyn P. Zimmerman, "Percept and Concept: Implications of Piaget," *Music Educators Journal,* 56, No. 6 (February, 1970), 49.

## TEACHING FOR MEANING

Learning of the kind just described is dependent on the *personal experience* of the learner. In all cases the learner must be actively involved with the material to be learned. As a general rule, *personal experience forms the basis for meaning*. This principle has several implications for the music teacher.

1. The teacher must provide many and varied opportunities for the learner to experience the concepts, skills, cognitions, affections, or attitudes to be learned *for himself*.

2. Such actual involvements must be progressively differentiated and articulated. This should promote an increasing level of refinement and sophistication with the learning. For example:

a. The ABA principle might first be encountered in a small three-part song.

b. After sufficient contact with this concept of *statement–departure–return*, a longer three-part song form can be profitably encountered.

c. Following more perception and analysis of this longer song form; a Sousa march with a *song form–trio–song form repeated* can be undertaken.

d. Then the *minuet–trio–minuet repeated* can be introduced and investigated.

e. And so on, continuing to the sonata and fugal principles, and other such tripartite structures and their various ramifications.

Of course, not all of this sequencing would occur within the period of a few days or even a few weeks. It probably would be spread over many months, interspersed with other learning—textures, keys, techniques of development, augmentation, diminution, and so forth—all of which would work together toward a more complete understanding of the musical art.

After such progressively differentiated and articulated contacts and experiences with each of these different—yet similar—manifestations of the ABA principle, each stated in behavioral terms that insure that every learner has in fact grasped the application at hand, then the learner is well prepared to respond to this principle with greater understanding and insight. The conceptual bases underlining this musical device will be best established for each individual who has responded appropriately in each activity. It will have "meaning" for the learner.

Meaning results from personal experience. Thus, the ideas of hot and cold have different "meanings" for an eskimo and the natives of the Amazon rain forests, each according to his own personal experience with temperature variations.

3. The teacher must, therefore, do more than just provide the opportunity to apply such concepts or skills as the ABA principle. Learning will be more focused and more effective if:

a. the teacher, through probing questions, provocative statements, and exploratory activities, leads the learner to discover the concept or skill by himself at his own level of learning and rate of speed:

b. the teacher provides ample opportunity for such discoveries to be applied, interpreted again, reapplied, reinforced, and refined; in other words, provides the opportunities for the discovery to be related to the aural experience of music.

4. Meaning is most profoundly achieved through *direct inductive experience* rather than through *indirect vicarious experience*. The best kind of experiential learning cannot be effectively implemented by a teacher using the lecture method: the lecture, for many learning experiences, is the least efficient and effective method of teaching, especially in large group situations. The technique is not improved by making of the lecture a lecture-demonstration. The demonstration facet can, with not a small amount of doublethink, be regarded as "experience" for the observers, but the opportunity for personal application, interpretation, reapplication, refinement, and so forth, is still missing.

There is a great difference between periodic explanation and qualifications by the teacher and the consistent use of lecturing for the purpose of dictating notes on musical information. Verbal elucidation, *when needed*, can assist the learner only when it enhances his ability to: (a) understand and conceptualize the learning under consideration; and (b) relate the learning to actual skilled performance or aural experience. Of this, one psychologist has written:

> Whether or not an explanation is helpful depends on the learner's ability to relate the words to experience. The teacher cannot expect to communicate if he talks about things that have no connection with the pupil's experience. A sea chantey is "a rhythmic song sung in chorus by a ship's crew"—but this is a pallid image to the pupil who has never heard one. He still wouldn't recognize a chantey. A rainbow, a banana, or a baby defies description; only experience with the real thing acquaints a person with its characteristics.[6]

The implication is clear: learning the musical art must consistently involve *direct experience* with music as sound, not as an organized discipline of more or less objective facts and information presented as *vicarious experience* in verbal form. Such verbalizing reflects only on the experience of the speaker, and need not have meaning for the listeners.

It should be noted at this point that—except in the case of musical learning for its own sake (as in musicology, for instance)—most musical experiences, learning, and phenomena *do* defy description. In general, if any art, especially music, could be put into words, could be explained or paraphrased, there would be little reason for its existence. Imagine, to illustrate this fact, trying to convey the musical experience to a deaf man by using words; or

---

[6] Cronbach, *Educational Psychology*, p. 368.

9

conveying the experience of a painting, sculpture, or architectural edifice to a blind person, using only words.

The great advantage of the arts is that they must be experienced as they were intended. One can study and analyze them, but the eventual response, significance, meaning, or as Langer put it, "artistic import," will be realized only through direct contact with the art object.

It is plainly futile to explain the meanings you experience in a musical work or any work of art to another person. Some means must be devised whereby the learner can actively and consciously experience the essential significance of the art work at the personal level. To do otherwise is to deny the learner the ultimate advantage of the musical art: the personal meaning that results when each person affirms his own identity by the uniqueness of his own response the art object. This is not to say that the artistic response is totally subjective; it merely affirms that each individual has a response that differs in quality and sometimes quantity from that of other individuals. In fact, a given person will respond differently to the same art object at different times. This is fortunate, for it permits us to return and significantly respond to such works of art many times.

To assume that meanings can be dictated or explained is not only a questionable practice, and inherently unethical,[7] it is also a supreme disservice to any art form. If, as Langer maintains, the essence of art and of mind are those vague and fleeting, ineffable, nondiscursive states of mind called feelings, then the teacher involved in any aspect of esthetic education is obliged to provide the opportunity and means by which each learner can actively come into contact with, if not consistently experience, these feelings.

*GO TO FRAME 6, PAGE 20.*

---

## PERCEPTION AND CONCEPTION IN MUSIC

The key to understanding the conditions under which experience can lead to significant learning for listeners is found in the realization that the musical art involves (1) both *percept* and *concept*, and (2) *stimulus* and *response*. Music, being an aural art, requires some sort of sound event exterior to the human organism. Traditionally, this sound event has not been merely a simple, single sound source, but, rather, a complex of sound arranged into various sonorous structures. Such structures, or any part thereof, constitute the *stimuli*[8] of music.

*Perception,* then, is the process of becoming aware of the qualities,

[7] Unethical in the sense of imposing one's values and value systems on others, especially other people who are not yet able to defend themselves or their current value systems; unethical in that it can amount to indoctrination.

[8] *Stimuli* (pl.); *stimulus* (s): an objectively describable situation or event that occasions, however indirectly, an organism's response.

arrangements, and relationships in the sonorous structure of music. A *percept* is the mental product of such sense perception. What is perceived is influenced by prior experience. A related collection of such experiences is called a *set* or *preparatory set*. Thus, perception is an active process based in part upon *concepts* developed through many such prior experiences. In this sense, a musical response or musical learning involves some kind of behavioral activity of the organism in response to musical stimuli.

The musical response or learning may be *overt*; that is, it may involve *observable* movement or activity of some kind in conjunction with the musical stimulus and percept. Performance is a prime example, but foot tapping, dancing, and other such activities also manifest such an overt response.

The response may be entirely *covert*; that is, it may involve only responses *within* the organism, usually involving the thoughts, ideas, feelings, sensations, etc., of the listener. This is obviously the most common means of responding to music. It is also the aspect probably most ignored in current methods of musical instruction. To improve the situation, teachers must:

1. realize that contacts with musical stimuli, and the perception thereof, develop the musical concepts that make a musical response possible; and

2. devise means for making covert responses somehow observable as overt behaviors. This enables the teacher to observe the general nature of the musical response had by the learner, and to plan new experiences with musical stimuli accordingly. It also helps make learning in music seem more tangible to the student.

The results of learning based upon the perceptions and cognitions arising from personal experience, and evidenced by transfer of behavior and an increase in the frequency of a desired behavior, can be called concepts. A *concept* is a general thought tendency that results from:

1. the perceptions and cognitions of many particular personal experiences with the learning or skill to be mastered; and

2. the *transfer*, by accident or design, of certain learnings or observations from each of these particular personal experiences to other particular, but somewhat different, situations. Thus, a related web or complex of learnings or insights gradually evolve into a *tendency*.

3. Such tendencies promote *an increase in the frequency of a behavior*. This in turn is enhanced by the more frequent success the learner has in recognizing the invariant qualities of newer situations, and, thus, in dealing successfully with them.

Thus, any concept (of tonality, for instance) that an individual may have is dependent in part on:

1. All his prior perceptions and cognitions (in many particular instances of the phenomena of tonal center or key). This fund of prior experience, or lack thereof, indicates the learner's *readiness*[9] to undertake certain learnings (dealing with, related to, or dependent upon the concept of tonality).

---

[9] Readiness may also refer to the learner's physical or kinesthetic preparedness for a given learning task.

2. Whether the learner is able to transfer learning from one experience to a dissimilar one (his perception of "tonality" and its role and effect).

3. Whether the many perceptions and cognitions of tonality and successful opportunities for transfer have resulted in an increase in the desired behavior (the ability to recognize and identify the key tone or tonic chord).

The music teacher's responsibility for each of these facets of conceptual learning is to:

1. Provide the occasion for such perceptions through personal experience.

2. Provide the occasions, and organize them to enhance the operation of transfer.

3. Provide increasingly refined situations, each of which has an overt phase.

From this it should be clear that significant musical learnings and skills will only result when:

1. The *readiness* of each learner for the percepts and concepts has been taken into consideration (that is, has developed to the point where the new experience *can* meet with success).

2. Experiences are planned that are conducive to the continual *refinement* of the percept and the development of the concept.

3. Means are devised for directing attention to the percept(s) under consideration.

4. Means are provided for recognizing or identifying the concept at hand.

5. Means are developed for allowing both the teacher and learner to *evaluate* (or at least observe) the student's awareness of the percept, and the accuracy of his concept. For instructional purposes, this usually involves some kind of overt application of the concept, which results in some kind of overt behavior.

In sum, then, musical learning is most significant and most effective when it proceeds from actual experience with sonorous structures as the stimuli for musical responses. The arrangement by the teacher of particular learning experiences can assist the student in effecting transfer, and, thus, enhance conceptual development. Both the teacher and the student profit from the strategy of planning for overt applications of otherwise covert responses. The teacher is able to observe the effects of instruction (if any), and the student finds learning in music to be more tangible (that is, more readily observable). Being somewhat pragmatic, young people thus find this kind of learning more rewarding.

Musical concepts result only from a learner's interaction (experience) with musical percepts. They cannot be

. . . handed around from one person to another in a verbal package. A concept has no transportable substance, and it has no form or physical structure of its own.[10]

[10] Asahel D. Woodruff, "How Music Concepts Are Developed," *Music Educators Journal*, 56, No. 6 (February 1970), 51.

As a result, concepts cannot be learned solely by verbal explanations or lectures. In fact, in the mistaken sense that teaching means the transfer of knowledge from one person to another, *they cannot be taught. They can only be learned,* and by each individual at his own level, according to his own prior perceptual experiences and his resulting fund of concepts.

An aspect of this process that often goes unnoticed is the fact that each person's experiences and mental functioning are unique to that person. In addition to the formal musical experiences the teacher provides in school, each person has a host of additional informal musical experiences outside of school. Add to this the unique biological equipment and mental characteristics (intelligence, learning style, and so forth) that causes each formal and informal experience to be somewhat different for each individual, and it is easy to see that concepts differ in various degrees from person to person.

These differences may be slight, or they may be great. There is usually a certain ground of agreement within a given society, for many experiences—formal or informal—are similar. But the concept of "freedom," for instance, means many things to many people depending on whether they are black or white, prisoner or a soldier, youngsters or adults. The same is true of musical concepts.

Let us momentarily digress from music to consider a nonmusical concept known to everyone: love. Everyone develops a unique concept of love. Through personal experiences with parents, a concept of parental love is developed; experiences with brothers and sisters add another dimension to this concept of love. Both of these aspects of your concept of love are affected by your perception of certain relevant cues in your experiences with your family. There are often certain physical manifestations, such as a hug or a kiss, that not only relate to your concept of love, but also provide a means of expressing love beyond the purely "spiritual" level. Each experience of this kind that you have further refines your concept of love. To some people the relevant cues may be entirely material or tangible: they expect or give gifts or physical expression as their manifestation of love. Others may regard inner qualities and feelings as the most important indexes of love. As you grow older, your concept of love is applied to members of the same and different sexes. From such experiences you learn further percepts relating to your concept of love. These too may often have certain physical manifestations that provide a means of expression.

The nondiscursive, nontransportable quality of such a concept is demonstrated when someone asks you to verbally respond to such questions as "What does love mean to you?"; "How do you know you're *really* in love with him?"; "How do I know that you *really* love me?" These questions are really unanswerable; or, at least, there is little if anything you can *say* to meaningfully communicate your concept of love to your questioner. And when it comes to showing your love for another person, even "I love you" can soon come to sound meaningless and redundant. A hug, squeeze of the hand, a smile, a gesture—these kinds of symbolic expression are among the many ways people communicate their concepts of love for their loved ones.

As you can see, a concept is a very complex thing indeed. You should notice, most significantly, that concepts are continually being developed and modified, sometimes dramatically. Learning in the conceptual sense, then, seldom if ever occurs at one time or one place in your personal history. It is ongoing, and ever growing.

Similarly, musical concepts result from all prior experience with music. These musical experiences are also unexplainable, not capable of meaningful verbal transportation from one person to another. They, too, result from each person's perception of relevant cues in each musical experience. They, too, are part of the symbolic expression that results from music.

> They enable the person to *perceive what he is doing,* in the case of conditioned responses, which are fairly automatic behaviors. They are the basis of *deterministic control* of what he is doing in situations where subliminal concepts guide the response. When concepts are recognized and verbalized, they provide the capacity for critical analysis and *deliberate and conscious decision making.*[11]

To perceive what you are doing, to determine the control of what you are doing, and to be able to critically analyze and make deliberate and conscious decisions are as much a part of the operation of musical concepts as they are of choosing a husband or wife on the basis of your concept of love.

The phrase in the Woodruff quote immediately above, "When concepts are recognized and verbalized," should not be mistaken to mean that concepts can be verbally communicated from one person to another. It refers, rather, to the developed ability to consciously think about things conceptually, and since we think in the same verbal language in which we speak, this usually amounts to a kind of private conversation with ourselves that is based on certain concepts.

In some instances, our concepts will have some objective equivalent in the stimulus situation. For instance, our conceptual feeling for tonality is affirmed when the harmony of a composition finally resolves to the tonic key after a long transient modulation. The objective fact of resolution to the tonic key after a modulatory passage can then be noted, written down, or explained verbally. However, this verbal process has meaning only for its formulator; such verbalization about resolution to tonic after a modulatory passage will have no significance to the youngster who has no concept *of his own* about tonic keys, resolutions, modulatory passages, and the like.

On the other hand, there is the tendency among some teachers to assume that the ability to name something verbally or to describe it according to certain canons exemplifies mastery of a discipline. This may be true as far as the artificial requirements of the discipline may be concerned. Yet it is likely that many people may have the requisite conceptual development without either the need or the desire to categorize such concepts verbally in terms dictated by the discipline.

[11] Woodruff, "How Music Concepts Are Developed," p. 51.

14

Many professionals within the musical discipline, in verbally or systematically formulating their own concepts of certain musical phenomena, have effectively thrown much confusion on many issues. They have their own personal concept of certain musical processes, and insist on convincing the world of the merit of such views. Rather than clarifying an issue, this approach often leads to confusion.

Witness the confusion of the music student who in reading one text is told that an AABA arrangement of phrases with a certain kind of cadence formula for each is called *rounded binary* form. Then he turns to another source and finds it called *incipient ternary* form. In either case, he may have a quite clear conceptual understanding of what is taking place in the music he is considering, but is confused unduly by having to label his concept verbally with someone else's designation. Though it is necessary to have some common or understandable means of reference in certain musical situations—certainly in teaching music—it seems possible, too, that various individuals may communicate their understanding in various ways. Some may prefer to refer to the phenomenon in question as simply AABA form. Others may prefer to merely describe objectively what happens in terms of phrases and cadences. Either can adequately convey the essence of the musical process.

Unfortunately, the teaching of music, both in public schools and at the level of higher education, too often amounts to nothing more than a teacher conveying his own concepts in his own conceptual terms (or those he must use because of available texts), rather than aiding the learner to experience the musical process himself and to arrive at his own conceptual understanding of it. Through personal experience, the individual student may see the merit or relevance in the designations commonly used within the discipline. Thus,

> When concepts are regarded as cumulative tendencies based on the consequences of antecedent experiences, there is only one place they could be formed: in direct interactive experience with each environmental substance that is to be known.[12]

In this sense, the use of verbal description is of use only as an adjunct to "direct interactive experience," and should by no means either supplant such experience or become the central purpose of the teaching process.

*GO TO FRAME 8, PAGE 21.*

---

## SUMMARY

As you have seen, behavioral objectives can be well written in terms of fulfilling the formal conditions of a behavioral objective, but they may still be

[12] Woodruff, "How Music Concepts Are Developed," p. 52.

unsuitable for a given learning situation. There are two general conditions under which this might occur.

1. The behavioral objective may serve poor educational, learning, or philosophical principles.

Example: Given separate mixed lists of fifty names of famous composers, their dates, and five famous compositions of each, each student will correctly match all the composers with their dates and their famous compositions within fifteen minutes.

> Faults: Emphasizes memorization and recall; is not indicative of conceptual learning; does not provide for transfer or conservation; is not founded in aural experience that emphasize percept and concept; none of this information is likely to contribute to the apprehension of felt life, expressive form, artistic symbol, or artistic import.

2. The behavioral objective may be ill suited to the particular class, their level of interest and readiness for the learning, or to the situation.

Example (for a third-grade general music class): Given the recorded example of *La Mer*, the student will be able to write a 250-word essay describing his conception of "how the music fits the title," and to make three lists of contrasting adjectives describing the mood of each of the three sections.

> Faults: Composition is too long for the attention span of third graders; no provision for physical activity or involvement; calls for a level of abstract thought not yet developed in children of this age; calls upon verbal skills not yet well enough developed.

You should note also that an activity ill suited to a particular class or situation is therefore also inappropriately serving educational, learning, or philosophical principles. Why? Because the readiness of the learner and the nature of the situation should be a part of both educational and philosophical considerations.

A successful music teacher must combine several ideal qualities into an effectively operating synthesis of teacher behavior. He cannot, and should not, avoid taking a point of view on the esthetic and philosophical aspects of the musical art. Without some clear notion of what the musical art involves, and what it can or should contribute to those he teaches, the teacher's efforts are likely to lack commitment and conviction. The result would likely be a mere "going-through-the-motions" kind of teaching. This chapter has introduced some points of view for your consideration; others will follow in subsequent chapters.

The music teacher must be thoroughly practiced in the theory and use of current educational psychology. Much research that has been done is directly relevant to the efficiency and effectiveness of musical learning. Many teachers fail to take advantage of such new and relevant insights, but continue to teach as they were taught, or to teach "by the seat of their pants." Several principles of learning in music have thus far been considered. Soon, several more will be undertaken. Approach these as though your success in teaching depended on your mastery of them. To a large degree, it does!

The music teacher must know the many psychological and sociological aspects of the age group taught and of the locale of the school. Knowing what to expect from various age groups, and their corresponding learning capacities, is fundamental to good teaching. Understanding the community is necessary as well. Subsequent chapters will deal with the former consideration; locale, however, is too great in variety to warrant comprehensive treatment here.

Last, but not least, the music teacher must be a competent musician. To those who teach, and teach well, it is obvious that all good musicians are not good teachers, but that every good teacher must be a good musician. There are those who prefer to denigrate teaching as a profession and as an avenue for serious study; they would deny that anything can be taught (learned?) that can assist a musician in becoming a good teacher. This is patently false, and belies the ignorance or prejudice, or both, of such persons concerning the many areas of competence a music teacher must have. Such misconceptions often result from the false assumption that learning to teach requires only the learning of a few teaching formulas, called "methods," which are thereafter applied mindlessly to a variety of situations, with only the content and materials varied. If you believe this, read no further. If you disagree, read on.

*From page 3*

It is important at this point to see if you have grasped the essence and implications of this line of thought.

According to Suzanne Langer's position, which of the following approaches in a music class would be most conducive to enhancing effective musical knowledge?

A. Lectures on the music of the more significant composer in relation to their lives and times. Go to Frame 10.

B. Progressively refined musical involvement with the elements of musical expression. Go to Frame 19.

C. Teaching all youngsters to perform music. Go to Frame 27.

Mark this page with your other bookmark. Then, as with all others like it throughout, turn to the frame number that follows the answer you have chosen. Always follow the direction in the frame to which you have turned. If your answer proves to be inappropriate, you will be returning to this page to answer the question again. If it is appropriate, you will be directed elsewhere in the book.

*From page 3*

If, as it has been said, "Music sounds the way emotions feel,"° then it is incumbent upon the music educator to provide those learning activities that allow youngsters to react and respond to *musical sounds,* and to come to the awareness that music, and all the arts, objectify and symbolize the unspeakable realities of life. This process also entails exposure to a wide variety of music since different types and styles of music embody different kinds of feeling.

With all of this in mind, which of the following is probably *least* suitable to the domain of the music class?

A. The exclusive teaching of performance skills to provide for an aural response to music. Go to Frame 11.

B. The use of listening experience to provide for an aural response to music. Go to Frame 20.

C. The use of creative experiences with many facets of music to provide for an aural response to music. Go to Frame 28.

° Carrol C. Pratt, "Design of Music," *Journal of Aesthetics and Art Criticism,* 12 (1954), 296.

*From page 4*

On this basis, which of the following descriptions does *not* constitute definite learning?

After many experiences rehearsing a given passage in a choral class,

A. Some individuals sing it correctly thereafter with consistency. Go to Frame 12.

B. Some sing it incorrectly the same way all the time. Go to Frame 21.

C. Some sing it incorrectly, but different ways each time. Go to Frame 29.

---

From page 7                                                          Frame 4

Let's review for a moment.

Which of the following behavioral objectives most clearly makes provision for "transfer" or "conservation"?

A. Given the list of descriptions and diagrams studied in class, the student will be able to identify successfully those that best apply to:
   1. the sonata principle, or
   2. the fugal principle,
by placing an *s* or an *f* before the appropriate choices. Go to Frame 13.

B. Given the recordings of the first movement of *Eine kleine Nachtmusik* and the Little Fugue in G minor heard in class, the student will be able to identify:
   1. their titles,
   2. the composer of each, and
   3. the operative principle for each.
on a written test with ninety percent accuracy. Go to Frame 22.

C. Given a series of five unfamiliar recorded examples, the student will be able to determine successfully whether they exemplify:
   1. the sonata principle, or
   2. the fugal principle,
by defending and explaining his choice in class discussion. Go to Frame 30.

---

From Frame 30                                                        Frame 5

Let's apply these same principles to a learning situation in a performance ensemble class. Which of the following behavioral objectives shows that the director has *not* made it clear in his mind, or those of the students, the need for "transfer" or "conservation"?

A. Given the basic rhythms $\frac{6}{8}$ ♩ ♪♩ ♪ and

$\frac{4}{4}$ ♩. ♪♩. ♪ (M.M. ♩ = 60) in (names of two compositions), each student will be able to consistently perform them correctly. Go to Frame 14.

B. Given the basic rhythms $\begin{smallmatrix}6\\8\end{smallmatrix}$ ♩ ♪♩ ♪ and

$\begin{smallmatrix}4\\4\end{smallmatrix}$ ♩. ♪♩. ♪ (M.M. ♩ = 60), each student will demonstrate his understanding of each by consistently performing them correctly. Go to Frame 23.

C. Given the basic rhythms $\begin{smallmatrix}6\\8\end{smallmatrix}$ ♩ ♪♩ ♪ and

$\begin{smallmatrix}4\\4\end{smallmatrix}$ ♩. ♪♩. ♪ (M.M. ♩ = 60) and $\begin{smallmatrix}3\\4\end{smallmatrix}$ ♩ ♩ and two or three minutes to inspect each new composition, the student will indicate his comprehension of each by identifying and locating it by measure number(s), and will perform each correctly on his first attempt. Go to Frame 31.

---

*From page 10*

Let's see if you really understand these important distinctions that we just discussed.

Which of the following descriptions of class activities would *not* provide a firm and direct basis of experience for conceptual and "meaningful" learning?

A. Mrs. X structures an activity in which the class creates an ABA form out of sound material of all kinds found in the classroom. She then assigns each member of the class to score an ABA sound form as a homework assignment. After she has evaluated the homework, several of the better compositions are performed in a subsequent class period under the directorship of the composer, tape recorded, and discussed. Go to Frame 15.

B. Mrs. Y has her class sing a song that uses the ABA principle. By means of probing questions, hints, and the like, she leads the class to discover like and unlike phrases and periods, and hence to the operative ABA principle. They sing the song again with class members representing each of the three parts by standing when their part is sung. As homework, she assigns the class the task of finding, among the songs familiar to them, other examples of songs in ABA form. The class then discusses one another's contributions during their next meeting, and several are sung. Go to Frame 24.

C. Mr. Z provides his class with an explanation and diagram of the ABA principle. He finds a recorded example that exemplifies the principle and plays it for the class, telling them to direct their attention to the *statement–departure–return* of musical material. Then he chooses a song from among those the class knows which exemplifies this formal principle, and has the class sing it. Each member of the class is then instructed, as homework, to be able to describe, explain, and diagram the ABA principle. During the next classes, Mr. Z solicits descriptions from class members and discusses their accuracy with the entire class. Go to Frame 32.

Let's apply these same principles to a performance situation.

Which of the classes in the following descriptions is *weakest* in providing a meaningful basis of experience?

A. Early each year Mr. A spends much rehearsal time analyzing and sight-reading the music that will eventually be performed in concert. The group spends several minutes looking over their parts; then they sight-read nonstop. Mr. A then takes one logical section at a time for closer consideration. The group is asked to try to identify their own errors, and to suggest the means for correcting them. The problems are then worked out, and Mr. A rehearses whatever necessary refinements the group missed. And so on through each piece. Of course, this process takes a considerable amount of time. Go to Frame 16.

B. Mr. B doesn't have as much rehearsal time as Mr. A, so early each year he carefully chooses music that involves typical, important musical and performance problems. These problems are isolated before they are performed. Mr. B draws from the group the possible solutions to the problems; the group tries each; and in conjunction with Mr. B, a solution for each problem is decided upon. The piece is then rehearsed, and goes quite well because of the prior work. Refinements are done by Mr. B. Subsequent classes continue to emphasize these same problems and others, according to the same procedures. Go to Frame 25.

C. Through the year, Mr. C progresses rapidly through much music. He is able to do this by identifying all the problems of his students as they occur; then he directs the group's attention to these problems, prescribes the remedy, and rehearses it. The group overcomes each problem area effectively. Using this method, Mr. C puts on many concerts and assembly programs. The performances, due to his approach, are always of high quality. Go to Frame 33.

---

After studying the three behavioral objectives below, identify which choice of sequence represents a progression from the *least* successful teaching for conceptual growth to the *most* successful.

Least      Most

A. 3, 1, 2.
B. 1, 2, 3.
C. 2, 3, 1.

When you have your choice in mind, go to Frame 17 to confirm your answer.

1. Given two unfamiliar aural examples, the student will (a) identify which one is in the Romantic style, and which is in the Classical style; and

(b) compile a list of characteristics in his own words, which identifies the differences between the two styles.

2. Given a mixed list of characteristics given by the teacher in class, not all of which are applicable, each student will identify correctly those that apply to the Classical style, and those that apply to the Romantic style.

3. Given a mixed list of characteristics, not all of which are applicable, the student will identify, upon hearing two unfamiliar aural examples, those that apply to the Classical example, and those that apply to the Romantic example.

---

*From Frame 17*

Next, try this problem.

In a music appreciation or general music situation aimed at enhancing listening perception and cognition, which of the following behavioral objectives provides for activities that would be most suitable in enhancing the *aural perception* and *conceptual understanding* of the formal role of full, half, and deceptive cadences?

A. Given several unfamiliar aural examples, the student will be able to aurally comprehend the formal role of the cadences by (1) listing in order of occurrence the types of cadences heard, and (2) explaining verbally and in writing his personal explanation of how the cadences used contributed to the evolution of the form. Go to Frame 18.

B. Given several unfamiliar aural examples, the student will be able to comprehend the use of cadences by providing the symbol I, IV, V, V⁷, or VI— whichever best represents the chords used at the various cadence points. Go to Frame 26.

C. Given a matching question, the student will identify cadences by matching the symbols I, IV, V, V⁷, and VI with the types of cadence they represent, and describing how each of these cadences is best used in evolving a musical form. Go to Frame 34.

D. Given a poem, the student will demonstrate his cognition of cadence usage by (1) identifying where he would locate the cadence points in setting the poem to song, (2) identifying the type of cadence he would use at each point, and (3) giving the reasons for his choices. Go to Frame 35.

---

*From Frame 1*

You answered that lectures on the music of significant composers in relation to their lives and times would be the approach most conducive to enhancing effective musical knowledge in a music class. This is not likely to be correct.

To study the biography of a composer is to learn many details of his life that: (1) are not all relatable to his music, (2) are not relatable to the musical style of the age, and (3) are not relatable to all music in any age. And even if the study of a composer's life were made somehow significant to his music, the major source of study is still likely to be the composer, and not the music. To take this position implies that the knowledgeable listener, or the appreciating listener, would have to know the biographical details of each composer whose music he encounters. Furthermore, it is dangerous to make any one-to-one cause-and-effect relationship between a composer's life and his music (or, in fact, between most extra-artistic facts and any specific artistic changes). For one thing, it obscures the historical continuity of the internal dynamism of musical change by relating all musical phenomena to extramusical considerations.

Such a study also takes on factual or informational overtones that seem to preclude increasing *musical* insight. The degree to which facts and information are studied will be the degree to which the students are not given the opportunity to experience feelings toward the music they hear. Such teaching provides little or no basis for progressively articulated and differentiated "feeling" responses to music. Furthermore, those students weak in verbal, reading, and memorization skills are not likely to be able to undertake such a factual study effectively; hence, they profit little from such a study, and all too often are lost forever to the art of music. This tragic condition occurs daily in countless music classes across the country as students with academic problems are denied entrance to the pleasures of music by having an academic study made of it.

Finally, with this means of teaching there is no way of assessing whether or not each student has been able to associate the facts with the aural experience.

Go back to Frame 1, try the question again, and see if you can come up with a less problematic answer.

---

*From Frame 2*                                                                    Frame 11

You selected choice A, that the exclusive teaching of performance skills to provide for an aural response to music was the least suitable to the domain of the music class. This is probably correct.

Briefly, the reasons for this are that (1) performance is not suited to all youngsters; (2) performance does not necessarily develop skill or insight in listening; (3) performance can become a self-sufficient act performed for its own sake, and not for the sake of significant responses while listening; (4) musical contact with a large repertory is limited; (5) professional-quality performances are seldom encountered in school music situations; (6) opportunities for performance after graduation are limited, while opportunities for listening are not as limited; and (7) this type of approach, which has been operative during the entire history of public school music, has not made as much progress in the development of the taste and listening habits of the population at large as we might have hoped.

Go back to page 4 of the text, below the line.

The individuals who sing the passage correctly after rehearsing it and do so correctly thereafter *have learned* it. Therefore, your answer that this kind of behavior does *not* constitute learning was itself incorrect.

The only special concern here is that the teacher should not assume that he or she is entirely responsible for the learning, or that the same teaching technique would work with these same individuals at all times. Some may have learned it as a result of the rehearsal activity; others may have learned it through independent action in spite of the class activity; some may have merely imitated their neighbors; still others may have been able to perform it correctly from the start.

In any case, the fact is clear that these individuals have indeed learned to sing this passage accurately. To put it in terms of the definitions given on page 4,

> as a result of the experience of having the problem passage identified and practiced, their behavior has been changed so that the frequency of the desired behavior had increased to the point that they consistently performed it accurately thereafter.

Go back to the question in Frame 3 and select another description that clearly does *not* constitute learning.

---

Your choice of the behavioral objective that clearly makes provision for "transfer" or "conservation" was A:

Given the list of description and diagrams studied in class, the student will be able to identify successfully those that best apply to:

    1. the sonata principle, or
    2. the fugal principle,

by placing an *s* or an *f* before the appropriate choices.

This is not a good choice. This is a good example of a well-written behavioral objective designed to serve poorly conceived principles of learning. Descriptions and diagrams can be memorized and thereafter easily recognized. Learning descriptions and diagrams does not necessarily guarantee that the student will be able to *aurally* perceive the existence of a formal principle in a wide variety of compositions. When listening to recorded music, or live music at a concert, no one will provide the learner with a diagram or description. The important principle here is that these skills or cognitions should be learned in the context in which they are most usually experienced. Listening should be approached as an aural skill in conjunction with certain cognitions. Cognition without aural application and practice is useless in terms of effective learning. The learner may know more *about* music, yet not respond to it any better when encountering sound patterns in real listening situations. Too often, general music classes at all levels (elementary, junior high, and even high school appreciation and theory classes) have suffered in this way.

Therefore, this behavioral objective not only fails to provide for transfer or conservation, it also fails to provide for the acquisition of aural skills. It substitutes factual learning for conceptual learning. Now don't be misled here. It often can be helpful to diagram and describe musical phenomena in the early stages of learning aural discrimination. It helps to provide a visual, graphic (tangible) framework to guide the formulation of the student's concepts. But the process will go for naught if it is not followed by frequent and varied aural applications where the learner has the opportunity to apply and test his aural discrimination.

This must be provided by an additional behavioral objective. It is one of the remaining two: go back to Frame 4 and try the question again.

---

*From Frame 5*                                                      Frame 14

You chose example A as being *unclear* about the need for "transfer" or "conservation."

a. Given the basic rhythms $\frac{6}{8}$ ♩ ♪♩ ♪ and

$\frac{4}{4}$ ♩. ♪♩. ♪ (M.M. ♩ = 60) in (names of two compositions), each student will be able to consistently perform them correctly.

You are correct. By limiting the performance of those rhythms to the two compositions specified, the director has *not* made provision for the abundant number of other compositions that employ these same basic rhythms and that will inevitably be encountered by his group.

Now it may seem obvious that many students, after the emphasis on these two compositions, will likely be able to transfer or conserve these learnings. But it is equally likely, as any experienced teacher can affirm, that as many will not be able to demonstrate this behavior consistently and, thus, will not have learned it effectively.

The most notable weakness in this highly problematic behavioral objective is that it reveals that the director has not consciously planned to actively follow-up this learning session with ample, varied, and progressively refined opportunities for his group to apply such learnings. If he were planning to do this, he would have applied either or both of the other two objectives given.

Another grave weakness is the lack of reference to any covert behavior (inner, mental activity). By eliminating any intent for this lesson to develop broad conceptual mastery, the teacher has left the door wide open for purely imitative, rote learning. In fact, the omission of such covert behavior seems to indicate an intent to approach the problem through rote means. This teacher would, very likely, have to similarly "program" his group each time they encountered these rhythms in subsequent compositions. This is an extremely common, but inefficient and ineffective method.

Go back to page 8 of the text, below the line.

Your choice of the class that did *not* provide a firm and direct experiential basis was A. You must be a little confused because the class described *did* provide very well for the kind of direct experiences that leads to conceptual development and meaningful learning.

Don't be unduly alarmed by the fact that this creative activity did not use traditional musical sounds and traditional notation. The fact is that the class created a sound object, a sound "form" that exemplified the ABA principle. Musical sounds, "found" sounds, electronic sounds—it really doesn't affect the conceptual development of these learners, for all of these are sounds that can be assembled into an abstract formal object having a *gestalt*.° Therefore, the members of the class would actively experience the principle of ABA. What better way is there to conceptualize and understand such musical phenomena as sound forms than by actually manipulating sound and creating of it such a sonorous form? Because sound seems relatively intangible, youngsters often have difficulty understanding the concept of sound having a form because they often think of form in terms of a tangible *shape*. In fact, sonorous form is a rather abstract idea; this is all the more reason for involving them with this abstraction in such a way as to make it somehow more tangible. Creating their own sound forms is *one* very excellent approach.

The activity that followed the creation of the sound form provided well for individual needs and interests, and provided the means by which the teacher could evaluate each learner's understanding of the learning at hand. The class discussion of the better compositions would also help those who still were somewhat confused—especially if the teacher encouraged the composers to explain their own compositions, and encouraged the less successful ones to alter theirs in light of these explanations by their peers. A *learner will often understand explanations given by a peer when they don't understand those given by the teacher.*

All would be for naught, however, if the teacher never followed up, reinforced, and reviewed this lesson with other activities designed to refine their understanding and handling of the ABA principle.

Go back to Frame 6 and try the question again.

° An arrangement of separate elements of experience in a pattern, form, or configuration that is perceived to be so integrated and to function in such a way that it appears as a unit or whole that is more than the sum of its parts.

You said that Mr. A was not providing a meaningful basis of experience. Indeed he was!

Mr. A was providing a basis of experience in preparing his musicians to function in an *increasingly independent and self-sufficient* manner. The time he spends early in the year is easily made up as the year goes on by the savings in time he realizes as the group becomes increasingly more independent and more expert in:

1. identifying problems in advance;
2. knowing the probable solutions to those problems;
3. knowing other solutions in case their first interpretation turns out poorly;
4. judging their own performance independently of the teacher, and making corrections themselves; and
5. recognizing the kinds of refinements possible in given situations.

In general, Mr. A's *structure* helps his students develop musicianship, rather than training them according to rote means to be dependent upon him. Thus, they are continually provided with independent *experiences in problem solving*. Most problem solving entails:

1. recognizing the existence of a problem;
2. an interpretation, and selection of a possible solution;
3. a tentative trial (which the teacher should provide);
4. reinterpretation if the trial proved unsuccessful (the necessary *means* for such self-judgment on the basis of observed feedback must be provided by the teacher); and then
5. the application of a new solution; more feedback; and so on.

The more independent a performer is, the more likely he is to continue with music *on his own* outside of and/or after graduation from school. Thus, it would seem that such an approach is a highly meaningful way of approaching the performance class.

Go back to Frame 7 and try the question again.

---

*From Frame 8*

Frame 17

Behavioral objective number one is the *most* successful because it provides for the learner *to apply his own concepts* of Romantic and Classical, and to explain (verbalize) his own concepts in his own terms. This allows the teacher to evaluate each individual's conceptual level; for although the entire class may respond correctly, their levels of conceptual understanding may vary greatly. One learner may respond mainly to the melodic differences, another to differences in orchestration. Some may respond to several, and even many of the prime differences. The teacher is able to assess conceptual understanding by examining such responses. This approach also provides well for the transfer of such concepts, which theoretically would have been derived from prior aural experiences of this type, to unfamiliar aural experiences.

Number two seems *least* successful for it emphasizes *recognition of verbal descriptions* phrased in the teacher's words. Should a student perform well according to this objective, it would indicate only mastery of certain verbal or memory skills, and would not *necessarily* involve conceptual understanding or musical behavior. Also, this approach does not provide for application of such concepts, regardless of how they were reached, to an unfamiliar aural experience. Most serious of all is that this behavioral objective does not indicate that any aural experience was part of the learning situation. Thus, it is unlikely that a teacher working from this point of view would provide any actual music for listening. Rather, such a teacher would be likely to explain these characteristics verbally.

Number three has some of the advantages of number one, but some of the disadvantages of number two. It is good in that unfamiliar aural examples will serve as the bases for the experience; but it is weak in that the basis for differentiation is a prepared list of characteristics expressed in the teacher's words. Thus, the teacher has not permitted the learner to apply *his own* concepts of Romantic and Classical (or at least his own verbal formulation of those concepts), nor has he provided a means for evaluating each individual's conceptual level.

Therefore, the most appropriate sequence should have been choice C: 2, as *least* successful; 3; and 1, as *most* successful. Go to Frame 9, page 22.

---

*From Frame 9*                                                                    Frame 18

You chose example A as *most suitable* in providing for a conceptual understanding of cadences in a situation designed to enhance listening perception and cognition.

Good. This is correct because this behavioral objective (1) provides for listening perception and cognition, and (2) provides a behavioral means for the teacher to evaluate the learner's understanding of the role of cadences in creating musical forms.

However, if you will reread the other choices, you should now notice that they also provide other kinds of conceptual learnings, which are suitable in situations other than the one described.

For example, choice B– read it again on page 22–is not suitable to the situation described because it is not necessary for the general listener to be able to identify by chord symbol the chords used. It is much more effective to provide for a conceptual understanding of the *sound* of a full, half, and deceptive cadence without going into an exercise in harmonic dictation. This technique might, however, be suitable in a theory class.

Choices C and D also deal at the conceptual level—read them again— but they are not suitable when listening perception and cognition are the tasks at hand. They would, however, be good preparatory exercises in a theory or general music class that is progressing to individual and original compositions.

At this point, you should note that all the objectives given specified the covert response quite clearly; yet only the first specified that the student be able "to aurally comprehend." Thus, this objective is the most suitable for situations designed to enhance listening skills.

Finally, you should note that there are many kinds of activities that are conducive to conceptual development; the kind you will implement will depend on the kind of conceptual development required for the students in a given situation. Therefore, not all such activities are well suited for all learning situations. You must first identify the kind of conceptual development you wish to encourage, then design an activity specifically to meet that need. The technique of using behavioral objectives ensures this, for the objective should in each case specify a covert behavior. This covert behavior, whatever you choose, should indicate what kind of learning you are seeking.

Go back to page 15 below the line.

---

*From Frame 1*                                                    Frame 19

Your answer that progressively refined musical involvement with the elements of musical expression would be conducive to enhancing knowledge in a music class is correct.

The reasons for this seem sound and self-evident. Contact and involvement with music is the best way to develop an awareness of the inherent expressiveness of music. A study of facts as ends in themselves cannot do this.

But mere contact and involvement, as in musical performance classes, is obviously not enough, at least for a formal learning situation. It is important to structure the learning contacts with music so that they are progressively refined. If, as was noted earlier, "Feeling is an aspect of evolving reality which emerges gradually within the system of nature, becomes progressively differentiated and articulated, and achieves its fullest expression in the rhythm, patterns, and symbols of art," then the formal structuring of learning situations designed to foster the process of progressive differentiation and articulation will be of most value in esthetic education.

For these reasons, and others to be discussed later, mere participation in a performance ensemble does not necessarily guarantee the kind of contact and involvement that enhances the learner's ability to progressively respond to music, whether as a performer, or especially as a listener. Performance classes too must be highly structured in order to properly benefit the student. Merely rehearsing or playing through the music is much too casual a contact, however else it may contribute to attitudes and impressions.

Go to page 3, below the line.

---

*From Frame 2*                                                    Frame 20

Your answer that the use of listening experience to provide for an aural response to music is *least* suitable to the domain of the music class is probably quite removed from the truth.

In fact, one of the most important guiding principles in the formulation of teaching objectives is to create learning situations that provide the learner with experiences of the same or a similar kind that he will eventually encounter. Thus, if the teaching of music for both performers and nonperformers is ever to achieve the realization and apprehension in youngsters of "felt life," the "artistic symbol," "expressive form," and "artistic import," the kinds of learning situations structured for such learnings must increasingly or eventually be oriented toward listening, since this is the behavior that is required for such responses to occur.

Go back to Frame 2 and try the question again.

---

*From Frame 3*          Frame 21

If some individuals incorrectly sing the passage the same way all the time, as you answered, then they have in fact learned it, however incorrectly. They have not learned it correctly, but *they have learned it incorrectly,* because their behavior has become more frequent in this regard; in fact, it has become consistent. Therefore, learning has occurred, and your answer is off base.

This kind of learning (call it "negative" or "nonproductive" learning if you will) goes on every day in all kinds of music classes. When it happens, many teachers often assume that the learner is at fault: that he is lazy, dumb, inattentive, unmotivated, not musically talented, or all of these. Though these factors might be present to some degree, in almost all instances the teacher shares at least some, if not all, the responsibility for such nonproductive learning.

If the teacher described in this example was working with a good behavioral objective in mind, then some positive result could still be possible. If nothing else, the teacher might find that the passage and therefore the composition, is beyond the present level of ability (i.e., of readiness) of this particular group.

Since the chorus did not meet the criteria for success that the teacher had in mind (that is, they did not show the anticipated behavior as a result of instruction), and assuming the music is appropriate for the readiness of the group, either more experience with this passage and others like it should be provided in order that they have the opportunity to learn the correct response, or the learnings necessary to attain this level of proficiency should be undertaken before attempting this passage again. It would also seem wise to vary the rehearsal technique. Since the previous approach did not succeed, there is no reason to expect or assume it will succeed if applied again. This has the additional advantage of providing review and reinforcement for those who initially performed the task correctly.

With this in mind, go back to the question in Frame 3 and select a choice that clearly does *not* constitute learning.

---

*From Frame 4*          Frame 22

Your choice of the behavioral objective that clearly makes provision for "transfer" or "conservation" was B.

Given the recordings of the first movement of *Eine kleine Nachtmusik* and the Little Fugue in G minor heard in class, the student will be able to identify:

1. their titles,
2. the composer of each, and
3. the operative principle for each,

on a written test with ninety percent accuracy.

This is not a good choice. This, like one of the other choices is a good example of a well-written behavioral objective designed to serve poorly-conceived principles of learning. The fault with this objective is that the learner is being called upon to recall a composition previously heard, and then to recall certain information about it. It does not provide the opportunity for the teacher to evaluate whether or not the learner is able to transfer or conserve his understanding of the sonata and fugue principles to new and unfamiliar compositions. It also puts an inordinate emphasis on memorization (of titles and composers) rather than on conceptual learning applied to aural perception.

An additional disadvantage is that the behavioral objective indicates the use of methods and materials within very narrow limits, namely the two compositions specified. Therefore, it is likely that a teacher using this particular behavioral objective would involve the class with only these two examples of the two formal principles.

Furthermore, evaluation of learning must take place in ways other than, or in addition to, testing. Testing, and the grading that inevitably accompanies it, often tends to:

1. make the passing of the test a goal in itself, rather than placing a premium on the acquisition of the learning; and
2. create pressures, tensions, and anxieties regarding the test and the learning to be tested. This often results, regardless of the outcomes of the test, in continuing attitudes about music, music class, or the learnings at hand that are not conducive to the goals of music education.

Go back to Frame 4 and try another choice.

---

*From Frame 5*

You said that example B was *unclear* in its provision for "transfer" or "conservation."

B. Given the basic rhythms $\frac{6}{8}$ ♩ ♪♩ ♪ and

$\frac{4}{4}$ ♩. ♪♩. ♪ (M.M. ♩ = 60), each student will demonstrate his understanding of each by consistently performing them correctly.

Example B is, contrary to your answer, a good example of a well-written behavioral objective that is conceived in accordance with accepted learning theory.

It clearly specifies the learnings to be undertaken (the two rhythms), how such learning is to be judged (performing them correctly), and the proficiency expected (consistent correct performance). It also provides well for transfer and conservation by clearly indicating that such learnings must be displayed in *all* or *any* compositions encountered in class. Thus, it is likely that the teacher, keeping his own behavioral objective in mind, will frequently and consistently follow the initial experiences with others designed to review, reinforce, and refine these rhythms.

Further contributing to the likelihood of transfer and conservation is the specification of a *covert behavior* (inner mental activity) that deals with conceptualization rather than rote imitation. This provision—"demonstrate his understanding of each"—will promote transfer by placing emphasis on the general concepts involved, rather than on the specific imitative execution of the rhythms on one or two occasions.

Go back to Frame 5 and try the question again.

---

*From Frame 6*  

You chose example B, Mrs. Y's class, as the one that did *not* provide a firm and direct experiential basis. Since this class has the potential to provide such experiences successfully, you may be confused.

Mrs. Y has the class sing the song; that is experience. She leads them, by questions and hints, to discover the ABA principle; that is experience. They sing the song again with members of the class graphically representing the three parts; that is experience. She assigns them to find other familiar songs that exhibit the ABA principle; this is experience using the "inner ear." The class discusses one another's contribution; this represents more experience with the concept. So, in each case the class is actively involved in the perception and cognition of the ABA form.

Plenty of opportunity is afforded the teacher for assessing the progress of each individual learner; by having the peer group discuss and explain their own contributions, provision has been made for identifying and clearing up any confusion. A learner often will understand explanations given by a peer when they don't understand those given by the teacher.

By itself, this one class would not necessarily prove mastery of the ABA principle. Mrs. Y would have to follow this lesson with many others designed to review, reinforce, and refine the learnings undertaken in this first lesson. After many experiences with the principle, it is likely that most of the youngsters will indeed have experienced meaningful learning.

Go back to Frame 16 and try the question again.

---

*From Frame 7*  

You said that Mr. B was not providing a meaningful basis of experience. Given the rehearsal schedule he had to work with, he *was* doing a commendable job.

By carefully choosing his music for its educational and musical merit, he is making good use of the time allotted him. He *structures* the situation so that his group encounters the kind of typical problems that will confront them throughout the year. By making the class aware of the nature of these problems, he effectively prepares the class to solve them throughout the year. By isolating the problems, drawing solutions from the group, and experimenting with each solution, he provides for a considerable degree of musical independence.

When these problem passages are finally put back into context, the amount of time required to learn the piece, and other similar pieces, is small. Both the time factor and his group's continually refined mastery of these problems, and others introduced along the way, improve as Mr. B follows the same process in subsequent classes.

The experiences here are experiences in *problem solving*. Most problem solving entails:

1. recognizing the existence of a problem;
2. an interpretation, and selection of a possible solution;
3. a tentative trial (which the teacher should provide);
4. reinterpretation, if the trial proved unsuccessful (the necessary *means* for such self-judgment on the basis of observed feedback must be provided by the teacher); and then
5. the application of a new solution; more feedback; and so on.

The provision for this kind of problem-solving experience clearly leads to musical independence. The more independent a musician is, the more likely he is to continue with music *on his own* outside of and/or after graduation from school. Thus, it would seem that such an approach is a highly meaningful way of approaching the performing class.

Go back to Frame 7 and try the question again.

---

*From Frame 9*

You chose example B as *most suitable* in providing for a conceptual understanding of cadences in a general music or music appreciation situation designed to enhance listening perception and cognition. Though it is true that your choice does represent an activity that would enhance a conceptual understanding of cadences, this activity is not well suited to a situation that seeks to enhance listening perception and cognition.

The reasons for this are quite simple. It is a demonstrable fact that it is not necessary for the general listener to be able to provide the chord symbols that identify cadence patterns. With experience and practice, they are easily able to conceptualize the mere *sound* of the varieties of cadence. Thus, they are able, if called upon, to identify them by such descriptions as half, full, or deceptive, without resorting to the labeling of chords. Making the activity one of harmonic dictation only confuses the situation unnecessarily.

Since the goal of any listening that aims at improving aural perception and understanding does not include the mastery of difficult analytical skills, it seems unwarranted in this kind of class to so heavily emphasize this particular system. What is important is that the students recognize and understand cadences. Describing their understanding in non-technical language will allow the teacher to sufficiently evaluate whether or not they have heard as they should have, and whether they have heard well.

Go back to Frame 9 and try the question again.

---

*From Frame 1*

Your answer was that teaching performance skills to all youngsters would be most conducive to enhancing knowledge in music classes. This argument involves several serious questions.

First, performance of music does not necessarily imply or involve an understanding or significant feeling for or from music. This should be evident when considering the large number of youngsters who discontinue their performance contact with music upon graduation, and whose "taste" or listening habits have not been significantly effected by their membership in a performance ensemble. This is true even in many college music programs where performers whose experience has been limited to "bands" too often have too little understanding, insight, or appreciation of choral or orchestral music.°

Second, not all youngsters are suited to or interested in performance skills, especially if those skills involve singing. In our culture, this tendency becomes increasingly evident of boys as they approach and pass through pubescence.

Third, this approach may not provide for an extensive enough contact with different musical media, styles, and forms. This is especially true of much of the singing and rhythmic activities undertaken in general music situations where a quality repertory is next to nonexistent.°

Fourth, this approach may not provide for an extensive contact with quality performances of various kinds of music. No matter how advanced the performance group in public school, it is still far removed from quality performances by collegiate and professional groups (a fact that causes great dissatisfaction among teachers who have entered the profession to satisfy their own musical needs).°

Last, this approach may not necessarily provide for the aural apprehension of the musical "whole." Performance does not necessarily lead to intelligent or knowledgeable, not to mention enjoyable, listening. Hence, many public school performers enjoy the act of performing—for various reasons, sometimes unrelated to music—but never develop a liking or skill for the act of listening to music while not performing.°

Go back to Frame 1 and try the question again.

° See, Charles Benner, *Teaching Performing Groups* (Washington, D.C.: MENC, 1972), pp. 5–25, for a more detailed exploration of research findings related to these issues.

---

*From Frame 2*

You answered that the use of creative experiences with many facets of music to provide for an aural response to music was *least* suitable to the domain of the music class. This is probably not correct at all.

34

Creative experiences in which youngsters work, experiment, and create "sound objects" with the standard and "advance-guard" elements of music have great relevance and applicability to the listening response. A music teacher can lecture for years about the ABA principle in music, but when the learner creates such a form of his own or in conjunction with other peers, he then has the beginnings of a working conceptual knowledge of this principle. He is better prepared to perceive it, respond to it, and enjoy its musical benefits. However, one such experience would never be enough. Many and varied experiences with creation according to this principle, with continued refinements and applications, would lead to the reinforcement and transfer of learning that indicates effective mastery. Yet no matter what value these creative activities may have, they must eventually contain or be related to listening, since this is the manner in which *all* people can relate to music.

Caution must be exercised in such creative activities, however, for the experience must be well structured in the minds of the teacher and students. The musical principle or concepts being dealt with must be clearly evident during or at the completion of the activity, or else the lesson is likely to degenerate into meaningless activity with no viable or positive result. Furthermore, all musical or "sound" creations should be performed, and thus used as a listening experience. To merely have such activities end as notated exercises defeats the notion of creativity in music. There is no creativity in music unless some sonorous product results from the creative activity.

Go back to Frame 2 and try the question again.

---

*From Frame 3*                                                                                    Frame 29

You said that singing the passage incorrectly a different way each time does not constitute learning, and you are basically correct.

This is so because there is no increase in the frequency of any particular response. Each performance is incorrect, and is so in a different way. Conceivably, some of these individuals might at any given time sing the passage correctly, but either be unable to know that they have done so, or be unable to repeat it.

Therefore, a good behavioral objective would have helped to eliminate the possibility that a teacher, upon hearing the passage sung correctly by the group on one occasion, would assume that the passage had been learned once and for all. If the objective in mind had been this one:

> Given the name of the composition, each member of the chorus will attend to the notation of pitch, rhythm, and phrasing by singing it accurately and with consistency thereafter.

then the possibility of such an accident happening would have been minimized. With the specification "accurately and with consistency thereafter," the teacher is made aware of the need to regard the frequency of a behavior as a prime indication of mastery of a skill. Additionally, such a specification entails both some way of evaluating each individual, and provision for the performance of this passage at several different and widely separate times.

Go to page 4, below the second line.

---

*From Frame 4*

Your choice of the behavioral objective that clearly makes provision for "transfer" or "conservation" was C.

Given a series of five unfamiliar recorded examples, the student will be able to determine successfully whether they exemplify:

1. the sonata principle, or
2. the fugal principle,

by defending and explaining his choice in class discussion.

Good. This is the best choice. Since the students are being called upon to identify formal principles from among other unfamiliar examples, transfer or conservation will be indicated for those learners able to respond correctly. Or will it? Maybe! If this were the one and only time you provided this opportunity, it would not necessarily indicate anything. Some students could have guessed the correct answers; others could have responded correctly for the wrong reasons.

In part, the last segment of the objective given helps to clarify these possibilities; for as the students defend and explain their choices in class discussion, the teacher will be able to assess the merit of the individual responses.

Even this is not sufficient. The teacher is still obliged to continually follow such experiences with others designed to reinforce these learnings for those who indeed have learned as anticipated. The same subsequent opportunities will identify those who are still unable to consistently perform the desired response, while at the same time giving them the opportunity to master and refine these responses.

Go to Frame 5, page 19.

---

*From Frame 5*

You said that example C was *unclear* in its provision for "transfer" or "conservation."

Given the basic rhythms $\frac{6}{8}$ ♩  ♪♩  ♪  and

$\frac{4}{4}$ ♩.  ♪♩.  ♪ (M.M. ♩ = 60) and $\frac{3}{4}$ ♩  ♩ and two to three minutes to inspect each new composition, the student will indicate his comprehension of each by identifying and locating it by measure number(s), and will perform each correctly on his first attempt.

Contrary to your answer, this behavioral objective is well written, according to good learning theory. It clearly specifies the learnings to be undertaken (sight-reading three rhythms after first identifying and locating them), and how such learning is to be evaluated (correct performance on first attempt). It also provides for transfer and conservation by the fact that it does not indicate any specific pieces. Therefore, any and all pieces are liable to this treatment. Thus, it is likely that the teacher, keeping his own behavioral objective in mind, will frequently and consistently apply this activity when and where possible or desirable, thereby insuring review, reinforcement, and refinement.

Of major importance is the fact that this objective specifies a *covert behavior* (inner mental activity) designed to enhance the possibilities for transfer to subsequent situations. This specification—"will indicate his comprehension"—would tend to promote transfer more than would the choices "to imitate" or "to follow directions."

Go back to Frame 5 and try the question again.

---

**From Frame 6** Frame 32

Your choice of the class that did not provide a firm and direct experiential basis was C. You are quite correct.

Mr. Z explains the principle; this is vicarious experience and there is no way of telling whether the class understands his verbal explanation since there is no way for them to respond or directly experience the principle. Mr. Z plays a recorded example; many teachers do this, yet it is always futile because, first, the example will be of little use to those who didn't understand the initial explanation; and, second, there is no provision for them to respond actively to the music and thereby display their covert understanding or perception in an overt behavior.

In other words, just playing the example provides no means for either the teacher or learner to know whether or not the factor to be experienced (1) has in fact been perceived by each and every individual; or (2) what the sources of error and confusion are for those who inevitably will not achieve the desired response. Without these two factors, Mr. Z has no basis for restructuring and representing the lesson. Hence, those learners who inevitably will be lost as to the learnings at hand will remain lost; and subsequent experiences, even if predicated on this earlier one, will hold little meaning or profit for them. As a result, it is likely that their attitudes will not be favorably disposed to music or the teacher. With each subsequent lesson, this will more likely become true.

Go to Frame 7, page 21.

---

**From Frame 7** Frame 33

You said that Mr. C was probably *least successful* in providing a meaningful basis of experience. You are correct.

Mr. C's class does seem to be attaining a high level of performance. But he has little way of knowing whether or how anyone is profiting from such experiences. He is operating under the common assumption that quality performance automatically guarantees meaningful musical learning.

The problem is that he has not specified, by means of behavioral objectives, what that learning is to be or how he will evaluate it. He may think that the learning he is dealing with is excellence of performance, and that the manner of evaluating it is by judging the performance quality and improvement of the group as a whole over the year. But what does this prove? Merely that the group's performance has improved; it says nothing about what this improvement is to bring about in each member of the group or how they are supposed to profit from such improvement.

Meanwhile, Mr. C may very well be programming musical robots. It seems likely that they play well because:

1. he identifies each mistake for the class;
2. he always tells them how to correct their mistakes;
3. he always tells them when they have satisfactorily mastered the problem;
4. and he always drums this into their heads for each separate piece.

This kind of teaching seems unlikely to lead to musicianship, or musical independence (which may be the same thing). An added difficulty is the fact that a considerable amount of time is spent in ironing out problems; and the same problems continue to reappear in different pieces since the group is never enabled to understand, identify, and solve the problems themselves. That is, they are not able to transfer or conserve because they are not truly understanding why or how they are able to play well; they are just responding to rote processes. Thus, considerable and valuable time can be wasted in drill and rote learning. The ensemble music in such situations frequently serves as the basis for private or group "lessons" as well. And the end result of performance for its own sake as an educational philosophy still remains suspect, for the group learns very little about music or its performance.

If you have not already done so, read Frames 16 and 25; then go to page 10, below the line.

---

*From Frame 9*

You chose example C as most suitable in providing for a conceptual understanding of cadences in a general music or music appreciation situation designed to enhance listening perception and cognition. Though it is true that conceptual learning is involved in example C, this particular activity has little or nothing to do with the *aural skills* involved in developing listening perception and cognition. Furthermore, without some kind of subsequent activity involving actual experience with composing, performing, or listening, the structuring of the present activity is unsatisfactory.

The matching portion might have some value for students headed toward collegiate study in music. It is made more valuable for all by being followed by the activity of describing the role of cadences in evolving form. But some further activity involving a musical stimulus is needed to apply this learning to an actual musical situation. Thus, what to this point is conceptual learning of a verbal nature can become truly *musical behavior* in some way.

To date, far too much learning in music education at all levels has been verbal; far too little has involved *musical behavior*.

Go back to Frame 9 and try the question again.

---

*From Frame 9*

You chose example D as most suitable in providing for a conceptual understanding of cadences in a general music or music appreciation situation designed to enhance listening perception and cognition.

Though it is evident that conceptual learning would enter into the completion of the task described in example D, it is not true that this activity is well suited to providing for a conceptual understanding of cadences in a learning situation designed to enhance *listening* perception and cognition.

In a theory class, or some such specialized situation, this activity does have some aural relevance if it assumes that (1) the student uses his "inner ear" to identify the cadence points, and (2) uses the same faculty in deciding upon cadences to be used. However, it would be difficult to assess whether the inner ear was hearing what it was supposed to (or whether the student had successfully guessed) without going on to a subsequent activity. If this subsequent activity involved actually composing a melody that accorded with the preselected cadence points and cadence choices, then a greater insight would be provided to both the teacher and the student. Many such activities could conceivably result in a better trained ear.

There is a better and more direct choice than this; go back to Frame 9 and see if you can find it.

# CHAPTER TWO

# *teaching music*

*Instruction is the choice of circumstances which facilitate learning. . . .*

*A . . . major illusion on which the school system rests is that most learning is the result of teaching. Teaching, it is true, may contribute to certain kinds of learning under certain circumstances. But most people acquire most of their knowledge outside school, and in school only insofar as school, in a few rich countries, has become their place of confinement during an increasing part of their lives.*

*Most learning happens casually, and even most intentional learning is not the result of programmed instruction.*

Ivan Illich, Deschooling Society (*New York: Harper and Row, 1972*), *pp. 16, 18.*

Perhaps the greatest of all the traditional educational fallacies is to assume that what should be learned can be taught. This manner of thinking is fallacious to the degree that teaching is regarded as

the process of transferring or communicating knowledge from the teacher to the learner.

Given this definition, can you imagine the impossibility of "teaching" someone who has never seen ice about the nature and "feeling" of ice? You could communicate much knowledge about the physical character of ice, its uses, its creation, and the conditions under which it is found; but would the learner have a real understanding of the feel of ice, the look of ice?

Of course these are extreme examples, but they point out one fact: teaching is something well beyond the mere imparting of knowledge or information. Given this point of view, it is easy to see why most things that should be learned cannot be taught. But they can be learned! How? By creating the conditions under which learning can occur. By structuring learning situations that permit a choice or series of choices among possible actions. By structuring learning situations that give the learner the opportunity to implement in practice his choices of possible actions.

Although it may seem like a semantic nit-pick, two other words describe such learning processes better than the above definition of teaching. They are:

1. to educate—"to draw out or develop the mental powers";[1] and

2. to nurture—"to furnish the care and sustenance necessary for physical, mental and moral growth."[2]

These terms (or at least thinking in these terms) are preferred because they seem to specify or imply the active participation of the learner in the learning process. They imply consent and involvement on the part of the learner. They affirm the role of the teacher as a facilitator of learning. The traditional notion of teaching seems to imply brainwashing.

This thinking of the teacher as a facilitator of learning seems to be especially needed in regard to music, where, as was pointed out earlier, an inherent stimulus-percept, concept-response situation exists at all times. Except for scholars involved in the pursuit of scholarship *about* music and its history, the musical art involves:

1. The existence of the aural *stimuli* that constitute the composition being performed—or heard—and the *perception* of those stimuli.

2. A developed web of musical *concepts*—some of which, for example prejudices adopted from parents, are not developed as a result of direct contact with music—concepts that result in a variety of possible responses in musical situations.

---

[1] *Funk and Wagnall's Standard Dictionary*, International Ed., p. 401.
[2] *Ibid.*, p. 1287.

Performance of music is even more complicated than that, for here the experience involves:

1. Beginning with the perception of *relevant cues* in the stimulus situation (notation, conductor, other players) that constitutes the composition being performed.

2. Then a series of *mediating responses* that result in individual or collective performance of the notation;

3. Then the *perception of the aural stimuli* resulting from such performance (feedback).

4. Concluding with *confirmation or contradiction* regarding the musical accuracy of the response, and a suitable readjustment if necessary.

## LISTENING

Let us consider the nature of each of these two kinds of musical experience separately.

The musical art is an *aural* art: its *raison d'être* is determined by the sense of hearing (audition).

Thus,
because the perception of the aural stimuli that constitute the composition being performed is an inherent part of the listening (consumptive) experience,

Then,
the teacher who proposes to create the conditions for musical learning must structure situations where:
1. *aural stimuli* are either present or planned; and
2. a means of evaluation is devised that assesses the nature of the perception of these stimuli by each individual.

Therefore, structured learning experiences that are intended to foster the perception of the musical art must consistently provide the opportunity for contact with and perception of the musical stimuli.

Under certain conditions, initial experiences might not actually involve musical stimuli. For example, certain musical concepts that are important in the listening experience might first be explored in visual terms—through the study of scores, diagrams, or examples of forms and styles of the visual arts. Such activities should not, however, be planned or undertaken without full realization of the nature and means of eventual aural application, where each individual student will:

1. encounter the musical concept by means of an aural (musical) percept; and

2. will be assessed as to the accuracy of his perception, and the nature of this concept; the teacher will accomplish this by observing the overt signs of his response, or by devising an activity calling for an observable response.

Thus, both aspects of the listening experiences in music are provided:

(1) the aural stimulus and resulting percept, and (2) the variety of possible responses to the perceived stimuli.

*GO TO FRAME 1, PAGE 51.*

---

If you really understand the principles at hand, you will easily recognize that a lecture-demonstration lesson suffers from several faults. First most important, by lecturing, the teacher is eliminating the possibility that each student will arrive at his own understanding of the visual examples. To use the visual examples as the stimulus for having the individual class members discover for themselves the form in question would be one of many proper ways of approaching this problem.

Second, just playing musical examples makes no real provision for learning. The teacher has no idea who is or how many are really listening (as opposed to merely hearing), or what each individual is able to perceive. The solution to this problem is to structure a situation where the class is *directed* to try to perceive certain stimuli, and where some means are devised for allowing an observable response.

Example:

Teacher: "You told me that the picture of an arch that we just studied got its form or construction by starting low, gradually getting higher, then gradually getting lower again. I'm now going to play two familiar songs for you: on your paper, write which of them seems to have a melody that is like the visual example of the arch.

(plays "Do–Re–Mi" and "Scarborough Fair")

"How many of you thought it was 'Do–Re–Me'?" (Hands raise.) "How many thought it was 'Scarborough Fair'? I'll play the examples again. This time, use your hands to design the melody as it gets higher or lower: when the melody goes up your hand should go up; when the melody goes down, your hand should go down." And so on, until each individual is able to draw a line on his paper that accurately captures the formal design of the melodic direction of "Scarborough Fair."

In a subsequent lesson, this could be reinforced by a similar activity with several other songs that have a similar melodic shape, such as "Michael Row the Boat Ashore." As an assignment, you might have the class identify other familiar songs that use this process.

## PERFORMANCE

What of the steps leading from the stimulus to the eventual response in the performance of music? How are they developed, and in particular, how

43

do they relate to preparing the individual for intelligent listening in situations where he is not actually involved in performance—where, as is most typical, he is a consumer?

Earlier, it was pointed out that in the *performance* of music, the ideal sequence of stimulus leading eventually to a response is more complicated in some ways than *listening* responses. It involves:

1. Beginning with the perception of the *relevant cues* in the visual stimuli involved in the situation; these include the notation that constitutes the composition being performed, and, in ensembles, the director or leader.

2. Then a series of *mediating responses* and cues permit the individual to transform the visually perceived stimuli into their sound equivalent. Mediating responses are those intervening mental processes that, when linked, connect the initial stimulus (the visual perception of the score) to the initiation of a response. Thus, each mediating response serves as a kind of stimulus for another mediating response. (For example, "What is the name of that note? How am I supposed to finger it?" These are necessary and separate mental operations for the novice.) This chain of associations results in the terminal response of the performance of musical sounds.

3. Then, ideally, each individual *perceives and assesses the aural stimuli* (more relevant cues) that result from the performance. This would include not only the performer's own playing, but also the playing of others in an ensemble.

4. Finally, each individual *assesses the accuracy* of the performed musical sound, and if *confirmed,* continues on in the same manner; if contradicted (that is, if mistakes are perceived), he makes the necessary readjustment based on what was wrong.

All is not as simple as it appears in outline. For example, the mediating responses referred to are a complex and, thus, essential consideration. In part, *skilled learning involves the elimination of the step-by-step process of mediating responses,* and the achievement of an immediate response to the initial stimuli.

Each such response in a chain of mediating responses is something that each learner must perceive. His perception of these stages, and the next response, is conditioned in large part by his conceptual understanding of each step. A *fully normalized or immediate response* also involves conceptualization. When this stage is attained, all the required steps are understood as a single entity, rather than as a series of separate steps. Nonetheless, each step is implicitly understood, and can be isolated for purposes of analysis, diagnosis, or reinterpretation in the event of an error. Thus, the greater the degree of conceptualization present, the more musical independence the student can manifest.

Not all performance of music is, or should be, involved with the visual stimuli presented by means of notation. There are many kinds of music and many instances where performance without notation is desirable. Aside from memorized music, these might involve improvisation, as in jazz and other styles of music, and, in general, the ability to "play by ear." Since it has been established that people who learn to "play by ear" are more likely to continue performing outside of or after graduation from school, and since such ear training is of great help in sight-reading music, it seems that this form of musical learning should be increasingly undertaken in public school music training.

Whether notation is used or not, expertise in musical performance increases to the degree that the performer is:

1. more efficient at recognizing the relevant visual and aural cues;

2. increasingly able to eliminate his conscious or specific attention to mediating responses; and

3. increasingly able to evaluate the accuracy of his performance on his own, and make adaptive behavior if necessary.

In each case, the mastery of these skills indicates greater speed in learning the music correctly. In addition, there is the very real question of musicianship. Musicianship involves conceptual understandings that condition what the performer regards as relevant visual and aural cues, what he considers appropriate or necessary mediating responses, and what he uses as criteria to evaluate his performance and to respond adaptively. Musicianship also involves how well-developed the "inner ear" of the performer is, how quickly and accurately he can "read" rhythms, and similar behaviors that depend both on much prior experience and well-developed comprehension.

In performance, visual and aural *cues* direct the effort of the performer. Visual cues entail all notated symbols, the visual implications in playing the instrument (if there are any), and the conductor (if there is one). Aural cues include any other musical part(s) that may be present (for instance, questions of intonation,[3] blend,[4] ensemble,[5] and so forth), and the *aural feedback* the performer perceives from his execution. The quicker and more efficient each performer is in attending to these visual and aural cues, the more successful and expert his performance will be.

The elimination of mediating responses involves elimination of the slow step-by-step processes necessary at beginning levels of skill development. The student lifts the instrument to his lips, and after several adjustments (each a mediating response) finally arrives at a viable—if not perfect—embouchure. Then he looks at the music and identifies the first note: he thinks, "Second line of the treble clef is G; hmmmm? . . . that is played with this fingering." Then he generates a sound as he fingers the notes, and so on for each note, rest, and symbol he encounters. Is it any wonder directors have difficulty in encouraging such performers to watch the conductor?

An expert performer, of course, is ready to play at an instant and is able to read (i.e., see and "hear") large patterns of notes at once. Often he anticipates his vision by hearing in advance of his eyes what should be next. A good pian-

---

[3] The accuracy of pitch with regard to a standard pitch source.

[4] The impression of pitch accuracy that results from various mixtures of timbres, vileratos, etc.

[5] The collective accuracy of rhythm when several instruments play the same rhythms together.

ist will not need to direct his attention to each of the notes (cues) in a ten-note chord that constitutes a stimulus. With only a glance, he perceives the entire chord as a unit, hears the sound of the chord in his inner ear, and then plays it. At the stage his hands are playing the chord, and his mind is hearing and evaluating the chord, his eyes are already moving on to the next stimulus on the notated page; and so on. Hence, the eye, mind, and ear are always several steps ahead of the actual performance, and the many mediating responses of the novice are eliminated in favor of what *seems to be* an almost automatic stimulus–response sequence. Do not forget, however, that the well-developed concepts constituting the performer's musicianship condition this entire procedure. Without considerable training of the faculty of the "inner ear" and conceptualizing of chords and chord progressions, this seemingly simple stimulus–response sequence cannot occur effectively. The separate mediating responses have not disappeared; rather, with conceptualization they can be isolated and refined, and, thus, can work more quickly, and as a unit.

Expertise is always shown by the performer's increased ability to *independently assess* the accuracy of his own performance and to make *adaptive behavior*. The concepts and skills related to this kind of *feedback* are often the most severely neglected in music teaching at all levels. Too often, directors perform this service as an expediency for the individual or group, always identifying the mistakes, giving the means for correcting them, and confirming the degree of accuracy in the corrections made. Is it surprising that true musical independence is difficult to develop under these conditions?

Earlier, in relation to theories of learning, we identified the use of feedback by the performer as *musical independence*. Actually, performer feedback is only one phase of musical independence; another is the ability to study a score to resolve matters of style, interpretation, and so forth. Most significant is the greater likelihood that the musically independent student will continue to perform after leaving school. One wag has said, "What the world needs is more talented amateurs and fewer semitalented professionals!" There is great merit in this view, and it seems a worthy goal for music educators to realize. A more musically active populace will not only enhance the current status of music in the economy, but should also have great bearing on matters of public taste.

*GO TO FRAME 2, PAGE 51.*

---

## WHY TEACH PERFORMANCE?

Now that you have seen the reason for including in the learning situation the kind of musical stimuli that the student is likely to encounter in either performance or listening situations, a major question remains: What, in fact, is the purpose of training student performers in music? What long-range effect is such training to have on their future development or involvement with music? Three answers seem possible.

1. One purpose of training student performers in music should be to identify, encourage, and improve those musically talented individuals who might consider music as a *vocation*. Implementation of this goal requires all of the factors previously cited: contact with solo and ensemble literature, ear training (playing by ear), music theory appropriate to the performer, contact with a large amount and wide variety of music, appropriate insights into matters of technique and how technique serves musical expression.

Rote training, excessive contact with a small or narrow repertory, use of large ensemble music for private and group lessons—none of these will help the young and talented musician who might consider music as a vocation. It will not prepare him for study beyond high school, and runs the risk of having a negative effect on his attitude.

A corollary here is that music teachers must avoid encouraging the not-so-talented performer to regard music as a serious vocation. In order to do this, the music teacher must himself be an accomplished musician and must be nonprovincial enough to recognize that the best performers in his school system are not necessarily good enough to achieve a musical vocation. Only the exceptional individual should be encouraged, and even then with realistic counseling regarding the availability of musical vocations in what is becoming an increasingly difficult job market. This leads to the question: "Well, what good is it to have the less-than-exceptional musicians trained in the first place?"

2. The answer to this question leads to the second major reason for training student performers in music: to encourage and provide for those musically talented and interested individuals who might find music a source of keen *avocational* pleasure and involvement. The major problem with this provision is that performance groups for avocational musicians do not exist in any significant numbers outside of high schools, colleges, or churches. It is hard to tell whether this is a case of the chicken or the egg: Do such groups *not* exist because music education has *not* encouraged interest in music as an avocation? Or does an avocational interest in the performance of music suffer because such groups do not exist outside of high school?

Whatever the case, music educators must act. Either they must foster these outside performance groups themselves, or they must foster the musical independence necessary to start, support, and sustain such groups. In the long run, only both possibilities acting together will have any significant effect. In addition to this, all the other factors previously mentioned must be implemented. Most notable among these, of course, are those that enhance the development of *musical independence*[6] and *individual musicianship*. These include all of the same situations recommended in providing for a musical

---

[6] See T. A. Regelski, "Toward Musical Independence," *Music Educators Journal*, 55, No. 7 (March 1969), 77–83.

vocation, except that here, playing by ear becomes a viable alternative in those situations where no organized performance groups exists.

3. The third purpose often voiced in justification of training student performers in music is that such performance develops understanding, taste, discrimination, and appreciation for music. Although it is seldom specified, this line of thought seems to imply the application of the above qualities to a listening situation where the individual is not a member of a performance group.

While this goal is both laudable and achievable, it seldom comes to fruition because of the assumption that mere participation in the performance of music automatically and necessarily breeds more perceptive listeners. This assumption is implicit in a much elementary and junior high school general music teaching as well, especially among teachers who focus exclusively on singing and reading the score. If this assumption were true, we could expect a much more musically sophisticated population than is now the case.

Given enlightened teaching, it is possible that greater perception might be developed, especially in terms of those listening skills necessary to a good performance; but even here it is not necessarily true that performers would be intelligent listeners in a situation where they were not performing. This is especially true to the degree that school music performers are permitted or encouraged to develop increasing pleasure from the mere *act* of performance, to the detriment of their ability to perceive and respond to music in purely listening situations. Thus, such students will perform "good" music when the occasion is made available and convenient to them. But they are not inclined to actively seek contact with "good" music as listeners, even when it *is* made available and convenient to them (for instance, by recordings, local concert series, and so forth).

Performance must be enjoyable, but it must also include an extension of effort beyond the mere "fun" level. And the degree to which students become band-, chorus-, or orchestra-oriented is the degree to which they hinder their ability to perceive and respond to music they hear performed in a medium other than the one to which they belong.

Furthermore, they will also be hindered by the fact that the school music repertory is relatively limited in comparison to the total repertory available in listening situations. This is most notably true of so-called "concert" and "symphonic" bands and large wind ensembles. Precious little opportunity exists to hear such music performed outside the public school or university. Though there are a few contemporary composers who have composed significantly for these media, much of this music is too difficult for many high school groups. The repertory of this music is rather meager compared to the wealth of music in the choral and orchestral realms, and the opportunities to hear recorded or live examples of such "band" music are relatively rare.

How then can this third goal of using music performance to prepare intelligent and responsive listeners be attained? Without going into great detail, a few suggestions can be made. First, it seems obvious that increased opportunity to listen to music under the conditions described earlier (p. 42ff.)

48

must be provided; and they must be provided in quantity, with a variety of styles and media considered, and with quality performances.

Second, the performance ensemble should be regarded as a course in the study of music, not merely a course in the performance of music. Once established, such a more broadly based course could provide many diverse opportunities for musical learning and contact, especially because it would be directed toward a student population that theoretically is well motivated toward music and is well able to perceive and intelligently discuss its elements and concepts. Those students unwilling to undertake such concerns are likely to be uninterested in music as an art. Though music education should in no way begrudge them the pleasure of performance, it is a fact that even the most accomplished of professional performers derive equal pleasure from listening to and studying music.

Third, increased contact with live, professional-caliber music in a listening situation will constitute giant strides in the proposed direction. Even bringing student groups of various kinds together to listen to one another (not, emphatically, just to be adjudicated by an anonymous audience of one to three adults) would help greatly.

Fourth, regarding the performance ensemble as a kind of laboratory that applies and expands musical learnings acquired in the study of theory, history and appreciation sessions will also advance this cause, and at the same time make membership in such a group infinitely more rewarding and of much greater practical benefit for the future.

Last for now, applying all the principles of learning and good teaching to the performance class will enhance each member's ability to profitably respond to the aural experience as a listener.

*GO TO FRAME 5, PAGE 52.*

---

## SUMMARY

Thus far, we have discussed the nature of learning in music and the nature of teaching music. Learning in music was seen to involve change in *musical behavior* or change in the frequency of a musical behavior. On the other hand, teaching music was seen to include the need for frequent contact with a variety of musical stimuli. From these frequent contacts, which constitute personal experience for the learner, the percepts that result are increasingly conditioned by a developing framework of concepts. These concepts are then understood as generalizations or tendencies resulting from the learner's increasing ability to find relevant relationships among past experiences, and to relate these generalizations or tendencies to present and future experiences. As this conceptual framework develops, the student's responses will be increasingly affected by his conceptual understanding.

Teaching music also involves commitment to the idea that musical performance has three possible consequences in an educational setting. It prepares the performers for a possible vocation, for avocational use, and for knowledgeable and sensitive listening. Therefore, musical performance in school music must never become a solitary end in itself. The teacher must provide the kinds of learning experiences that enhance the possibility that each student becomes as musically independent as his talent and interest allow. This independence includes skills and learnings related to listening to music as a nonperformer. Above all, the needs of the individual students must take precedence over the musical and personal needs of the teacher. Seeking personal accolades through student performing groups can no longer be tolerated as a teaching behavior. If one is to judge such teaching behavior in terms of demonstrable learning, it seems all too evident that many teachers have "learned"—in the sense that the frequency of their behavior is on the increase —that the plaudits of other teachers of similar persuasion is the overt evidence needed to evaluate the success of a performance program in music. Thus, performance excellence is automatically equated as the sole criterion of successful teaching.

Until this attitude, and others as well, are modified along the lines suggested here, the music education profession will experience difficulty in achieving any impact on public taste and listening habits. Until music education again becomes a process that embraces all aspects of music and serves the needs of all students, and not just those relative few who are a part of the performance program, it cannot hope to reach the various lofty goals proposed by individual teachers and their professional organizations. Teaching music, as in all teaching, must begin to focus less on the teacher's goals, and more on the goals of those students who presently pass unaffected or disaffected through the total music program.

*From page 43*

Which of the following behavioral objectives *best* provides for structuring a musical listening experience in a general music class in an elementary or junior high school?

A. Given a list of characteristics, the student will be able to consistently identify those that apply to the four major sections of the orchestra. Go to Frame 6.

B. Given several contrasting visual examples of architectural forms, the student will accurately identify those that best represent the *forms* of unfamiliar aural examples. Go to Frame 11.

C. Given the song, "Cotton Needs a-Pickin'," the student will:

1. discover its formal construction
2. by singing the song.

Go to Frame 16.

*From page 46*

Which of the following is *best* suited to developing expertise in musical performance according to the above analysis of stimuli–response sequences:

A. Early in the year, upon assessing the abilities of his band, the director chooses music for the spring competition festival and other music to be performed in concert throughout the year. This relatively small number of compositions is worked upon extensively, and results in a very high level of apparent expertise and competence. Go to Frame 7.

B. Another director insists that his students work out their own band parts at home, although he is willing to help solve any especially difficult problems during private and group lessons. Otherwise, the band covers a lot of music during the year, more than is actually performed in concert or at the festival. Private and group lessons are devoted to solo and ensemble literature. Most of it is never played in concert; the best of it is. Go to Frame 12.

C. In order to develop the ability of his band to perform music with a high degree of expertise, this director prepares for and reinforces band rehearsals by studying each individual's part in their private or group lessons. He feels he is killing two birds with one stone: improving his band helping each individual to play his instrument better. Go to Frame 17.

*From Frame 12*

Which of the following choices best represents the sequence leading from stimulus to terminal response that is involved in a typical performance of music:

A.  aural stimuli
    response
    feedback
    mediation
    adjustment. Go to Frame 8.

B.  visual stimuli
    feedback
    mediation
    response
    adjustment. Go to Frame 13.

C.  visual stimuli
    mediation
    performance
    feedback
    adjustment. Go to Frame 18.

D.  aural stimuli
    mediation
    performance
    readjustment
    feedback. Go to Frame 21.

---

*From Frame 18*                                                                    Frame 4

Which of the following is *not* a true or reliable indication of expertise in musical performance:

A. Increased ability to eliminate attention to or need for mediating responses. Go to Frame 9.

B. Increased efficiency and attentiveness regarding feedback. Go to Frame 14.

C. With time, the ability to develop a piece to the level of high competence. Go to Frame 19.

D. The ability to more quickly respond to the visual and aural cues in the situation. Go to Frame 22.

---

*From page 49*                                                                     Frame 5

Which of the following best provides for *all three* major long-range effects (vocation, avocation, appreciation) given earlier in justification of the inclusion of musical performance in music education?

A. Given the unfamiliar composition *Suite Francaise* by Darius Milhaud, each member of the band will study the score for two minutes; read it through nonstop at half the given tempo marking; study the score for two minutes more; read it through nonstop at about three-quarters of the intended tempo; study and master their parts at home; and show mastery of the notated score by correctly executing it at almost full tempo at the next rehearsal. Go to Frame 10.

B. Given the unfamiliar composition *Suite Francaise* by Darius Milhaud, the band will be able to play through it nonstop at almost full tempo, with correct execution of notes, rests, rhythms, and all other elements in the score, by the end of the rehearsal; they will demonstrate this ability plus a good tone and dynamic sensitivity in their next private lesson. Go to Frame 15.

C. Given a hearing of Darius Milhaud's *Suite Francaise*, each member of the band will follow his own score while listening; study his score for two minutes; be able to "get through it" at a reasonable tempo; and demonstrate the ability to perform the work with accuracy and expression at the next rehearsal. The recording will also be available for use outside of class.

Go to Frame 20.

---

*From Frame 1*

You said that choice A best provided for structuring a musical listening experience in an elementary or junior high school music class.

Somewhere along the line, you have become confused and missed the point, for this example provides for no aural experience whatsoever. Not only are such aural applications not provided or planned, they could not even be successfully included in this situation. It is unlikely that verbal descriptions of instrumental characteristics would be of any use in the perception, identification, and aural response to the instruments of the orchestra. Imagine trying to explain or describe the tonal differences between the oboe and English horn in such a way that the listener could then distinguish between them.

Review pp. 42–43 and then try the question in Frame 1 again.

---

*From Frame 2*

You chose A as the approach you felt was best suited to developing expertise in performance according to the previous analysis of stimulus–response sequences.

Perhaps you did not fully understand the scope and implications of the earlier discussion, for your choice here seems inappropriate.

This director violates several aspects of the stimulus–response sequence. Most notable is the inordinate amount of time spent on the same music. The less contact his group has with new music (new notation-stimulus situations), the less able they will be to develop effective skills in the perception of the relevant visual cues. They will *not* have had enough experience. Thus, they will not have had the practice that would lead to the elimination of mediating responses when encountering new music, and each new composition would require the same lengthy process of dealing with each cue and mediating response separately.

You may ask, "But didn't they achieve a high degree of expertise?" Yes, that is true, but the rejoinder is "How?" By drilling on parts in rehearsal (during which the majority of band members do not play)? By rote repetition of the same music, during which the ability to attend to cues and eliminate mediating responses is learned, *but only for that music*, and only with excessive and what may be boring repetition? It might be asked, "At what price progress?" The point is that it is possible to "program" an individual or group to play well, without providing them with the skills that properly constitute expertise, or with the concepts that facilitate transfer of learning.

In some instances, the amount of time necessary to "perfect" a performance can serve as an indicator of the degree of skill development of learning. For example, if two bands receive the same performance rating on the same composition, yet one had to rehearse three months to perfect it while the other rehearsed only half that time, it is quite safe to say—all other things being equal—that the latter group has evidenced more learning and skill development. They are able to eliminate the mediating responses, monitor their own feedback, and make corrections more efficiently. These are the primary signs of skilled learning.

Go back to Frame 2 and choose another answer.

---

*From Frame 3* Frame 8

Your choice was A:    aural stimuli
response
feedback
mediation
adjustment

Aside from the fact that most performance responses begin with visual stimuli, there are other difficulties involved in your choice of this sequence. They tend to indicate that you do not yet understand these ideas.

Since a firm knowledge of this learning process is fundamental to the music teacher, go back and review pages 42–46. Then answer the question in Frame 3 again.

---

*From Frame 4* Frame 9

You answered that the increased ability to eliminate attention to or need for mediating responses was *not* a true or reliable indication of expertise in musical performance.

On the contrary. This is a good indication of expertise or progress toward it.

Review page 44 and answer the question in Frame 4 again.

---

*From Frame 5* Frame 10

You chose behavioral objective A as the one that best provides for *all three* possible long-range effects that justifying the inclusion of musical performance in music education.

This is probably *not* correct; but it is not too far off base either. What this objective indicates does provide well for the first two possible long-range effects—vocational and avocational application of performance. The techniques implemented here would help to develop a degree of independent musicianship that would help to encourage and permit such long-range effects to occur.

However, it does not provide for the third possible justification—the obvious fact that many if not all the members of the band *will* almost certainly have the opportunity some day to apply certain listening skills. This lesson does not seem to provide in any way for this.

Do not be misled into thinking that all such objectives must provide for all three contingencies. This objective would in many instances be very satisfactory. The challenge given you in this question is an artifice designed to see if you can perceive the missing elements. It is important, however, that you realize how important it is to include learnings for performance groups that can influence their later listening habits and skills. Thus, not every objective must aim at fulfilling all three conditions; an objective may include one or two. The rule of thumb should be that your total efforts should manifest a well-rounded balance of learning experiences designed to enhance vocational, avocational, and listening possibilities.

Go back to Frame 5 and choose a more appropriate answer.

---

You said that choice B best provided for structuring a musical listening experience in an elementary or junior high school music class.

Good! This behavioral objective implies several things: first, that visual examples of architectural forms will be a part of the structure of the learning experience; second, that during the learning experience these visual examples will be co-ordinated with appropriate aural experiences; third, that these visual and aural examples will be used to assess each individual's perception and response to the aural experience.

Here, the visual examples can be predicted to serve two purposes: (1) They provide a tangible representation of formal concepts (for instance, Gothic cathedrals are typically ABA; two steeples separated by the main body of the structure). (2) They provide a *means* of identifying musical percepts in overt terms. Such a technique need not detract from the desire a teacher may have to teach music *purely* for its own sake. But it can also provide avenues of entrance and exploration for those teachers who are disposed to some use of comparative arts, where such integration amplifies the musical experiences and at the same time relates or compares other (more tangible) arts to the musical experiences.

Thus, provision has been made for the perception of aural stimuli, and means have been devised for assessing the accuracy of such perception. (The response will indicate the nature of the perception, and of the conception that serves as the basis for an interpretation of the percept.)

One further point should be made: The wise teacher, upon devising such a behavioral objective, structures learning experiences that prepare the student for the eventual learning (that is, musical behavior) that the objective specifies. Conceivably, a teacher might seize upon the objective considered here and do the following:

1. present, by means of lecture/demonstration, visual examples of architectural forms that are related to musical forms (the ABA form of the typical Gothic cathedral, for instance);
2. then play for the class musical examples of each of the visual examples presented;
3. then test the class on the same material.

Hopefully, you are not asking yourself, "What is wrong with that?"
Go to page 43, below the line.

---

*From Frame 2*                                                                    Frame 12

You chose B as the description best suited to developing expertise in performance according to the previous analysis of stimulus–response sequences.

This is correct. The students are encouraged to encounter and master their band parts individually and independently. Refinements, or problems beyond their current level of competence may be handled during private and group lessons on a kind of diagnostic or remedial basis. These lessons also preview the new lesson material in order that the home practicing can be most effective, and the chances of "learning" something incorrectly are minimized. Thus, lesson time is devoted to musical problems, and band rehearsal is not wasted on learning notes, and otherwise dealing with the score. The musical and expressive content of the music is what the teacher is most involved with, and this is as it should be.

At the same time, best use is being made of private and group lessons by devoting these situations to the encountering and perfection of solo and small ensemble literature. This doubles or triples the amount of music that each learner encounters during the year. This fact, plus the increased independence called for by solo and small ensemble music can dramatically improve the learning of performance skills.

In addition to the advantage of developing musical independence, this structure also provides each student with a viable means of musical participation outside of school or after graduation, when the opportunities for performance in orchestras, bands, and choruses are greatly diminished. It also enables the individual to encounter the musical experience at a more personal level.

It seems unarguable that every student musician should have ample opportunity to perform solo literature with some kind of accompaniment, and ensemble literature requiring one performer per part. Both provisions entail and encourage musical independence, and individual musicianship. Any and all such efforts in private and group instruction can only enhance the eventual performance caliber of the full group, as well as the chances of exerting a continuing influence on the future musical involvements of young musicians.

Go to Frame 3, page 51.

---

*From Frame 3*                                                                    Frame 13

Your choice was B:    visual stimuli
                      feedback
                      mediation
                      response
                      adjustment.

The first and last are really all that you have in correct order here. Feedback cannot occur without some discernible prior response, which in turn results from certain mediating responses.

Because it is imperative that each music teacher have these steps firmly in mind, review pages 42–46, and then answer the question in Frame 3 again.

---

*From Frame 4*                                                                    Frame 14

You answered that increased efficiency and attentiveness regarding feedback was *not* indicative of expertise in a musical performance.

Not so. These qualities are indeed good indications that the student is at least making progress toward a condition of true expertise.

Review page 44, and then answer the question in Frame 4 again.

---

*From Frame 5*                                                                    Frame 15

You said that behavioral objective B was the one that best provided for the three possible long-range effects that justify the inclusion of musical performance in music education.

This is really quite far removed from the truth; are you reflecting your own experiences here, or are you trying to implement the above discussion of the three possible long-range effects? If it is the former, then it is understandable, for the approach described in this objective is far too commonly used. If it is the latter, then you do not yet understand the earlier discussion of long-range effects.

This objective suffers in many ways. To be able to play this new piece as well as the objective indicates within the confines of one period would entail working on this piece the whole period, drilling and learning parts by imitation, and avoiding any real learnings about either the music at hand, performance skills in general, or listening skills. Obviously, none of the methods used in this lesson will help provide for any of the three reasons for including musical performance as part of music education.

This objective also entails using band music as the basis for private and group lessons; and this is also a poor basis for providing the skills and learnings necessary to justify the inclusion of performance in music education. The lesson should feature study material built around specific pedagogical needs plus solos and small ensemble materials. All of these will help develop musical skills that have relevance in many situations. Learning the notes of band music serves much narrower, short-term goals. See Frame 17 for more explanation.

Go back to Frame 5 and try the question again.

---

*From Frame 1*

Frame 16

You said that choice C best provided for structuring a musical listening experience in an elementary or junior high school music class.

This, unfortunately, is a very common mistake. It assumes that after discovering the form of the song—which, by the way, is a good approach—that the mere singing of the song thereby connects in the minds of each student the form and the aural experience.

No! This is not necessarily so nor even likely. For one thing, youngsters could so enjoy the act of singing the song that their attention is not attuned to the aural perception of the form they are singing. As a general rule, the younger or more inexpert the musical learner, the less able he is to devote his attention to more than one musical factor at a time. Thus, by being involved in the act of singing, these children would be less likely to be able to focus aural attention on the form of the song. Even assuming that they could, there is no guarantee that they could visually or aurally perceive and respond to this form when they encounter it in a pure listening experience, or in another song.

Go back to Frame 1 and try the question again.

---

*From Frame 2*

Frame 17

You chose C as the description best suited to developing expertise in performance according to the previous analysis of stimulus response sequences.

Unfortunately, the situation described is too often true. Your response (and the methods of such directors) leads to several difficulties.

The use of band material for private and group lessons has serious faults. First, such parts, even when learned adequately, are not learned in a musical context. That is, a given part or section is learned outside of the expressive whole of which it is only a small component. Also, by rehearsing parts separately, the student is denied the needed opportunity of the aural cues other than his own part that are necessary to an apt performance, and which are provided by the missing parts.

Second, this teaching procedure serves only to train a "group" performer, rather than a self-sufficient, independently capable *musician*. Someone ought to write a book called "The Loneliness of the Fourth Trombone Player" or "I Was a Teen-Age Second Violin, Fifth Desk, Second Chair."

Go back to Frame 2 and try the question again.

---

*From Frame 3*

Your choice was C:   visual stimuli
mediation
performance
feedback
adjustment

Good: this is correct. The only conditions under which this might not be entirely true are those where a performer is not using music (that is, where he has memorized the music or is playing by ear). In these cases, the visual stimuli would be replaced as controlling forces by more subtle factors such as the inner ear and the intellect.

Go to Frame 4.

---

*From Frame 4*

You answered that the ability, with time, to develop a piece to a level of high competence is *not* a true or reliable indication of expertise.

This is decidedly so: a student may spend an inordinate amount of time practicing a piece to the degree that he may play it well. But this does not indicate that the various factors indicative of expertise have been truly or fully developed. It only means that he has mastered these factors for this one piece. This is no indication that he will be able to efficiently or effectively transfer such learning to another composition.

There is also the possibility that the teacher is training the student by rote drill alone. That is, the teacher may be explaining or demonstrating and the student may be imitating without knowing why; if this is the case, the student will not be able to transfer this skill independently to a different composition. Though it is true that in many instances the very early stages of skill instruction in music do involve rote imitation by the learner, the teacher is obliged from the beginning to use these occasions to develop in the student a fund of personal experience upon which he will be able to build his conceptual framework of understanding. In other words, the student should be increasingly developing and applying his understanding, and rote processes should become less and less necessary and desirable.

Remember, the amount of time a learner takes to master a given skill or composition is often indicative of the stage of skill development he has reached. In part, this development is indicated by a decrease in the time necessary to perform the skilled behavior. This is related to the elimination of mediating responses, and the increased efficiency in using feedback and making adjustments where necessary.

Go to page 46, below the line.

*From Frame 5*

You answered that choice C was the one that best provides for the three possible long-range effects that justify the inclusion of musical performance in music education.

Good: this answer is most correct. The score study and sight reading are means to two important ends: they help develop the independence and musicianship necessary for all three long-range goals; and they ensure that the students will read the work through several times until they are able to perceive its expressive whole—without, on the other hand, rehearsing the piece for an inordinately long period of time.

Listening to a recording of the composition—an experience the director is obliged to make available by whatever means the physical situation permits—will further enhance the students knowledge and ability to respond to its expressive whole. It gives them an idea of the expressive whole in terms of a degree of excellence they must work for (a goal). It also provides needed experience in the skill of listening to music as a nonperformer.

This experience and the home practice that might be expected to occur are then checked by the performance of this work at the next rehearsal. The listening experience might even be more successful if the students were directed to provide a written response to certain elements in the music, such as tempo, interpretation, and so forth.

Go to the summary on page 49.

---

*From Frame 3*

Your choice was D:    aural stimuli
mediation
performance
readjustment
feedback

In addition to the fact that most performance situations begin with visual rather than aural stimuli, you have confused other parts of the sequence.

Since it is imperative that all music teachers be able to work effectively with these ideas, review pages 42–46, and then attempt the question in Frame 3 again.

---

*From Frame 4*

You said that the ability to more quickly respond to visual and aural cues in the situation was *not* a true or reliable indication of expertise in performance.

Your answer indicates that you are confused.

Such an ability would indeed indicate significant progress, at least, toward the attainment of expertise. What it means is that the student is able to eliminate time-consuming mediating responses, and is better able to monitor his own feedback and make adjustments where necessary.

Review page 44, then answer the question in Frame 4 again.

CHAPTER THREE

# *music education*
# *for the individual*

. . . the student too often uses the map, the lab, the encyclopedia, or the microscope only at the rare moments when the curriculum tells him to do so. Even the great classics become part of "sophomore year" instead of marking a new turn in a person's life. School removes things from everyday use by labeling them educational tools.

If we are to deschool, both tendencies must be reversed. The general physical environment must be made accessible, and those physical learning resources which have been reduced to teaching instruments must become generally available for self-directed learning.

Ivan Illich, Deschooling Society (New York: Harper and Row, 1972), pp. 115–16.

In stressing the point of view of the teacher thus far, we have seen that music is an art involving stimuli and responses conditioned by the developing fund of concepts that arise from personal experience. Earlier, you saw the various educational principles that help the teacher provide and recognize real learning. The nature of conceptual learning was covered, as was the need for it to supplant purely factual learning undertaken for its own sake.

You were also introduced to several important facts about the learner: he must be actively involved (a participant) in a musical experience; he progresses according to his prior background (readiness) and his own level, and at his own rate of speed; he benefits most from learnings that he can transfer to new musical situations; the greater the number and variety of prior experiences, the more likely it is that transfer will effectively occur.

Finally, you should now be more aware of the philosophical need to develop the ability in youngsters to respond in terms of "expressive form," the "art symbol," "artistic import," and "felt life," as they apply to the musical art. None of these depend on factual learning; they all arise from conceptual learnings and the feelings or affections attached to or arising from those learnings.

Beyond these factors are several others that are of great importance to the teacher. But they are even more important to the student, for they affect the ability or attitude of the *student* in learning situations. Sometimes the student is acutely aware of these things at a very conscious level; and if poor provision is made, he may openly rebel, sullenly acquiesce, or just "drop out" mentally. At the unconscious or preconscious level, certain attitudes unfavorable to music and/or the teacher may be nurtured.

Young teachers often assume that students whose musical attitudes or skills are lacking do not like music, or do not like the teacher. The former is seldom true; the latter is sometimes true, but not in the personal sense. What is at stake is the student's dislike of studying music. The teacher is the symbol of this activity. This condition most likely arises when the student is not interested or challenged by the teacher. It is probably this failure to provide interesting and challenging learning situations which may result in the selection of activities that are too simple and unchallenging—and thus boring—for the more intelligent, interested, or musically able class members. On the other hand, the choice of learning activities may be too challenging or just inherently uninteresting to the age group.

In the case of the more musically or academically able students, the teacher's failure to create or sustain interest or challenge in learning often results in the problem behavior associated with young people trying to interest themselves. Thus, it is not just the poor or unmotivated student who may develop unfavorable attitudes and disruptive behavior.

Since learning is manifested in the increased frequency of a response, or the ability to transfer a learning to a new and different situation, it should be easily recognized that (1) experiences (activities; learning situations) devised to provide for such responses; (2) the learner's ability to cope with the experience and the envisaged response; and (3) his desire to actively engage himself in the activities there are prime among the factors that influence both the teacher's planning and execution of lessons, and the reaction of the student to such lessons. These are not the only factors, but consider them first, for without a proper understanding of them, the other factors may never become operative.

### 1. Readiness

Perhaps first in order of importance is the readiness of the individual to learn. Readiness involves all the prior experiences, learnings (concepts developed as a result of experience), and attitudes of the learner that affect his ability to complete a task. Abilities that are developed through earlier experiences may prepare the individual to successfully respond to a situation. In other instances, the individual may not have had enough of the proper prior experiences, and so his ability to deal with the situation is limited.

The responsibility of the music teacher with regard to readiness entails two choices:

a. Situations must be structured that can be satisfactorily completed by every member of a class. In order to work, such activities should involve *multiple outcomes,* one of which will be suited to and successfully achieved by every member of the class.

b. Or, situations must be created that allow each individual to respond at his own level, for a class is composed of many individuals, each with a different level of readiness for any particular activity. This is true even with classes that are supposed to be homogeneously grouped, for such grouping can be done on the basis of only one standard common to the entire class. This may be IQ, reading ability, musical ability, or any of a number of other variables. No matter which is used, such a constituted group will display considerably different levels of readiness and interest.

Failure to implement one of these two alternatives may result in the selection of learning situations that are too difficult. As a result, most students complete them unsatisfactorily and are thereby liable to develop unfavorable attitudes toward music and even the music class as such. Equally troublesome are activities that are too easy and thus uninteresting to an individual or class.

Every music class will manifest a wide variety of levels of readiness and degrees of interest in any given situation. By structuring situations that allow each individual to respond at his own level, those who are more advanced or more ready for the learning will not be left unchallenged. Frequently, activities that can satisfactorily and uniformly be completed by every member of the class tend to aim at too low a common denominator. Thus, the more advanced students are left unstimulated and uninterested by the activity.

A further problem arises when one considers the other effects of activities that call for uniform behavior. It is difficult to imagine, in any kind of musical learning, any situation where a uniform behavior can be expected. The very few "objective truths" in music all involve information *about music,* rather than dealings with musical stimuli as such. Therefore, those teachers

64

who "teach" lessons in which all students are expected to complete an activity in the same way or to arrive at some uniform result most usually deal only with information about music. Classes that involve compiling notebooks and passing tests are usually geared this way.

Part of the special magic of music (and all the arts, for that matter) is the kind of responses elicited, which, though not usually totally subjective, are very personal. When asked if a passage appeared to be musically tense or relaxed, all students might agree that it was one or the other. Yet, we could readily accept that the degree and quality of tension was unique for each. It is the lack of uniformity, or, put another way, the lack of conformity, that characterizes the artistic response. In fact, a given individual may respond differently to the same work of music at different times. This provides another rationale for the uniqueness of the response, for it is unreasonable to expect an entire class to respond in the same way, and to do so at all times.

GO TO FRAME 1, PAGE 79.

1. Readiness
2. **The Activity** (experience)

The second factor in the teacher's planning of a lesson, and the student's reaction to that lesson, is the *activity* itself. An activity, in a music class, is an *experience* that requires active participation by each learner in the completion or solution of the learning task. In most instances, active participation involves both covert and overt behaviors.

Cronbach has cogently described what he calls the "situation":

> The situation presents alternatives requiring choice. Situations offer opportunities to satisfy wants.
> The situation consists of all the objectives, persons and symbols in the learner's environment. Experience in one situation prepares a person to respond to similar situations in the future. Curriculum planning is, in essence, the selection of situations (tasks, lessons, questions, objects) to which the pupil should learn to respond and the arrangement of them in the best sequence.[1]

The need to increase the contacts with learning situations and objects that too often remain within the control of only the teacher seems to be among the main arguments of the quotation that opened this chapter. The facts seem clear: teachers must stop regarding songs, recordings, and performance scores as the "tools" of musical learning, and begin regarding them as real musical contacts for learners. These contacts are personal experiences with music, and as such it is impossible to limit in any way the many learnings that may result. This is not to say that the teacher may not wish to focus on a given aspect of the situation; it does affirm that other learnings not be re-

[1] Cronbach, *Educational Psychology*, pp. 69, 73.

65

garded as secondary by-products or ancillary benefits. These learnings are in many ways even more important than those planned, for they arise from student self-direction with the musical stimulus. This is but another application of the need for *multiple outcomes* in any given learning activity.

Similarly, and continuing along the lines suggested by Father Illich, music teachers should make scores, recordings, instruments, and so forth, more available for students to learn with on their own. This should also include guidance for rock groups who seek help.

If learning involves and results from responses to learning activities, then such activities that are devised must call for observable responses. If learning is shown by a change in behavior as a result of some experience(s), then such experiences that are provided must allow both teacher and learner to evaluate the resulting behavior. If learning is shown when a desired response becomes more frequent than others, or than before, then opportunity must be provided for its occurrence in order to determine the frequency of that response. If there is no opportunity, there is no response and no learning. If learning is observed when *transfer* to an unfamiliar situation occurs (i.e., the learner can correctly interpret and act in this unfamiliar situation), then situations must be provided that are conducive to developing the concept, and that provide the opportunity for transfer to occur.

Thus, a point made earlier, that the teacher is really a facilitator of learning, is made even more clear. The teacher facilitates learning by creating the conditions from which learning can occur.

Thus, the role of the music teacher has many dimensions. The teacher must create and design activities that properly consider *readiness,* and that permit each individual to *actively experience* the musical skill or concept to be learned. Such activities must be well structured; that is, they must provide for individual needs, individual responses (behavior), individual evaluation, and *bona fide* involvement on the part of each individual. The means for implementing the activity must be clearly and wisely laid out in advance, and must accord with the best principles of learning. The concepts or skills to be experienced and learned must be made as clear and as uncomplicated as possible. No unnecessary barriers must be allowed to operate. For example, excessive reliance on verbal responses or well-developed verbal skills (as is the case with note taking) will unduly hinder and prevent a *musical response* in those learners who are deficient in verbal skills, but who are capable of having a significant musical response.

The several activities that make up a given lesson should be related to past or future activities in the same or other lessons. Thus, development, refinement, reinforcement, and transfer are all planned. This kind of planning has several different names—developmental, sequential, spiral—all of which mean about the same thing in practice. Furthermore, the activities that make up a given lesson should be well arranged in the order relevant to the learnings at hand.

The many activities that constitute a year or curriculum must be well selected and arranged, to provide for maximum learning on the part of each individual. This entails knowing where you are, where you have been, and where you are going *at every moment* during the year. Though the future never works out the way we may plan it, the focus and thrust of such teaching results only from long-range planning that specifies long-range behavioral objectives.

The activities making up a curriculum must be organized into a plan that provides for continuous and sequential learning for each music course. A general music curriculum should provide a continuous, well-planned sequence of learning experiences from kindergarten through grade 12. Likewise, performance curricula should provide for continuous and sequential development from preinstrumental classes and elementary chorus through graduation.

Far too often, the freedom given music teachers in organizing their own curricula has been taken as a license for having no curriculum (or an improvised one). If the teacher does not know at any given step what he wishes the student to learn, or where the current activities fit in the long-range sequence of necessary learnings, it cannot be expected that the student will have a clear and self-directed idea of such goals.

Because they are so important, here is a summary of the many responsibilities of the teacher in arranging and selecting learning activities (situation).

1. *Considers readiness,* and on that basis, plans for relevant *experiences* or *responses* for each individual.
2. *Structures activities* on the basis of:
   a. individual needs;
   b. individual responses (behavior);
   c. individual evaluation (on the part of both teacher and learner);
   d. *bona fide* involvement by each individual.
3. Clearly *plans in advance* the means for implementing the activity, in order to avoid unnecessary confusion in the completion of the activity.
4. *Relates each activity to past or future activities,* and works out the most efficient and effective ordering of the multiple activities within a lesson period.
5. *Provides a curriculum of activities* planned well enough in advance to know at every moment where he is, where he has been, and where he is going.

*GO TO FRAME 2, PAGE 79.*

---

1. Readiness
2. The Activity
3. **Student Attitude and Interest** (motivation)

Another factor that influences the teacher in selecting and arranging activities is the attitude(s) held by the learner(s). Since actions usually arise in reaction to certain goals, the teacher must try to *motivate* the students to recognize some future reward, some satisfaction, some positive consequence in the completion of the proposed learning activities. In truth, the teacher cannot directly motivate the students to do anything. He can only create situations and so structure them that students are more likely to be motivated by the very nature of the learning activity and its goals.

Before this subtle side of motivation is revealed, the several different kinds of motivation should be considered.

*Intrinsic motivation:* incentive or interest is aroused by appealing factors within the prospective *musical experience* as such.

*Extrinsic motivation:* incentive is aroused by *nonmusical* factors such as the desire to do well, the desire to please, intellectual challenge, threats, and so forth.

*Self-motivation:* incentive generated by inherent interest within the individual; can be intrinsic or extrinsic.

*Imposed motivation:* incentive generated by people—such as teachers or parents—who are in a position to influence the actions of the individual through rewards, punishment, or any other available leverage.

Of these, of course, intrinsic motivation and self-motivation are usually more successful and most desirable in the learning process. Many lessons should be learned from young rock musicians who spend many hours learning to play, sing, and arrange by ear through intrinsic and self-motivation.

However, extrinsic and imposed motivation can be useful if effectively handled. Questions arranged as a crossword puzzle or a bingo card provide a much more motivating experience than a traditional homework assignment or quiz, just as a spelling bee is always more fun than a spelling test. It is essential, however, that these two forms of motivation be used sparingly and always with the most positive and beneficial overtones. For example, it is usually not too difficult to motivate students (extrinsically and imposed) to work hard for good grades, to avoid penalties, to avoid personal embarrassment, and so on. This, in fact, is what people seem to mean when they say an individual student is "well disciplined" or that a teacher is a good "disciplinarian." The implication seems to be that the teacher is very crafty in applying (imposing) various kinds of extrinsic motivation and that the student responds well and reliably to these motivations. A very independent student is in the same way branded as "difficult."

Many of the current problems affecting the secondary schools and colleges stem from the increased independence of students in terms of their own goals, and their increased unwillingness to regard grades and academic attainments as worthy goals. Attendance is required in schools where it is imagined that the possible penalties (such as failing the course) will "motivate" the student to attend class, and that by his very presence he will learn. Though the student may learn in such circumstances (this is by no means assured, or in many cases, likely), it seems increasingly doubtful that learning so motivated and acquired is significant.

The effective teacher realizes that no motivation will exist in those situations where the student sees no possibility:

1. of interest (euphemistically called "relevance" or "meaning");
2. for success;
3. for satisfaction;
4. for significant or tangible progress.

The effective teacher also recognizes that an *individual may have many goals at once*. He may truly enjoy music, but feel obligated to toe the line indicated by his peer group. Thus, his goals are in conflict, and the teacher must attempt to structure the learning situation so that a solution results that favors music but does not damage the individual's peer group image. The wise teacher also recognizes that *within a class a wide range of goals is likely*. Everyone has his own preferred music that he wants to study, sing, play, or hear. The teacher must effectively temper demands and effect compromises. Such compromises may even involve the teacher's own goals for the class.

Some teachers who perhaps intuitively recognize the goal-oriented nature of motivation try to "motivate" the class to accept those goals that the teacher has set for the class. Though this is often sound, it is usually more successful for the teacher to co-ordinate his teaching goals with those held by the students. Since the teacher is also a member of the group and has goals in mind, he must also recognize that the students have goals that are different and very significant to them. Similarly, the students must be encouraged to recognize the goals of others in the group, including, not incidentally, those held by the teacher. The attitude of the teacher to these issues will more than likely determine how goals are set and used in music classes of all sorts.

The teacher who tactlessly imposes teaching goals on a class usually courts danger in the form of problem behavior or insignificant learning by the class. The teacher who assesses and evaluates student goals and then co-ordinates teaching goals with them is much more likely to engage student interest and attention, and to then have the opportunity of extending these goals beyond the original dimensions held by the class. For example, the teacher who wishes to undertake a study of the singing voice in "art" music would begin to project well by investigating all types of singing, from rock and folk, through pop and musical comedy, finally culminating in art song and opera. Aside from the importance of this approach in terms of motivation and class goals, the approach would be more significant in terms of *present and future* benefits for the learner.

Thus, the truly wise teacher creates ways of using already existing student interest and goals to serve musical learning of much greater consequence. Examples for study are selected with the taste of the class in mind. Learnings are undertaken that accord well with, yet increasingly extend, the status quo of student taste and interest. And, above all, the students' musical goals, tastes, and interests are never belittled or denigrated. The wise interlocutor or proselytizer always makes clear his acceptance of the values of his audience. Just witness a typical political campaign if you need evidence of this psychological fact.

In the past, schools of education often required student teachers to begin each lesson plan with some kind of "motivation." The unfortunate result was often that the neophyte teacher understood this to mean the need *to create interest* in the learning to be undertaken. However, motivation properly understood should involve taking present student interest into account and relating teaching goals to those already held by the student. Even when motivation has been successful, the teacher is advised to carefully inspect the situation to try to determine whether the interest is intrinsic or extrinsic.

Frequently, the small matter of a grade can make much difference. In tests and homework, for example, the grade can become a most disturbing influence. If the teacher's own motivation is to assess individual understanding or progress and to provide the student with diagnostic evaluations of progress, then grades seem unnecessary. It makes far more sense to regularly correct the work without assigning grades. Thus, the student is motivated by musical accomplishment and the satisfaction of learning, rather than by grades. In other words, the students are able to observe the degree of success represented by the corrected work, and may derive various degrees of satisfaction from such an approach without the arbitrary and abstract matter of grades.[2]

"Since goals direct effort, the teacher's problem of motivation is essentially one of arranging situations in which the learner will see goals he wants to attain."[3]

*GO TO FRAME 3, PAGE 80.*

---

So far we have covered three factors:

1. Readiness for an activity
2. The activity (or activities)
3. Motivation and attitude toward an activity.

There are several other considerations; the teacher should be aware of them because they are fundamental to the learning experience and because the class is likely to be aware of them as well (this has important consequences that will be discussed later).

### 4. Decision Making and Problem Solving

If the activity is suited to the appropriate levels of readiness and is well structured, and if the learner is motivated, then actual involvement with or in the activity most profitably takes the form of selecting, from the possible actions offered in the activity, the one that promises the most satisfactory results.[4]

[2] More on grades on pp. 119–120 and 301–305.
[3] Cronbach, *Educational Psychology,* p. 73.
[4] Example G in Frames 3 and 8 illustrates a decision making, problem solving activity.

In this sense, a good activity is a problem, structured so that the process of solving the problem will contribute to effective conceptual or skilled learning. Such activities are *challenges* that the learner must overcome by interpreting and selecting those responses that will best complete the task or solve the problem.

This *interpretation* by the learner is in part his attempt to transfer learning (to use prior learning in a new situation). It is predicated on the belief that this activity (situation, problem) is related to some prior personal experience, and that the response that was successful in the earlier situation will have the same satisfactory result in the present activity. It also depends on the ability of the learner to direct his attention to those cues in the present situation that resemble those in the earlier one(s) (transfer of learning).

The *interpretations* made by the learner in decision making and problem solving make several important demands on the teacher of music. First, the activities should be so structured as to provide for decision making and problem solving on the part of each individual. Teachers who do so directly enhance the likelihood that transfer of learning will take place. They also insure that students will be *actively participating* (covertly and overtly) in the lesson. The degree to which information is imparted—when for instance, the teacher provides the correct interpretation and dictates the responses—is the degree to which the activity will fail to provide for real learning to occur.

Second, every attempt should be made to enhance each individual's ability to direct his attention to the relevant cues in every situation. Thus, activities calling for personal involvement must be planned, and a means for evaluating each individual's "decision" or "solution" must be devised. Without these guidelines, learning—if it occurs—is likely to be haphazard.

Third, in order for a learner to be able to interpret present situations in terms of past experiences, both relevant past experiences and continual refinement of such prior learnings must be planned. Thus, you come full circle to the question of *developmental* or *sequential* learning. Every activity should have a significant and sequential place in the past, present, and future development of each individual's ability to respond to music.

Thus, the last requirement: All such activities should meet the above three requirements as much as is practical for *each individual student.*

*GO TO FRAME 4, PAGE 81.*

---

Note that potentially successful problem-solving activities are predicated upon prior experience. Thus, the student is able to make his decision, his interpretation in the present situation, on the basis of past experience. The teacher, in judging each student's response, will then be able to assess:
1. the progress being made by each student,
2. the success of those earlier activities,

3. what further learnings (activities) might be necessary or logical for future class experiences, and

4. what review and reinforcement might be necessary in the way of activities.

Each behavioral objective should also specify in some way that *each student* be able to complete the assigned task. In each case, therefore, there should be the understanding that the teacher gives each student the freedom to make a mistake, and thereby learn that his interpretation was not successful.

Some teachers tend to give hints, either consciously or unconsciously. For example, in objective (a), Frame 4, many teachers will raise their eyes with expectation when they hear the places where the students' hands should go up. The class, noticing this, obediently responds to the teacher's hope by raising their hands each time the teacher looks up and around expectantly. This practice exemplifies the "self-fulfilling prophecy" at its worst.

In other activities, there is usually a strong temptation to help individual students with the interpretations necessary in solving the problem. Though this is beneficial in the very earliest stages of problem solving, it must be increasingly avoided thereafter. Clarifications that enhance the student's efforts to recognize cues or recall past actions must be used carefully and judiciously, lest the student become dependent on the teacher and, thus, unable to function independently.

Also, necessarily inherent in the idea of freedom is the freedom to learn from mistakes. Without this ingredient, one's ability to monitor oneself becomes increasingly difficult.

1. Readiness for an activity
2. The activity
3. Motivation and attitude toward an activity
4. Decision making and problem solving

The next step to be considered in terms of the individual student and learning in music should not be new to you.

### 5. Observable Behavior

Actually, we have assumed in the foregoing discussion that, on the basis of the learner's decision (interpretation) regarding the problem (activity), a certain *action* (overt behavior) would result. In each objective specified in Frame 4, page 81, the desired overt behavior was clearly indicated.

Example A. *Raise hand* when each statement of the subject or answer is heard.

Example B. *Identify* meter, *place* measure lines, *notate* rhythm—all of these correctly.

Example C. *Compose* and *notate* (with original notation), and *perform* as notated.

Example D. *Select* a good example of unity and variety, and unity in variety, and *explain* it.

Example E. Write (*compose*) a suitable countermelody and *arrange* it for SA and TB performance.

Example F. Correctly *perform* notation and expressive markings.

Example G. *Identify* errors from tape recording, then correct in *performance*.

If you were really perceptive, you may have noticed that some of these overt behaviors may be thought of as covert behaviors. For example, "to identify" may, under certain conditions, exhibit no overt behavior. It is quite possible to identify something to your satisfaction, purely as a mental activity. This would be true as well for choosing or selecting: we frequently choose or select things we would or will buy if or when we have the money. Often, each such choice does not immediately realize itself in an overt behavior. These kinds of situations represent a kind of "double-think," and the teacher is advised to be well aware of such confusions in order to avoid structuring activities that call only for a covert response. With this qualification, Examples A–G above each provide an observable response behavior.

One further statement should be made about the observable response that results from decision making and problem solving: such behavior does not always constitute a definitive action on the part of the learner. Sometimes when the learner is unsure or the teacher has not provided enough prior experience, the learner will try a tentative or provisional response. This tentative act will then undergo evaluation as feedback. If successful, it will be retained; if unsatisfactory, it should be withdrawn and a new interpretation or decision made and acted upon.

Thus, in many kinds of music classes, responses are frequently *provisional* because so much of the musical art is new to the learner. The beginning and even intermediate performer has very little to be truly sure of, truly secure with. This is perhaps even more likely in general music classes, where very few specific learnings and skills have been undertaken.

For these reasons, musical learnings are best accomplished in a class atmosphere where the freedom to make a mistake is well recognized by everyone, especially the teacher. Grading all responses severely inhibits this kind of learning. Teachers who do not provide the opportunity for any kind of overt responses or who give inordinately strong hints will find that this "freedom-to-make mistakes" phase of the learning process will go undeveloped. Students either will not be able to respond or will respond only when they are absolutely sure of their responses. There will be no ad*venture*some thinking and behaving and, hence, no self-discovery. Learning will become dull and routine without the excitement and challenge of discovery learning.

Making mistakes and being able to monitor these mistakes in terms of available feedback is an absolutely crucial factor in the learning process. What is so good about making mistakes? "Mistakes" imply the recognition of the *consequences of an action.* This is the next step in the sequence of learning that we are considering:

1. Readiness for an activity
2. The activity
3. Motivation and attitude
4. Decision making and problem solving (interpretation)
5. Observable behavior
6. **The Consequences of an Action**

When an action results in *confirmation* of the initial decision or interpretation, *reinforcement* will occur, and the learner is thereby more likely to apply the same interpretation to similar musical situations in the future. When an action results in *contradiction* of the initial decision or interpretation, *negative reinforcement* will occur, and the learner becomes doubtful about his interpretation and is inclined to avoid it in the future.

Because the consequences of an action are so essential to the learning process, and because the learner is often very sensitive to potential success and failure, the teacher is again presented with several responsibilities: (1) to aid the learner in developing the capacity to *accurately and independently observe the consequences of his actions* (that is, the results of his interpretations); (2) to foster a positive attitude toward mistakes and to make the entire class aware of the fact that considerable learning results from mistakes—sometimes more than from success; and (3) to encourage, assist, and provide for adaptive rather than non-adaptive behavior.

1. Readiness for an activity
2. The activity
3. Motivation and attitude
4. Decision making and problem solving (interpretation)
5. Observable behavior (overt behavior as a terminal response)
6. The consequences of an action
7. **Adaptive or Nonadaptive Behavior**

This is the final step in the network of factors that constitutes active learning for each individual student. When the consequences of an action contradict the learner's interpretation, his attempt to make the correct decision or to correctly solve the problem has been thwarted or frustrated. Here again the question of motivation is important, for if the student is not positively motivated—if he is forced to respond or if he responds because that is the easiest way out of an unpleasant situation in contrast with making a response because of a real desire to learn, to succeed musically—he probably will be satisfied with producing *any* action. This usually happens whenever a student acts because of imposed or extrinsic motivation.

When a learner is so easily satisfied, his behavior is nonadaptive, as a result of contradiction and thwarting. Nonadaptive behavior may also result from instances where the learner is not able or has not been given the opportunity to accurately or independently interpret the consequences of his action.

This occurs very frequently in a multitude of situations, both performance and nonperformance, across the entire range of music education.

In a general music situation, this might occur when a teacher does not teach sequentially (base all activities on past and future experiences). Thus, when a number of students do not do well on an evaluation, then:

1. The learnings are not returned to, so there is no opportunity to reinterpret the situation and act again.

2. In any case, without future activities to further clarify the situation and direct the learner's attention to the relevant cues, he has no basis for a new interpretation or a new action except a wild guess. Usually he gives up. This is nonadaptive behavior.

Traditionally, tests have been used in this way to merely assess the learner's progress. When a number of grades are poor, those receiving less than C or its numerical equivalent are seldom assisted in overcoming their weak performance on the test. Far too frequently, the teacher continues forward, leaving these people behind forever. This can only happen when the teacher considers teaching to be a matter of covering a certain amount of material in a given order in a given time, rather than a matter of guiding and developing the musical behaviors of students.

In schools whose performance programs consist mainly of large ensembles, the learner is also faced with the following problems: (1) He is often unable to accurately and independently interpret the situation because his part is swallowed up in the general mass of sound. (2) By not having the opportunity to play solos or small ensemble literature where he must master an exposed part, he is unlikely to ever develop the ability to correctly interpret the musical consequences of his actions or to know or have the opportunity to *reinterpret* and *act again*. Furthermore, the director is faced with the prospect of wasting considerable time by continually having to stop, correct, advise, and rehearse those individuals or sections who continue nonadaptively (probably because the source of the error and how to correct it has not been learned conceptually).

Thus, the responsibilities of the music teacher are clear. Adaptive behavior in situations where contradiction has led to thwarting should be encouraged by: (1) providing the kind of *individual attention* that helps to identify and overcome the causes of difficulty; (2) providing the students with the *means or guidance* (at first) necessary to reinterpret the problem; (3) *reducing any emotional tension* or personal difficulties that might result from thwarting or from the reaction of other members of the class to such thwarting; (4) above all, providing and structuring those situations, those opportunities, that enhance the learner's ability to (a) monitor his own actions, (b) develop self-diagnostic capacities, and (c) achieve some measure of success. Failure to provide for adaptive behavior can result in all kinds of errant behavior, and without doubt, is responsible for many of the problems that confront music educators continually.

The easiest way to provide for adaptive behavior, a course that is followed by too many teachers, is often rote training: the teacher demonstrates the correct response whenever an incorrect response occurs, and then has the class repeat it and practice it so many times that the difficulty seems overcome finally. Though this kind of teaching seems to realize the most immediate results, it does not eliminate errant and multiple forms of nonadaptive behavior in the long run, and is thus neither the most efficient nor the most effective method.

It is not efficient because of the inordinate amount of time it takes to drill the correct responses into the heads of individuals or classes. It is also inefficient because drilling must occur *virtually every time* an incorrect response is made. This constitutes a waste of valuable time. The method is thus inefficient because far too much time is taken up, and no real learning results. Hence, the risk of boredom or satiation is ever present.

Also, this rote method of providing for adaptive behavior is ineffective because no real learnings conducive to musical independence and musicianship are developed. Hence, the overwhelming number of school musicians whose interest, involvement, and contact with good music ceases upon graduation from high school. Such musicians are unable to continue performing (even where situations for such performance exist) because they cannot deal independently with musical problems; or their interests are captured by other pursuits, which offer long-range possibilities of success and pleasure in areas in which they have developed independence—something that their musical studies never afforded them.

The solution is not difficult. At the beginning stages, the teacher judiciously blends corrections that he identifies for the student with the so-called "Socratic" method. This method involves the leading-question approach: "What is the meter of the piece?" "What meter were you playing?" "How many sections should a binary form have?" "How many did you compose?" As the student progresses, the Socratic method should ever so gradually replace any corrections identified and made by the teacher. Eventually, the student should locate and correct most of the mistakes by himself, with the teacher applying the Socratic approach only as a means of continuing refinement or of isolating problems overlooked accidentally by the student.

Too many teachers are interested in immediate results—presumably to fulfill their own needs—to the extent that music education has not had the impact on public musical taste and involvement that it can and should have. Nowhere is this more tragic than with the large number of students not actively involved in musical performance groups, but who are intelligent enough and/or interested enough in music to have a genuine and significant response to music as listeners. Were they interested in musical performance, they would join the appropriate musical organizations (assuming, of course, that all such organizations are not selective). Yet at all levels of their general music classes, they are subjected to a barrage of performance skills that usually involve singing and reading music. Teachers usually do this under the guise of providing actual experiences with music that are necessary to develop concepts. The problem is, of course, that performance is not the only way of personally experiencing music, nor necessarily the best, considering the needs of all youngsters. Couple this with the fact that if personal experience with music is to result in concepts of music that are valuable in listening, it must occur under certain conditions. In many programs, these are seldom realized.

Due consideration of needs, interests, motivations, and goals would be a step in the right direction. With such an approach, activities can be undertaken that are more fruitful in terms of the eventual impact of music on the individual as listener. It would necessarily be a process where contradiction and thwarting are regarded as positive factors in the learning experience,[5] not one where such experiences are used only to arrive at a grade for the course. When contradiction and thwarting are used in the latter way, they are often generalized, and associated with certain emotions, after which they become attitudes that disclaim any affection for music as an art or as a serious avocational pursuit in terms of listening or performing.

*GO TO FRAME 5, PAGE 81.*

---

## SUMMARY

As you may have noticed in the previous exercise, this book attempts to employ many features of the kind of active learning recommended in its pages —to the degree that this is possible in a book. Many books present questions or problems at the end of the chapter: this is better than no problems at all, but leaving the questions until the end often creates difficulty, especially in books that are sequential and in which each learning is predicated on the previous learning. Any lack of understanding in the early stages of the chapter, and the reader is likely to be lost throughout. Rereading the chapter may be necessary; but not only is this time consuming, there is no guarantee that the verbal explanation misunderstood the first time through will be understood the second time.

Another failing of such texts is the fact that possible answers, especially to "discussion" questions, are seldom forthcoming within the book itself. Here, where possible, you are given suggested answers in terms of the material previously presented. Following the outlining of material, each activity is usually followed by the answers. This not only gives the reader the opportunity to find out whether his interpretation of the problem is confirmed or contradicted, it also considers where contradiction has occurred, and the possible reasons for the misinterpretation. Where possible, a brief re-presentation of the material in somewhat different terms is given as well. Thus, the reader is better able to understand the reasons for his mistake, and to make

---

[5] Such as where the last part of a lesson (a behavioral objective) offers multiple opportunities for discussion, revision, and other forms of eliciting or reinforcing appropriate learning.

adaptive behavior. This adaptive behavior is possible because in the event of a mistake the reader usually is directed to return to the problem and, in light of what he may have learned from his mistake, to reinterpret the situation and act again by making another choice. And the process is repeated. When the correct choice is reached, the reader proceeds to the next section of text. This kind of process atempts to overcome some of the limitations of teaching by means of a written text.

Why would anyone go to the trouble to organize a text in this way? For the same reasons that all teachers must take whatever steps are necessary to improve their instruction. If reading a text is to be considered learning, then the experience of having read the text should have some influence on the behavior of the reader. Here, that would entail increasing the frequency of your correct responses, and, above all, having a positive influence on your teaching behavior.

Which of the following behavioral objectives best fulfills the above two responsibilities of a general music teacher with regard to *readiness?*

A. Given a directed listening lesson containing twenty responses, the student will be able to demonstrate at least one satisfactory response in each of the following categories:

1. physical response
2. affective (mood) response
3. imaginative response
4. intellectual (cognitive) response

Go to Frame 6.

B. Given the song "When the Saints Go Marchin' In" each student will participate in singing it, and sing the pitches and rhythms accurately. Go to Frame 12.

C. Given the rhythm pattern

the class will clap it correctly while counting aloud; clap it correctly while counting silently; clap it correctly while singing "America" from *West Side Story;* and clap it correctly while listening to "America." Go to Frame 15.

---

Because it is imperative that each music teacher have these responsibilities clearly in mind, try this review activity. Which of the following lists *best* represents the many responsibilities of the teacher in lesson planning that we have covered so far?

The teacher must plan in terms of:

A. class readiness and needs;
an activity involving *overt behavior* by all;
*efficient means* of implementing the activity;
evaluation by the *teacher;*
evaluation by the *class or individual;*
relating an activity to others in *past* classes;
relating an activity to *future* activities during the year;
relating an activity to the future in terms of *curriculum and life.*
  Go to Frame 7.
B. readiness and needs of each individual;
an activity involving *overt behavior* by all;
efficient and effective *implementation* of the activity;
evaluation by the *teacher;*
evaluation by the *class or individual;*
relating an activity to others in the same class period;

relating an activity to *past and future* activities during the year;
relating an activity to the future in terms of *curriculum and life.*
Go to Frame 13.

C. class readiness and individual needs;
an activity involving *overt behavior* by all;
*efficient means* of implementing the activity;
evaluation by the *teacher;*
evaluation by the *individual or class;*
relating an activity to *past* activities during the year;
relating an activity to others in the same class period;
relating an activity to the future, in terms of *curriculum and life.*

Go to Frame 17.

---

From page 70                                                  Frame 3

On a piece of scrap paper, characterize each of the following examples of motivation as either *strong* or *weak;* also, identify the kinds of motivation that are involved in each: intrinsic, extrinsic, self-, or imposed motivation. Consider each carefully.

A. A teacher undertakes a listening lesson on the recognition of instruments with the remark, "You'd better concentrate hard because you'll have to know this for the quiz next week."

B. The author of a book for teachers writes, "Perhaps you should close the book for a moment and see whether or not you can recall all of these principles, for it is certain that your effectiveness as a teacher will depend on your continual awareness of them."

C. The band director announces, "This new composition we will study will be challenging, but I am confident that you will do well with it."

D. A general music teacher, beginning a lesson on musical form, says, "It is very important for each of you to be able to understand and perceive musical form in order to properly appreciate and evaluate music."

E. A high school theory class is assigned to create a four-part choral arrangement of any song of their choosing, as an exercise in harmonization and part writing; after corrections and a decision by the class, the most successful ones will be sung in chorus.

F. An elementary general music teacher preparing for a listening lesson on Ravel's *Bolero* tells the class, "I am sure you will like this piece; it has lots of interesting rhythm, two nice melodies, and uses many interesting instruments."

G. A junior high school general music teacher beginning a lesson on theme-and-variation form says, "Today we will divide up into groups of three. Each group will have five minutes to find as many different kinds of rectangles in the room as they can and list them. Make sure you don't let another group steal your list."

Go to Frame 8 to check your answers.

On a sheet of paper, briefly note the merits and/or weaknesses of the following behavioral objectives with regard to their effectiveness in providing for decision-making and problem solving.

A. Given Bach's Little Fugue in g minor, each student will be able to identify each statement of the subject or answer by raising his hand when he hears it.

B. Given a copy of the poem "Night" by William Blake and a correct reading of it by the teacher, each student will demonstrate his comprehension of rhythm and meter by determining in musical terms the meter of the poem, by placing measure lines between the appropriate words or syllables, and by notating the rhythms of the words using standard musical notation.

C. Given a time limit of twenty minutes, groups of ten students each will compose and notate (with original symbols) a second rondo form (ABACA) from "found" sounds in the room, and will perform it for the remainder of the class.

D. Given the task of selecting an architectural example in town which manifests (1) unity *and* variety; and (2) unity *in* variety, each student will demonstrate his perception of these principles by explaining his selection to the class; they, in turn, will "critique" each explanation.

E. Given the song "Where Have All the Flowers Gone?" each student will write a suitable countermelody and place both in a range suitable for SA (soprano, alto) *and* TB (tenor, bass) performance.

F. Given a trio of their own choosing and three weeks preparation, each of three students will correctly and independently learn his own part, and the group will rehearse the work on their own, correctly and musically performing all notation and expressive markings for the teacher.

G. Given three minutes, each section of the band will correct its major errors after hearing a tape recording of the composition (or section thereof) in question.

When you have answered each example, turn to Frame 10 to review the possibilities.

---

Think back for a moment and see how well you can interpret and decide upon the proper response, by choosing the example(s) below that provide(s) well for the conditions of: observable response behavior, consequences of actions (contradiction or affirmation), and, in the event of contradiction, adaptive behavior.

A. Given the song "Kum Bah Yah," each member of the class will sing the song with correct pitches and with a pleasing tone. Go to Frame 11.

B. Given the titles "Rainbow" and "Waterfall" and the choice of "found" or self-generated sounds, each student will choose a title, and compose and notate an original composition of approximately thirty seconds which embodies his musical interpretation of the title he selected. The entire class will perform and discuss each composition, and for homework each member will create another composition for the other title. Go to Frame 14.

C. Given new exercises 37–40 in his instrumental methods book, the student will (1) practice them each day at home; and (2) play them correctly at the next lesson. Go to Frame 18.

D. Given a tape recording of "Say ye to the righteous" by Randall Thompson, made during an earlier rehearsal, the chorus will identify on a sheet of paper the overall weaknesses of the performance, the weaknesses of their particular section, and the overall merits of the performance; these will be handed in to the teacher, after which the work will be performed again with significant improvement; discussion will follow. Go to Frame 9.

E. Given the use of the tape recorder after school and during free periods, each student will choose one of the following forms of processes: arc form (*Bogenform*), figure and sequence, theme and variations: create a composition of self-generated vocal sounds that exemplifies the chosen form; and tape record his performance of this composition, which will be played to the class and graded by the teacher. Time allotment, ten school days. Go to Frame 16.

---

*From Frame 1*

You chose A as the behavioral objective that best fulfills the two responsibilities of the general music teacher with regard to *readiness*.

Good; that is correct. It is correct because each student will most likely be able to fulfill the minimal criteria specified, yet all will be able to respond at their own level. Some will far surpass the minimal criteria. Thus, both the strongest and the weakest will be provided with relevant learning possibilities.

The affective (mood) response might be to check an adjective that best describes the music, or to choose a color that seems to reflect a mood similar to the music. In both cases, should the teacher ask, the student should be able to explain the reasoning supporting these choices. The imaginative response might involve suggesting a title for a programmatic composition whose title has been left unannounced. With a sufficient explanation, practically any suggested title might be satisfactory, and, thus, everyone should be able to derive both satisfaction and success in these areas.

The intellectual or cognitive response (identification, analyses, discrimination, etc.) and the physical response (conducting meters, tapping rhythms, etc.) can be included by providing opportunities ranging from simple (which could be a review or reinforcement for the advanced and a chance for success by the less advanced) to difficult (which would be a challenge for everyone) and, especially by providing needed stimulation for the advanced.

Thus, again, all would be capable of a considerable amount of successful responses at their own level. By such means, each would progress from different conceptual levels at their own rates of speed.

Go to page 65, below the line.

You chose A as the list that best provides for each of the responsibilities of a music teacher in planning lessons.

Unfortunately, were *you* to use this list in planning your lessons, you would have overlooked several important factors. Let's consider the list you chose:

1. Class readiness: Here you should be concerned with individual readiness. No class of individuals no matter how homogeneously grouped, will be equally or uniformly "ready" for all activities.

2. Class needs: Again, it is individual needs that are important. No single need will represent the will of the entire class, so it is better to think in terms of an activity that will have *multiple outcomes or multiple levels of achievement.* This can meet more (but seldom all) individual needs.

3. An activity involving overt behavior by all: This is true and as it should be if you want to be sure that learning is taking place in accordance with your goals.

4. Efficient means of implementing the activity: This is again good sense, for it will minimize confusion and thereby maximize the effectiveness of the activity.

5. Evaluation by the teacher: Again, true and easily done if the third responsibility (above) is followed.

6. Evaluation by the class or individual: True, since musical independence requires the student to be able to monitor his own or the class's joint performances and to successfully evaluate such performances.

7. Relating an activity to others in past classes: True *in part*. It is also helpful to think in terms of relating an activity to others (past and future) in the *same* class period; this insures continuity, order, development, sequence, logic, and so forth for each class period.

8. Relating an activity to future activities during the year: As with the responsibility immediately above, this is only true *in part,* for the future (if readiness is considered) is always dependent upon the *past* activities in the learner's experience. Thus, this provision should specify both past and future activities within and outside the present class period.

9. Relating an activity to the future in terms of curriculum and life: Good; in other words, you must determine how this activity provides for the goals of the total curriculum and how it provides a life-influence for the student.

Go back to Frame 2 and try the question again.

Reread each description in Frame 3 before you read the answer that goes with it.

A. This motivation is very weak: it is both *imposed* and *extrinsic.* It makes no attempt to intrinsically involve the class in the activity *for its own value.* It does not provide for self-motivation, except to extrinsically impose the threat of a quiz and grade.

B. This motivation—given the conditions—is stronger than it is weak. It, too, is extrinsic and imposed, but it makes a strong attempt to arouse intrinsic and self-motivation in the reader by suggesting and clarifying the importance of the activity to an audience in a position to make a valid decision on the matter. It also operates on the likelihood that readers of such a book have an interest and a stake in learning to be better teachers, and, thus, that such a suggestion will be seen as useful and significant.

C. This motivation is *strong:* it is extrinsic to the degree that it appeals to the sense of challenge of the age group, but it is also likely to encourage self-motivation necessary to complete the task. Contributing to the motivation is the director's honest optimism. If it is not honest optimism and if the director has continually said this about compositions that the band has not been able to learn well, not derived satisfaction from, or had to work on for so long that they became bored, then, of course, all is for naught. The crux of this situation is the choice of the piece. Is it a composition that will appeal to the age group? And, will they do well with it?

D. This motivation is weak, even though on the surface, at least, it appears to be similar to choice B. Unlike B it is *not* addressed to a group in a position to make a valid decision on the matter. The teacher has already made the decision for the class, and it is perfectly obvious to them that they have no choice in the matter. They may not be concerned that "proper" appreciation and evaluation is what does or should interest them. Most adolescents, especially during the early teens, cannot see the abstract future as being of much importance or interest. They are frequently more interested in short-term goals and short-term results.

E. This motivation is strong: in a sense, all the factors of motivation may be present. It is extrinsic because of the challenge to do well. It is imposed to the degree that the initiative for the activity came from the teacher. If it has come from the class, it would have represented self-motivation. It can involve self-motivation to the degree that the individual is interested in the task and sees some possible relevance in its completion: this is likely in a theory class. It also involves intrinsic motivation since the class knows their compositions will be performed by the class, and possibly chosen for performance in chorus. Thus, the *theory* experience will eventually become a *musical* experience. Last, it is intrinsic to the degree that it is not a mere academic exercise. It will involve *musical behavior* (behavior dealing with musical and musically expressive problems) during both its composition and performance.

F. This motivation is awful: the teacher is imposing her choice on the class. She is also imposing value judgments *a priori* (such as "lots of *interesting* instruments"). Foresight, in any case, would warn that the piece is too long, too repetitive, for the attention span at any level of elementary school. Thus, even if interest were aroused by this statement, it would likely be "turned off" as the activity wore on, and the confidence of the class in the teacher would thereby suffer.

G. This motivation is strong. It is extrinsic because the content is not truly musical *as yet;* but it has many advantages. Because it provides for group (peer) activity, and because a competitive attitude is likely to develop (especially as a result of the last part of the statement), considerable self-motivation (for each group and individual) can develop. As a preparatory activity, it will provide a viable basis for intrinsic motivation when the theme-and-variation process in music is finally undertaken.

The motivation described in G is often successful in general music classes, where students are studying music as a curricular requirement rather than on an elective basis. It operates on the premise of creating extrinsic interest by means of a preparatory activity that will then be applied to a more intrinsically musical situation. This kind of strategy is sometimes called a *venture*, though not because the usual meaning of the word infers risk or hazard. It is used in the sense of an ad*venture*, an occasion for opening up new vistas of interests. Ventures, thus, are best planned and undertaken with a sense of challenge and adventure at the possibility of some exciting or interesting discovery or activity. Members of such classes often have no real goals or interests yet developed regarding music or its study. Therefore, a successful preparatory activity in which they find success and interest often becomes a firm basis for more serious musical undertakings.

Go to page 67, below the line.

---

From Frame 5

You chose D as one of the choices that provides well for observable response behavior, consequences, and adaptive behavior.

Given a tape recording of "Say ye to the righteous" by Randall Thompson, made during an earlier rehearsal, the chorus will identify on a sheet of paper the over-all weaknesses of the performance, the weaknesses of their particular section, and the overall merits of the performance; these will be handed in to the teacher, after which the work will be performed again with significant improvement; discussion will follow.

Your interpretation and response are confirmed; you are correct.

Observable response behavior is provided by the written identifications and by the repeat performance.

Consequences of the taped performance are provided by the same means. (How economical!) Consequences of the second performance will be provided by the discussion that follows.

Adaptive behavior is built into this activity by the fact that the second performance, based on their prior observations, is undertaken with improvement specified as its anticipated outcome. Therefore, adaptive behavior is strongly encouraged by the very nature of the activity; if it does not come to fruition, the teacher may repeat the entire activity. More fruitful would be the inclusion of other experiences designed to enhance their readiness for the repetition of this activity.

If this was your first correct choice, go back to Frame 5 and choose again, because there is another correct answer. If you have already chosen both correct answers, go to page 77, below the line.

Before you review each of the following answers, reread the corresponding behavioral objective in Frame 4.

A. This kind of activity is frequently employed. On the surface it appears to provide for real problem-solving or decision-making behavior. However, it is subject to one pitfall: it permits the unsure or weaker students to copy the actions (reactions, behavior) of the more confident students. Such "group thinking" is not conducive to the kind of independent interpretation required in order for problem solving and decision-making to be effective. The simple modification of having the class close their eyes improves the activity immeasurably. Other devices can be used to overcome the weaknesses of such activities that rely on the raising of hands.

B. This activity provides well for the kind of independent interpretations that lead to effective learning. Because the behavioral objective given clearly specifies the steps of the activity and the order in which they are to be taken, the teacher is able to observe the individual interpretations as the activity progresses. Thus, with probing questions and individual guidance where helpful, each individual must complete this assignment essentially on his own. The teacher should not, however, give so many or such complete hints that the interpretation is virtually accomplished for the individual.

C. This is an interesting activity, but it suffers from the fact that the large-group process is likely to hinder individual participation: in almost every group of this size, there will be leaders and followers. In this activity, the followers will not make significant progress unless the group is much smaller. To do this the behavioral objective might have specified what each of the group members is to do—for instance, "each is to 'discover' or create at least two different sounds"; "each should be prepared to capably direct the performance"; "each should be able to perform each of the separate parts of the notated score."

D. This too is an interesting activity, and would successfully provide decision making and problem solving to the degree that each student's parents cannot or do not help with the assignment. The class activity seems to provide well for this by calling upon each student to explain his selection and defend it in discussion. Contributions made during discussion will also display the learner's mastery of this problem, and will give the teacher the opportunity to introduce refinements and additional ideas.

This is also another example of a *venture* where certain nonmusical and more tangible concepts are undertaken prior to their application in a musical setting. The interest (and perhaps even pleasant disagreements among class members) that can arise from such a venture stems from the open-endedness of the problem, which has *no single correct answer*. This kind of problem is ideal for sparking interest in ideas that will *immediately* be followed by some musical application.

E. This activity plans well for individual interpretations. It must be completed individually, and the final result would be considerably different from student to student, thus proving that a variety of interpretations and decisions are possible in many musical situations. Finally, all the various interpretations add to the conceptual fund of experience of each student, thus enhancing the possibility of successful transfer in other situations. Obviously, this activity seems most appropriate to a theory class.

F. In terms of performance situations, this activity provides very well for independent problem solving and decision making, with one very important addition. In the group rehearsal, each individual will have to consider other group members, and thus the situation unique to chamber music, that of "independent" *group solutions* of musical problems, is also practiced.

G. This activity again provides successfully for "independent" group solutions of musical problems. This, like the preceding activity, is likely to enhance *musical independence*. This activity is in contrast with situations where the director insists on pointing out all errors at all times and dictating their remedies.

If you are satisfied with your answers, go to page 71, below the line. Otherwise, you may wish to return to and review pages 67–70, before going ahead.

---

*From Frame 5* Frame 11

You chose A as one of the choices that provides well for observable response behavior, consequences, and adaptive behavior:

Given the song "Kum Bah Yah," each member of the class will sing the song with correct pitches and with a pleasing tone.

Unfortunately, the consequences of your own interpretation are about to be contradicted and thwarted, for you are not correct.

This activity provides for observable response behavior only in that singing occurs. It would be difficult to assess the correctness of the pitches and whether each child's tone was pleasing.

No provision is made for student monitoring of the consequences; and without this, adaptive behavior is not likely. If the teacher monitors consequences (which, as was said above, would be difficult), then any adaptive behavior that might occur would be teacher-directed and thereby ineffective. Also, correcting the mistakes of the pitch-deficient students (formerly known as monotones) or those with "poor" tones° might very well lead to embarrassment. And what would the successful students be doing while the teacher is "working with" the students who did not do well?

Go back to Frame 5 and try another selection.

---

° A value judgment such as this might better be supplanted by the teaching goal of allowing each student to use his voice naturally, even if the end result is not especially "pleasing" to the teacher. Though everyone should be able to sing well, not all will have "pleasing" voices in the sense that seems implied by so many teachers who use this as a teaching goal.

---

*From Frame 1* Frame 12

You chose behavioral objective B as the one that best fulfills the two responsibilities of the teacher with regard to *readiness*.

Of the three objectives, this one probably would least provide for readiness. Why? Because not all students may care to participate at this time. This would be especially true if the class included students with adolescent changing voices. Furthermore, in most cases you can anticipate that each student will not be able to sing the pitches and rhythms correctly.

Other than these objections, this behavioral objective fails to provide for a means of evaluating whether or not each child is singing accurately. It would be difficult to be sure: the teacher would either have to repeat the song many times as she wandered among the class listening to each long enough to evaluate, or solos would have to be solicited. Neither technique is recommended, of course: the first tends to boredom and meaningless repetition, the second to embarrassment and poor attitudes.

Even if evaluation were obtained, what could be done with those who performed incorrectly? And in a philosophical vein, how is this activity supposed to enhance the individual's ability to experience "felt life," "expressive form," the "artistic symbol," or artistic import?"

Go back to Frame 1 and try the question again.

---

*From Frame 2*

You chose B as the list that best provides for each of the responsibilities of a music teacher in planning lessons.

You have done well, but let's review the list briefly to make sure you made the correct choice for the correct reasons.

1. Readiness of each individual: no class of individuals, no matter how homogeneously grouped, will be equally or uniformly "ready" for all activities. Thus, the readiness of each student must be considered.

2. Individual needs: No single need will represent the will of the entire class. Thus, activities that have multiple outcomes are likely to meet more (though seldom all) possible individual needs.

3. An activity involving overt behavior by all: The overt behavior helps insure active involvement and provides a satisfactory means for observing progress.

4. Efficient and effective implementation of the activity: The more efficient the implementation, the less confusion is likely to result. The less confusion, the more learning is likely to occur effectively.

5. Evaluation by the teacher: The overt behavior specified in the third responsibility (above) provides the means for achieving this.

6. Evaluation by the class or individual: The more tangible evidence of learning provided by the third responsibility helps the learner to monitor his own performance or that of his group. This leads to musical independence.

7. Relating an activity to others in the same class period: This insures continuity, sequence, and logic for each individual class period.

8. Relating an activity to past and future activities during the year: In conjunction with the responsibility immediately above, this will unify the year's efforts, and provide the necessary focus and opportunity for transfer of learning to occur.

9. Relating an activity to the future in terms of curriculum and life: Does the activity fit into long-range plans for the year? How does the curriculum in its totality have any significant bearing on the effective incorporation by each individual of these musical learnings and their relevance to effective living?

Go now to page 67, below the line.

---

*From Frame 5*                                                          Frame 14

You chose B as one of the choices that provides well for observable response behavior, consequences, and adaptive behavior.

Given the titles "Rainbow" and "Waterfall" and the choice of "found" or self-generated sounds, each student will choose a title, and compose, using original notation, a composition of approximately thirty seconds which embodies his musical interpretation of the title he selected. The entire class will perform and discuss each composition, and for homework each member will create another composition for the other title.

Good, your interpretation is correct and your response is thereby confirmed.

Observable responses are provided by the notation, performance, and discussion parts of the activity.

Consequences are also provided by the discussion that follows the performance.

Adaptive behavior is provided by the post-assignment that allows the opportunity to apply what was discovered during the discussion, and to improve the second composition.

An added benefit here is the likelihood that each student will discover that many interpretations can be equally successful.

This question had two correct answers. Go back to Frame 5 and make another choice if you have not already done so. This is your opportunity to reapply and hopefully reinforce your own insight. If you have found both correct answers, go to page 77, under the line.

---

*From Frame 1*                                                          Frame 15

You chose example C as the behavioral objective that best fulfills the two responsibilities of the teacher with regard to *readiness*.

Decidedly not so. If you understood the position outlined earlier, you would have seen that the activities proposed here would entail the following:

1. The activities could not be satisfactorily completed by every member of any given class and, thus, could not take their readiness into account.

2. The activities would not allow each individual to respond at his own level (the readiness level of some would allow them to perform these tasks

only with a considerable amount of error, probably accompanied by frustration and disaffection).

3. Those whose level of readiness is not suited to these tasks would also likely be uninterested and what we may call, for our present purposes at least, unmotivated.

The activities suggested are also extremely likely to encourage the weaker students to imitate and follow the more advanced. Thus, while they might conceivably perform all these activities "correctly," they would not have done so by themselves, and, thus, would profit little, if at all, from the experience. Under the described circumstances, it would be difficult to tell which students were independently successful and which imitated the leaders.

This objective is also liable to a philosophical challenge: What contribution does this skill-oriented activity have in developing concepts that allow the individual to have a significant response to music?

Go back to Frame 1 and try the question again.

---

*From Frame 5*

You chose E as one of the choices that provides well for observable response behavior, consequences, and adaptive behavior.

Given the use of the tape recorder after school and during free periods, each student will choose one of the following forms or processes: arc form (*Bogenform*), figure and sequence, theme and variations; create a composition of self-generated vocal sounds that exemplifies the chosen form; and tape record his performance of this composition, which will be played to the class and graded by the teacher. Time allotment, ten school days.

Not bad, but not entirely correct. After reading the explanation below, you are called upon to manifest adaptive behavior of your own.

Observable response behavior is present in the form of the tape recording. Score one for you!

Consequences are provided to the degree that the learner will have the opportunity to hear his own composition and those of his friends. Score two for you! No basis for evaluation seems to have been provided, however. No discussion or other activity has been suggested that would allow the student to improve his ability to monitor his own actions.

Adaptive behavior, therefore, is not well provided here. As a result of the teacher's grade, and his comments, if any, the student will only know whether he has done well or not; he will have no follow-up experience that would allow him the chance to reinterpret the situation and act again.

The teacher may someday repeat this kind of activity, but if this is not specified in the behavioral objective, the future activity is likely to be haphazardly and weakly, if at all, related to this activity. Hence, transfer, as well as adaptive behavior, is unlikely.

Now that you have been given a basis to aid you in reinterpreting the problem, go back to Frame 5 and make another interpretation and response; manifest adaptive behavior of your own.

---

*From Frame 2*

You chose C as the list that best provides for each of the responsibilities of a music teacher in planning lessons.

Not all of these are appropriate choices. Let's see why.

1. Class readiness: Here, you should be concerned with *individual readiness.* No class of individuals, no matter how homogeneously grouped, will be equally or uniformly "ready" for all activities.

2. Individual needs: This is true. No single need will represent the will of the entire class. Thus, activities that have multiple outcomes are likely to meet more (though seldom all) possible individual needs.

3. An activity involving overt behavior by all: This too is correct. Such behavior helps insure active involvement and provides a satisfactory means for observing progress.

4. Efficient means of implementing the activity: This is good: such planning will minimize confusion and maximize learning.

5. Evaluation by the teacher: The overt behavior specified in the third responsibility (above) provides the means for achieving this. Your choice here is good.

6. Evaluation by the individual or class: This is an appropriate choice also. This kind of individual or group evaluation is made easier by the more tangible evidence provided by the third responsibility. It leads to musical independence as it becomes progressively refined.

7. Relating an activity to past activities during the year: *This is insufficient.* Every activity *should* be related to past experience, but should also lead to *future* goals. Both past and future must be considered.

8. Relating an activity to others in the same class period: A well-organized lesson, each segment of which has a logical and perfectly clear relationship to others in the same class period, can establish connections between previously unrelated ideas or skills. Your choice is correct.

9. Relating an activity to the future in terms of curriculum and life: A good choice. Every activity must have long-range goals, and must enhance the possibility that the learning will become a life-influence for the learner.

Go back to Frame 2, and try to clear up the two errors found in this list by making another choice.

---

*From Frame 5*

You chose C as one of the choices that provides well for observable response behavior, consequences, and adaptive behavior.

Given new exercises 37–40 in his instrumental methods book, the student will (1) practice them each day at home, and (2) play them correctly at the next lesson.

You should now be contradicted and thwarted because your interpretation and response were wrong.

Observable response behavior is provided in the form of performance at the lesson. Theoretically, this will determine the kinds of responses that occurred during home practice.

Consequences are less well provided because no indication is given of *how,* or, in fact, *if* the student will monitor his own performance. This condition results from the teacher's unfortunate oversight of neglecting to preview and to make sure the learner has a basic understanding of the problems confronting him in the lesson materials. He may, in fact, practice incorrectly all week long.

Adaptive behavior was also overlooked, for no mention is made of providing the opportunity for the learner to reinterpret and act again on similar problems that are new to him. So even if the student and teacher were cooperatively able to iron out any difficulties, there appears to be no provision for evaluating the learner's supposedly new insight. Exercises 41–45 may not even be used after the previous four exercises.

There are two correct choices in Frame 5. Go back and make another choice.

CHAPTER FOUR

# *understanding and guiding student behavior*

*Authority that has to use force has already lost its authority. . . .*

*What conventional schooling does mainly is replace curiosity with conformity, vitality with docility, and honesty with hypocrisy—and what is so surprising is that young people didn't rebel against this distortion of the educational process generations ago.*

Sydney J. Harris, syndicated columnist

# A GOOD OFFENSE IS YOUR BEST DEFENSE

To many teachers, the considerations undertaken here may seem unbearably idealistic, unrealistic, or, at the least, unwarranted. There seems to be so much work, so many considerations to be thought about, that it hardly seems worthwhile. A student teacher once questioned, "Why can't you just teach them to appreciate music?" Too bad it is not that easy.

In truth, teaching is not an easy profession. No successful teacher has ever indicated otherwise. It is a profession precisely because there are so many serious responsibilities that must be dealt with by the teacher at the personal level. These responsibilities exist in addition to the mastery of the musical discipline, and they are what makes a good musician a good music teacher.

The title of a novel and also of a once-popular song could well serve as the motto for this book on teaching music: "I Never Promised You a Rose Garden!" But on the other hand, there are certain reasons why the adoption of the considerations recommended here are worth the serious attention of every music teacher. Sooner or later, most teachers of music will experience the many-headed beast known euphemistically as "discipline problems." This, among all possible problems, is the one that seems to concern young and beginning teachers the most. They want to know all the ready-made formulae for "What should I do if this happens?" or "How should I handle this problem?"

Some problem behavior can always be expected, the degree, quantity, and severity of which depend upon many factors. This fact precludes any simple remedies for specific problems. However, many behavior problems can be either eliminated or blunted by the efforts of the teacher before the fact. The means by which this is achieved *is* susceptible to a simply stated formula: "A good offense is your best defense!" The formula is simply stated, but the process is complicated and difficult. The means for implementing a good "offense" have been dealt with in some detail already. Study the following check list when preparing or evaluating your lessons: if you use it you can eliminate many problems in advance.

1. Is provision made for the realization of the "art symbol" or "expressive form" that leads to the apprehension of "felt life" or "artistic import"? Or have you provided only for the dissemination of information about music?

2. Is provision made for the apprehension (listening) and/or manipulation of sound, musical and otherwise? Or is the class confronted mainly with teacher-generated verbalizations?

3. Has provision been made for stating the objectives of the lesson and observing its success in behavioral terms? Or does it merely state and assume the success of vaguely sought results?

4. Does the lesson provide for each learner to have personal experience with the musical object(s) and behavior(s) to be learned? Or does it deal with diagrams, memorization, and other nonmusical behaviors?

5. Does the lesson provide for transfer or conservation of learning? Or are no conceptual relationships planned in a developmental manner?

6. Does the lesson provide for actual and personal involvement on the part of the learner(s), involvement that is progressively differentiated and articulated and that results in an increasing level of refinement and sophistication? Or are lessons randomly strung together as self-sufficient entities?

7. Does the lesson adopt the discovery method or problem solving as means of leading to musical independence? Or does it consist mainly of "explanations" in the format of the lecture-demonstration method?

8. Does the lesson key on *concepts* related to the musical art as percept and concept, stimulus and response? Or does it deal purely with information and/or performance skills such as singing and music reading?

9. Does the performance class emphasize such skills leading to musical independence as efficiency in recognizing visual and aural cues, elimination of mediating responses, capacity for self-judgment and self-diagnosis, and ability to make adaptive behavior? Or does it emphasize rote training through imitation in an all-out attempt to realize a high level of performance quality?

10. Do your performance classes:

a. Identify, encourage, and improve those musically talented individuals who might consider music as a vocation?

b. Do the same for those who might consider music as a keen avocational interest?

c. Develop understanding, taste, discrimination, and appreciation of music?

Or do your performance classes result in very little carry-over into adult life or out-of-school activities?

11. Is your performance class a course in the study of music in all its aspects and ramifications? Or is it merely a course that leads to performing "robots" with little taste, discrimination, love, or understanding of the music they play?

12. In designing your lesson(s), do you consider the readiness of the class and the individuals who make it up? Or do your lessons appeal to or suit only a small segment of the class?

13. Are your classes (that is, the situations you create) well organized, do they provide for individual involvement and response, and are they arranged into a curriculum? Or are your classes inefficient in their use of time, poorly planned in terms of personal involvement, and void of long-term curricular thrust?

14. Do you provide the factor of motivation so that the student sees a possibility of interest, success, satisfaction, and significant progress? Or does your motivation consist of exhortations and threats?

15. Do the situations you create provide for free decision making and problem solving? Or do you impart the information and provide the correct interpretations and responses?

16. Do your lessons provide for actions (overt behavior) resulting from

the learner's decision making? Or are your students busy trying to master information or the rote-performance skills you offer them?

17. Do your lessons provide for the consequences of an action (confirmation and reinforcement, or contradiction and negative reinforcement) by aiding learners to interpret their own actions and by fostering a positive attitude toward mistakes? Or do you diagnostically interpret their actions for them and adopt no specific strategy for helping them to overcome mistakes?

18. What provision do you make for adaptive or nonadaptive behavior? Do you unburden yourself by ignoring those who are not able to either succeed or adapt?

Attending to the positive aspects of all the foregoing considerations can result in a "good offense." Failure to do so can result in a situation where no amount of defensive strategy will have *positive* results. Many if not most problems of class control in teaching, and especially music teaching, stem from poorly conceived lessons that fail to interest and actively engage the attention of the members of the class. When students' minds begin to wander, when they lose sight of the purpose(s) of the lesson, they must resort to their own means to rid themselves of their boredom. For some this means nothing more than daydreaming, staring about, or doodling in their books. For others it entails good-natured fooling around with other friends when the teacher's back is turned. A few will amuse themselves by baiting the teacher or stirring up some kind of "action." Some may become actively arrogant, and others will have various kinds of personal difficulties aggravated by the ineffective and uninteresting teaching. For instance, slow learners and poor readers (often the same people) frequently have great difficulty in writing as well. Classes that emphasize or depend on note-taking and cognitive tests further compound their problems.

At the other end of the spectrum, the very intelligent and quick learners are often bored silly with meaningless rote drills and mechanical copying of notes from the board. They frequently put their intelligence and creativity to use in other ways. Can you blame either group?

The same results accrue when a class activity, no matter how well intended, is poorly organized and inefficiently implemented. Far too often pandemonium breaks loose, merely because the teacher and the class are unsure of how to progress: there is no clear goal or means for achieving any specific goal.

To this point, no mention has been made of "evil" or "malicious" youngsters. Most teachers are truly unable to identify any of their charges as being truly "bad" at heart. However, there are many youngsters who are essentially unmotivated toward the concerns of the school. Some are unprepared or not ready for the learnings at hand. Some have physical or emotional handicaps that prevent them from positive participation in an activity. Some are just "devils," by which most people mean good and intelligent youngsters, from good families, who are full of spirit and energy. Very few are openly rebellious and disrespectful. Even if they are, there seems to be no good reason to blame or punish them. Blame their family situation and environment, blame society, blame the school situation that has permitted such behavior to continue; blame the teachers who have put the student in uncompromising situations where the only "honorable" alternative was for the student to openly rebel against the teacher's authority.

No positive good accrues from regarding such individuals or groups of students as "bad" at heart. Especially disheartening are those teachers whose weaknesses and failures as teachers lead them to think that the class or certain individuals are "out to get me." They take every instance of poor behavior as a personal affront, casting blame for problem behavior in all directions except the most probable one: the teaching processes used. This kind of teacher frequently punishes the entire class for the misdeeds of one or a few. It does not take much thought to realize that seldom, if ever, will an entire class be at fault; or to realize the damage done to the attitudes of those who were not to blame.

Such teachers eventually end up in a rut, not really liking teaching, sometimes actively dreading each school day. They become professionally inactive; they put in their time, collect their salary, and search for meaning and relevance elsewhere in their lives. They do not understand (or perhaps even like) their colleagues who derive great pride and pleasure from the act of teaching and from contact with the youngsters they teach. They deeply suspect anyone who could be sincere and well meaning in this profession.

## DISCIPLINE REDEFINED

The sincerity, pride, and pleasure of those for whom teaching is a profession of great responsibility usually results from their more correct understanding of *discipline* as a factor and function in the educational process and in group dynamics. In order to understand some of the problems of group interaction and behavior, it is necessary to inquire into the nature of the term, for herein lies the difficulty. Most dictionaries, and teachers, define discipline in terms similar to these: control or submission gained by enforcing obedience or order. This sounds like the behavioral objective of an obedience school for dogs. It implies mastery of unpleasant tasks, punishment, threats and exhortations, and the establishment of law and order. These, of course, may be involved to a small degree, but, obviously, cannot be all that is involved in the problem of discipline. *The purpose of discipline and its end result is the fostering of intelligent self-direction.* This is especially true as youngsters grow older. As they mature, they are less susceptible to threats, corporal punishment, and the like. As their powers of abstract reasoning improve and become an effective part of their functioning, artificial devices designed to overcome or prevent problem behavior become less and less reasonable to them. They also become better prepared to deal with and circumvent such means of control.

Most teachers falsely consider discipline to be the ability, on the part of the teacher, to treat *the symptoms* of problem behavior: class interruptions. Dealing with symptoms still leave the source of the problem untouched in most cases, and the behavior recurs. Hence such teachers find themselves engaged in a constant battle of wits over behavior problems.

Separating talky girl friends may seem to the novice teacher to be a reasonable and good way of overcoming or preventing further problem behavior. But to teen-age girls whose powers of abstract thought are considerable, the passing of notes becomes an interesting and challenging alternative to sitting together. When one of these notes becomes intercepted or pirated by another girl (or worse yet, by the boy who is the subject of the note), then the problem, in fact, has been compounded. So the "control device" that deals only with symptoms itself becomes a contributing factor to the causes of poor behavior. Thus, the teacher's concern with discipline should not be one of inventing or learning devices for dealing with the symptoms of poor behavior. It should, rather, manifest itself in constructive motivation of the student toward intelligent self-direction.

The question of *patience* is also of special interest here. Often, teachers are told that they must develop patience with the youngsters they teach, usually in reference to adolescents, preschool, and primary grade children. A closer examination of patience reveals that it is based on the *expectations* of the teacher. The teacher becomes impatient when expectations are not met; or when no clear idea exists of what to expect from the age group concerned.

Misbehavior results when the behavior expected by the teacher and the behavior actually achieved by the class do not agree. Thus, much problem behavior results when teachers' expectations are too high, false, or just plain uninformed. Viewed in this light, you can see that much problem behavior is in large part the responsibility of the teacher rather than of the class.

It has been traditional in American education to expect classes at all levels to sit perfectly still, to speak only when questioned or after being recognized, and to pay close attention to all that is being done. This approach is being seriously questioned at all levels of education today. At worst, it leads to an undesirable conformity that especially deters the interests and involvements of the more gifted and creative youngsters. At best, this method has made possible the continued functioning of the lecture method, which, by its very nature, requires this kind of atmosphere in its execution: "discipline" has been extracted from countless generations of youngsters in order that the teacher can lecture and tell them all the facts and information it is assumed they should know.

There is every reason to suspect that, especially in music classes, this approach has no good reason for continued existence. Though a classroom should not be chaotic, a music class in which each student is actively involved in the pursuit and completion of a learning activity would exhibit a slight din, some movement about the room, and a considerable amount of (musical) sound. Because music, like all the arts, depends on individual responses, conformity to any given behavior hardly seems to be recommended any longer. Music, like all the other arts, requires some kind of personal involvement (cognitive, affective, or psychomotor); and this often eliminates the possibility of conformity, silence, and so on.

It is only when individual behavior begins to impinge on the ability of others to properly function that steps might be taken to clarify the situation and permit each to continue his work unhindered by others. Normally, music instruction is not truly objective. And, perhaps most importantly, neither is uniformity or conformity likely or desirable in young people.

## GROWTH-TYPICAL BEHAVIOR

The teacher's knowledge and perception of *growth-typical behavior* is extremely important. It is the quality that conditions the teacher's expectations and, hence, his patience.

It is unreasonable to expect a group of primary school youngsters to sit absolutely still without squirming, wiggling, and offering unsolicited and often totally irrelevant comments. It is equally unreasonable to expect junior high school age youngsters to sit submissively quiet while the teacher lectures (or "explains," as it is euphemistically called).

Certain behavior can be expected which is growth-typical, but which is not actual problem behavior. Through age fourteen or so, it can be expected that youngsters will be highly energetic; therefore, they will need to be active, even to the point of physical involvement. This is especially true of boys, who like their fathers do not seem destined to sit still in one position. Consequently, it seems reasonable to structure class activities that allow for this youthful energy.

Though we are not dealing here with the psychological development of young people, one critical stage thereof should be especially noted because it strikes such fear into the hearts and minds of so many parents and teachers: adolescence. This period in child development begins with pubescence generally somewhere between sixth and eighth grades—ages ten–eleven to twelve–thirteen—and ends with adulthood. Pubescence (sometimes called preadolescence) is the period of about two years, and the physical changes then occurring, that precedes *puberty*. Some children are pubescent as early as the late-intermediate elementary grades. Puberty is the period marked by the maturing of the primary sex characteristics, the development of secondary sex characteristics (body hair, etc.), rapid physical growth, and an assortment of other physical and mental changes that accompany the arrival of sexual maturity.

Adolescence is a long period of time for the individual, a period during which the individual gradually leaves the ways and things of childhood behind and advances toward the ways and things of adulthood. In some societies, a ceremony conveniently signals the end of one phase and the beginning of the other by identifying puberty as the arrival of adulthood. Our society, however unfortunate it may be seem to some, has culturally determined that the process should involve more than the arrival of sexual maturity. We, of course, still have some ceremonial vestiges to recognize or symbolize this event (such as *bar mitzvah* or confirmation), but by and large our ever-changing cultural determinants of adulthood make this a period of psychological and social turmoil for the adolescent, who experiences the problems, drives, and needs of adulthood without the means to successfully cope with them.

Problems of adolescence, then, confront virtually all but the primary grade teacher, for adolescents can be encountered anywhere from the fifth grade through college, even beyond. Communications and media being what they are, however, some teachers will discover even younger children who sometimes emulate their older brothers and sisters, at least outwardly. Thus the physical and social problems of pubescence are also of special concern to the teachers of all but the youngest children. Of utmost importance in both pubescence and adolescence is the *peer group,* which involves a social function as well as sexual awareness.

For the teacher, adolescence means a lot of students experiencing a lot of inner turmoil, self-consciousness, physical ebbs and flows, and intense social drives. It also means that each class is composed of *individuals* at varying stages of physical, and social, and intellectual maturity. It is not rare to see sexually mature boys and girls in the sixth grade, or boys in the tenth grade still waiting for their voices to change fully.

The trick of teaching such psychologically, socially, and intellectually heterogeneous classes is to (1) recognize growth-typical behavior and (2) structure activities and curriculums along the lines already covered in detail— namely, in ways suited to the needs, abilities, and interests of each individual —and to do so in behavioral terms. Classes that are structured to have *multiple results* will better serve the requirements of a multifaceted collection of individuals. If they are oriented toward overt behavior, the results will be more tangible to the learner and, thus, more accessible to the social nature of the adolescent. A word of caution: the more an adolescent advances chronologically through adolescence, the more adultlike (that is, less childlike) and relevant (to adulthood) the activities and learnings must be (or appear to be).

The teacher who sets sail on a course of conformity and uniformity in learnings and lessons is destined to run afoul. It is not in the nature of adolescence, especially when taken as a classroom group, to conform or to be uniform in any regard. Homogeneous grouping, or attempts at it, seldom have more than a negligible effect. Regardless of the common factor used to group adolescent students, it will be far less common than the fact of each student's inherent uniqueness.

Given the various drives among the adolescent peer group, and given the alternation between extremes of energy and lethargy that characterizes the growth spurt, the need for a highly active approach by the teacher seems even more appropriate. The beginning or new teacher is advised to regard this age group as a challenge, not an impossibility. Many teachers find personal rewards in meeting this challenge in extremely exciting and fulfilling ways. They regard the challenge as one of channeling and redirecting energy and enthusiasm, rather than as one of stifling it. They regard the inevitable conflicts of this age as necessary and useful to the natural and fruitful growth required of this development stage.[1] They recognize that adolescents need a "psychological moratorium" where they have time to find a healthy identity without having permanent penalties imposed on them by a society obsessed with striving for success.[2] In sum, they try to both understand growth-typical behavior and use it in the best interests of young people.

*GO TO FRAME 1, PAGE 128.*

---

The junior high school was conceived to deal especially with the most problematic years of pubescence-adolescence. In some places it includes grades seven through nine; in others, only grades seven and eight. The junior high school is sometimes a facility separate from the senior high school. In smaller school systems, the two often share the same facility, but have separate faculty and schedules.

Now, the trend seems to be away from the junior high school and toward what is perhaps more accurately called the "middle school." This trend reflects the social and physical facts that youngsters in the fifth and sixth grades are entering pubescence in larger numbers than before and, as a result, are more socially mature or aware than in the past. Middle schools are less well defined than junior high schools, however, since they encompass various combinations of grades five through eight and different uses of facilities. It appears now that only the so-called primary grades still constitute the elementary school. And with the advent of non- or ungraded schools, boundaries are even further obscured.

The course of study for grades seven and eight has, at least since the advent of the junior high school, been oriented toward the exploration and introduction of possible vocational or avocational pursuits in addition to the four R's (reading, 'riting, 'rithmetic, and rigors of science). Music, art, "shop," home economics, "gym," and others all became segmented courses given special emphasis. Clubs and other extra- or co-curricular activities abound. All this to give the adolescent the chance, in the form of a "psychological moratorium," to explore his interests, hone his skills, and begin to decide on his adult role in life.

This, at the very latest, is where the thrust toward the arts either

---

[1] See Edgar Friedenberg, *The Vanishing Adolescent* (New York: Dell Publishing Co., Inc., 1968) and *The Dignity of Youth and Other Atavisms* (Boston: Beacon Press, 1966).

[2] See R. Muus, ed., *Theories of Adolescence,* 2nd ed. (New York: Random House, 1968) pp. 178–80.

succeeds or fails to make a significant positive impact on most people. This is where to start: at the end of childhood, the last chance!

## CURRICULAR ORGANIZATION: THREE STYLES

There are three ways of viewing the organization of curriculums:[3]

1. Perhaps the most common involves the *acquisition of a body of knowledge* within each of the disciplines in a curriculum. Emphasis is placed upon the gathering and ordering of information for storage and retrieval. The utilization of this information and its availability for integration in life is not an aim, nor necessarily a result. It is revered for its own sake, and its relevance to life is rather unpredictable.

2. Another quite common curricular organization involves the attempt to "school" students in socially acceptable modes of thought and behavior. In other words, *conformity or uniformity in terms of societal norms* is the aim. It invariably involves acceptance of currently prevalent social patterns of thought, values, taste, and behavior. The result can be acquiescent behavior, conscious or unconscious. In terms of its efficacy for improving future life, for overcoming social misconceptions, for reconstructing society along improved lines, this kind of curriculum is extremely conservative, if not reactionary.

3. The third curricular style, and the one recommended here, organizes learnings in ways designed to enhance the possibility of their *integration in life*. Thus, only those learnings are sought that tend to satisfy personal wants, to create understandings that allow the student to knowingly develop and apply values, tastes, and actions in line with his concept of effective living. In this kind of curricular orientation, learning activities should be realistically related to the life situations the individual is likely to encounter as he matures and is integrated into adult society. Perhaps more important are learning activities that directly relate to the adolescent's present understanding of effective living, to his personal wants and interests, and to his practical life situations.

If learning activities can be made to serve both present and future life situations, then the curriculum can be regarded as truly relevant.

*GO TO FRAME 2, PAGE 128.*

---

As you have seen, a curriculum oriented toward effective living does not necessarily have to revert to some onerous form of pragmatism where

[3] These categories owe much to the unpublished working papers of Asahel Woodruff, educational psychologist and past advisor to MENC (Music Educators National Conference) and MMCP (Manhattanville Music Curriculum Project).

only those things that have practical use are taught. Such a curriculum, rather, plans for the development of present interests and capacities, as well as for the continuing refinement of other latent capacities, attitudes, values, and tastes. Remembering that a prime characteristic of adolescence is its introspection, its quest for identity, its awareness of self and all the problems and tensions the self is experiencing, it should be clear that a curriculum designed to manifest and develop every aspect of every "self" is likely to engage the interest, attention, and involvement of the various individuals who make up the class.

The failure of the teacher to engage in learnings relevant to the student's present and future life situations, the failure to make such learnings interesting and profitable as short-term aims, the failure to enhance the acquisition and development of significant concepts and their transfer to future situations —these failures on the part of any teacher will lead invariably to problems of class control, euphemistically known as "discipline problems."

With most individuals, and most classes, there is one dominating cause of control problems: boredom. Thus, the reminder again that a good offense is your best defense.

By now, you should realize that the teaching, and not discipline, is more frequently the problem. It is not necessarily the students who are to blame for their lack of self-discipline or response to authority. It is often the fault of the teacher who has been unable or unwilling to provide the conditions of self-discipline. (These conditions were treated at length in Chapter Three in the discussions of the kinds and processes of motivation.)

Although it is true that youngsters—adolescent or not—who have physical problems or are in some way socially, emotionally, or even intellectually maladjusted (even "maladjusted" has implications of social conformity!), are more difficult to understand and accommodate; it does not necessarily follow that they cannot be made an integral and profitable part of any learning activity. In fact, the more the activity allows for successful completion at a multitude of achievement levels, the more likely it is to encompass every student in the class regardless of his personal difficulties. Such difficulties must always be handled on an individual basis, and usually require the assistance of the school psychologist, physician (or nurse), or guidance counselor.

In addition to those mentioned above, there are other factors that pertain to the discipline and control of individuals and classes. Were these not considered in their turn, this entire discussion would doubtless be construed by many as idealistic.

## ADOLESCENT TRAITS

First, even the best students or classes are not consistently receptive to learning. There are several possible reasons for this: it may be the first warm and sunny day of spring; it may be the last class before the week-end; the class before may have been unruly, and it carries over into your class. These are just a sampling of the variables that affect how a class will behave and that explain how a class may react differently to a learning activity on two different occasions.

Second, every adolescent is, to a degree, constantly fluctuating between conformity and independence. Even though the question of degree is difficult to deal with, it is possible to isolate, if only for purposes of emphasis, several more or less clearly defined *syndromes*.[4]

From time to time, the adolescent is likely to be self-centered. At times such as this, he is likely to be more interested in *independence* than in the completion of teacher- or peer-directed tasks. At other times the adolescent may be *conformity*-minded: he will tend to place a disproportionate emphasis on conforming to the interests or behavior of the peer group. This may be an insecure time for the adolescent, one of seeking peer group approval, peer identification, a feeling of belonging. Then, too, there are times when this same adolescent may lean toward what used to be called "apple polishing"— *conscientious* behavior, sometimes overly or irrationally so. During this syndrome, the adolescent may be seeking recognition by the adults in his life (he may also be laying a smoke screen for some future or past behavior). Under these conditions, he is likely to derive satisfaction from responding to authority. This frequently happens in situations that are totally unfamiliar and where authority provides stable guidelines.

These three states of being—independence, conformity, conscientiousness—are balanced to some degree in the stable adolescent. He fluctuates among them from day to day, hour to hour, even class to class, depending on the conditions or the situation, or how he "feels." Though "fluctuation" hardly seems an apt description of the condition of stability, it is so in this context because fluctuation is the growth-typical behavior of this age group. After all, even adults experience fluctuations of this sort, though perhaps not as frequently, intensely, or dramatically. Perhaps "adulthood" could be described as the condition of possessing the means for dealing with these fluctuations of mood.

Though the stable adolescent experiences all of these moods at various times, he is able to exert some control over them depending on the circumstances or situations. Thus, such behavior is within the control of reason and may be called *rational*. The same is true of the stable and rational adult: a delicate balancing act is performed so that no one of these tendencies becomes ascendant.

This is not the case with unstable and irrational adolescents, with whom one of the syndromes is likely to be dominant in his personality and behavior. It is easy to see how the self-centered *independence* syndrome can cause disruptive behavior. Here, the adolescent balks at authority or at any outside

---

[4] A set or aggregate of concurrent symptoms indicative of a state of being or mind; in the present discussion, symptoms of various *moods* experienced by young people.

direction in his quest for personal independence of thought and action. The teacher who backs such a student into a corner where a graceful and face-saving exit is not possible is in for difficulty.

The *conformer,* involved as he is in a game of follow the leader, follows the actions of the peer group (which will have a recognized leader—a youngster likely to be manifesting independence). Regardless of family environment, academic skills, or other such factors, this individual is likely to become involved in any disruptive behavior initiated by the peer group. He is afraid of losing face, friends, and the security of "belonging" to the group. Similarly, if the peer group is involved in productive learning activities, the conformer will follow suit, though not always with a clear or correct understanding of the goals at hand. His goals may not be those set by the teacher and agreed upon by the peer group, but may be, rather, only those that conform to the actions of the peer group, thereby winning their approval. Under these conditions significant learning is not as likely to occur, though the resulting behavior may be exemplary. Many teachers are thereby misled to favor such an apparently well-behaved student. ("He's such a nice, well-behaved boy, he must be learning! He just needs more help!")

Even the adolescent who seems consistently *conscientious* may be a source of difficulty. Again, the question of motivation arises. Is this behavior conducive to learning because the individual wants to learn? Or because he wants your approval (usually in the form of a good grade), or the approval of his parents? If it is the latter, the student may manifest many different kinds of problem behavior. Such an individual may cheat because he dares not risk failure—and, hence, disapproval by the teacher or his parents—by acting independently. Or he may become a tattletale, thereby causing other problems for the teacher.

The stable and rational adolescent is better able to assess a situation and to adapt his "mood" and behavior as the occasion seems to demand. Such youngsters can be "guided" by the teacher, who merely has to emphasize the needs of the situation. For example, if the decibel level reaches a point of distraction that seems to jeopardize the success of a group activity, the teacher advises the class of this fact. Those stable and rational members of the class usually respond quickly (though, admittedly, this clarification might have to be repeated once or twice more during the period, adolescent energy being what it is).

Unstable and irrational adolescents are likely to consistently manifest most of the characteristics of their syndrome, whichever one of the three it may be. Some of the means for dealing with this will be considered shortly. The point here is to recognize that both types of behavior, stable-rational and unstable-irrational, are to a degree growth-typical. It would be difficult to prove which of the two is *more typical,* but most teachers would probably agree that most adolescents are both stable and rational. In either case, problem behavior resulting from any of the three syndromes we have discussed is not a sign that the youngster is headed toward juvenile delinquency, is evil, or is out to get the teacher. Rather, it is a quite natural and expected result of the process of growing up.

*GO TO FRAME 3, PAGE 129.*

---

In summary, then, there are really *four* syndromes related to adolescent behavior:

1. self-centered and independent
2. conformity-minded, and peer-oriented
3. conscientious and adult-oriented
4. stable and rational

Since unstable and irrational youngsters quite consistently manifest one of the first three syndromes, while stable and rational youngsters fluctuate among the first three, it appears that there are really only two broad categories of which the teacher must be aware. The real skill, however, is realizing whether one of the first three behaviors is causing unstable and irrational behavior, or whether it is merely a phase that a stable and rational adolescent is experiencing at a given moment. In most cases, analyzing problem behavior in these terms will point to its solution.

It is perhaps unfair and culturally biased to even think in terms of a category of unstable and irrational behavior. Since each individual is nurtured in a different environment, depending on his family and their socio-economic status, interests, and motivations, each individual is bound to manifest different sets of behavior. But in the context of classroom control, it is a fact of teaching life that the student who consistently exhibits one type of problem behavior is of more concern than the student who can control his behavior to some degree. The problem is not solely one of conforming to the authority of the teacher, because as you have seen this in itself can constitute a problem. Many teachers seek to develop independence in students; yet even when their tactics have realized some degree of successful self-motivation, there are still times when the individual must accede to the needs or demands of the larger group. This pattern is standard in life in general, so it too constitutes education toward effective living.

Above all, the teacher must not under any circumstances definitively categorize students into groups of those who are problems and those who are not. Each child should be considered individually, to whatever degree that is possible or necessary. Self-motivation, self-respect, self-understanding can arise only from situations where confidence in one's self is realized. Situations in which a class is approached as a collection of individuals best furnish the conditions for such self-realization.

Adolescents manifesting *independence* need the opportunity for constructive, positive applications of independence. Therefore, activities, or the student's role in activities, should be so structured as to allow or sustain such independence. At the same time, such individuals must learn sooner or later to cope with rules and authority. Therefore, activities should also have some guidelines that must be followed. Since social interaction with the peer group is also characteristic of the stable and rational adolescent, activities might also involve group processes or, at least, the sharing of their projects with the group for collective discussion or use.

The same remedies are suitable for the *conformity-minded, peer-oriented* student. Activities that provide ample opportunity for independence help foster this trait. Often, one successful independent venture will be enough to reassure the individual that he can succeed independently yet still retain the security of the peer group when the success of his independent act is brought to their attention. And, as above, minimal rules and guidelines must direct his efforts, and his work must be scrutinized and evaluated by the teacher. The teacher should maintain a spirit of "honest optimism."

The *conscientious and adult-oriented* youngster can be aided in learnings (and in life) by group activities that in some way call upon him to work within a small group on a particular problem. Often, placing students together with the same problem works well and precludes harassment by others in the class. Certainly, independent action leading to a better self-image is also called for by whatever means the teacher can devise. Above all, the teacher is warned to politely ignore various "apple polishing" routines and other evidence of adult orientation that the student might manifest.

In all instances of student problem behavior, whether rational or irrational, what the teacher does usually makes the difference. What should be done? Scold, punish, threaten, ignore? There are some general guidelines that can help the teacher handle a wide variety of situations. If teachers would take the time and interest necessary to understand such guidelines instead of seeking ready-made formulas that apply in all instances, they would find the task greatly simplified.

## GUIDELINES FOR DEALING WITH BEHAVIOR PROBLEMS

Psychologists have sought to systematize certain principles that people have been applying intuitively throughout history. Unfortunately, some of this intuition (such as the Judeo-Christian maxim, "an eye for an eye") has either been misunderstood or misapplied, with some rather unexpected consequences (witness the general failure of penology in our own age as well as the past). Therefore, how is the teacher to cope with various situations of student conduct?

*Positive reinforcement* invariably aids in the retention of a behavior; *negative reinforcement* might do the same, for when the student is thwarted he might, as you saw earlier, continue to act nonadaptively. *No reinforcement* (or *nonreinforcement*) has been demonstrated to eliminate unwanted behavior more effectively (and, incidentally, more efficiently) than punishment. Thus, in each instance of problem behavior, the teacher must be careful to neither positively nor negatively reinforce the unwanted behavior.

It is amazing how many teachers reinforce unwanted behavior in some way without realizing it. Frequently, when a teacher loses his "cool," is visibly annoyed, or allows the class to "get his goat," he positively reinforces the behavior that brought about the situation by giving pleasure or satisfaction to those who instigated it.

The teacher can use positive reinforcement much more wisely—for example, he may have a student experience some *pleasant consequence* as a result of a desired behavior or performance. To the underachiever, "honest optimism" (for instance, "That's not bad; it's really quite good; of course there are still some things to be ironed out, but you are really making progress," said sincerely) can be a tremendous source of motivation toward the desired behavioral response.

On the other hand, it is equally amazing how many teachers follow the futile course of *negative reinforcement*. This happens when an *unpleasant or unwanted consequence* that the student wishes to avoid results from problem behavior. Though this kind of conditioning has some value in certain situations, and can be used to train house pets, it certainly does not have the intended effect that many teachers *imagine* when they apply it to problem behavior.

Scolding and punishment are the prime forms of negative reinforcement; some teachers never seem to notice that they are using these tactics over and over again, usually for the same individuals or classes. They may quiet things down or resolve a particular crisis for the moment, but they seldom cure the problem behavior altogether. Treating the symptoms does not eliminate the cause.

Thus, in problem behavior situations this kind of negative reinforcement serves only as a temporary pacifier. Teachers who must, from time to time, take their turn supervising "detention" halls after school are often surprised when the same students continually reappear for this punishment! The technique is about as successful as scolding or punishing a dog at supper time for his poor toilet habits at breakfast. It is generally agreed that this system does not work as its originators believed it would, yet it continues. Ironically, it is useful only with those youngsters who do not really need this kind of treatment in the first place: the stable and rational adolescents. If teachers only realized how many students actively seek to be kept after school to avoid work at home, to be with a friend, to avoid (gracefully) a bully waiting outside, they would begin to think along other lines.

Since various emotional problems[5] and tensions associated with adolescence are frequently the cause of a student's problem behavior, it is his

[5] For a moving insight into some of the most important of these problems, in the form of actual letters written to parents by teen-agers, see Earnest Larsen, *You Try Love and I'll Try Ajax* (Ligouri, M.: Ligourian Books, 1970).

feelings toward the situation at hand that must be taken into account. Thus, any action taken by the teacher must avoid *further* heightening the tension or the emotional reaction of the student. Of all possible approaches by the teacher, punishment is least likely to solve problems arising from typical adolescent tensions and emotions. There are several reasons for this.

First, only the stable and rational child can accept punishment, and then usually only when his peers know nothing of it. Second, punishment increases conflict and hostility and temporarily disrupts rational thought. Third, punishment or the threat of it almost invariably interrupts and disrupts the class. Last, punishment breeds antagonism: antagonism of the individual student and even the entire class toward the teacher; antagonism toward the subject being taught; and, eventually, increasing antagonism by the teacher toward problem individuals or classes, or even toward all youngsters, as a result of continual episodes of punishment.

> The trouble with punishment that is used regularly as a means is that before too long, without realizing it, it becomes an end in itself, gratifying the wielder far more than it chastens the culprit.[6]

Scolding, censure, shouted commands—all suffer from the same weaknesses that punishment does, though perhaps to a lesser degree. They also run the risk of becoming positive reinforcement if they represent the intended result of the problem behavior.

*Nonreinforcement* usually proves most effective in eliminating problem behavior, not only during moments of "crisis" but over longer periods of time and even permanently. It is distinguished from positive and negative reinforcement by the fact that the problem behavior is followed neither by pleasant and gratifying results, nor by punishment, censure, or other consequences the student wishes to avoid. In fact, not much happens; nothing, at least, with the intensity associated with positive and negative reinforcement.

The teacher may apply nonreinforcement in several ways:

1. Stop everything entirely and wait for things to calm down. This period of apprehensive silence, coupled with an "evil eye" or stern expression, often works wonders. If anything, the class comes to realize that they punish themselves: one of the things an adolescent dreads most is total silence and inactivity.

2. A low-key verbal appeal or statement may have the intended result. Usually, this entails identifying for the student or the class the problem behavior and what the teacher conceives to be the various solutions to that behavior. "There is too much noise over in that section of the room; no one else can concentrate or even hear himself think. Now let's hold things down a bit so we can all work." Or, "I can't hear what John is saying if there is other talking going on!" Each can work wonders. The student certainly can receive little gratification from such cool responses by the teacher; nor should he feel

[6] Sydney J. Harris, syndicated column.

scolded or censured—just advised. (Advised should not be the same as warned!) Such verbal appeals should never reach the point where they become a status symbol for the problem student.

3. Often, the simplest way of handling such problems is to try to discover their causes. Since it is not within the purview of the peer group to appear *too* eager or interested, problems or questions often go unnoticed by the teacher. Problem behavior thus results as the student tries to handle the problem by himself, by "illegally" conferring with a neighbor, or by some other means. Often, nonproductive participation in a learning activity may be a simple matter of having no paper or pencil. Often, too, a given student may be just plain lost and will not understand what is happening (this is not unlikely, considering the daydreaming among adolescents and the short attention span of younger children). In either instance, and countless others like it, the student may actively seek solutions to his or her problem from those nearby, rather than by asking the teacher. The easiest way to get to the source of such matters is to ask, "What's the problem, John?" This will elicit either the answer you were after, or a response of "Nuthin'." If the latter, then the problem is most likely student generated and related to emotional rather than practical issues.

4. Another way of applying nonreinforcement is simply to ignore certain kinds of behavior. Many teachers cause their own problems in this regard by constantly admonishing individuals or classes for the slightest unexpected or undesirable behavior. If the behavior does not detract from the ability of others to successfully involve themselves in the learning activity at hand, and if it is not constant, then it is often best to ignore it. Speaking out of turn, for example, is best cured by ignoring offenders, rather than by continually scolding them.

*GO TO FRAME 4, PAGE 130.*

---

Perhaps the greatest source of problem behavior lies in anciently held beliefs about teaching. It was mentioned earlier that the lecture method of teaching is no longer relevant to the principles of learning, especially learning that involves youngsters formulating their first concepts of music. Yet even those teachers who accept this fact still insist that the class sit still and quiet. This, more than anything else, is likely to encourage the garden variety of control problems: too frequent trips to the lavatory, restlessness, feet up on the desk ahead, books knocked to the floor, whispering, and so on.

When instead classes are busily engaged, in the form of small groups or as individuals, in projects and learning activities, there is bound to be some noise, some movement, some activity. It is only when this noise, movement, or activity becomes annoying to others that it should receive the attention of the teacher. This kind of class requires considerable skill in motivation on the part of the teacher and, eventually, self-direction and self-discipline on the part of the students, who must see, recognize, and accept the goals at hand and be interested in working toward the successful completion of those goals.

The air of freedom engendered by this kind of teaching scares some experienced teachers who have become accustomed to and can even handle the more traditional concept of a music classroom. But being able to "handle" this kind of classroom—by which is meant being able to control the behavior of the class—is not what determines successful teaching. In an *autocratic atmosphere,* learning is very unlikely to be oriented toward individual needs and interests. Such teaching always has overtones of a curriculum oriented toward *conformity* or the acquisition of a *disciplined body of knowledge.* Younger teachers and beginning teachers, themselves bored silly by sixteen years or so of this kind of teaching, are usually more inclined to take the leap of faith necessary to try the approach that emphasizes student self-motivation and individual accomplishment.

Following such a leap of faith is a period of adjustment as the teacher learns how to cope with this *activity-oriented* format. During this period, the young teacher learns how to teach in ways other than he was taught, and this is sometimes difficult. Once the teacher is able to conceive of projects and learning activities in behavioral terms—along all the lines recommended thus far—and is able to effectively set them in motion and see them through to completion, the battle is won. It is a battle not against recalcitrant students, but against tradition and an unresponsive system of education. Teaching can thus become a true joy because you will see interest, excitement, and challenge in the eyes of your students, replacing the dull, bored faces we are all too accustomed to seeing.

In this kind of teaching, positive reinforcement is its own reward in terms of the satisfaction it gives to the student who successfully completes (at his own level of ability, remember) an activity or project. Best yet, when such reinforcement is self-induced, the question of conditioned behavior ceases to have the onerous overtones usually associated with it, for the teacher is not reinforcing or determining behavior directly. With sensible structuring of class learning activities, the students can find success and satisfaction on their own. No artificial, imposed, or extrinsic reinforcement is needed in the way of grades, colored stars, and so forth.

And therein lies the secret to problem behavior or "discipline problems": What a person thinks *about* what he learns is often more important than *what* he learns. Attitudes are emotional states of varying degrees of intensity that accompany concepts or concept objects. Therefore, it is not difficult to understand that attitudes, values, and taste all result in part from "what a person thinks about what he learns." A modification of this might also hold true: What a person thinks about *as* he learns is often more important than *what* he learns.

Thus, positive reinforcement relates to the individual: what he thinks about; what his interests, goals, and needs are; what his readiness is; and other such factors relating to personal identity. It stands to reason that activities that provide the opportunity and means for an individual to derive satisfaction are likely to enhance the kinds of learnings and attitudes all music teachers should encourage.

Values do not arise in a vacuum, but, rather, from established networks of behavior that come to be preferred by the individual. Since values are a way of codifying behavior, it stands to reason that musical behavior that is self-rewarding, self-fulfilling, even self-determining should be encouraged. It is this kind of behavior that will be carried over into adult life to become a part of the value system that regards music as an ingredient in effective living.

With activities that induce positive attitudes and values, the resulting development of self-direction and self-discipline should make discipline problems the exception rather than the rule. Somewhere in the large expanse between conformity and permissiveness, there *is* a middle ground in which the best of each is dialectically synthesized. More and more schools, such as the Wilde Lake Middle School (grades six through eight) in Columbia, Maryland, are converting practically their entire curriculum to activities-oriented formats. The Wilde Lake School has been described in *Time* magazine, and in the process a useful term was coined to describe this new concept of discipline:

> The air of freedom neatly defines away what Principal Charles L. Jones calls "the garbage discipline problems—kids with feet in the aisle or getting up to sharpen pencils." But self-discipline is another matter. To encourage it, the teachers try to steer a middle course. They refuse to insist on old obedience, which often prevents kids from learning the consequences of their own choices. Even so, the teachers also shun the pure permissiveness that says if a child is allowed to goof off long enough, he will decide for himself that work is more satisfying. The resulting hybrid might be called "permissipline."[7]

*Permissipline*—a synthesis of enough discipline and not too much permissiveness—is the means by which learning can be most fruitful for the individual, and teaching most rewarding for the teacher.

The fuel that will keep permissipline operating is a mixture of suitable activities, successful motivation, and satisfaction bred by positive reinforcement that is self-realized, not imposed. In situations where the goals of the class or teacher are in competition with those of the individual, the "reward" (in terms of satisfaction) for achieving the former must clearly outweigh the anticipated rewards of the latter. In other words, successfully completing the activity must result in greater satisfaction than fooling around, goofing off, and other problem behavior.

*GO TO FRAME 5, PAGE 131.*

[7] *Time* (June 21, 1971), 54.

## CLASSROOM TEACHING STYLES

Teaching style is determined mainly by the teacher and the kind of learning he wishes to impart. There are several different styles a teacher may adopt in a class. A *teacher-dominated* or *autocratic* class style has goals, means, and reinforcements that are determined by the teacher. The teacher manifests an autocratic attitude in one of two ways: He either controls class activities in order to proceed in an orderly and systematic way, or he dominates the class in order to enforce conformity and obedience. In and of itself, a teacher-dominated situation need not be as bad as the term may sound. In fact, in certain musical situations this kind of teaching is common, if not necessary. Such situations invariably involve large musical performance groups. The director (who is more than just a conductor) must dominate and control the rehearsals and performance activities to a large degree. It is within his purview, however, to adopt many of the techniques recommended so far for developing independent musicianship.

However, the autocratic method is usually unsuitable in general music situations, where interests, needs, and readiness vary considerably. In such situations, a single-handed approach is likely to have singular results: conformity, obedience, acquiescence, stultification, or problem behavior. Such a teacher assumes that he and only he knows what is best for the class and what the class wants and needs. Though this may be true with very young children, and though it was true in the past when society was more homogeneous, it is seldom true today because of the tremendous diversity within society as a whole. Hence, the class will accede to the demands of an autocratic teacher, or will rebel in some way. Neither behavior is conducive to effective or efficient learning. Even though efficient use of class time is most often advanced as a rationale for this kind of teaching, inefficiency can result if the learnings undertaken are never mastered because of student reluctance, or because of lack of relevance in such learnings.

Contrasted with the teacher-dominated or autocratic classroom is the *undirected* or *permissive* classroom. As you have seen, this approach involves letting the students do what they want or what they think is best. *Discovery* and *creativity* are usually advanced as a rationale for this kind of teaching. A trial-and-error process involving personal searches for solutions to self-realized problems may be important, but its inefficiency opens it to some objections and qualifications. One criticism is that long-term developmental processes designed to foster continually refined concepts and their transfer are not adequately considered, if at all. Also, the assumption that discovery and creativity can occur only in a totally free atmosphere is open to serious doubt. Its correlative in the arts insists that "personal expression" and "creativity" take precedence over the demands of craft, technique, and mastery of the medium, all of which have been seen by the greatest of artists not as impediments but as fundamentals to be given the deepest consideration.

Rather, creativity and discovery often can be best encouraged and developed in a situation that is well structured or well controlled. In the process of discovering these insights in completing an assignment, the neophyte develops the means for applying himself creatively at times in the future when he *is* functioning with total independence. Such a situation invariably involves the selection or suggestion of a task that challenges the student, allows a great degree of personal freedom in exploring and discovering through trial and error, and contains new learnings or refinements of previous learnings. These processes usually involve, as well, criteria that the teacher can use to help the student evaluate the fruits of his labor.

A third kind of teaching approach is the so-called *democratic* or *group-controlled* classroom. Here, the class is often a part of the decision-making process that sets goals, means, and reinforcements. The class is encouraged to discipline and direct itself in many aspects of its endeavor, and the role of the teacher is much like that of the driver-training teacher: he can see what is happening, advise and suggest, and put on the brakes when he needs to. But he cannot drive, and he accepts the inevitability that some bumps and scrapes of varying degrees will occur.

With this approach, unfortunately, much time is consumed in group planning, thereby leaving less time for group projects and activities. The teacher is also hopelessly unable to bail out when things seem headed the wrong way up a one-way street; all he can do is break the tryst with democracy and resort to a benign or beneficent autocracy until things are set in order again. This, of course, can create serious problems of class attitude, not to mention the possibility of "revolution."

However serious its flaws, the group-controlled approach does bring to light one important factor that should be emphasized. In terms of group dynamics, *the teacher is a member of the group.* He may adopt the role of hero, leader, friend, one of the boys, or dictator. The role he adopts will determine to a large extent how the group as a whole functions. The role most recommended, because it is most successful and most satisfying, is that of friend. A friend is sympathetic, empathetic, understanding, and usually fair. A friend can make mistakes and still be forgiven. Friends are easier to get along with and they are easier to understand. They are seen as being human, possessing all the strengths and weaknesses implied thereby. And since adolescents look forward to impending adulthood, and generally seek some kind of adult approval and respect, what better thing than to have the teacher as a friend.

Many young teachers who, by intent or because of personality, effectively implement this role are often unnerved by the large number of adolescents of either sex who come to them with personal problems. It is unfortunate, but not unnatural, when an adolescent feels he has to turn to a teacher for help rather than to his parents or clergyman. Nonetheless, it is true; and

114

though it is disconcerting, it proves the effectiveness of the role of friend adopted by the teacher.

Teachers who contemplate establishing themselves in the role of friend must avoid phoniness. An adolescent can smell a phony at a hundred paces. Many young or inexperienced teachers fall into this trap when they act the role of friend without or before really feeling and believing it. They view it as a means to class control, not as an end worthy in itself. To teach, you must truly like, respect, and care for the young people whom you will teach. And young *people* they are, subject to most of the same problems and pressures as the rest of us, but experiencing such difficulties more intensely and with less means for doing so. On the other hand, they experience most of the same joys, pleasures, and satisfactions that we all do; and here also, frequently more intensely. (What could possibly be more intense than a teen-age crush or puppy love?)

The sooner the teacher realizes that he is dealing with sensitive and feeling human beings, and not conditioning mere animals to respond on direction, the sooner he will achieve quite naturally the role of friend, with all its many rewards and satisfactions. Furthermore, the class will respond more readily, naturally, and favorably to the important role of the teacher in the group processes of classroom learning.

If the teacher-dominated or autocratic classroom is subject to the fault of breeding conformity and obedience; if the undirected or permissive classroom breeds permissiveness and unfocused, inefficient learning; and if the group-directed or democratic classroom leads only to group spirit and mutual friendship, where or how is the atmosphere of permissipline established? By the judicious combination of all three of these forms of teacher-class involvement or interaction; sometimes all within the same class period, or applied to the same class activity. Sound ridiculous, impossible, or contradictory? Well, it is possible and even sensible once the possibilities and processes are understood. You have had considerable experience with just this kind of teaching in your study of the examples recommended thus far. Thus, you should be well on your way to having some sort of concept of your own.

## PERMISSIPLINE RECONSIDERED

If the class is engaged in projects and learning activities that give them considerable freedom of action, independence, self-reliance, self-direction, and self-discipline, then the beneficial conditions of *permissiveness* are present. If these activities are given specific criteria and guidelines, and are set in motion and even guided from time to time by the teacher, then the best aspects of efficiency and structure in *teacher-dominated* classes are present. If the teacher takes a periodic inventory of the interests of each class, solicits suggestions for class learnings, and builds and orders class activities *at least in part* around expressed student interests, then the strongest incentives of the *group-directed* class are present. Furthermore, the small groups in this learning situation are democratic microcosms of the larger class: each is free to direct and complete activities in whatever way it decides. So even if the activity is entirely teacher-conceived and directed, the democracy of the small group directing itself is still present.

Thus, *permissipline*, as a classroom approach to the interaction of the teacher and the students, results from learning activities and projects that include:

1. Considerable freedom of action, independent problem solving and decision making, self-reliance, self-direction, and self-discipline on the part of each student (permissiveness).

2. Structure, criteria, guidelines, and a conceptual relationship of the present activity to past and future activities—all given by the teacher (teacher-dominated).

3. Some activities or facets of activities generated by student interest, and the possibility of the various small groups directing their own participation in them (group-directed). Activities that incorporate all three of these approaches fulfill most beneficially the conditions of permissipline.

Many such activities are possible. For instance:

> Given recordings of Bach's Fugue in d minor (from the *Well-Tempered Clavier*) by the Swingle Singers, the Moog synthesizer (*Switched-On Bach*), and Wanda Landowska, and given fifteen minutes, each group of three students will identify the stylistic difference among the three approaches, and as individuals, indicate which version they prefer, and why.

The activity and materials are obviously contrived by the teacher, but with student interests (and hopefully, student readiness) in mind. The students are free to offer varying descriptions of stylistic differences; this is inevitable. Yet, there will be sufficient similarities among them for the teacher or the class to agree on wording and to arrive at a valid list. On the other hand, each individual is called upon to make a personal value judgment, and to support it with some reasoning. If nothing else, this can lead to aesthetic or affective thought by each individual, and to lively discussion among the entire class.

This activity could lead to another one—perhaps by teacher suggestion, but in any case with the group's consent and direction—in which the same process is followed with three recordings of the same popular or rock tune by three different performers or groups. Or the study of what is involved in musical style might be extended to having students play their own or others' "sound compositions" in varying, but significantly different styles.

In structuring a curriculum of permissipline, laws and guidelines need not impede freedom of action and independence of behavior. Democracy and freedom, even as practiced in our adult world, operate most usually under some kind of law, direction, or guideline: we are not free to shout "Fire!" in a crowded theater or to exceed speed limits. But within these *minimal* strictures of a democratic and free society, there is great latitude for personal action.

In some circumstances, the three orientations discussed above might be combined within the same class period, in the form of two or three separate but related activities. For example:

Given the topic "theme and variations" and ten minutes, each group of three students will choose a shape or color within the classroom and list and present to the class as many variations of that shape or color as they can find.

Given a recording of variations on the theme of "Pop Goes the Weasel" and directed-listening sheets comparing the theme and first two variations, each student will successfully identify at least five ways in which the original theme is varied in the two variations.

Given the limitation of self-generated sounds, each student will compose a "theme" and two variations of that theme as a homework assignment, to be completed and discussed with the whole class at the next class meeting.

In this class period, the first activity involves considerable group direction in the completion of the activity. The members of each group must decide and agree upon whether a shape or a color will be considered, and then must cooperatively search the room for the appropriate variations.

The second activity is purely teacher-dominated. The teacher has selected the material and the criteria, and has prepared the means for completing the activity in advance, without class consultation (though with class interest and readiness in mind).

The third activity, though guided by the two minimal requirements of "self-generated vocal sounds" and "theme and two variations," gives extreme latitude to each student. The results of this kind of project are often mixed. Some compositions will be excellent and may often exceed the minimal requirements (here, two variations); others will be merely competent but not exceptionally creative; still others will be mediocre or even weak; and inevitably someone will neglect (through desire or accident) to do the project at all. All of these results must be anticipated in any such project or activity, and means for dealing with each must be well thought out before the activity is undertaken. In any event, each student is able to complete the project at his own level of ability and interest, and to profit accordingly. In completing such a project, the student will "discover" much about variation techniques, and perhaps will manifest creativity.

There are times, too, when any *one* of the three kinds of classroom style might be applied to class period. The provision here must be that subsequent class periods or future contact with the teacher involve one or both of the other possibilities, for balance. This is the usual and recommended situation in teaching music performance ensembles. Because of the nature of group performance, the director *must,* dominate the class during rehearsals and performances. He does so, however, as a benevolent despot, and hopefully avoids the autocratic role ascribed by many professional musicians to professional conductors.

In group and private lessons, however, the teacher must emphasize the more democratic and undirected approaches. He must give his students the latitude to practice and learn their music themselves, after first previewing it with them. Much too often, lesson time is spent in what might be called "supervised practice": the student plays through his lessons—frequently being stopped, corrected, and admonished by the teacher—and never really has an opportunity to monitor his own errors and correct them himself. Students must be given some freedom to choose the material they will study. This can be done in two ways, and usually both are combined: the student is given the opportunity of choosing among pieces or studies recommended by the teacher, any of which the teacher has determined will profit the student; or the student is given the opportunity of choosing a "recreation piece" in accordance with his own interests, tastes, and abilities. In both instances, the student is more or less free to make independent decisions.

Solo and small-ensemble work should be a regular feature of individual or group lessons, where possible. Again, rather than the teacher directing all preparation and rehearsal of the music, the student(s) should be solely responsible for mastering, at the least, large parts of the notation and technique. However, he should be free to discuss and decide any matters of interpretation with the teacher.

Of special merit in democratic and undirected activities is the need for much experience in sight reading and playing by ear; and for those who are interested and able, improvisation. In such activities, students are given the opportunity to read through much music for the sake of reading, not for the sake of perfection. They may even choose the pieces to be read. Students are also asked to prepare by ear tunes of their own choice. (For instance, "This week see if you can figure out how to play _____ by ear." And later, "Good! Now see if you can play it in the key of A major.") Those who are able can, if they wish, also be encouraged to "fool around" and vary the tune by ear, creating at first simple and then more ambitious improvisations.

*GO TO FRAME 6, PAGE 132.*

---

You are probably well aware by now that it is not really easy or natural to break down a well-conceived plan such as this into clearly defined categories. Perhaps in trying to complete the activity you have gained additional insights into the almost inextricable wedding of the elements that constitute classes designed to foster *permissipline.*

A behavioral objective is only an abstract formulation until it is put into operation. It is quite conceivable that the teacher who is not clearly aware of the educational and philosophical bases covered thus far will attempt to autocratically implement every facet of this objective by trying to dictate *how* the activity is to be completed, or by imposing his own tastes and values on the finished projects. This, of course, defeats the purposes of the objective. Thus, much depends on the attitudes, insights, and intent of such plans.

Very closely related to the issues of teacher attitude, classroom atmosphere, and motivation and reinforcement—factors in class behavior that we have covered before now—is the matter of how student progress (behavior in terms of overt responses to projects and activities) should be evaluated and recorded. It is a difficult issue, not so much because of philosophical or psychological factors as of the entrenchment of certain well-established attitudes toward and means of using grades.

## THE PROBLEM OF GRADES

Grading systems were initially meant, and are still used from time to time today, to summarize and evaluate a student's work; grades were symbols of the degree of value the teacher attached to the learning of each student. This system is being called into doubt in practically every corner of education today because it is clear that student progress is at least in part related to or determined by the nature of the teaching the student has received. Thus, grades in part place a label of value on the teacher as well as the student.

But even when the system of grading was the only workable means of evaluation (others are increasingly being devised today), it was put to notoriously poor use. The most flagrant abuse of grades—for which parents, as well as teachers, stand abundantly guilty—was to use them as motivation. The reward for completing a desired activity successfully became valued as a high grade. The satisfaction of positive reinforcement was found not in the completion of the activity, but in the receiving of the high grade. Thus, incentives that lead only to the desire for the reward, not for the learning that accrues from the activity, must be avoided. Grading too frequently performs such a function, and far too many students, in public schools and colleges alike, strive for grades as their satisfaction.

You may ask, "So what? Why not use whatever motivation is useful in making the student work?" Several things are wrong with this approach. First, such learning may be only memorized and, thus, quickly forgotten after the grading situation passes. Second, since the grade is the end in sight, students may use whatever shortcuts are necessary, including cheating. Last, life situations do not have grades as their rewards; a student motivated only by grades in musical situations, for instance, is not as likely to derive satisfaction from nongraded musical situations later in life.

The real problems arise when enlightened students begin to realize the disparity between what they learned (sometimes in spite of the teacher) and what grade they were awarded. Sometimes they find easy ways of attaining good grades, and then tend to follow other more interesting concerns of their own (which may or may not be profitable).

A similar problem arises when grades are used as negative reinforcement: poor grades are accorded for what the teacher considers to be poor learning. The assumption is usually that low grades will encourage and motivate the student to "try harder" or "work more." This is patently false, for several reasons. First, what is an "A"? Is it a value placed on the highest achievement within given limits? Or is it a value placed on the efforts of a solitary individual? Might not an "A" be awarded to the least able student on the basis of his improvement? Otherwise, how are grades supposed to motivate the student who is inherently less capable? What does the poor student think who gets a "D" after much travail? What *can* he do? Second, grades do not tend to motivate except perhaps in negative or unproductive ways. They unnecessarily discourage a student, or they unnecessarily help him to classify himself as incompetent in a certain discipline. What else can an individual think when he tries as best he can but receives consistent "D's" or "60's" in music class? How often have you heard people remark that they didn't like music because they were not "good" in it in school—whatever that means?

The issue of grading in music classes is, to say the least, a touchy one. How do you grade a freshman trumpet player in the high school band, which also has senior trumpet players who are presumably better? What possible criteria can you use for arriving at grades in general music classes? Until newer grading systems (such as bar graphs, pass/fail, and anecdotal accounts) become more widely accepted, music teachers in secondary schools and colleges, at least, will be forced to continue to use the prevalent grading systems. Given the use of behavioral objectives that specify minimum competencies yet permit successful fulfillment at varying levels of achievement, *grades should be relative to individual progress and should accurately reward effort.* Only in a curriculum designed to teach the "discipline" of music as an absolute body of objective information could grades be postulated in *absolute* terms. Never, in any case, should they be used as inducement or motivation; nor should they be used as punishment.

If music is taught in order to enhance effective living, grades should not impede this aim. Grades in music classes, except for those going on to professional studies in music, seldom have any positive value in effective living. If anything, the students whose music grades are low may be unnecessarily encouraged to think that they are not suited for music, or it for them. The competencies specified in behavioral objectives should be recognized by an "A" or its numerical equivalent. Thus, everyone can get an "A" even though various degrees of ability are manifested. Many will far surpass the minimum requirements, and the effort of each is rewarded mainly by the satisfaction of achievement itself.

In sum, then, the use and role of grades should be de-emphasized to whatever degree the school situation and conditions allow. To be sure, this will be difficult in music class if grades are heavily emphasized in every other sector of the school.

120

*Physical Problems*

Another type of problem behavior is attributable to physical discomforts or problems. This is more than a matter of room temperature, though this often may have a bearing on general unrest. More often, you are likely to encounter more specific physical difficulties. The student sitting near the back of the room who cannot hear what is being said in the front of the room is a common example. A similar case is the student whose eyesight is poor and who cannot read the chalkboard without straining. It is not uncommon in either case, and others like them, for the students experiencing such difficulties to mentally "drop out" of the class activity.

Youngsters have one common physical difficulty: sitting still. This is virtually physically determined for children from kindergarten through grades four or five, but with pubescents it becomes partially psychological as well. The problem becomes most acute in grades six through eight, and is most noticeable in boys (who even as adults seem least comfortable sitting still for any length of time exceeding a few minutes). Activities that involve or permit occasional movement around the room, or a classroom atmosphere that allows students to "stretch their legs" now and then will save many spurious trips to the lavatory.

*Singing*

Keep in mind, also, that adolescents are acutely aware of the physical changes occurring in their bodies. Any incident or activity that results in embarrassment or discomfort related to physiology is likely to cause an emotional scar, if not problem behavior. For this reason, extreme care is advised when undertaking *singing* activities in general music classes during the time when boys' voices are changing. The difficulties are greatest here rather than in a junior high school chorus, where the same vocal problems exist but are overcome by the youngsters pleasure in singing and music. In the general music class, you can assume in most cases that if the interest existed, the youngster would be in the chorus. So without an inherent interest or strong goals, the discomforts of singing (both physical and psychological) often outweigh whatever possible advantages the youngster may see in the singing activity. Problem behavior often results.

Listed below are recommendations and cautions that experience has proven useful for teachers who deal with this age group (ten through fourteen).

1. Carefully choose the music in terms of range, making sure that parts sung by boys do not exceed their existing range.

2. The above condition implies regular, if not frequent, voice testing,

which is best done while the class (or chorus) is singing by walking around the group and listening to individual voices.

3. If the chorus is divided into parts, make sure that the boys whose voices are changing sit next to the section toward which their voices are moving. When a boy's voice has changed sufficiently, he may begin to sing with the lower section.

4. Make the fact of voice change common knowledge to the entire class, emphasizing that it is quite natural and not a source of ridicule.

5. Perhaps above all, choose music that is likely to capture the interest or fancy of the boys in the group: music that, by its nature, encourages them to continue singing through this difficult period of physiological change and psychological discomfort. It is best not to force anyone to sing and, above all, not to use singing as punishment. Strange as it may seem, teachers have been heard to threaten, "If you don't behave, you'll have to sing a solo!"

The issue of singing as a major strategy in the teaching of music is a topic worthy of major consideration. Music education in this country began as instruction in singing and reading music. Ever since, music education has been, to some degree, influenced by this ubiquitous legacy, though under continually changing rationales. Suffice it to say here that the use of singing as an avenue for student participation in a musical experience does not automatically guarantee success. Many people who can neither carry a tune nor read music do enjoy and appreciate music in all forms as an aural experience, not as a performance experience.

Moreover, singing has often been used as a means to acquiring certain information about music, the thought being that the more one knew about music, the more one was likely to understand and enjoy it. This is patently false. It is not information relating to music and musical notation that is important. Rather, musical concepts, attitudes, and feelings derived from personal musical experiences, as well as the process of music learning, determines whether music will play a significant role in effective living. Singing is only one among literally hundreds of ways of personally experiencing music and developing musical concepts. As an isolated pursuit it runs the danger of encouraging children to think of music as being made up solely or mainly of singing. It risks equating musical enjoyment with active musical performance, so that youngsters (especially in elementary grades) become so enamored of singing that listening seems rather boring, or at least strange. It also runs the danger of gradually losing the interest of boys, who, physically and psychologically, are often less and less inclined to regard this as the sole or the most satisfying means of musical involvement.

Finally, adolescent boys are frequently prone to think of singing as a sissy or girls' activity. They seem to ignore the fact that most rock and pop vocalists are male. It is difficult to say whether they get the attitude from their fathers or from older boys, or whether it is a "reasoned" decision relating to the nature of the songs they are asked to sing. The fact remains, though, that teachers who insist on basing significant portions of their class activities or lessons on singing run an increased risk of encountering problem behavior.

What do you do when a boy absolutely refuses to sing? Or fakes it by merely moving his lips? And what would happen even if you found a way of cajoling or forcing him to sing? Would whatever he supposedly "learns" from this experience be a reward strong enough to outweigh the damage done to his attitude toward you and the musical art you represent?

Generations of youngsters go through school thinking that music class is a singing class. Anyone who has done much junior high school teaching can vouch for the fact that even six or seven years of singing instruction in the elementary school does not often result in youngsters who can read music, who can sing in tune, and who like to sing.

Yet when approached sanely and with caution, singing can be one device among many for personally involving young people in musical experiences designed to develop musical concepts. The main requisite is to put singing in a proper perspective: it should be employed only when it can achieve something no other kind of musical experience can, or when it can achieve something better than another kind of experience. Proper perspective also involves the careful choice of songs. Without doubt, teachers who have learned or devised means for teaching youngsters to compose their own songs have found that singing becomes a natural and rewarding outgrowth of the composing activity.[8]

It is important to keep boys singing through this difficult age, and to maintain or sustain their interest in it, if only to people the bass and tenor sections of high school and church choirs. It is more important, however, because singing is a form of music and music educators should not be responsible for "turning off" young people to any aspect of the musical art.

### Special Problems of Girls

Adolescent girls have their own physical problems. With the onset of menstruation (menarche), and at regular intervals thereafter, their physiology plays a significant role in their moods and how they relate to their environment. They are also prone to fooling around with their present "loves" if they are in the room, or writing notes about them if they are not. It is not unusual, either, for adolescents of junior high school age to have crushes on their male teachers.

Girls seem somewhat more clannish than boys do at this age. They may collectively plan their wardrobes, and manifest other signs of group cohesiveness. They frequently prefer to work together with other friends in their group. Although this must be allowed from time to time, it is not generally wise to divide the class into smaller groups on such bases. Such groups of close girl friends are more likely to become unproductively concerned or diverted by other group concerns or interests (for instance boys!).

Both boys and girls are likely to attempt to teasingly antagonize each other. This is normal, and though it should not be allowed to disrupt class

[8] See Henry Lasker, *Teaching Music Creatively* (New York: Allyn and Bacon, 1970).

activities, it should not be a source of major concern for the teacher. Often it can be a useful tool in the structuring of activities that involve some form of natural competitiveness. This is but another instance of recognizing "growth-typical behavior, and turning it to teacher advantage rather than making a major problem of it.

### Seating

Class seating is also an interesting matter. If the new or young teacher observes how classes seat themselves, two patterns will emerge. Either the girls seat themselves in the front of the class (usually because the boys rush to the back rows!), or the pubescent boys and girls take the back rows, leaving the front of the room for the prepubescent youngsters. If anything, the teacher is advised to reverse this tendency, placing the boys and/or pubescents in the front of the room and the girls and/or prepubescents toward the rear. Under the closer scrutiny of the teacher, boys and pubescents are less likely to engage in unruly behavior. Furthermore, if the teacher frequently subdivides the class into smaller working groups, he should make sure that the new arrangement does not overly disturb the group.

In most general music situations, where the physical plant permits, a semicircular floor plan with desks only two or three rows in depth is far more preferable to traditional arrangements. This permits greater flexibility in all regards, yet avoids sectional seating arrangements and permits no students to be so far removed as to feel comfortable in engaging in undesirable behavior. This is also a successful singing format if the students are divided by voice.

### Attention Span

Related to both physical and psychological causes of behavior problems is *attention span*. As long as the class is actively (intellectually, physically, or both) involved in the class *activity* (which, incidentally, is the reason why the activity format is so important with this age group), as long as the activity is not drawn out over too long a period of time, and as long as the activity has enough variety built into it to sustain interest, then there is little cause for worry. In such a well-planned activity, the wise teacher is ever alert for signs of waning interest and ever ready to invigorate the activity with a new line of pursuit or to switch to another activity.

### Passive or Active Listening?

Listening activities are by their nature subject to problems relating to attention span. Not only does listening to music involve sitting still for a period of time (which can encourage the adolescent to think that listening is *passive* in nature rather than highly active, in terms of mental involvement), it also requires more intense concentration than students are accustomed to.

124

Several recommendations for avoiding problems—and enhancing learning—can be made in regard to listening.

1. All listening should be directed listening. That is, before the class listens, they must be directed to try to perceive and/or think about certain features of the music they are about to hear. This insures active rather than passive listening and thus minimizes problem behavior. Directed listening may be accomplished in any of several ways. First, a list of questions or directions (a "directed-listening sheet") may be devised to direct student attention to specific elements in the music. "What instrument plays the main theme?" "What color do you think goes with the opening section, and why?" "If you had to create a title for this piece, what would you call it, and why?" "Raise your hand when you hear the A section return—and no looking around!" "Do you think you like this kind of music? Why or why not?" These are all appropriate questions. It is best to mix questions calling for cognitive, mood, creative, physical, and aesthetic responses, respectively represented by the above questions. Second, oral questions of the same nature may be given; this is usually most appropriate for shorter or simpler compositions. Third, other specific directions, not in the form of questions, may be given, such as to conduct a beat pattern, clap a rhythm, or move to the music.

2. The music chosen should be appropriate to the interests and readiness of the class. For instance, complicated compositions, or ones that change mood rapidly, are appropriate only for older students (in theory class and beyond). An advantage of this approach is that successful listening can minimize disorder; on the other hand, overly difficult music can cause the student to "give up" listening and seek some form of amusement.

3. Related to readiness is the length of the composition. Compositions of two to three minutes are recommended for elementary-age children. For junior-high-school-age youngsters, a time of four to five minutes, or less, is most successful. This is true even for older musical neophytes. Compositions of longer length can be profitably undertaken only if the student is seriously interested in music and motivated to study it; otherwise, problem behavior will arise from lack of attention and boredom.

4. The less expert the student, the less likely he is to be able to concentrate on more than one thing at a time. Therefore, a composition should be heard several times, not during the same lesson, but with enough intervening time for the class to receive it freshly. Before each subsequent listening, students should review their previous insights; then they can direct their attention to other elements in the music. Not only does this enhance the probability of transfer of learning, it permits refinement of the aural skills by which students can learn to hear ever more subtle elements of the music. A further benefit of repeated hearings is the resulting idea that good music can be returned to several times because it has more information, more to listen to or for; this is true even of simple music of high quality. Such a conclusion which does not have to be dictated by the teacher, can lead the student to begin his own value system. Above all, this kind of approach guards against the possibility of snap value judgments made on the first hearing. Even experienced musi-

cians recognize that an unfamiliar composition should be heard several times before a judgment is made.

5. It is most desirable, if circumstances permit, to hear each selection twice in a listening lesson. The first listening is analytic; that is, attention is directed to specific yet separate musical elements. This should be followed by discussion (and disagreement, if necessary) among the teacher and class of the problems or activities completed in conjunction with the listening. Then the selection is heard again, after which any lingering questions (some of which the teacher may have encouraged) are dealt with; the student is also better able to hear the music as an expressive whole, in terms of the prior listening, the intervening discussion, and the ideas he picked up as a result. The second listening thus helps establish a relationship between the elements perceived in the initial hearing and the expressive use of those elements in the composition as a whole. Thus, this sequence: analysis—discussion (resulting in more analysis)—synthesis.

### Community and Administration Attitudes

The final determinants of discipline and problem behavior that we shall discuss are the nature of the community and the attitude of the school administration. These are among the most important things that a teacher should investigate before accepting a position.

Rural communities, larger villages or towns, centralized or consolidated school districts, suburban areas, large-, small-, and medium-sized cities all have widely different influences on how a teacher plans. The socioeconomic background of the area, opportunities for cultural experiences, ethnic and racial determinants, and other factors as well, play a major role in the kinds of activities you plan.

The attitude of the administrators, how they have organized the schools, and the kinds of attitudes and behaviors they allow or encourage on the part of both teachers and students will indicate and perhaps limit, depending on the circumstances, the types of activities you should plan. Some schools may be notoriously intolerant of extending any freedom to students, whether it be in terms of dress codes, conduct in the halls, or otherwise. Other schools are equally intolerant of traditional means of teaching and working with youngsters, and it may be difficult to meet their ever-changing philosophies and demands.

Behavior—problem or otherwise—is not a factor that is directly attributable to any single source. Therefore, it is not controllable by any single agent. Youngsters are not masters of their own destinies, but are still in the grips of the dual forces of nurture and nature: nurture, to the degree that their environment—which includes their parents, their neighborhood, and all they come in contact with—influences their development and behavior; nature, according to the capacities and potentials they have inherited and the stage of psychophysical development they are currently experiencing.

126

Teachers, in turn, are similarly affected by the results of their own contacts with nurture and nature and by their resulting personalities and developed abilities. They are further controlled by teaching schedules, the physical plant, budgets, "administrivia," and other such factors that are outside their control.

Administrations have all of these problems plus those of dealing with boards of education and with parents. And the adult community brings us full circle to the nature and nurture that influences the adolescents you teach.

## SUMMARY

Thus, there is no disciplinary panacea designed to be applied mindlessly and to work perfectly in all teaching situations. Teachers who earn recognition as "good disciplinarians" usually fall into one of two categories, the second of which is eminently more desirable than the first: (1) those who by threats, physical force, or whatever, enforce obedience and conformity in their classes with an "iron fist" and the hard head that accompanies it; and (2) those who teach well and, thus, keep their students so busily and profitably engaged in learning that there is little time or cause for problem behavior. When disruption occurs, the latter can deal with it swiftly and surely because such behavior is the exception and not the rule. Such exceptions are obvious and thereby easier to deal with.

In order to avoid charges of unmitigated idealism, we should emphasize that no class is ever as controlled, motivated, and self-directed as a teacher may wish. There will be poorer classes and better classes. Much depends on what the teacher wishes. If the wish is for a totally obedient and silent class, in which everyone always does as they are told or asked, then this wish is bound to be unrealized. Instead, untold bitterness, anxiety, pressure, and frustration are likely to result. If the teacher's wish is to have a collection of youngsters busily engaged and interested in learning activities, and if the means are provided for such ends, then this wish can prove to be most satisfactorily fulfilled.

The tolerance, stability, and limen for "pain" of each teacher will also affect how they feel about their classes. And it can only be emphasized once again that the teacher's best defense is an active and successful learning offense. Within these very general guidelines, specific problems that are not attributable to factors in the classroom or to the manner and content of the teaching can be dealt with as individual and unique problems, along the lines we have recommended.

It was mentioned earlier that what a person *thinks* about what he learns is often more important than *what* he learns. This can now be expanded to include how a person *feels* about what he learns. The same may be said for the teacher, for what the teacher thinks and feels about what the class thinks and feels will, without doubt, be the key to his success and to their learning.

Which of the following behavioral objectives seem to provide *best* for the growth-typical behavior of pubescents in a general music situation:

A. Given a series of aural examples and explanations, the student will learn to identify the instruments of the orchestra. Go to Frame 9.

B. Given songs to sing, analyses of those songs and follow-up listening experiences, the student will display his knowledge of melody, harmony, rhythm, texture, and form in music by:

1. defining each writing,
2. identifying each in an unfamiliar song,
3. achieving a grade of at least seventy-five on an identification test of these concepts. Go to Frame 18.

C. Given fifteen minutes of preparation and their short sound compositions from the previous class, groups of three students each will display their understanding of style by performing the composition in at least three different styles, manipulating all but the fixed elements of the composition, and discussing each stylistic variant with the class and teacher. Go to Frame 27.

---

Here are some examples of curricular viewpoints for you to examine. Identify each as to the curricular orientation it most clearly manifests: body of knowledge, social conformity, integration in life. Check the discussion of each, one at a time.

A. Mrs. J spends considerable time each year with a unit of study on musical forms. Her junior high school classes analyze the forms of songs they are singing in class, listen to recorded examples of the most important musical forms, and compile a notebook of diagrams, descriptions, and explanations of these forms. The unit concludes with a unit test. The notebooks, too, are subject to her scrutiny and grading. Go to Frame 10.

B. Mr. R is fortunate in having band rehearsal five times a week and time for one group lesson per student each week. He uses this time to prepare his students on the music for upcoming concerts, festivals, and so forth. His use of this time and his persistence with this approach have brought him many accolades and much respect for the excellence of his band. Go to Frame 19.

C. Miss F, recognizing the futility of ever teaching a mastery of the considerable body of information that constitutes music, decided that she would devote her energies to elevating the taste of her students. Thus, her classes involve much listening to the classics and a study of the history of musical style. Since she wants her students to attend and enjoy concerts, each listening lesson is treated like a concert (except for clapping) and her students are taught how to understand the printed program and other niceties of concert attendance. Go to Frame 28.

D. Mr. Y's classes spend most of their time completing various creative activities. One involves the composition of original songs, another the creation of "sound forms," still another the discussion of vocal practice and singing styles in all vocal forms from folk to art song. Each of these activities is evaluated, and individual grades are given on the basis of effort and improvement. Go to Frame 37.

E. Mr. H directs the string program for grades seven through twelve. Students study solo and ensemble music appropriate to their level of ability, and briefly review difficulties they have with their orchestra music. The junior high school orchestra often implements his version of musical chairs, especially following concerts. At such times, the students within each section exchange parts several times, so that each eventually plays every part within his section. The high school orchestra is augmented in concert programs by various smaller ensembles drawn from the full orchestra. Eventually, everyone plays in a smaller group. Playing by ear and sight reading are given special emphasis throughout the year. Go to Frame 45.

---

*From page 106*                                                                      Frame 3

To be sure that you are clear about adolescent traits, examine the following descriptions of adolescents in action. Identify each as (a) stable and rational or (b) unstable and irrational. Also, identify which of the three syndromes or developmental phases—self-centered and independent, conformity-minded and peer-oriented, conscientious and adult-oriented—is manifested. Assume for now that the teaching is both good and successful. Turn to the appropriate frame to check your analysis of each youngster, before going on to the next example. Your accuracy should improve as you progress through the list.

1. John, who is ordinarily well behaved in class, becomes involved one day in some general horseplay. The teacher reacts with the practiced "evil eye" technique, and his total silence makes the class quickly aware of impending action. John is among the first to respond. Go to Frame 11.

2. Anna comes from an old-world, distinctly ethnic background. She seems to be the model student. Her work is always done neatly, thoroughly, and usually before it is due. Although her work is not superior or outstanding, it is good, and she becomes quite concerned when the teacher indicates it is not up to her usual par. Sometimes she even questions the teacher about the accuracy of the grade. Go to Frame 20.

3. Harry is fourteen going on fifteen, and in the eighth grade. His most frequent behavior in class is sulking, though he takes part in some of the activities that he seems to judge as not being beneath him. He cannot be goaded or pushed into anything, for he openly rebels under these circumstances. He is on friendly terms with almost everyone in the room, except that no one is really his friend. Go to Frame 29.

4. Janice, whose family ardently supports the arts, is a flutist in the junior high school band. She also plays piano, as does the rest of her family. In the band and in her group lessons she excels in musical performance and behavior. In general music class she is a constant source of agitation, usually in the form of gabbing, note passing, boy teasing, and wanting to go to the lavatory. Go to Frame 38.

5. Adella is a constant source of wonder to her music teacher. During some group activities, Adella is likely to really go out on a limb in attempting to solve the problem at hand. Sometimes she is successful, sometimes she is not. Either way, she does not seem to be affected. Yet at other times, she manages to be drawn into the "goofing off" of some of her friends, and she heartily joins in the fun until the teacher steps in. But never does she openly rebel against the teacher, for she usually recognizes her role in things. Go to Frame 46.

6. Tim is an eighth grader whose voice has not yet changed, and who has yet to undergo the rapid and dramatic physical changes already experienced by the majority of his class. Thus he is the shortest member of the class, high-pitched in voice, and generally younger-looking than his peers, even though he is as old or older than they. He seems the model student and takes part in all activities with gusto. He gets picked on a lot by the others because of his size and his interest in class activities, but he is always quick to advise the teacher of the offense. Go to Frame 51.

7. Tom is too energetic to even describe. He is bright, comes from a secure family background, and has many interests (not the least of which are girls, sports, and motorcycles). He vacillates between teasing girls, passing notes, reading motorcycle magazines, and doing good work in class activities (which is the most frequent when his mind can be distracted from his many other interests). Aside from his diverse interests, it is not beneath him to occasionally involve himself in high-spirited fooling around, especially when he thinks he won't be caught. But he usually responds quickly enough to the requests of the teacher to cease and desist. Go to Frame 56.

---

*From page 110*                                                                      Frame 4

The following are examples of reinforcement. Identify each as positive reinforcement (pos.), negative reinforcement (neg.), or nonreinforcement (non.).

A. John, during an activity in which he is to function independently, is engaged in active discussion with a neighbor. The teacher asks: "What's the problem, John?" and finds that John just didn't understand the assignment. So the teacher explains and clarifies it again for John, and he busily engages himself in work.

B. Archie is too eager to volunteer his frequently excellent answers, and continually shouts an answer when a question is asked of the class. He seldom raises his hand, and when he does, he does not wait for the teacher to call on him. The teacher is continually bringing this to Archie's attention by remonstrating in this manner: "Archie, when are you going to learn to wait until you are called upon? Are you deaf, or are you just naturally impolite? I want this silliness to stop immediately!"

C. Janice is boy-crazy. She is forever passing notes about boys and boy friends to her girl friends in the class. When possible, she talks to her neighbors about boys; she even carries on conversations across the room about boys, using hand signals where appropriate. She is a constant source of annoyance to Miss J, who looks with disfavor on such unladylike and disturbing behavior. One day, finally, Miss J becomes visibly upset at these goings on and heatedly berates Janice in front of the class, telling her that the proper concern of the class is music, not boys.

D. Jimmy is a very active seventh grader. But with constant urging from the teacher, he has increasingly become a productive member of the class by devoting his energies to the fruitful completion of class activities. One nice spring day, however, he boils over again, but is quickly quelled by the teacher. As he leaves class, the teacher says: "You know, Jim, I was kind of surprised at your behavior today. You have been a real contributor to class activities recently; I'd hate to see you become a poor influence. Let's chalk this one up to the sunny weather, O.K.?"

Now which of the following sequences best fits the above anecdotes?

1. Pos., neg., pos., non.   Go to Frame 12.
2. Neg., non., pos., non.   Go to Frame 21.
3. Non., neg., pos., pos.   Go to Frame 30.
4. Non., non., neg., pos.   Go to Frame 39.

---

*From page 112*

Frame 5

Since the proper use of reinforcement is essential to establishing the climate of "permissipline," see if you can determine which of the following activities best encourages

    a. conformity/obedience
    b. permissiveness
    c. permissipline

1. Given the march "Stars and Stripes Forever" and one week of practice, each member of the band will master his own part in terms of notation and musicianship, and will perform it correctly *a tempo* with the other members at the band rehearsal.

2. Given the song "The Marine's Hymn," each eighth grade student will sing the pitches and rhythms correctly at sight.

3. Given a few minutes of the film *The Leaf* (an art film tracing the trip of a dead leaf after it falls from the tree), shown without its sound track, each group of three students will present a description to the class of the kind of music they would compose for the sound track.

4. Given only sounds found or generated within the classroom, each student will compose a "sound form."

Which of the following best identifies the above behavioral objectives?

A. b-a-c-a. Go to Frame 13.
B. a-c-b-c. Go to Frame 22.
C. a-a-c-b. Go to Frame 31.
D. c-a-c-b. Go to Frame 40.

---

*From page 118*

To test your understanding of these various kinds of teaching styles, decide whether the following behavioral objectives is likely to result in:

    a. Teacher-directed activity.
    b. Group-directed activity.
    c. Undirected activity.
    d. Permissipline (which combines the previous three).

Given the patterns $\frac{6}{8}$ 𝅘𝅥𝅮𝅘𝅥𝅮𝅘𝅥𝅮 𝅘𝅥𝅮𝅘𝅥𝅮𝅘𝅥𝅮 | $\frac{3}{4}$ 𝅘𝅥 𝅘𝅥 𝅘𝅥 | , $\frac{4}{4}$ ("*foot*-ball *play*-er"), and $\frac{5}{4}$ ("*ten*-nis *tour*-na-ment"), each student will independently perform each correctly, while clapping or speaking the pattern and tapping his foot on the accents.

    a. Teacher-directed. Go to Frame 32.
    b. Group-directed. Go to Frame 47.
    c. Undirected. Go to Frame 41.
    d. Permissipline. Go to Frame 52.

---

*From Frame 32*

Here are some additional examples. For each, identify the teaching styles it represents:

    T. Teacher-directed.
    U. Undirected.
    G. Group-directed.
    P. Permissipline.

1. Each student in the class selects a musical composition or idea and "teaches" or "explains" it to the class.

2. The class is divided into groups of two students each; each group is responsible for choosing either the AB, ABA, or ABACA pattern and creating a "sound composition," traditionally notated or improvised, that clearly and correctly exemplifies the chosen pattern.

3. Each student in the class is charged with (a) the responsibility of creating a visual design that illustrates the principle of "unity in variety" and one that illustrates merely "variety"; and (b) the task of being able to explain and defend the rationale behind each.

4. The class sings the song "Puttin' on the Style" being conducted in turn by selected individuals.

5. Part of the high school band concert includes a performance by a brass quintet, whose members joined forces through mutual self-interest, and who developed a number largely by themselves just for this occasion.

6. The chorus begins work just after the Christmas concert on the music chosen by the director for the spring competitions, and after considerable rehearsing, wins the highest possible ratings. This music is also a part of the spring concert.

If you need to, reread all of these examples before making your final selection. When you think you have the best possible set of identifications, turn to Frame 57 for a discussion of each.

---

*From Frame 57*                                                    Frame 8

Here is another problem to test your understanding of the various teaching styles. After studying the behavioral objective below and the letters that identify portions of it, select the answers that most accurately identify the aspects of permissipline present in the objective.

A            B
(Given simple, pitched rhythm instruments), (a choice of other sounds in the
C            D
room), and (the full period), (each group of three students) will (create,
E
notate, and perform) at the next class a composition (that interprets the
F
title "The Sounds of Silence" with a suitable style and mood), and, upon
G
completion, (discuss and defend) their rationale.

Solve each section before going on to the next.

A. a. teacher-directed. Go to Frame 14.
   b. undirected. Go to Frame 23.
   c. group-directed. Go to Frame 33.

B. a. teacher-directed. Go to Frame 44.
   b. undirected. Go to Frame 50.
   c. group-directed. Go to Frame 55.

C. a. teacher-directed. Go to Frame 16.
   b. undirected. Go to Frame 25.
   c. group-directed. Go to Frame 35.

D. a. teacher-directed. Go to Frame 42.
   b. undirected. Go to Frame 48.
   c. group-directed. Go to Frame 53.

E. a. teacher-directed. Go to Frame 15.

b. undirected. Go to Frame 24.

c. group-directed. Go to Frame 34.

F. a. teacher-directed. Go to Frame 43.

b. undirected. Go to Frame 49.

c. group-directed. Go to Frame 54.

G. a. teacher-directed. Go to Frame 17.

b. undirected. Go to Frame 26.

c. group-directed. Go to Frame 36.

---

*From Frame 1*                                                                                                                     Frame 9

Your choice of the objective that provides best for growth-typical behavior was A:

Given a series of aural examples and explanations, the student will learn to identify the instruments of the orchestra.

Of the choices given, this is probably the *least* appropriate.

For one thing, it is not a well-written or well-conceived behavioral objective. The word "learn" is not qualified or given criteria; thus, even if this activity were carried out, what would constitute learning? How would you determine if, and what, they had learned? How is the identification to be carried out? What kind of observable response will you try to elicit?

Aside from this objection, this kind of activity—which is all too common in music education today—does not in the least take the growth-typical behavior of this age group into consideration. The activity entails sitting still, and probably taking notes while listening to examples and explanations of each of the instruments of the orchestra. Aside from the fact that doing this in one class period is unrealistic, this kind of activity is not geared to the interests and physical energy of this age group.

The activity also suffers from the point of view that regards learning in music as segmented: first you learn to recognize the instruments, then the forms, and so forth. This is not true! Though these goals may be emphasized at any given time, such learnings must be returned to often, sequentially and developmentally, if they are to have any real impact. Such planning enhances the likelihood of transfer of learning. Nothing is really ever "learned" once and for all at a given time. Almost everything is subject to refinement as new concepts and experiences are encountered.

Go back to Frame 1 and answer the question again.

---

*From Frame 2*                                                                                                                    Frame 10

A. This curricular orientation is most assuredly based on the acquisition and ordering of information within the musical discipline. Though the analysis of songs and recordings might seem to be worthwhile activities, they are subject to strong criticism in this context.

134

First, by restricting these activities to a specific *unit* of study occurring at a specific moment in time, Mrs. J has severely limited the probability or possibility of transfer to other situations later in the year, or later in life. Second, by requiring her students to compile a notebook, she has introduced an unnecessary verbal factor that will cause difficulty for those in the class with weak verbal skills or for those not inclined to this kind of busywork. This is especially true when verbal skills are used to collect, organize, and recall information, rather than to express ideas or feelings in discussion. Strong students are as likely to become bored by this as are weak students to become frustrated. Third, diagrams, descriptions, and explanations must be related and continually applied, refined, and reworked in light of new experiences, or they will almost certainly be forgotten within a few days or weeks. Last, the grading of the notebook and the tests based on the notebooks put a premium on memorization and recall as ends in themselves, and have no necessary relevance to music or musical behavior per se. Recall is no indicator of understanding or appreciation, and seriously threatens the (musical) attitudes of the less academically talented students, who invariably have difficulty with this kind of teaching but who can (and do, under other circumstances) learn, understand, and enjoy music at their own levels of readiness.

Go back to Frame 2 and analyze situation B.

---

*From Frame 3*                                                                                          Frame 11

1. John is obviously a stable and rational adolescent who is undergoing a conformity-minded, peer-oriented moment—during this class at least. He quickly joins in the rowdiness on this occasion, but as quickly responds to the teacher's stern "evil eye" look and to the silence and the mysterious future that silence seems to portend ("What will he do?").

Go back to Frame 3 and tackle example 2.

---

*From Frame 4*                                                                                          Frame 12

You listed sequence 1—pos., neg., pos., non—as the one that best identifies the sequence of anecdotes given. Sorry; only two of the four are correct. Let's consider them in order briefly.

You said that anecdote A involved *positive reinforcement.* Positive reinforcement would have resulted in some pleasant consequence for John; but though he may have felt better, finally knowing what was going on, it is obvious from what happened that his problem behavior was not intentional and that in misbehaving he was not seeking any particular consequence. The problem, thus, was isolated and eliminated; it was not positively reinforced in any way.

You said that anecdote B involved *negative reinforcement,* and here you are correct. Archie was scolded and censured for his behavior. This is an unpleasant consequence, one he probably wished to avoid. Had he been seeking such attention from the teacher by his actions, it might have been positive reinforcement because he visibly annoyed the teacher. But since he was apparently a good student with frequent answers of quality, it is likely that he was just overanxious. The negative reinforcement to what Archie surely considered a positive contribution he was about to make might result in his discouragement, or in stultifying his future willingness to answer. Non-reinforcement would have been a better solution: just ignore Archie until he learns to wait his turn.

You said that anecdote C involved *positive reinforcement,* and you are right again. Janice's preoccupation with boys was obviously a feature of her personality that she wished to make more widely known to her peer group; thus, her continual conversations with practically anyone who would listen. The teacher succeeded in finally bringing this fact to the awareness of the entire class, and this, most likely, was what Janice intended to do one way or another. Thus, the results were likely to be gratifying, and she may very well continue this ploy in the future.

You said that anecdote D involved *nonreinforcement,* but this is not correct. Nonreinforcement would have involved no positive or negative action on the part of the teacher. In this instance, the teacher did act with apparently well-conceived pointedness.

Go back to Frame 4 and, after rethinking A and D, make another choice.

---

*From Frame 5*                                                                 Frame 13

Your answer was A, that the sequence b-a-c-a best describe the identification of the behavioral objectives given. You have only two of the four correct.

1. You said that this activity exemplified *permissiveness.* Permissiveness would entail virtually no controls, or even criteria, letting the student be totally responsible for his motivation and direction. This is not the case here, for the material to be learned, the criteria that such learning must meet, and the conditions under which the learning will be performed and evaluated are all specified.

2. You said that this activity exemplified *conformity/obedience,* and you are correct. Given the nature of eighth graders, all are not likely (a) to be able to fulfill the behavior as expected; (b) to be motivated to sing this particular song; and (c) to accept the correct performance of pitch and rhythm as relevant, valuable or worthy of their concerted or individual efforts. Furthermore, the very "commonness" of this song obviates the possibility of sight reading since many, if not all, will probably know the song by ear. The inevitable result would be some problem behavior and a conformity/obedience crisis.

3. You said that this activity exemplified *permissipline* and you are again

correct. The air of freedom and individuality characteristic of the permissive part of permissipline is present in the free choices set up by the activity, in the independent and individual response made possible by small-group work. Discipline or authority is present in the form of the criteria and the selection of the learning materials by the teacher.

This activity puts a premium on aesthetic insight, creativity and individuality, but it also depends to a degree on verbal skills. Therefore, the teacher should compose the groups wisely, making sure those who are weak in this area are placed with more competent peers. It would also help to follow this activity either with a similar one involving the actual creating of an appropriate score, or with the repetition of the activity, resulting in "sound compositions" that fit the group's initial descriptions.

4. You said that this activity exemplified *conformity/obedience*. That is quite removed from the truth. In fact, this activity has virtually no controls or criteria aside from the specification of "only sound found or generated within the classroom." With no standards, then, there is nothing to conform or be obedient to.

Go back to Frame 5, reconsider items 1 and 4, and make another choice.

---

*From Frame 8*                                              Frame 14

You said that part A of the behavioral objective was teacher-directed. This is correct. Factors that are "given" usually imply teacher decision, structure, and control of an activity. Go back to Frame 8 and check your answer to part B.

---

*From Frame 8*                                              Frame 15

You said that section E of the behavioral objective was teacher-directed. Not really; though it specifies "notation" and "performance," it does not include guidelines as to the kind of notation (original or traditional) or the kind of performance (improvisatory, based on notation, or with strict control). Go back to question E in Frame 8 and make another choice.

---

*From Frame 8*                                              Frame 16

You said that section C of the behavioral objective was teacher-directed. This is correct. The teacher has specified a time limit in advance. Now check your answer to question D in Frame 8.

You said that section G was teacher-directed. Not so, unless you assume that the teacher planned to dominate the discussion. If the discussion involves the entire class, as it should, then this is clearly not a teacher-run aspect of the activity. The teacher must be prepared to handle any of the possible directions in which the discussion might lead, without unnecessarily cutting short the discussion or imposing his values in it. Go back to question G in Frame 8 and try another answer.

---

You chose B as the behavioral objective that best provides for the growth-typical behavior of preadolescents in a general music situation.

Given songs to sing, analyses of these songs, and follow-up listening experiences, the student will display his knowledge of melody, harmony, rhythm, texture, and form in music by:

1. defining each in writing,
2. identifying each in an unfamiliar song,
3. achieving a grade of at least seventy-five on an identification test of these concepts.

Unfortunately, there are many problems in this objective that are likely to lead to behavior and control difficulties. For example, even if this activity is spread over several classes—which it would have to be—the teacher will have a serious problem of motivation. How do you motivate students to be interested in this sort of information? How do you convince them that it is interesting, useful, and necessary to their own personal listening habits? How do you interest them in the activities necessary "to get across" such information. The answer is that you truly cannot do any of these things—especially not by asking for definitions and by posing the threat of an examination.

If, in fact, a teacher wants a class to *conceptually* refine their understanding of these elements, it is necessary to implement a host of activities calling for the actual involvement of the students in manipulating and creating music or sound forms that manifest various kinds of melody, harmony, rhythm, texture, form, and timbre. This would have the added advantage of variety and personal (even physical) involvement. Such activities, if planned as group activities, would also provide for the creative and energetic needs of this age group.

Defining concepts such as these is literally impossible, for by definition concepts have no such transportable substance. Identifying these factors in unfamiliar songs would have validity if it were ongoing and continually re-fined. To identify these features in one song (if one could even be found that manifested all) would have no true bearing on learning. Passing a test, as each reader must appreciate, is no guarantee of having learned anything.

Go back to Frame 1 and try the question again.

---

*From Frame 2*

B. The curricular orientation of Mr. R and the way he teaches his band is, as in situation A, subject to criticism. This approach has overtones of both the disciplinary mastery of learnings and skills and of the approach that values acceptable modes of thought and behavior. In his teaching there is little relevance for present or future life situations. Even considering the fact that his group is highly advanced, they are not given the possibility of developing independently as musicians because band music is the only basis of their instruction. Denied solo and ensemble participation, playing by ear, and encounters with a larger repertoire, they are being programmed with the skills and learnings directly related to the music at hand, and, thus, are being taught to conform to the musical modes of thought and behavior that are acceptable to the teacher (who represents "musical" society). Unfortunately, they will probably not be able to participate in "band," or wind ensembles after graduation, nor will they have much opportunity to listen to such groups. In any case, Mr. R did not provide practice or experience with the skill of listening.

Go back to Frame 2 and analyze situation C.

---

*From Frame 3*

2. Given her background, Anna seems, for the time being at least, *unstable and irrational*, even though she seems a model student. Her behavior indicates that she is, if anything, too *conscientious* about her work and too sensitive about the success of her work. Though this is not by any means invariably true, the cause may be her family background and the understandable emphasis her parents may have given to academic and social success in school. On the other hand, it is quite possible that Anna is a stable and rational child who has a poor understanding of grades and what they mean, or perhaps her goals are a bit too high. Either case requires teacher assistance.

Go back to Frame 3 and try example 3.

You listed sequence 2—neg., non., pos., non—as the one that best identifies the anecdotes given. Sorry; you got only one of the four correct. Let's take them in order briefly.

You said that anecdote A exemplified *negative reinforcement*. If this were true, John would have received unpleasant consequences that he wished to avoid. He might have wished to avoid the work in question, but he readily began work when the situation was explained to him, so it seems that he received no unpleasant consequence whatsoever.

You said that anecdote B was an example of *nonreinforcement*. If this were true, the teacher would have taken no positive or negative action; he would have ignored Archie or inquired as to the source of the problem instead of scolding him as he did. Therefore, this cannot be an example of nonreinforcement; it is much too strong an action for that. Nonreinforcement does seem called for here: to ignore Archie until he learned to wait his turn would avoid discouraging his future willingness to respond.

You said that anecdote C was an example of *positive reinforcement*, and you are correct. Janice's preoccupation with boys was obviously a feature of her personality that she wished to make more widely known to her peer group; thus, her continual conversation with practically anyone who would listen. The teacher succeeded in finally bringing this fact to the awareness of the entire class, and this, most likely, was what Janice intended to do one way or another. Thus, the results were likely to be gratifying, and she may very well continue this ploy in the future.

You said that anecdote D was an example of *nonreinforcement*. Again, you are confused about this kind of reinforcement. Nonreinforcement (or no reinforcement, if that makes it clearer) involves neither positive nor negative action. In this case, the teacher did act with apparently well-conceived pointedness.

Go back to Frame 4 and, after rethinking A, B, and D, make another choice.

Your answer was B, that the sequence a-c-b-c best describes the identification of the behavioral objectives given. You have somehow managed to get all of them wrong.

1. You said that this activity exemplified *conformity/obedience*. This is true only to the degree that all musical performances by a group demand a certain amount of both behaviors by all members of the group. That is the nature of musical performance; it cannot be avoided in most situations. What can be avoided, and and what is avoided in the described activity, is

the unnecessary carry-over of such behavior to all the activities prior to the mastery of the composition in question. Here, you must realize that greater latitude should exist so that the student can develop individually and become independent of the teacher. By being given the opportunity to learn his part by himself the student is also given the opportunity to be wrong, and this too is an important ingredient in independent learning situations; the individual becomes aware of the consequences of his actions, and learns better how to monitor his own performances and how to use feedback derived from these performances.

2. You said that this activity manifested *permissipline;* this could not be further from the truth. Permissipline entails the discipline or authority of controls or criteria, yet puts each student in a position of exercising a considerable degree of independence. Such is not the case here, for the activity is highly structured, to say the least, with no room for independent choice or action.

3. You said that this activity manifested *permissiveness.* Not so. Permissiveness entails virtually *no* controls or criteria and, hence, no discipline or authority to guide progress. It places total reliance on independent motivation, goal setting, interpretation, and actions. The activity described does allow a considerable amount of independent choice and action, yet a certain amount of criteria and controls are prescribed.

4. You said that this activity manifested *permissipline,* and again your answer is incorrect. Since permissipline involves, in part, a degree of criteria and control, this activity hardly fits the bill. It has virtually no controls or criteria other than the choice of sounds to be used. Thus, there is no discipline or authority in the form of guidelines for the students to follow or for the teacher to use in evaluation.

Go back to Frame 5 and reconsider all the items; then make another choice.

---

*From Frame 8*                                                     Frame 23

You said that question A exemplified an undirected activity. Hardly; such "given" factors are not undirected because they in some way guide the student by limiting his choices within a prescribed framework. Go back to question A in Frame 8 and make another choice.

---

*From Frame 8*                                                      Frame 2

You said that question E exemplified undirected activity. You are close but not entirely correct. Even though "notate and perform" may seem to be explicit teacher-dominated directions, they are not; yet they do prevent activity from being totally undirected. They specify certain requirements, but do not dictate how these requirements are to be fulfilled. The notation may be original or traditional, and the performance may be spontaneous, rehearsed, improvisatory, and so on. Thus, the group is given great latitude in choosing their actions. Go back to question E in Frame 8 and try another choice.

---

*From Frame 8*                                                                            Frame 25

You said that question C exemplified undirected activity. Hardly! Time so rigorously controlled does not qualify as undirected. It is a "given" factor and, therefore, limits choices to those within the given framework. Go back to question C in Frame 8 and try another choice.

---

*From Frame 8*                                                                            Frame 26

You said that question G exemplified undirected activity. Though a discussion might seem somewhat free, it is not likely to be so, for it is conditioned by what has preceded. Thus, it is not totally free. Nor does the teacher totally remove his presence from such discussion, since he is a member of the group as well. He can guide it, stimulate the class with leading questions as needed, and even try to proceed elsewhere when the discussion has spent itself. Go back to question E in Frame 8 and try another choice.

---

*From Frame 1*                                                                             Frame 27

You chose C as best providing for the growth-typical behavior of pubescents in a general music situation.

Given fifteen minutes of preparation and their short sound compositions from the previous class, groups of three students each will display their understanding of style by performing the composition in at least three different styles, manipulating all but the fixed elements of the composition, and discussing each stylistic variant with the class and teacher.

You are correct. This activity provides for individual involvement, a certain degree of independence, creative and abstract thinking, challenge and competition (self-induced!) between groups, physical involvement, and valid musical learnings that will be useful in listening or performing. All of these are approached conceptually.

The concluding discussion gives individual students further opportunity to apply their knowledge or ideas, and gives the teacher the chance to evaluate individual understanding on the basis of contribution to the discussion. On the basis of the learning observed, subsequent activities can be planned.

Go to page 101, below the line.

---

*From Frame 2*                                                            Frame 28

C. The curricular orientation of Miss F is decidedly weighted toward social conformity and acceptable behavior, especially in terms of values and taste. She denies the existence of any values or tastes other than those that apply to the so-called classics. By devoting herself to "elevating the taste of her students," she has committed the error of not recognizing and accepting the current values and tastes of her classes. In any situation where attitudes are to be affected, the recognition of the point of view already held by those to be swayed has proven to be a prime requisite of success.

Miss F has also failed to provide for the current life situations of her classes, which during adolescence are likely to be the only ones of which they are aware or concerned. Their current readiness is the experiential and conceptual base upon which the teacher can begin to build and refine. Whether it is a "taste" for food, a "taste" for clothes, a "taste" for cars or colors, the whole question of taste involves an intricate and very personal system of values. Values cannot be imposed by teacher fiat; at best they can be broadened and refined by the kinds of learnings and activities undertaken. But even this is difficult, for the teacher has the student in class only a fraction of the time that he is interacting with the environment and developing or making value judgments. Many students, for example, will be influenced by the tastes and values of their parents; others will reject their parents' values.

Society is becoming increasingly diverse. Its fragmentation has led to what Susanne Langer has called "the ultimate unit,"* the recognition that each person is a unique entity. To try to "teach" taste is to impose your own tastes, values, and judgments on others and, thereby, to impinge upon their right and need to develop themselves fully as individuals. This is especially true in the arts, where each individual must come to grips with the artwork, and all it involves, by, and for himself. Teachers help provide the opportunities for this to happen, and aid each student to understand what is involved in the artwork or the medium. "Feelings," which are embodied or objectified in works of art and values attached to those feelings, are philosophically, if not pragmatically and ethically, outside the teacher's sphere of influence.

Go back to Frame 2 and analyze situation D.

* *Philosophical Sketches*, pp. 107–22.

3. Harry is, without doubt, unstable and irrational. His age alone indicates his position and role in the class. He is obviously much older than the rest, and is therefore neither a part of the peer group nor totally outside it. He is on the fringe. Thus, he sees some activities as childish. He sulks during these occasions, and in doing so manifests his *self-centered independence* for both the teacher and the rest of the class. This interpretation is further proved by his rebellious behavior when he is goaded or pushed by the teacher. Under these circumstances, such behavior clearly defines his disproportionate desire for independence, even at the risk of action by the school authorities.

Go back to Frame 3 and analyze example 4.

You listed sequence 3—non., neg., pos., pos—as the one that best identifies the sequence of anecdotes given. You are completely correct. Here is why.

In anecdote A no positive or negative action was taken by the teacher; thus no strong pleasant or unpleasant consequences resulted for John. The teacher *nonreinforced* John's behavior by inquiring about the source of the difficulty and then clearing it up.

In anecdote B a strongly *negative reinforcement* occurred. Archie was scolded and censured for his behavior. This is an unpleasant consequence, one he probably wished to avoid. Had he been seeking such attention from the teacher by his activities, it might have been positive reinforcement since he visibly annoyed the teacher. But because he is apparently a good student with frequent quality answers, it is likely that he is just overanxious. The negative reinforcement to what Archie surely considered a positive contribution he was about to make might result in discouragement, or in stultifying his future willingness to answer. Nonreinforcement would have been a better solution: just ignore Archie until he learns to wait his turn.

You said that anecdote C was *positive reinforcement*. This is correct, even though it is a kind of "perverse" reinforcement. Janice's preoccupation with boys is obviously a feature of her personality that she wished to make more widely known to her peer group; thus, her continual conversation with practically anyone who would listen. The teacher succeeded in finally bringing this fact to the awareness of the entire class, and this, most likely, was what Janice intended to do, one way or another. Thus, the results were likely to be gratifying to her, and she may very well continue this ploy in the future.

In anecdote D a *positive reinforcement,* in the form of "honest optimism," was used to nip in the bud, possible future problem behavior. The teacher does not exhibit unpleasant feelings to Jim (which would constitute negative reinforcement); nor does he nonreinforce the behavior by ignoring it or even inquiring into its sources; he in effect gives Jimmy the rather pleasant feeling that he has confidence in him, and that he has been noticing and approving of his recent work. The teacher even saves Jim the embarrassment of having to invent an excuse for his behavior by providing one ready-made. In all this, there is a note of positive expectation given to Jim by the teacher. This, more than any other treatment, has a good chance of success in the present situation.

Go to page 110, below the line.

---

*From Frame 5*                                                          Frame 31

Your answer was C, that the sequence a-a-c-b best describes the four behavioral objectives given. Not bad; you have identified three of the four correctly.

1. You said that this activity exemplified *conformity/obedience*. That is true only to the degree that all musical performances by a group demand a certain amount of both behaviors by all members of the group. This is a feature unique to musical performance in most situations. What is avoided in the described activity is the unnecessary carry-over of such behavior to all the activities prior to the mastery of the composition in question. Here, you must realize that greater latitude should exist, allowing the student to develop as an individual and become independent of the teacher. In this way the student is allowed to be wrong, and this too is an important ingredient in independent learning situations; the individual becomes aware of the consequences of his actions and learns better how to monitor his own performances and how to use feedback derived from those performances.

2. You said that this activity manifested *conformity/obedience*. This is correct. Given the nature of eighth graders, not all will be able to perform as expected, not all will want to, and not all will enjoy the song. Most serious is the fact that the familiarity of the song eliminates the possibility of sight reading. The results of this activity are likely to be poor behavior and a conformity/obedience crisis.

3. You said that this activity exemplified *permissipline*. This is correct. The activity has the air of freedom and individuality characteristic of the permissive part of permissipline and the guidelines or authority of the discipline part. In this situation, guidelines for student effort are minimal, and free and independent thinking is encouraged.

4. You said that this activity exemplified *permissiveness*. Once again you are correct. It is permissive because it specifies no controls or criteria, and, hence, no discipline or standards. The student is allowed to function almost totally free of any direction, other than the stipulation that certain sounds are to be used. In so arranging the lesson, the teacher would be placing each student in the position of generating his own motivation, and choosing his own goals, means, criteria. Though this might benefit some students to a degree (it would be difficult to assess such benefits without criteria), the nature of adolescence proscribes the use of this technique. Adolescencts, though seeking

145

adult independence, still covertly desire (and need) the authority represented by minimal guidelines.

Go back to Frame 5, reconsider item 1, and make another choice.

---

*From Frame 6*

Your answer was that the objective was likely to lead to a *teacher-directed activity*. This is correct.

The teacher has specified all the criteria, materials, procedures, and means of evaluation.

Even though each student will act "independently," this does not constitute the kind of freedom of choice or interest bred by group-directed or undirected activities. Nor would it result in permissipline as such, since while each separate performance (or more likely, multiple attempts at correct performance) was being undertaken, the other members of the class might become increasingly restless. Also, by the time several correct performances of each of the two patterns had been made successfully, many of the remaining class members would begin to learn the patterns by rote imitation (by ear) rather than by independent means (sign and concept).

Thus, in addition to its other failings, this objective does not even provide for significant learning. Also, unless this activity were better structured and related to learnings the class felt to be relevant; it would be difficult to postulate the philosophical goal of "effective living." This might be remedied, for instance, by having the students relate the first metric pattern in the objective to "America," from *West Side Story* by Leonard Bernstein; or having them create, from rhythmic chants, original polymetric or changing meter compositions.

Go to Frame 7, page 132.

---

*From Frame 8*

You said that question A was an example of group-directed processes. A "given" factor is more than likely not invented by the group. Add to this the fact that the class has been subdivided into smaller groups, and there is even less of a chance for class control. Go back to question A in Frame 8 and try another choice.

---

*From Frame 8*

You said that question E was an example of group-directed activity. This is the most suitable of the three choices, although elements of each are present. Creation implies independent action; but here, the individual must compromise his ideas with those of the other two members of the group. That notation is to be used is directed by the teacher; what kind of notation, however, is left to the group. It may be original or traditional, or even a mixture. The same holds true for performance: it is specified by the teacher, but may occur in any of several ways—spontaneous, rehearsed, improvised from very general notation, or clearly controlled by specific notation. Thus, this part of the activity is most clearly described as group-directed effort. Go back to Frame 8 and check your answer to question F.

---

*From Frame 8*                                                        Frame 35

You said that question C was an example of group-directed activity. As with the other "given" factors in this objective, it is unlikely that the class, either as a whole or in the form of several subgroups, would agree to so specifically delimit their choice. The singular control represented by these delimitations should not be ascribed to group direction or democratic procedures. Go back to question C in Frame 8 and try another choice.

---

*From Frame 8*                                                        Frame 36

You said that question G exemplified group-directed effort. This is correct, especially when you remember that the teacher is properly a member of the group. Therefore, even though the discussions will be necessarily conditioned by the nature of each performance, and even though the teacher can enter into the discussions, contributing his own ideas and suggestions, the course and content of these discussions cannot be predicted in advance. Nor do they qualify as undirected, since each will be directed to some degree by the performance and by the teacher's participation. Congratulations: you are finished. Go now to page 118, below the line.

---

*From Frame 2*                                                        Frame 37

D. Mr. Y's classes are strongly oriented toward *effective living*. His classes involve active encounters with music and musical phenomena. As such, they enhance the acquisition and development of concepts. Transfer of learning to new and future situations and to adulthood is thus more likely. His classes also aid students to satisfy present personal interests and to deal successfully with present life situations.

For example, the creation of original songs, no matter how simple, provides an outlet for creative urges, presents a challenge that can be overcome successfully (to different degrees, of course), allows for peer interaction (since many songs will be sung, analyzed, and so forth, by the entire class, or even created by small groups within the class), and provides for the specialized skills needed by those who are gifted enough (such as for their own rock groups, or other such ad hoc student activities). Similarly, the creation of sound forms provides for all of these things, though in a less precise and perhaps more conceptual vein. They are, however, more directly related to the directions in which music seems to be moving today, and will serve well to provide musical situations that learners are more likely to encounter in adult life. Aside from the many practical benefits of studying vocal practice and singing style (such as realizing that the voice is an instrument capable of various degrees of training and manipulation), the discussions involved in this activity provide some opportunity for applying musical learning and discrimination to forms of music relevant to the students' current level of taste (folk song, rock, popular and show tunes, jazz singing, etc.), while simultaneously providing an avenue to further musical refinements (opera, art song, etc.).

Above all, the teacher who structures learning activities to provide for individual involvement such as this recognizes the importance of "the ultimate unit" both in life and in art. Such activities allow each person to realize his individuality, with all that this might entail.

Go back to Frame 2 and analyze the last situation.

---

*From Frame 3*                                                                Frame 38

4. Janice seems somewhat *unstable and irrational.* Her behavior is consistently *conformity-minded, peer-oriented.* Given her family and musical background, she is probably a good student who is quick to learn, but easily bored. In band classes, where the peer group has a single well-motivated goal, her behavior is good. She and the remainder of the peer group have musical ends in mind that are mutually rewarding. In general music class, however, her constant interaction with the peer group indicates that, in this situation conformity takes precedence over learning. You might conclude that the teacher of this class is not doing a sufficient job. That may be true, but it may also be true that Janice is an exceptionally intelligent or talented student who needs especially strong challenges and decidedly individual attention.

Go back to Frame 3 and try example 5.

---

*From Frame 4*                                                                Frame 39

You listed sequence 4—non., non., neg., pos—as the one that best identifies the sequence of anecdotes given. Sorry; of the four, you have identified only two correctly. Let's consider them in order briefly.

In anecdote A no positive or negative action was taken by the teacher;

thus, no strong pleasant or unpleasant consequences resulted for John. The teacher *nonreinforced* John's behavior by inquiring about the source of the difficulty and then clearing it up. Thus, you were correct.

You said that anecdote B was an example of *nonreinforcement*. If this were true, the teacher would have taken no positive or negative action; he would have ignored Archie or inquired into the source of the problem instead of scolding him as he did. Thus, this cannot be an example of nonreinforcement: it is much too strong an action for that.

You said that anecdote C exemplified *negative reinforcement*. If this were so, a truly unpleasant consequence that Janice wished to avoid would have resulted. You think, "Well she was scolded, and that is unpleasant, isn't it?" This is one of the most common mistakes made by teachers; they assume that scolding, censure, and punishment are unpleasant and, therefore, will eliminate the poor behavior. These acts are unpleasant only when the student wishes to *avoid* them. When the student anticipates such a reaction by the teacher or even seems to actively seek such a response, then such actions by the teacher are not unpleasant. Students frequently think this way when the rewards they receive for their poor behavior outweigh any possible consequences, or when the reward is getting the teacher upset.

Janice's main preoccupation is making the boy-crazy facet of her personality known to her peer group. Thus, the teacher's response to her behavior is not likely to deter her from this kind of behavior in the future, for the teacher performed the task so well for Janice. Thus, she may very well continue to show off in this way.

You said that anecdote D was *positive reinforcement*. You are correct here because positive reinforcement, in the form of "honest optimism" was used to nip in the bud possible future problem behavior. The teacher gave neither unpleasant nor pleasant consequences; he merely conveyed confidence. He even provided Jim with an excuse, thereby saving the student from this embarrassment. This, more than any other treatment, has a good chance of success in the present situation.

Go back to Frame 4 and, after rethinking B and C, choose again.

---

*From Frame 5*                                                          Frame 40

Your answer was D, that the sequence c-a-c-b best describes the behavioral objectives given. Good; these are all correct.

1. You said that this activity exemplified *permissipline,* and it does. It provides the guidelines necessary for the discipline part of the hybrid. On the other hand, it provides the freedom indicated by the first part of the hybrid: the student will independently work on his own part, thus enhancing the possibility of his development as an independent musician. He is not able to copy or imitate the teacher or other students. He must rely on his own musical experience and insight. He is free to make mistakes and, thus, to learn the consequences of his action and how to better monitor his own performances. Thus, in working toward the conformity necessary in performances

by groups of musicians, the student is nonetheless allowed to develop as an individual.

2. You said that this activity manifested *conformity/obedience*. This is correct. Given the nature of eighth graders, not all will be able to perform as expected, not all will want to, and not all will enjoy the song. Most serious is the fact that the familiarity of the song eliminates the possibility of sight reading. The results of this activity are likely to be poor behavior and a conformity/obedience crisis.

3. You said that this activity exemplified *permissipline*. This is correct. The activity has the air of freedom and individuality characteristic of the permissive part of permissipline and the guidelines or authority of the discipline part. In this situation, guidelines for student effort are minimal, and free and independent thinking is encouraged.

4. You said that this activity exemplified *permissiveness*. Once again you are correct. It is permissive because it specifies no controls or criteria and, hence, no discipline or standards. The student is allowed to function totally free of any direction, other than the stipulation that certain sounds are to be used. In so arranging the lesson, the teacher is placing each student in the position of generating his own motivation and choosing his own goals, means, and criteria. Though this might benefit some students to a degree (it would be difficult to assess such benefits without criteria), the nature of adolescence proscribes the use of this technique. Adolescents, though seeking adult independence, still covertly desire (and need) the authority represented by minimum guidelines.

Go to page 113, below the line.

---

*From Frame 6*                                             Frame 41

Your answer that the objective was likely to result in an *undirected* class activity is quite far off the mark.

An undirected activity would involve a considerable degree of *permissiveness:* each student would decide for himself what he wanted to do, how he wanted to do it, or even if he wanted to do anything at all. It should be clear that the activity here does not in any way satisfy these requirements, for the students have virtually no freedom of operation at all.

Re-examine the objective in Frame 6 and choose another answer.

---

*From Frame 8*                                             Frame 42

You said that question D was an example of a teacher-directed activity. This is most likely correct, for the teacher should be responsible for subdividing the class into well-thought-out groups. To allow students to group themselves or to allow them to decide on the size of their group is to court trouble. Go back to Frame 8 and check your answer to question E.

You said that part F of the objective was teacher-directed. This is correct, but only to the degree that the teacher has indicated the nature of the task and the qualities that the class should strive to realize in their solutions to the problem. This is a good example of a teacher-directed activity that allows considerable freedom to the class to discover and create independently. The "suitable style and mood" should not cause any unnecessary stricture, for each group interpretation of the title is likely to be suitable in various ways and to various degrees. The determination, of course, will be found in large measure in the rationale that the group advances following their performance. Go back to Frame 8 and check your answer to question G.

You said that question B was an example of teacher-directed conditions. This is correct even though it allows student choice because the teacher has, in addition to stipulating "simple, pitched rhythm instruments," further limited the available means to "other sounds found in the room." Thus, the students cannot drag in garbage can lids, jackhammers, and so forth; instead, they must explore their immediate environment for sound-producing sources. This too is important, for it sensitizes them to a greater awareness of sound and of factors related to timbre. Go back to Frame 8 and check your answer to question C.

E. Mr. H, too, has oriented his curriculum toward providing for effective living. By including solo and ensemble literature in all lessons, he is aiding the development of musical independence. By briefly reviewing the orchestra music and by ironing out difficulties in the lessons, he avoids having to scold or correct individuals during the group rehearsals. He also saves time this way, and can include other relevant learnings (such as experimenting with interpretation) in the rehearsal. By allowing his players to switch parts, the less expert players can experience the more musically rewarding parts and experience the musical challenges and rewards that await them in their future. By including solo and ensemble opportunities in concerts, he provides the major basis for the existence of such solo and group activity outside of or after graduation. Solos and small ensembles are, in addition, the major avenues to independent musicianship.

Go to page 102, below the line.

*From Frame 3*

5. Adella is strictly *stable and rational*. She manifests some independence on the occasions when she goes "out on a limb," and accepts the consequences with equal aplomb. At other times she is conformity-minded and peer-oriented, either completing class activities within the intended parameters or joining in a session of good-hearted goofing off. But at all times she is entirely responsive to the request of the teacher. Thus, she is able to remain stable through her self-direction in each of these situations.

Go back to Frame 3 and analyze example 6.

*From Frame 6*

Your answer was that the objective was likely to result in a *group-directed* activity.

This is highly doubtful, unless you interpreted "group-directed" to mean that the group would become so undisciplined in the course of the activity that it would literally take over the classroom. Remember, group-directed activities entail democratic operation: students in a group decide and choose the materials, processes, or activities they wish to undertake; or, if the activities are suggested by the teacher, smaller groups choose and implement the processes to be used in the solution of the problem at hand. It should be clear that these conditions are not present in the behavioral objective given.

Re-examine the objective in Frame 6 and choose another answer.

*From Frame 8*

You said that question D was a form of undirected activity. Because the class will not know how to group themselves effectively, this kind of process is best removed from the domain of "undirected" class functions. Therefore, your choice here is inappropriate because the grouping referred to in the objective is implied to be a teacher function. In the rare instances where the teacher may wish to allow the students to group themselves, such a provision would have to be included in the objective because it must be assumed that such an idea would be used only in situations where some educational merit could be observed (for instance, to see if people with equal abilities or interests gravitate together). Go back to Frame 8 and try another choice for part D.

*From Frame 8*

You said that part F of the objective was undirected. Not quite right. Though there is considerable freedom for the class to discover and create independently, there are some direct guidelines and restrictions present. Their compositions must interpret the mood of a suggested title in a suitable manner. The fact of a predetermined title, and the direction to interpret its mood, eliminates the possibility of this portion of the activity being undirected. Go back to Frame 8 and try another choice for question F.

---

*From Frame 8*

You said that question B provided undirected conditions. This is probably the least suitable answer since the objective *limits* the group to "other sounds" found in the room. Conceivably, the class could bring this condition on themselves, but are not likely to do so. Nor would it be advisable to spend time deciding such issues as this when the period could best be used in actual composition, discussion, and so on. Go back to Frame 8 and make a more suitable choice for part B.

---

*From Frame 3*

6. Tim is in the unenviable state of being somewhat of an ugly duckling or a runt of the litter. The result is that his behavior is *unstable and irrational.* He is picked on by what should be his peer group; but he is apparently having difficulty finding the security of such a group and has determined instead to seek his *approval and recognition* from the adult world, in the form of his teacher. Thus, he is well behaved, overly eager in learning activities, and quick to tattle. As with Anna, Harry, and Janice, Tim's problems soon become the teacher's problems.

Go back to Frame 3 and consider example 7, the last example there.

---

*From Frame 6*

Your answer was that the objective was likely to engender *permissipline.*

Perhaps you are confused by some of the elements in the behavioral objective. Remember, permissipline should include facets of teacher-directed, undirected, and group-directed learning. This activity does mention that each student must be able to perform "independently," but you should realize that this does not refer to the free, "permissive" kind of independence characteristic of permissipline. All that is provided here is a kind of independent testing situation for evaluating each student accurately. Unfortunately, this will prove to be very time-consuming and redundant, and unless the performance is done privately, many students will begin to learn the pattern through rote imitation instead of conceptually demonstrating cognition of the metric tasks at hand.

Re-examine the objective in Frame 6 and choose another answer.

---

*From Frame 8*                                                      Frame 53

You said that question D has aspects of a group-directed or democratic activity. This is only partially correct, in the sense that the group must function democratically in order to complete the assignment. But why not have groups of two or four? The decision to have three students per group was not conceived by the class. Go back to Frame 8 and choose a more suitable answer for question D.

---

*From Frame 8*                                                      Frame 54

You said that part F of the objective was group-directed in conception. Though the groups of three would have to function democratically in order to complete the assignment, there is yet considerable latitude for independent thought and action. And it is obvious from the objective that the small groups or the class as a whole did not conceive the conditions of interpreting the mood of a suggested title. Go back to Frame 8 and choose a more suitable answer for question F.

---

*From Frame 8*                                                      Frame 55

You said that question B provided group-directed effort. Because choice is provided, it might seem that the group is free to exercise their democratic rights in this situation; but they did not decide by themselves to stipulate this choice. If time had been devoted to allowing the class or groups to decide this for themselves, considerable time that would be better spent in actual work would have been lost. Go back to Frame 8 and choose a more suitable answer for question B.

7. Tom is, in addition to being too energetic to describe, too typical to describe. He is from all signs, totally *stable and rational*. He shifts gears between interests and behaviors as rapidly as his dreams of shifting the gears of motorcycles. He constantly needs to be steered by the teacher, but once involved in class activities, he does well. When he does respond to the initiatives of peer group frolicking, he is equally direct in his response to the requests of the teacher.

Go to page 106, below the line.

---

Here are the answers and some rationale for the examples given. You may want to reread each example in Frame 7 before considering the discussion of it below.

1. **U.** This example demonstrates an *undirected* activity. The only direction given is the charge to prepare something, anything musical in nature, for the class to share. Each student is left entirely to his own designs and choices. Some might undertake very ambitious presentations, others extremely minimal ones. The danger, of course, arises from the chancy nature of the activity: the chance that some students will merely complete the assignment, and the chance that some will make incorrect presentations. This is not a bad feature because it allows the teacher to suggest corrections. What is weakest is the chancy nature of the probably unrelated morsels of musical information likely to be offered.

2. **P.** This example is clearly one of *permissipline*. Teacher-direction, small-group self-direction, and ample freedom within these conditions are all provided.

3. **P.** This activity, too, exemplifies *permissipline* since it involves teacher-direction; independence and freedom of action in completing the activity; and group processes in the form of class interaction, with the possibility of further group direction resulting from the class discussion.

4. **T.** This is clearly an example of a *teacher-dominated* activity. The teacher selects the piece, the students, and the manner in which the composition is to be performed and conducted. There is no chance for group-direction or free behavior and choice (except for the possibility of problem behavior).

5. **U.** As it is described, this activity is *undirected*. The group joined together and worked on the composition "themselves," presumably just for the concert; but the element of enjoyment was the probable motivation. Though the director might audit preparation and make suggestions at various stages, this in no way impairs the freedom of action of the performers in what is basically a self-directed learning experience.

6. **T.** This last activity is all too common: it exemplifies strong *teacher-*

155

*domination* in the choice of the music, its programming, and its use. The time used in preparing the music for competition and concert is unwarranted, even in view of the motivations involved. If the director had allowed the chorus to enter somewhat into the decisions regarding the music, and if he had reserved this much time in order to include learnings about the music and to involve the chorus in considerations of interpretation and accuracy, then the air of permissipline would be present.

Go to Frame 8.

CHAPTER FIVE

# a point of view
# on music
# and behaviorism

*From whatever different sensations the arts may de-
rive, from touch or vision, or hearing—on to whatever
the artists may project their visions, on statues or
murals or melodies—they are one in spirit and meaning. . . . The arts, like gesture and speech, are ex-
pressions of man; they confirm and corroborate in
their own individual ways, what their sister arts reflect: man's emotive reaction to stimuli from without
and within.*

Curt Sachs, The Commonwealth of Art (*New York:
W. W. Norton and Company, Inc., 1946), p. 17.*

*[In music] the assignment of meanings is a shifting
kaleidoscopic play, probably below the threshold of
consciousness, certainly outside the pale of discursive
thinking. . . . Because no assignment of meaning is
conventional, none is permanent beyond the sound
that passes; yet the brief association was a flash of
understanding. The lasting effect is, like the first effect
of speech on the development of the mind, to make
things conceivable rather than to store up propositions. Not communication but insight is the gift of*

music; in a very naive phrase, a knowledge of "how feelings go." This has nothing to do with "Affektenlehre"; it is much more subtle, complex, protean, and much more important; for its entire record is emotional satisfaction, intellectual confidence, and musical understanding.

Susanne K. Langer, Philosophy in a New Key (New York: New American Library, 1951), pp. 206–7.


Literary men pretend to believe that the enjoyment of the ear and the eye in music and painting is like that of the palate in the action of eating and drinking.

Eugène Delacroix, Journal of Eugène Delacroix, tr. and ed., Walter Pach (New York: Covici, Friede, Inc., 1937), p. 364. [Jan. 17, 1854].

## THE DILEMMA

The quotations that open this chapter are probably no great news to the musicians and music educators who have always believed that their art involves both the inner realm of feelings and the other realm of overt acts. They generally hold as well that because this subjective component exists, their art cannot be reduced to simply stated rules or explanations. Yet there are those—seldom musicians or artists of any kind—who would reduce the artistic impulse and response to pure, empirically measurable overt behavior. It is difficult to convince these scientists—notably the behavioral psychologists who uphold the pure behaviorism of Watson and Skinner—that there is even such a thing or experience as a real "inner life."

The teacher of the arts is faced with this paradox. On one hand, artistic insight—a nasty term to the behaviorist—implies that inner processes exist in the form of thoughts and feelings in the teaching, production, or consumption of fine art. On the other hand, the teacher has great difficulty in dealing directly with this inner life because it seems to be outside direct control. In music this is perhaps most notably true. Music, as sonorous patterns, is extremely transient and intangible. It is, therefore, difficult to account for its impact on the human consumer.

The purpose of this chapter is to clarify some of the difficulties involved in this apparent paradox. Early in the first chapter, I cited Susanne Langer in support of the notion of the feeling response, as it applies to music. Yet in other portions of this book, the use of behavioral techniques has been recommended in situations designed to foster learning in the musical art. Are these two points of view really irreconcilable? Perhaps not.

Various philosophers have emphasized that the greatest truth is often the synthesis of conflicting views. Indeed, most Oriental philosophies hold that existence is defined in terms of oppositions that only seem real, but in fact reflect an inherent unity. To them, hot can exist only in comparison to cold, up to down, and so on. Therefore, our task is made easier if we clarify certain issues surrounding behaviorism and enumerate the conditions under which it can be fruitfully applied to arts education.

## BEHAVIORISM

The basic tool of behavioral learning theory recommended thus far is the use of behavioral objectives. These are statements that describe the results of a given learning activity in terms of overt behavior. You should recall that earlier learning was described in terms of such overt, observable responses.

> Learning has resulted when behavior is changed as a result of experience.
> Learning has resulted when the frequency of a behavior increases.

Note that neither of these statements maintains that learning *always* results in overt behavior, or that overt behavior is the *only* indication of learning. Nor do they affirm that *all* learning can be measured. They merely state that when behavior changes or when its frequency increases, learning *of some kind* has occurred *to some degree*. Thus, behavior can serve as a reliable indicator of certain learnings.

People in the arts who have given considerable thought to the subtleties of the aesthetic or affective (that is, "feeling") responses find it difficult to reconcile the gospel according to certain behaviorists with the artistic experience or artistic education. The reason is simple: many behaviorists maintain that mental or inner phenomena *always* result in overt behavior, or that behavior is the *only* acceptable indication of learning. Some go so far as to try to measure scientifically the relevant overt signs of physiological functioning during aesthetic and affective moments—heart rate, breathing, and "galvanic skin response."[1] They proceed to evaluate this data, and to draw certain conclusions from it. Unfortunately, their results often fail to agree with the observations of artists.

This line of thinking results from a long history of regarding mind and body, psychology and physiology, as separate though related entities—from regarding psychical and physical experience as distinct, though related or interdependent in some unnamed way. Thus each psychical experience is thought to have its correlative physical experience, and vice versa; but each remains a unique version of experience. Psychical phenomena, it is held, can be acknowledged only by observing and measuring physical phenomena (behavior, response, action, and so on). Some behaviorists go so far as to insist that psychic experience does not exist or is not observable or measurable at all.

## CRITICISM OF BEHAVIORISM

Though behaviorism is too controversial and subtle an issue to be treated at any great length here, it can be noted that such attitudes and their educational consequences have come under critical scrutiny in recent years.

Humanist objectives for education cannot be readily assessed by current behavioral, performance-based techniques primarily because they are matters of personal meaning. Meanings are internal. They lie inside of persons and are not open to direct investigation. Since they do not have a direct one-to-one relationship to behavior, neither can they be adequately assessed by the familiar psychometric techniques. . . .

. . . How a person behaves at any instant is a function of what is going on inside him—especially his beliefs, feelings, values, attitudes, personal meanings, purposes, and goals. Permanent change in behavior is only likely to occur

[1] Measurement of the electrical flow produced by the chemical action of the body during stimulation or excitement—taken from the skin.

when these causative factors within the individual are changed. . . . Change in behavior with no change in perception is unlikely to remain very long. On the other hand, a change in perception may result in many behavior changes.[2]

Humanistic objectives are holistic or summational: they take into account the sum of human functioning. Similarly, arts-oriented objectives deal with behaviors that are the composite result of many inward states of mind, and not with simple, atomistic behaviors that have a mathematical or simple cause and effect. Neither humanistic nor arts-oriented objectives are subjectable to "objective" treatment.

> Certain fundamental beliefs contradict strict behaviorist theory—the belief that knowledge and values are dynamic, uncertain and relative, not fixed; that each human being is a unique individual with his own needs, purposes, and values; and that learning is a continual and often long-range process the purpose of which is the relating of personal knowledge to one's total environment of thinking, feeling, and acting.[3]

It should be expected that Langer, whose position on the feeling response was briefly considered earlier, would be one of the severest critics of the behaviorist position:

> The chief motive of this formulation is to establish psychology as a natural science distinct from physiology, . . . yet to give it the virtues of experimental research and so-called "objective" truth. But behavior has every appearance of being the macroscopic result of microscopic processes in the behaving organism; and no scientific research can restrict itself to any set of phenomena having causal connections with some other set, yet leave that other set alone. So the blessed word "behavior," while purporting to supply an "objective correlate" for the mental phenomena—feelings, thoughts, images, etc.—which are the original material of psychology, but stand condemned as "subjective," really creates methodological difficulties of its own.[4]

The fallacious logic that Langer observes in the position of pure behaviorists provides her with an edifice upon which she builds a strong case of her own. Her new view of "mind" and "feeling" promises to resolve some of the difficulties of these issues encountered by philosophers throughout. She regards "feelings" as

> *anything that may be felt*. In this sense it includes both sensation and emotion—the felt responses of our sense organs to the environment, of our

[2] Arthur W. Combs, "Educational Accountability From a Humanistic Perspective," *Educational Researcher*, 2, No. 9 (September 1973), 19–20. This entire short article is highly recommended.

[3] Richard C. Larson, "Behaviors and Values: Creating a Synthesis," *Music Educators Journal*, 60, No. 2 (October 1973), 42.

[4] Susanne Langer, *Mind: An Essay on Human Feeling*, Vol. 1 (Baltimore: Johns Hopkins University Press, 1967), pp. 16–17.

proprioceptive mechanism to internal changes, and of the organism as a whole to its situation as a whole, the so-called "emotive feelings."[5]

This thesis, first advanced in early exploratory writings and then worked out in her subsequent and unfinished work *Mind: An Essay on Human Feelings,* is of major importance for arts educators:

> . . . sentience (i.e., feeling) is a phase of vital process itself, a strictly intraorganic phase, i.e., *an appearance which is presented only within the organism in which the activity occurs.* [italics added] Each organism, therefore, feels its own actions if they enter this phase, and not any other creature's. Not many of the myriad events that make up a life are felt at all—probably only those of unusual intensity.[6]

From this explanation—very important for arts educators simply because the arts *do* cause feelings of unusual intensity—Langer further affirms the uniqueness of each individual "mind." She proceeds to define mind, knowledge, and experience in terms of "feelings" rather than in terms of the "objective" data of facts and information or of stimuli. Mind "feels," it does not "know."

> 'Feeling' in the broad sense here employed seems to be the generic basis of all mental experience—sensation, emotion, imagination, recollection, and reasoning, to mention only the main categories.[7]

Thus, mind and felt experience are aspects of life that evolve, develop, and are refined from the system of nature. They constitute life in its most basic form. Not all of the felt experiences of mind result directly in acts or in any other overt behavior. Some are begun and completed in the brain in the form of images. Others may connect with other mental acts that *do* result in some behavior, or they may cause us to perceive the mental actions that we call subjective feelings.[8]

> At the present stage of our natural history, the human brain seems to be constantly thinking, remembering, recording, or dreaming—most often, in the waking state, all of these together, or in kaleidoscopic successions. The result of this heightened and largely self-perpetuating activity is that we continuously feel our own inward action as a texture of subjectivity, . . . . That psychical continuum is our self-awareness. . . .[9]

*GO TO FRAME 1, PAGE 184.*

[5] Susanne Langer, *Philosophical Sketches* (New York: New American Library, 1964), p. 16.
  [6] *Ibid.,* p. 17.
  [7] *Ibid.,* p. 18.
  [8] *Ibid.,* p. 27.
  [9] *Ibid.*

162

All of these points of view illustrate the weaknesses of behavioral psychology when it deals with purely "felt," "inner," or "mental" phenomena. These subjective conditions form the real substance of the arts in general and music in particular. To carry this reasoning one step further: if mind and hence life is regarded as "feeling" rather than "knowing" then the field of aesthetics becomes central not only to an understanding of mind, but to all education and to the living of life. Mind thus finds its most complete expression in the "feelings" embodied and reified in art.

> The primary function of art is to objectify feeling so that we can contemplate and understand it. It is the formulation of so-called "inward experience," the "inner life," that is impossible to achieve by discursive thought, because its forms are incommensurable with the forms of language and all its derivatives (e.g., mathematics, symbolic logic). Art objectifies the sentience and desire, self-consciousnes and world-consciousness, emotions and moods, that are generally regarded as irrational because words cannot give us clear ideas of them. . . . I believe the life of feeling is not irrational; its logical forms are merely very different from the structures of discourse. But they are so much like the dynamic forms of art that art is their natural symbol.[10]

Thus, arts education can be seen as not merely a luxury to be offered to only the fortunate few, but as a necessity for effective living. The cultivation and refinement of feeling, and the view of reality as a "subjectification of nature" where our feelings project themselves on external reality and thus re-present the world to our minds in a highly personal manner[11] are crucial to effective living and the effective functioning of society.[12]

> . . . a wide neglect of artistic education is a neglect in the education of feeling. Most people are so imbued with the idea that feeling is a formless, total organic excitement in men as in animals that the idea of education feeling, developing its scope and quality, seems odd to them, if not absurd. *It is really, I think, at the very heart of personal education.*[13] [italics added]
>
> The arts objectify subjective reality, and subjectify outward experience of nature. Art education is the education of feeling, and a society that neglects it [or, it might be added, does it poorly] gives itself up to formless emotion. Bad art is corruption of feeling.[14]

[10] *Ibid.*, pp. 80–81.
[11] Like a lamp, our feelings cast their own "light" on external nature. The "light" that is reflected back to us is therefore a reflection of our own feelings, our own inner nature. In this sense, all reality is perceived in terms of our individual feeling-tone.
[12] Langer, *Philosophical Sketches*, p. 83.
[13] *Ibid.*
[14] *Ibid.*, pp. 83–84.

Thus, music educators and other teachers of the arts can stand back and proudly affirm their vitally important role in education. They must also stand back and reconsider their means of teaching. Though it is possible to "live"—to be alive—without experiencing art or cultivating the qualities of feeling, aesthetic educators must believe that those who do live life to its fullest. Those who are not permitted to cultivate the feeling response through art are prevented from living life to its fullest.

We must consider now the means of enabling aesthetic education to reach and directly influence almost everyone who comes in contact with art. We must not reach just the talented few, but must attempt to facilitate this cultivation of feeling for all our students. Given the present inability of music education to achieve such broad results, its processes need a dramatic overhaul.

## PURPOSES AND NATURE OF ARTS EDUCATION

Professor Langer suggests the course such aesthetic education should take:

> . . . to *discover* the phenomena revealed in music, painting or any other order of art, one has to know what *problems* the maker of the symbol encounters and how he meets them. Only then can one see new forms of vital experience emerge.[15] [italics added]

Notice the description of this process of arts education as one of discovery and problem solving. It is not the acquisition of facts or information, not the acquisition of rote skills, not the achievement of operant conditioning (that is, achievement of desired behavior by providing rewards outweighing the satisfaction of the successful completion of the task) that Langer recommends. It is, instead, the discovery of the facets of artistic symbol making by each learner for himself. Even more important, Langer indicates that such discovery should deal with the processes of artistic creation. This of course is what we have recommended in the form of activity approach, which seeks to involve students in the processes of creation or in activities that are meant to develop concepts of artistic creation. Through these activities, heightened sensitivity to artistic processes can be developed, and "feelings" about them can be cultivated.

Langer further describes and affirms what has been described at great length here as *conceptual learning*, the derivation of general thought tendencies from the cumulative effect of many particular experiences, and the continual refinement and development of such concepts as the student has new and more complex experiences. "Knowledge grows with *exploration*" she

[15] Langer, *Mind*, p. xix.

164

writes, "adding new facts, correcting old beliefs."[16] Her writings indicate that by facts she means not objective and scientific "truths" but anything that is believed or known to be so by the feeling individual. As the process of mental development continues, old "facts" (beliefs) are continually corrected and refined. "Knowledge becomes coherent only as more versatile and negotiable concepts replace the generalities with which all systematizing thought begins. . . ."[17]

By means of scientific knowledge, which characterizes the life of any culture, concepts are related into a series of demonstrable discoveries called natural law. In this sense, natural law involves "the most general facts we know about the universe."[18] This process of growth connects otherwise unrelated knowledge and becomes an integral factor in the knowledge we have about our world.[19]

It seems obvious, then, that "pure factual knowledge, however wide, would not constitute a mental life."[20] It excludes "feeling responses" or felt experiences, and is thereby not entirely suitable to an education designed to cultivate felt life. Rather, such an education should comprise the kinds of experiences that are "felt" in mental life. The function of aesthetic education, and hence of art, should be "an influence on individual lives."[21]

> This function is the converse and complement of the objectification of feeling, the driving force of creation in art: it is the education of vision that we receive in seeing, hearing, reading works of art—the development of the artist's eye, that assimilates ordinary sights (or sounds, motions, or events) to inward vision, and lends expressiveness and emotional import to the world. . . . The result is an impregnation of ordinary reality with the significance of created form. This is the subjectification of nature that makes reality itself a symbol of life and feeling.[22]

Arts education can therefore no longer luxuriate in the comfort of objective facts, information, and behavior of the pure kinds behaviorists crave. It must instead refine and extend the capacities for feeling "expressiveness," "inward vision," "emotional import," "subjectification of nature." Arts education should use the symbols of art to accomplish this, and should not convey mere facts and information *about* these symbols of art. Remember that these "symbols" are not the system of symbols by which music is notated, but the *expressive symbols* that constitute the felt experience of the entire artwork.

*GO TO FRAME 3, PAGE 184.*

16 Langer, *Philosophical Sketches*, p. 123.
17 Langer, *Mind*, p. xx.
18 Langer, *Philosophical Sketches*, p. 124.
19 *Ibid.*
20 *Ibid.*
21 Langer, *Philosophical Sketches*, p. 83.
22 *Ibid.*

## CRITICISM OF SOME PAST EDUCATIONAL PRACTICES

A tendency toward "objective" or "verbal learning" has been abundantly active in teaching music. The few purely factual things about music have been taught and retaught over the years: the decoding of the (encoding) system known as notation; composers' lives and the names and dates of their compositions; the names and schematic diagrams of typical musical forms; so-called objective guides for suitable, effective, or accepted interpretation of the musical score; and so on.

From the beginning, a second tendency has coexisted with the first: the desire to engage young people in musical performances of quality in order that they could personally experience the tensions, resolutions, and processes of the "felt life" embodied in the musical art. This practice was carried over to the general music classroom as singing and rhythm activities. In both instances, it was assumed that mere participation in the production of music or any involvement with the musical process *automatically and necessarily* developed an understanding and appreciation of the "feelings" involved in the musical art. What was meant by understanding or appreciation, and how if at all it was to be identified, seldom troubled the proponents of such theories. The tangible evidence of what students did musically outside of school, after graduation, or as adults was either blithely ignored or dismissed as beyond the teacher's control. Various by-products of this kind of thinking have continued to thwart any significant attempts to unburden music education of its dead weight:

1. Performance—especially quality performance—became an end in itself, an activity pursued for its own processes and not in order to develop feelings or the ability to respond as a listener in terms of feelings. Or, it was pursued in order to fulfill the personal needs, desires, and glorification of the director, rather than for any potential contribution to effective living *throughout life*.

2. Endless concoctions of singing games and other musical involvements, purportedly designed to foster the growth of concepts, were force-fed to youngsters, who willingly took part because it was "fun" yet profited little in terms of their feeling responses to music.

3. Music reading and singing became the major vehicles of teaching music by hiding behind the rationale that if all children could be made to perform music, they would thereby receive its mystical benefits.

4. Having created a special language and special skills, and having the means of learning exclusively in their possession, teachers created for themselves the role of guardians of music learning. This kind of "featherbedding," by which teachers created the need for their continued role in the traditional pursuits of music learning, is still a major force.

166

5. Aesthetics, emotions, and feelings were relegated to the psychic realm, just as most behaviorists have done, with the rationale that such factors were believed to be largely untouchable except as a matter of chance. It was complacently assumed that those who entered band, chorus, and orchestral programs were those who had been "reached" or who had some "innate ability" for the musical experience. The remaining masses (as much as seventy or seventy-five percent in many schools) remained ignorant and unenlightened, and thereafter untouched by the formal processes of music education or by significant musical experiences. This notwithstanding the fact that many of them were very competent and intelligent students with active interests in other art forms, who could develop an active interest in music as adults.

Because this mystical, undefinable quality of music makes its appeal to the seemingly unknown, unmanageable, and intangible "psychical" realm, teachers have been prone to conceive of musical learnings as having little or no control or criteria. A song featuring the interval of a perfect fifth would be introduced, and clearly listed at the top of the lesson plan would be the objective, "to teach the concept of a fifth." The song would be sung, perhaps many times. The interval might be identified, counted, sung in isolation, put back in context, and sung again. If the interval was mastered correctly in performance, if it entered the student's music-reading vocabulary, the teacher continued to think that the "concept" of a fifth had been learned once and for all, when in fact such was not the case.

Langer has already noted that a true mental life does not consist of this kind of atomistic, accumulative process: only the collection of tendencies known as "natural law" can be usefully knit together in this way. In terms of mental life, concepts are ever growing, ever refining themselves in light of changing circumstances and changing experiences. Seldom is anything learned once and for all because, as you have seen, it is not the nature of conceptual knowledge to arrive at a given mastery. It is ongoing, always spreading, always establishing new relevancies and connections with other parts of the framework of personal knowledge. And of what value, in any case, is the concept of perfect fifthness in developing or cultivating feelings and felt life?

These mistaken tendencies have stemmed from the confused method of using musical information to teach performance as an end in itself rather than using performance as *one* of the means of experiencing "felt life" in music, and of coming to an understanding of its life-giving processes. The confusion stems mainly from the same problems experienced by psychologists wishing to "objectify" their researches. Because the reality of mind and feeling seems so personal, subjective, undefinable, and undescribable in any terms (what Langer calls "non-discursive"), teachers and researchers turned to whatever objective and manageable ideas or dealings they could find. In the case of music, this involved teaching the most objective elements of music and judging each student by his ability to appropriately master each such element. This, of course, led to the acquisition of much useless information and the destruction of many attitudes. When youngsters did achieve some communion with music or the musical experience, it was often in spite of the efforts of music education and often a personal accident based on the conditions of their personal development.

Because of this emphasis on objectification, music teaching was increasingly viewed as a precise and organized system. Success in teaching—or in learning, depending on the attitude of the evaluator—was viewed in terms of student performance on tests. Curriculums were organized according to commercial concerns and were published with a built-in sequence of conceptual development determined to be appropriate for each grade level. Various new methods, ideas, and curriculums engulfed the profession, each claiming in its turn to be the panacea.

## CONDITIONS OF SYNTHESIS

It should be clear by now that in music education, as in all arts education, it is not possible to accept fully the claims of the behavioral purists and their emphasis on objective behavioral data (terminal behavior) as the sole or most accurate demonstration of learning. On the other hand, the understandable frustration of previous generations of music teachers with the "feeling" realm and the consequent inattention to its role in the musical sphere is equally unacceptable. As with so many other apparently antithetical propositions, the truth is usually somewhere in between, in the form of a synthesis.

You have already seen how a synthesis of opposites was achieved in the formulation of "permissipline." You should recall how inextricably entwined the three separate elements of autocratic, democratic, and permissive became—so much so, in fact, that they seemed to belong together from the first. The same holds true in resolving the apparent conflict of psychical behavior versus physical behavior.

The more covert psychical aspect of musical learning can no longer be left to chance. No longer can it be ignored. No longer can it be denied as a potential source of demonstrable evidence. It is the very essence of the feeling aspect of human behavior that forms the *raison d'etre*—the major objective—of music education and all arts education. To achieve the wedding of "inner" and "external" aspects of instruction,

> . . . we should use objectives for affective instruction to describe dispositions toward desired outcomes rather than to insist on specific behavioral performances. Instead of giving up the attempt at achieving some objectivity, we should tailor our demands in terms that are flexible enough to provide for the uniqueness of both the individual learner and the instructional context. . . . Purposes, aspirations, attitudes, interests, feelings, and beliefs should be seen as value indicators useful to instructional planning—not as terminal behaviors.[23]

[23] Larson, "Behaviors and Values: Creating a Synthesis," *Music Educators Journal*, 60, No. 2 (October 1973), 43.

Thus, instead of a closed system where overt behaviors are regarded as self-sufficient, we require an open system where highly specific ends are rejected in favor of more general goals. Open systems involve

> . . . problems oriented with ultimate goals established only in very general terms if at all. Operating in this way, teachers and students together confront a problem, and together seek solutions which neither knows precisely in advance. . . . Open systems direct the practitioner's attention to processes rather than ends. The goal is to confront students with problems that constantly keep them stretching and to join or assist them in the discovery of appropriate answers.[24]

In this spirit, the following requirements represent the manner in which music teachers can profit from the use of behavioral objectives in a music education program designed to direct due attention to the feeling aspects of music and designed, at the same time, to take advantage of those aspects of overt behavior that are useful in instructional planning.

1. Behavioral objectives are used in an *attempt to encourage an overt manifestation of a covert activity or behavior.*

In this way the teacher has *some*—not, to be sure, infallible—bases for evaluating the progress and needs of each individual. On these bases, curriculums can be planned that successfully provide learnings and opportunities for learnings based on the need to cultivate musical understandings in terms of feelings, felt life, and effective living.

By no means should such overt manifestations of behavior be used or regarded as absolute judgments, as though they were fully accurate indexes of the *quality* of covert mental processes. The teacher must accept from the beginning that each individual, because of the very process of learning, will learn musically and will manifest this learning in divergent ways. The goal here is merely to encourage where possible some overt manifestation of covert activity, and to use such indications in the selecting and ordering of experiences designed to enhance the cultivation of feeling in musical contacts.

2. Behavioral objectives are used as means *for eliciting demonstrable indications of conceptual learning.*

This does not imply that *all* such learning will be demonstrated, or that *only* that which can be demonstrated has been learned. It merely means that youngsters who have developed a concept of form, for example, no matter how incipient or general it is, are likely to be able to demonstrate this concept to some useful degree. Therefore, we can learn something about the nature of *their* concepts by some kind of overt demonstration in terms of behavior. This might entail creating sound compositions that exhibit some degree of cohesiveness; manipulating abstract ideas in discussion or activities—such as in finding variations on a shape or color in the room; or by conceiving of or manipulating visual demonstrations in terms of color, linear, or spatial relations.

[24] Combs, "Educational Accountability From a Humanistic Perspective," *Educational Researcher*, 2, No. 9 (September 1973), 20.

With such an approach the teacher is aware of the unique phase or stage of conceptual development that each student is experiencing; the uniqueness of the interest and needs of each student; and the need to plan in terms of each "ultimate unit." Thus, activities resulting in multiple outcomes are again recommended. By these means too, transfer and the frequency of certain responses can be observed, and future measures can be planned according to present outcomes.

3. Behavioral objectives are used as *clear indications to students of the goals* at hand, the *processes* and *criteria* to be used, and the means of *evaluating the eventual results*.

This is achieved not so much by reading or announcing a behavioral objective to a class—though this may often be done in certain instances—but by the clarity and direction that behavioral objectives encourage on the part of the teacher. Because behavioral objectives specify outcomes in terms of overt behavior or a resulting product (artifact, event, composition), they necessarily force the teacher to clarify in advance the means and process of attaining such ends, the relevance of such ends (otherwise, some goals will clearly appear to be useless in terms of expended energy and time, or in terms of effective living), and the relationship of these ends to individual readiness, needs, and interests.

Remember, too, that most students—be they youngsters or adult neophytes—respond well to practical or tangible indications of progress. When a goal is clear in advance, the attainment of that goal is obvious to all. When a goal is specified in terms of behavior or as a product resulting from behavior, then the existence of the behavior or product serves as evidence of attainment.

Notebooks—no matter how fat or how thorough—tests, homework assignments, and other graded products of behavior occur too infrequently and are too susceptible to imposed value judgments by teachers to be effective in the same way. Ideally, each individual assigns his own value to the fruits of his own learning; not, of course, in the form of a grade, but in terms of attitudes he develops, thoughts he thinks, or feelings he feels. Once again, how a person thinks or feels about what he learns is often more important than what he learns. Thus, the student's feelings about his learning are important in three ways: they affect his attitudes and thus his future performance; they can aid him in assessing his own progress in terms of his present aspirations; and they help him to set future goals and to organize his efforts to reach them.

4. Behavioral objectives are used to *develop situations where a feeling response is specifically elicited* and also to make such responses overt in some way.

For example, rather than structuring a listening lesson that is unspecific and purely covert ("Listen to this recording for the wonderful mood it creates.") and therefore unfocused and lacking significant consequences— What are "moods" in music? How is the child supposed to recognize one? How will you know what, if anything, he has heard, or what he has been listening to, or whether he sat still obediently and daydreamed during the recording?—the teacher can provide special instances where feelings and one's feelings about his feelings can be explored. For example, the child is asked to choose a color that he thinks ("feels") fits the feeling of the music; or to choose or create a graphic representation of the music; or to create or choose pictures or drawings that he feels exemplify the music; or to choose adjectives from a checklist commensurate with his vocabulary; or to make up a story that fits the feeling of the music; any number of other such activities can be devised. Each encourages the youngster to feel something and to respond overtly in some way. Often, it is best to follow such activities with discussions of the answers. Such discussion should not be an attempt to bring feelings to a discursive level (which is impossible). Rather, it should encourage the class to "think about their thoughts" or to "have feelings about their feelings," and should emphasize the tremendous variety of feeling responses that are possible and, indeed, likely in regard to a given composition. To conduct the same activity with the same composition on two widely separate occasions would introduce to their ongoing conceptual development the possibility of their having different "feelings" about the same composition on separate occasions.

These techniques allow students to respond to music for what it is or what it has meant to them, in overt terms not ordinarily available in a typical response to music. In this way their feelings, in general, are made more tangible, and thus more focused, and are thus more clearly perceived by the student *at that moment*.

5. Behavioral objectives are used to *encourage creative responses and discovery learning* by specifying and controlling the means, guiding principles, criteria, and general nature of the behavior or product. This is done without in any way dictating the specific results, but nonetheless provides some means for student, class, and teacher assessment.

Examples of objectives used in this way might include such tasks as discovering variations of a color or shape in the room; creating visual or sound forms in three parts, with the first and third the same, and the second different; or creating compositions or arrangements that interpret given titles, moods, or feelings, followed by a "defense" or discussion of the musical elements evoking that mood or feeling.

The need here is for the teacher to set the goal, or to give the class, group, or individual a choice of goals, and to provide enough guidelines or criteria to help direct the student's efforts. These criteria can be used to assess the resulting products or behaviors, not in terms of absolute judgment as such (though it is often difficult to avoid situations where the youngsters themselves make such judgments), but in terms of questions such as these: What musical element do you think worked well? Why do you think it worked? How do you think it worked? What do you think are some other creative possibilities? How do you think they might work, and why? If you had another chance, how would you do it—the same way or differently, and why?

Through these techniques, whether the class is a general music class or a performance class, the student is increasingly able to monitor his own performances and to make use of feedback because he soon learns the relevant questions to ask himself before he concludes the activity or project, and he can thereby act to remedy any self-discovered deficiencies. This is not a typical feature of the more traditional "homework" approach, where the student is usually not able to so assess his own work, but must wait until it is corrected (or "graded").

This use of behavioral objectives has the added advantages of reducing or controlling any variables that may be present, thereby allowing the student to efficiently focus his attention on the most important cues, processes, or materials.

6. Last, behavioral objectives are used to *encourage the teacher to consider goals in terms of practicality* and with due regard for the *readiness, interests, and needs* of the individuals in the class.

If certain goals seem laudatory yet defy any means of implementation in practical behavioral terms they may lack relevance in terms of the readiness, interests, and needs of the class. For example, a teacher may want the class to freely discuss the abstractions of "taste," "style," and "value," but such discussions must necessarily await an appropriate level of student sophistication: it would be impossible to implement this goal with, say, third-grade children. On the other hand, enhancing the acquisition or development of the *concept* involved in each abstraction is quite suitable for the readiness of third graders, and is limited only by the creativity of the teacher in devising appropriate strategies.

Moreover, certain goals may be inappropriate to the interests of a given group. "How can I involve the class in an analysis of sonata form?" is a question that will be answered only by considering the interests of the group; then, either discard the entire notion (because there is no possibility of class interest, and, therefore, little possibility of significant motivation), or lay a groundwork of several activities to prepare and motivate the class toward the desired goal. The latter process might entail working slowly—from involvement with the principle and processes of ternary part-forms, through experiences with the concepts of development, extension, and so on, and eventually culminating in mini-sonatas composed by the class. Conceivably, if time were available and interest were still sustained, the activity could include a complete application of its processes to a sonata from the repertory. All of this theorizing and planning will be considerably aided by the kinds of questions and considerations the teacher must undertake in conceiving behavioral objectives. The eventual goal may be reached by a long series of sequential behavioral objectives, each successfully completed before the next refinement is undertaken. As you should see, the very nature of behavioral objectives provides for considerable organization.

This is the last sense in which behavioral objectives are advantageous. They efficiently indicate the most important aspects of a learning situation. They eliminate the need for long, drawn-out "lesson plans." They successfully capsulize all the possible elements a teacher needs to consider in planning, and thereby tend to make planning more thorough because more time is available than was formerly spent in plotting lecture notes or in gathering information.

Applying behavioral objectives in these ways helps synthesize the strengths of covert and overt responses. Teachers involved in music education must concern themselves with cultivating, encouraging, and refining the feeling response. On the other hand, they must have some empirical evidence to indicate success or failure. Without such evidence neither they nor students and parents can estimate the true value of such an education. Planning subsequent lessons becomes largely hit-or-miss when the teacher cannot estimate the success of lessons oriented toward the feeling response.

The sole qualification is that behavioral evidence in the form of overt behavior must *not* be regarded as strict or absolute; it should instead be regarded as a general indication or tendency. Many occasions that encourage such behavior should be planned. This increasingly validates the teacher's interpretation of the overt behavior in question by subjecting it to repeated observation. So we are not concerned with total objectivity in the form of lower-level cognitions and skills.

> No amount of effort along these lines, . . . can possibly enable the social sciences to achieve the kind of objectivity that is mandatory in the physical sciences and any diversion of effort to this end from a search for patterns of analysis sufficiently subtle to embrace the complexity of human personality is regrettable. Social scientists are needed who have been trained to a capacity for subtle analysis of more subjective observation, and formulae must be found for reducing the intrusion of individual conditioning.[25]

We should not, however, ignore the need for some accountability in dealing with the higher-level learnings of the feeling domain:

> If we agree that some objectivity is better than none at all, we need to ask just how much is sufficient, and if a high level of objective reliability is always necessary or desirable. Certain things in our lives are useful precisely because they are somewhat vague, and it may be that we will have to re-admit some older notions of measurement to their proper places. For example, if you want to know what someone is thinking or feeling, just ask him.[26]

Since in music education we are inevitably involved with the covert feelings of our students, it is only natural that we should deal with these feelings by turning to the means that we use in our daily affairs with people. We do not subject feelings to totally objective, scientific scrutiny; we cannot. Situations in life are not as sterile and controlled as situations in the psychologist's laboratory. We cannot control our friends or our students as though we were training a dog or a pigeon.

[25] Lincoln Rothschild, "Scientific Expansion of Art Criticism," *The Pragmatist In Art,* 7, No. 3 (Fall, 1973), p. 2.
[26] Larson, "Behaviors and Values: Creating a Synthesis," p. 43.

Internal personal meanings can be defined and assessed by a simple process of "reading behavior backwards." If it is true that a person's behavior is a function of his internal beliefs, attitudes, values and the like, then it should be possible to infer these events from adequate samples of the individual's behavior. As a mater of fact, that is precisely what all of us do every day in trying to understand the behavior of people around us. We call it sensitivity or empathy, and inferences made in this fashion provide effective and useful bases for the control and directions of our own and others' behavior. Inferences made in this fashion are basic tools of the clinical psychologist, the teacher, social worker, and counselor.[27]

Thus, if behavioral objectives are used to deal with the feeling domain, as we recommend here, the overt results allow the teacher the opportunity to exercise human judgment. The process is one of inference, of "reading behavior backwards." Activities that result in overt behavior or in a product of some kind are seen as means to ends, not as self-sufficient ends in themselves. Such behavior is used merely as a tool for enhancing learning, for emphasizing the processes of learning, and serves both the teacher and student.

## OPERANT CONDITIONING AND BEHAVIOR

These six functions discussed above apply as well to performance situations, where the overt behavior (performance) is often confused as a self-sufficient end. It may very well be that for the professional musician. But in public school music programs we can no more be satisfied with such behavior as an end in itself than we can with the student who, unknown to the teacher, attains good grades by cheating.

When performance skills alone are the sole source of accountability for the teacher, there exists the very great risk of inducing mechanical, atomistic[28] *operant conditioning.* Operant conditioning is the practice of strengthening a desired behavior by providing the reinforcement of a reward only if and when the desired response occurs. It results in operant behavior, which is defined or directed by the nature of the extrinsic reward rather than by the stimulus object or occasion that prompted the behavior. Students who are in performance ensembles and who learn performance skills as a result of operant conditioning display mainly operant behavior. They are there and they learn only as a result of extrinsic rewards: to be with or near a boy friend or girl friend; because they like the uniforms; because they seek recognition from parents, friends, and adjudicators; because they seek the satisfaction of attaining a goal—any goal; because of competition and grading in contests; because they get to go on trips, or to play during the halftime show of a

[27] Combs, "Educational Accountability From a Humanistic Perspective," p. 21.
[28] An adjective describing any mental state or act regarded as being composed of simple and distinct components; such a state or act is viewed as resulting from a specific fusion or accumulation of these simple and distinct atom states.

nationally televised football game. When these extrinsic means of reinforcement are removed because of graduation, such young people are no longer inclined to perform music. Nor have they necessarily been prepared to consume music in their new role as adults. Thus, when the extrinsic reinforcement outweighs the intrinsic satisfaction derived from successful musical participation, operant conditioning has subverted the very premises and purposes at the heart of music education. Young people will not have learned to respond to music with increased insight; they will have learned to respond to external rewards.

Once the ensemble director is aware of this problem, the many situations in which operant behavior may develop can be eliminated or mitigated. A primary means for doing this is to employ behavioral objectives that emphasize or evoke certain positive cognitions and feeling responses as the covert conditions of successful and meaningful performance. Thus, increased understanding of music and increased feeling responses to music and performance go hand in hand or converge in the skilled performance. This is perhaps the perfect example of what is today called *confluent education,* the confluence (flowing together) of the cognitive, affective, and psychomotor domains. A student so educated will continue to embrace music even after the opportunities for performing it have long given way to a career and family.

Thus, whether considering general music instruction or skilled performance instruction—regardless of the level—the music teacher is strongly advised to regard overt behavior with caution. The teacher must judge whether or to what degree the overt behavior reflects the covert mental processes that are the goal of instruction.

In addition, and perhaps most important, the various kinds of covert "feeling" behaviors must be emphasized. The six conditions discussed above apply mainly to these kinds of behavioral responses. They assist the teacher to co-ordinate or concentrate on these kinds of responses because they are the most beneficial in cultivating and developing the mental processes that are most significant in musical situations. No claim is made, nor should any be understood by the reader, that such resulting overt behavior isolates, identifies, qualifies, or quantifies in absolute terms such mental states or all mental states. The only major requisite is that wish fulfillment should be replaced with behavioral evidences, according to the six conditions already presented. Teachers can no longer allow themselves the seemingly necessary or convenient practice of hoping, imagining, or guessing that the intuitive, perceptual, and conceptual operations of the mind—usually covert—are occurring as anticipated. They must rely more on the many devices of the behavioral approach recommended here for bringing covert "mental acts" to the stage of overt "physical acts." Only then can the teacher observe, differentiate, and select the next learnings or experiences necessary to the systematic development of student capacities. Only then can operant behavior be avoided or minimized. The teacher, in other words, must regard the teaching situation as involving not only student learning, but also teacher learning in the form of feedback. The teacher must encourage overt behavior and utilize the resulting feedback in order to systematically organize future experiences and instruction. In this way, the teacher can *learn* to be more effective.

*GO TO FRAME 5, PAGE 185.*

---

The history of music education in this country has proven well how operant conditioning and the resultant operant behavior can, in fact, elevate the performance quality of a group. Indeed, it can elevate the self-esteem of an entire profession. Such techniques have also resulted quite clearly in very little if any musical independence, and in very little carry-over to an out-of-school musical behavior used avocationally in "effective living." At best, it has isolated and developed the individuals who were probably already self-motivated for musical reasons and who, as a result, decided to pursue music as a vocation. Even here, though, success has not been unqualified: many such students drop out of music schools when they find that they do not really like to work hard studying music, or that they cannot do the work, or that they are not really as self-motivated as they used to be or thought they were. For this group, the fun of playing music has become grossly confused with the hard work of studying music professionally. This, too, can be fun, but it requires a certain dedication and self-motivation toward the inherent rewards of the craft of music. Because of poor instruction, many freshmen entering collegiate music programs will find that they do not have the requisite motivation.

It should also be mentioned that *true* musical behavior can result from certain kinds of reinforcement. Truly musical rewards can result in the establishing of a certain behavior. Though this acquired behavior is not necessarily to be faulted, it is subject to criticism if it is merely conditioned, and not independently understood by the performer. All musical performance skills should be conjoined with cognitions that allow the performer to apply techniques intelligently and independently. Far too often, expert student performers acquire a set of musical behaviors *for a given composition,* yet cannot transfer these behaviors to a similar but different musical problem.

The problem of behavior that appears desirable, but that may be occurring because of poor reasons (such as luck!) is solved by several means. First, continued application of behavioral principles will eventually show whether the behavior in question is consistent or haphazard. Second, proper attention to the cognitions involved in cognitive and psychomotor skills can demonstrate whether the observed behavior was supported by desirable understanding. Certain cognitions also stand behind many affective responses. And since the acquisition of most cognitions and skills is attended by some feeling component, even the affective sphere of behavior is susceptible to an inspection of student's rationale.

In all fairness, many teachers are innocent of the several charges of non-accountability or conditioning presented here. Whether by instinct, luck, or well-developed practical skills, some teachers quite readily learn to think in more accountable terms. But even this group—the recognized core of "successful" teachers who draw much personal satisfaction from their profession—can profit from the kind of discipline and orderliness resulting from the behavioral objective approach recommended here. Many of the difficulties of trial-and-error or "seat-of-the-pants" teaching can be overcome or eliminated in advance by the effectiveness and efficiency fostered by the use of behavioral objectives in the recommended manner.

There is no need to assume, either, that behavioral objectives must by their nature limit spontaneity or freedom. As with any form of teacher planning, the teacher should become neither plan-bound nor totally improvisatory. If a plan is failing, drop it, fix it, or change it in midstream. If a new direction arises in the completion of an activity, you may decide to follow it while the trail is hot, or you may make a mental note to pursue it at a more convenient time in the near future.

The only limitations that behavioral objectives place on a teacher are those that entail due consideration of almost all the learning theory, philosophy, aesthetics, and musical processes mentioned throughout earlier pages. How you go about making such considerations, ordering the results, and then implementing them will be our last major area of consideration and will be undertaken in the next two chapters. Suffice it to say here that if any teachers or prospective teachers consider this responsibility too much work or too difficult, they should reassess their dedication to a profession that involves the lives and minds of countless generations of young people, as well as the future of the musical art. This is nothing to toy with. The major professions that deal with people—medicine, dentistry, law, education—all have an ultimate obligation to reach the highest possible professional standards. In each profession, a considerable amount of training and a continual updating of that training in light of new discoveries is required of each person.

Each major profession has a written or understood code of ethics; each is built upon a guiding philosophical committment. Yet within each, the individual practitioner is free to adopt a unique point of view. In the profession of music education, the guiding philosophical commitment is to nurture the musical feeling response. Your unique point of view involves not only your personality and training but your own notions of how you can best achieve the goals of the profession.

## SUMMARY

As Langer has indicated, the philosophical and psychological guide that any teacher of the arts must comprehend and follow faithfully is that art formulates "feeling"—with all that that implies—for our contemplation and understanding. Art embodies or objectifies feeling by presenting the morphology—

the form and structure—of it without having to imitate it with a representational model. Musicians have always been at least intuitively aware of this, for music can only suggest various "things" in the actual world and then only vaguely. What it can do, though, is capture in perceptible forms "how feelings feel." The phrase "music sounds as feelings feel" in an accurate description of this.

In this embodiment or objectification of feeling it is necessary to remember that feeling includes everything that can be felt. Thus, all mental operations that the individual can apprehend—thought, emotion, affection, and the like—fall within the domain of art. Furthermore, the artist creates not an imitation or model of these feelings but an image of their *quality*, their intensity, their dynamic state, their vitality. How each individual relates to each artistic image, in terms of artistic import and the feeling response, is known and determined only by that person. Of this Langer says:

> This image, however, serves two purposes in human culture, one individual, one social: it articulates our own life of feeling so that we become conscious of its elements and its intricate and subtle fabric, and it reveals the fact that the basic forms of feeling are common to most people at least within a culture, and often far beyond it, since a great many works do seem expressive and important to almost everyone who judges them by artistic standards. Art is the surest affidavit that feeling, despite its absolute privacy, repeats itself in each individual life.[29]

The implications for education should be clear. It is the "feeling" embodied in art that we must help each individual realize, and on his own absolutely personal terms. At the same time, each person must realize the subjective universality of feeling because a culture, a society, has many feeling possibilities as common property, though never to the same degree or of exactly the same nature. Thus, "the direct perception of artistic import . . . is not systematic and cannot be manipulated according to any rule. It is intuitive, immediate, and its deliverances are ineffable."[30]

You may wonder how we can organize a music education designed to enhance the perception of felt life if artistic import is intuitive, nondiscursive, and not systematic. Fortunately, Langer also provides an answer to this most difficult question, an answer that seems most congenial and satisfactory when completely understood. "Artistic expression," she writes, "is essentially nondiscursive";

> but to yield negotiable facts its homogeneously present import has to be somehow analyzed and demonstrated. Experience has long convinced all scientifically inclined persons that no matter how exact and sure their artistic insights may be *there is no direct way of demonstrating them to other people* [italics added], no basis for arguing their validity. So we require an indirect approach, some parallel phenomenon which can be manipulated.

29 Langer, *Mind*, p. 64.
30 *Ibid.*, p. 65.

The art symbol itself furnishes this parallel, for the symbol is a work, and its elements are analyzable.[31]

Here, then, is the answer; the approach recommended is to use music (the form of art being considered here) as such, and not to accumulate facts and information *about* music in general, or to impose value and so-called correct responses on a class. A continuous sequence of experiences with the musical product as "art symbol" is the recommended path. There is further qualification, however:

> It is with created elements, then, that we are dealing when we consider the components of the art symbol, which is always the entire work; and one way to understand what passages or aspects of feelings (always understood in the broad sense of anything that can be felt) are expressed in it is to analyze just what the artist has done and for what purpose . . . it guarantees the close association of the import, which we know directly, with technical processes that do invite analytic study and objective demonstration of facts, . . . but once the more detailed expressions of psychical activity are tracked down, there is less and less disagreement about their purposes.[32]

Again, it should be emphasized that all such musical learnings must occur from contact with musical compositions and from other musical experiences, and not from the academic or disciplinary learning (often undertaken as memorization) of facts and information about music. The responsibility of the teacher is, then, to provide the occasions and opportunities for such musical contact with musical stimuli. This way, students can develop the increased ability to perceive, cognize, and judge the elements that enter into the creation of musical symbols. Above all, this process enhances the possibilities of musical learning occurring within a context of "feeling responses."

The musical work—be it a famous one from the traditional repertory heard in a listening lesson, an appropriate song sung by the class, or individual student compositions ("musical" in the traditional sense, or "sound" in the more contemporary sense)—is the *object*, the basis for research that aims to *discover* the factors involved in the "feeling" manifested by the work.

> Such knowledge cannot be gathered without some systematic device whereby observations can be made, combined, recorded and judged, elements distinguished and imaginatively permuted, and, most important, data exhibited and shared, impressions corroborated. The symbol of feeling permits such manipulation, although feeling itself does not.[33]

Thus, as Langer indicates, it is possible to talk discursively about the work of art as empirical object, but it is neither possible nor desirable to systematically manipulate feeling per se.

Likewise, in performance situations the purpose is to discover, dif-

---

[31] Langer, *Mind*, pp. 65–66.
[32] *Ibid.*, p. 66.
[33] Langer, *Mind*, p. 68.

ferentiate, and judge expressive elements in the music being performed. An additional requisite here is to learn through concrete experience the best means for conveying these elements in performance. Thus, technique is always seen as a means to *expressive ends,* not as an end in itself. "Digital dexterity" or "facile fingers" should coincide with, not outrun, expression and expressive awareness. These remarks, of course, are predicated on the need for inherently expressive music rather than banal study material, atomistic exercises, or an entire page of playing whole note G's.

Finally, the entire question of the feeling response and the means for attaining it with much greater regularity in music education is conditioned by the six guidelines for using behavioral processes. Though feelings may never be as susceptible to overt observation as lower-level learnings, they are not immune to such observation. We "read" people's feelings daily through what they say, how they look, what they choose to do. Similarly, we can begin now to be somewhat more objective and controlled in our cultivation of the feeling response in music education by observing the same kinds of overt signs. All we really need to do is devise means for externalizing what otherwise would be feeling responses that never reached an overt phase. Once the nature and extent of this problem is realized, the only other caution is to regard such overt manifestation in nonabsolute terms. Regard them just as you would your inferences in daily life. In teaching, however, you must practice sharpening your acuity, and subject it to repeated observations of similar responses. The more observations that confirm your assessment, the more valid it is likely to be.


## ONE ADDITIONAL CONSIDERATION: AN EDITORIAL


One further caution can be advanced. You must always appreciate the fact that young people have a unique felt life of their own. Sometimes this may, through circumstances unique to the individual, encompass interests and "feelings" comparable to those embodied in the standard repertory. A more likely probability, if we are to use their avowed musical preferences as indices, is that the "youth music" of any generation or year most completely fulfills the desires they have to understand and contemplate their "feelings." It is also understandable why such music may not adhere to the forms, structures, and various means of embodiment of other styles of music. It is because youthful feeling is organized characteristically along different lines. It is dynamic, ever changing, intense, yet repetitiously the same in its predictable unpredictability. All feelings have these same qualities, of course, but not to the same degree as those experienced by adolescents.

Thus, in cultivating students' perception, cognition, and contemplation of their feeling responses to the art symbols of music, you must at all times consider the feelings typical of the age-group with which you are working. Above all, you must not belittle or denigrate their feelings; instead, use them in whatever way helps the individual to increasingly refine his understanding of "feeling" as it appears both in the art symbol and in life. This is why so much emphasis has been placed on teaching for effective living. Since the major concern of young people centers in the life of feeling—all the tensions and emotions they feel, all the thoughts they have, all their hopes and aspirations —any teacher who centers all musical instruction in the apprehension of "feeling" and the means by which feeling is presented in the art symbol will enjoy a captive audience, as long as growth-typical feeling is a duly considered end. Not to do so is perhaps the greatest failing of teachers in general, and music teachers in particular: the sin is greater among us, for our entire reason for existence is to consider, develop, and refine our students' capacity for the feeling response.

In the long run, the study of mind and the concerns and operations of mind as formulated and presented in the art symbol may lead us to an understanding of several distinct types (not necessarily levels) of artistic experience. For example, in the art of music it would appear that true folk music has always formulated the feelings of the ordinary man in any society, especially agrarian societies. Even the phenomenon of present-day urban folk music—reflecting issues of war, love, peace—indicates the presence of such "feelings" in the collective mind of our more urban society.

The same would necessarily hold true for "youth music" of any age, including our own rock music and, even more recently, the music of the "Jesus movement." The great appeal this music has for young people, both here and on opposite sides of the Atlantic and Pacific, would seem to indicate its efficacy in formulating and presenting to their intuitions the felt life and feelings of adolescence. The same thought seems suitable when considering the great hold country-and-western music has on a large segment of our society: it reflects some of the everyday feelings common to this group. That these feelings seem mundane is no reason for disqualifying the music; even the highest art form deals with feelings apprehended daily. Last, the evident appeal of soul music and its firm basis in gospel song, spirituals, jubilee music, and West African musical practice bespeaks the artistic import of this music to black Americans. It is truly interesting to speculate upon how and why this music, and rhythm and blues in general, has been appropriated by various styles of rock music and by youth of all racial and ethnic groups. Somehow, it must embody the feel of life that young people intuitively recognize and respond to. It may be that this music expresses the uninhibited, free, and spontaneous nature of adolescent inner life in a manner unrelated to societal norms and strictures, to geographic, national, or racial delimitations.

It is important to recognize the existence of distinct styles of artistic symbols as distinct styles and not as different levels of excellence. "Levels" implies a hierarchy of value or achievement. Those who are well-trained in the musical art too often adopt a quasi-aristocratic and superior demeanor about the level or degree of their "taste," and assume, as a result, that all other forms of music are "below" this level, and hence not really music, or art. Jazz improvisation is often so regarded. However, all of the styles of music enumerated above are distinct styles, each of which has some degree of validity for various people, or at various times.

The role of music education is not, therefore, to develop in every human being the ability to respond to music with so-called "advanced degrees of feeling" inherent to the cumulative development of the standard repertory in Western civilization, but instead to enable every individual to cultivate and refine whatever capacity for "feeling" as nature and nurture permit at a given time of life. It is not a valid purpose of music education to develop a single standard of taste, or to propagate a single type of music. Rather, the job at hand is to take the expression "Let each become all he is capable of being" and modify it to read "Let each *feel* all he is capable of *feeling*."

To necessarily limit such an education to any one type of music would be a contradiction of purposes: different and distinct kinds of feeling are embodied in different and distinct kinds of music. Many people are capable of relating to several styles. And this could be the final goal: to permit each individual to choose among musical types or styles as the occasion demands, or as he will. In this sense, the "aristocratic" musician who regards music as stopping with the last quartets of Beethoven is as much to be pitied as those who would devote all their musical pursuits to one style and close their minds to all others.

Frequently, a closed mind is unfortunately based in past experiences. The large number of young people who are "turned off" by so-called serious music are also "turned off" by many of the values of the "establishment." Anything smacking of the imposition of aristocratic values results in "turning them off" not only because of the lack of relevancy to their own inner life but also because it is in the nature of adolescence—and the current generation in particular—to attach emotional connotations to the value systems of their elders.

Marshall McLuhan has provided valuable insights into the source of this problem.[34] He distinguishes between what he calls "hot" and "cool" media. Music and teaching are both media, since both are "extensions of man." Music teachers, therefore, have twice as much at stake. A "hot" medium is charged with information. It requires very little activity by the consumer. A "cool" medium contains little information and thus requires the consumer to participate by drawing relationships, by "filling in the gaps," so to speak.

McLuhan feels that certain media are *invariably* "hot" or *invariably* "cool"; but if instead these two qualities are *variable*, some interesting possibilities arise. For example, it would seem that any given musical work could be either "hot" or "cool," depending on the consumer. This may be what bothers "aristocratic" musicians, who regard music as "cool" (that is, intellectual), and who therefore disparage those who regard some or all of it as "hot" (more immediately expressive). On the other hand, adolescents and many adults—particularly those who are musically untrained—find much of the

[34] *Understanding Media* (New York: New American Library, 1964).

standard repertory too "cool." Such music requires too much mental effort, which they are unwilling or unable to expend. Oddly, many well-trained musicians react this way when they encounter *avant-garde* music that is outside their previous experience and thus frustrates their attempts to understand it intellectually. But they also seem incapable of responding to it in a "hotter," more immediate sense.

It seems as though our continuing contact with certain kinds or styles of music can make them even "hotter." As we familiarize ourselves with a given style or idiom, many of the "cool" features that first demanded our conscious attention seem to have a more immediate, a "hotter" impact. Certainly, this has been true with compositions such as Stravinsky's *Le Sacre du Printemps*. Originally, it was received with a clamorous outburst of indignation. Today it almost seems "hot" (immediately expressive) to even the trained listener.

Thus, the teacher of music should not be surprised if student reaction to music listened to or played in class is less than immediate or spontaneously enthusiastic. For the uninitiated, the "art music" repertory, this medium, is very "cool." It not only lacks immediate appeal, it requires an effort of perception and thought. Perception and thought presume some kind of learning. This is what they do not have, and what you are to provide. That is music education; not the inculcation of values and taste.

Just as music may be "hot" or "cool," depending on variable factors, so may teachers—the medium of man educating man—be understood in similar terms. "Hot" teachers provide information to essentially passive students. "Cool" teachers facilitate or guide students in the active pursuit and discovery of meanings. They encourage as much participation by the students as is possible within the formal structures of public education. The music teacher who recognizes the importance of felt life in the musical values of young people, who takes care to avoid authoritative pronouncements on musical values, and who carefully and systematically approaches many styles of music—such a teacher enhances the possibility that each student, now and later as a functioning adult, will be able to choose the musical involvements that most truly reflect his idea (feeling) of effective living. The trick is in simply using their present ideas about musical expression as bases for more comprehensive and wide-ranging involvements.

This goal can be best accomplished if music teachers can realize in this proposal a new role. The music teacher must stop being a "hot" medium, dispensing all the information and encouraging students to believe that they have no responsibilities at all for their own learning other than sitting still and paying attention. Instead, the music teacher must become a facilitator of learning, a "cool" medium, whose role is to actively engage young people in the processes and content of learning. This would prove exciting for all involved.

From the following descriptions choose the one(s) that best complete the statement.

According to the preceding explanations, the tradition of strict behaviorism holds that:

A. Behavior always arises from the impingement of the environment on our mental faculties, and, thus, results in some overt manifestation of both the mental faculty and the environment. Go to Frame 7.

B. Mental behaviors, if observable at all, can be acknowledged only by observing and measuring physical phenomena. Go to Frame 14.

C. Two levels of experience exist—psychical and physical. They are related or interdependent in that each experience in one realm has a correlate in the other. Go to Frame 20.

D. Mental operations (actions) are self-induced and often result in no observable or measurable overt physical behavior. Go to Frame 27.

Of the choices below, choose the one(s) that best complete the following statement:

Susanne Langer, in arguing against the prevalent theories of the behaviorists, maintains that:

A. Feeling, as the prime function of mind, is a strictly intraorganic and vital phase of human existence, is largely self-perpetuating, and can be self-induced. Go to Frame 8.

B. Only those manifestations of feeling that are susceptible to scientific verification can be regarded as true evidence of a mental life. Go to Frame 15.

C. The mind, and the feelings it deals with, is continually in the process of thinking, remembering, recording, and dreaming, which results in the apprehension by the subject of the subjective state called self-awareness. Go to Frame 21.

D. Behavior can be measured, observed, qualified, and quantified by means other and better than those currently employed by the behaviorists. Go to Frame 28.

Which of the following statements can be properly attributed to Langer's definition of the function of art.

A. An outlet for pent-up desires, emotions, and moods, which, in the hands of the artist, takes the symbolic forms of inner experience and inner life without their accompanying problems. Go to Frame 10.

B. A means by which the artist embodies the irrational and illogical aspects of human consciousness or self-awareness in logical and rational symbolic forms. Go to Frame 17.

C. To objectify feeling so that we can contemplate and understand it, and to formulate those inner experiences of life that elude expression by discursive language, our usual means of understanding and communication. Go to Frame 23.

D. To capture the complex logic of human feelings as dynamic forms; to embody the structure of those feelings in a way that the logical structures of discourse cannot. Go to Frame 30.

---

Frame 4

Which of the following statements was *not* mentioned by Professor Langer as a reason for arts education?

A. To see new forms of vital experience emerge through discovering and understanding the problems the artist overcomes and how he overcomes them in creating the art symbol. Go to Frame 11.

B. To provide a vehicle or avenue for personal expression and creativity, and by these means to introduce order and control over the inner life. Go to Frame 18.

C. To educate individuals in feeling through art the objectification of subjective reality and the subjectification of the outward experiencing of nature. Go to Frame 24.

D. To prevent the corruption of feeling and the formless emotion represented in bad art. Go to Frame 31.

E. To appreciate art in terms of its programmatic suggestion of specific objects, stories, and ideas. Go to Frame 33.

---

From page 176                                      Frame 5

Assuming that the purely objective, scientific data sought by the behaviorists is not suitable (especially when considering arts education), but assuming nonetheless the need for some way of dealing with and giving direction or focus to the inner or feeling responses of young people in music education, which of the following choices *do not* represent one of the six applications of behavioral thought recommended earlier as a synthesis of the best facets of both the internal and the external aspects of the musical response?

Go through the list in order. Confirm your choices by turning to the directed frame for each item you choose as *not* representing one of the six recommendations.

1. To use behavioral objectives as means for eliciting observable signs of conceptual learning. Go to Frame 9.
2. To use behavioral objectives as bases for value judgments concerning the "inner life" of individuals. Go to Frame 16.
3. To use behavioral objectives to encourage an overt manifestation of a covert activity or behavior, and to use such overt behavior as means of evaluating progress and as a basis for planning. Go to Frame 22.
4. To use behavioral objectives as clear indications to students of the goals at hand, the processes and criteria to be used, and the means of evaluating the eventual behavior (or resulting product). Go to Frame 29.
5. To use behavioral objectives to develop situations where a "feeling response" is specifically encouraged and to make such responses overt in some way. Go to Frame 34.
6. To use behavioral objectives to elicit demonstrable evidence of the totality of learning achieved by each student. Go to Frame 12.
7. To use behavioral objectives to encourage the teacher to consider goals in terms of practicality and with due regard for the readiness, interests, and needs of the individuals in the class. Go to Frame 32.
8. To use behavioral objectives to encourage creative activities and discovery learning by specifying and controlling the means, guidelines, criteria, and nature of the terminal behavior or product without in any way dictating the specific results, yet providing means for assessment by student, class, and teacher. Go to Frame 25.
9. To use behavioral objectives to enable the teacher to impose order and control over the activities and behaviors of the class, and by so doing, to guide each student to most effectively develop appropriate "feelings." Go to Frame 19.

---

*From Frame 19*                                                                 Frame 6

The deficiencies of pure behaviorism in dealing with the so-called inner life have received much attention, as have the situations and conditions in music education where the use of overt behavior is recommended as a constructive means rather than a self-sufficient end. Yet in the realm of performance skills, the music teacher must be aware that the use of overt behavior (performing) as the only evidence of learning is fraught with difficulty and potential harm to the espoused aims of the music education profession.

To see whether you understand the bases for exercising these precautions, explain briefly in the space provided what each of the following is and why each should probably be avoided in a music education program designed to nurture the feeling response. As you complete each one, turn to the directed frame and compare your answer to the discussion there.

*Atomism:*

Go to Frame 13.

*Operant conditioning:*

Go to Frame 26.

*Operant behavior:*

Go to Frame 35.

---

*From Frame 1*                                                                 Frame 7

Your answer was A:

Behavior always arises from the impingment of the environment on our mental faculties, and, thus, results in some overt manifestation of both the mental faculty and the environment.

You must be somewhat confused as to the behaviorist position, for this statement is basically a confused and even contradictory one. It seems to postulate that the environment acts on the human body via some physical realm of experience, which is then converted into the "mystical" quality of mental or "psychical" process. It also directly implies that such mental operations will always result in some overt manifestation of the mental state, and that this manifestation will also somehow reflect something about the nature of the stimulus in the environment.

Although there may be an air of "mysticism" in the reasoning of certain behaviorists, they do not uphold this view. In fact, much of this statement is in direct contrast with the position defended by many behavioral thinkers.

Go back to Frame 1 and try another choice.

---

*From Frame 2*                                                      Frame 8

You said that Langer maintains that feeling, as the prime function of mind, is a strictly intra-organic and vital phase of human existence, is largely self-perpetuating, and can be self-induced.

You are correct. The essential thrust of this affirmation is that there are not two separate realms of existence or experience—one biological, physiological, or organic (physical), and the other metaphysical, mysterious, or unknown (psychical). Mind itself is biological and organic and has evolved in the form of "felt experience"

> elaborated in the course of high organic development, intellectualized as brain functions are corticalized, and socialized with the evolution of speech and the growth of its communicative functions.*

Furthermore, mind is capable of perpetuating itself and inducing itself to act without the need for external stimuli and without resulting in necessarily overt behavior. In other words, it can and often is self-sufficient.

This question also had two correct answers; if you have not already identified both, go back to Frame 2 and choose again. If you have, go to page 163, below the line.

* Langer, *Philosophical Sketches*, p. 18.

---

*From Frame 5*                                                      Frame 9

1. Your answer is incorrect. The use of behavioral objectives as means for eliciting demonstrable conceptual learning *was* one of the recommended compromises. Before proceeding, reread the appropriate discussion on pages 169–170.

Remember, the implication in using such objectives is not to regard the presence or absence of such observable *proof* of the presence or absence of learning. What is suggested is that the teacher who attempts to elicit overt behaviors that indicate conceptual learning will, through the sheer frequency of such attempts, help provide the greatest assurance that such overt evidences are accurate. Also, the overt evidence of conceptual development or understanding should be a constant reminder of the uniqueness of each student's conceptual framework, of the need for activities that give each framework full scope to operate, and of the need to provide it with frequent opportunities for transfer.

Go back to Frame 5, and consider the next choice.

---

*From Frame 3*                                                                        Frame 10

You answered that Langer defined the function of art as an outlet for pent-up desires, emotions, and moods, which, in the hands of the artist, takes the symbolic forms of inner experience and inner life without their accompanying problems.

This is not quite correct. First of all, Langer denies that art functions as a purgative or catharsis of pent-up emotional states struggling for release. This is the "bohemian" or "beat" image of the artist's role, which has survived from the Romantic era. Art does not need or deserve this rationale. Its role and function is much more positive. Instead of functioning as medicine or therapy, art allows us to experience more keenly the dynamic forms of our felt life. It does this by objectifying—that is, making an object (visual arts) or latent event (music, dance)—of the subjective "felt life." This object or latent event is then offered to us for our contemplation.

Thus, you are correct that the artist is engaged in symbolic activity: the created object or latent event is the art symbol. But the rationale of expurging emotions in order to avoid the problems of emotions is incorrect. The old adage, thankfully used infrequently today, "give a boy a horn to blow and he won't blow a safe" is based upon this common misconception of the social or psychological benefits of artistic experience. Though art does have many social and psychological relevancies and by-products, it does not deserve justification in those terms any more than the by-product of teaching, money, justifies it as a profession.

Go back to Frame 3 and choose another answer.

---

*From Frame 4*                                                                        Frame 11

You said that Langer did *not* recommend art education in order that students, and hence society, can be led to see new forms of vital experience emerge through discovering and understanding the problems the artist overcomes and how he overcomes them in creating the art symbol.

Your choice is inappropriate since this *is* one of the specific recommendations made by Langer in her explanation of the function, role, and importance of art and arts education. (See page 164). You are reminded too that the process was specified as one of *discovery*. No mention is made of the acquisition of rote skills, information, or "knowledge" for its own sake. The implication was clearly one of personal discovery by each individual of the problems and processes of artistic symbol making. This is but another way of saying that concepts, and in this case artistic concepts, are developed only through personal experience. Through such personal interaction with music and musical processes, each individual can become increasingly sensitive to the form of human experience or feeling that the work of art embodies. This, not the accumulation of facts or skills related to the discipline of music, is what music education is all about.

Go back to Frame 4 and make another choice.

---

From Frame 5                                                    Frame 12

6. Your answer is correct. The use of behavioral objectives to elicit demonstrable evidence of the totality of learning achieved by each student was not recommended because it is neither possible nor desirable.

Much learning is autogenetic; much mental activity and "feeling" never reaches the level of consciousness, let alone overt physical response. Therefore, there is no possibility of using behavior as the sole or even prime indicator of the totality of learning. In any event, as we have reiterated several times, how a person thinks about what he learns is often more important than what he learns. In this sense, regarding learning in terms of quantity is futile and self-defeating.

Go back to Frame 5 and consider choice 7.

---

From Frame 6                                                    Frame 13

Atomism is a theory that holds that mental operations and acts are a fusion of previously simple and distinct components. In practice, this amounts to assuming that a fact or skill is learned, is then added to another fact or skill, and so on in a purely linear progression. In atomistic terms, a simple and almost mechanical cause-and-effect relationship is assumed to exist between the stimulus and the responses. There are assumed to be no intervening thought processes.

According to the theory of mind we have discussed so far, it should be apparent that the capacities, functions, and operations of the mind are considerably more complicated than that. It is very likely that many more factors are involved.

Therefore, this approach should be avoided because musical behaviors involve much more than the simple addition of separate accomplishments. This is the "madness" behind some of the "methods" books used in instrumental instruction: they progress one lesson at a time in a specific order and assume that once a given lesson has been mastered, the student possesses the knowledge or skill for all time.

Music educators are concerned not only with the response, but also with the mediating covert mental processes that involve cognitions and feelings. This concern helps avoid those situations—and they are far from infrequent—where the response *seems* incorrect, but has resulted from desirable mental processes. For example, a third grade girl who had chosen yellow as the color she felt expressed her feelings about a funeral march just heard explained that it reminded her of her recently deceased canary. Her answer seemed inappropriate only until her thoughts and feelings were externalized.

Avoiding atomism amounts to avoiding the mistaken notion that something is learned once and for all and is then added to other learning. Learning grows not by addition, but by the expansion of the generalizations and tendencies known as concepts. Thus, you never learn once and for all time *the* concept of rhythm. You are always refining your concept of rhythm.

Go back to Frame 6 and attempt the next definition.

---

*From Frame 1*                                                 Frame 14

Your answer was B:

Mental behaviors, if observable at all, can be acknowledged only by observing and measuring physical phenomena. Your choice for this answer is correct.

But it is this idea that most bothered Professor Langer, who held that two separate realms of experiences, psychical and physical, do not exist as such at all. Though it may sometimes be convenient to refer to them as separate aspects of the human existence, they are better thought of as different sides of the same coin.

Langer therefore advances a biological theory of mind, which views mental phenomena as the natural result of intraorganic evolution, processes, and development. She was especially bothered by the lack in behavior theory of the so-called "subjective" phases of human functioning: what she calls "feelings." It is feeling to which she attributes the prime character of mind, not knowledge of so-called "objective" or scientific facts. Accordingly, the mind *feels*, rather than *knows*.

If you haven't selected a second correct choice, go back to Frame 1 and choose again. If you have identified both correct answers, go ahead to Frame 2, page 184.

---

*From Frame 2*                                                 Frame 15

You said that Langer maintains that only those manifestations of feeling that are susceptible to scientific verification can be regarded as true evidence of mental life.

This could not be more removed from the truth. Somewhere, your attention has slipped. Earlier, Mrs. Langer was quoted as saying:

> The chief motive of this formulation is to establish psychology as a natural science distinct from physiology, . . . yet to give it the virtues of experimental research and so-called "objective" truth. But behavior has every appearance of being the macroscopic result of microscopic processes in the behaving organism; and no scientific research can restrict itself to any set of phenomena having causal connections with some other set, yet leave that other set alone.\*

Instead of the objective and impersonal sterility of the psychologist's laboratory, she affirms that life is a complex of felt experiences—felt intraorganically only by the feeling individual—and as such are not susceptible to the abstractions of science. Science uses abstractions to arrive at conclusions; it does not, and should not, take the tangible or intangible stuff of life, and force-fit it into an abstract methodology.

Go back to Frame 2 and try another choice.

\* Langer, *Mind*, p. 16.

---

*From Frame 5*

2. Your answer is correct. The use of behavioral objectives as bases for value judgments concerning the inner life and feeling responses of individuals was decidedly not recommended as a successful synthesis or compromise.

In fact, to so regard the use of behavior is to fall into the web of problems experienced by the behaviorists who must deny the existence of an inner life, or who acknowledge and measure inner life only in terms of behavioral evidences. Furthermore, even if one could accurately measure the many aspects of inner life, the problem of value and of the imposition of value judgments on the inner life would remain. It is not defensible under any conditions to attach value judgments in this way, given the manner and nature of the development of the mental faculties. Mental operations are unique to each individual since he and only he can feel them. Thus, he and only he can attach a value or level of significance to them. The only place where this might not be true is where individual value systems and feelings about such value systems collide with the collective or traditional value systems of a society. Laws are made to handle these situations, but the laws frequently change (though slowly, and perhaps deservedly so) in order to reflect changing values.

No such composite, recognized, or "law"-characterized value system exists for the arts. Thus, it is not within the domain of the teacher to attach value judgments to aspects of inner life. Value judgments may be made on the more empirical, exterior aspects of an art, such as whether or not the correct pitches were played, because such aspects are subsumed under a more or less objectively based system of tradition. It is this specific fact that leads teachers to regard the teaching of notation and other empirically objective facts about music as true music education. They feel they cannot foster the development of tastes and values without unduly dictating them; this is not true, and the use of behavioral objectives that encourage subjective expression can well provide for the development of a value system.

Go back to Frame 5, and find another choice that does *not* represent one of the six recommended applications of behavioral practice.

---

*From Frame 3*                                                                    Frame 17

You said that Langer defined the function of art as being a means by which the artist embodies the irrational and illogical aspects of human consciousness or self-awareness in logical and rational symbolic forms.

This is not really correct. Though art does embody aspects of human consciousness and self-awareness, Langer does not regard these as irrational and illogical. Nor does she feel that the forms of art are thereby purely rational and logical formulations, in comparison. She says quite clearly:

> Art objectifies the sentience and desire, self-consciousness and world-consciousness, emotions and moods, *that are generally regarded as irrational because words cannot give us clear ideas of them* [italics added]. . . . I believe the life of feeling is not irrational; its logical forms are merely very different from the structures of discourse. But they are so much like the dynamic forms of art that art is their natural symbol.[*]

Thus, the making of art does not involve giving logic or rationale to unstructured, illogical, and irrational content. It consists of giving the different logical order of feelings an objectification (making from or of it an object or latent event), which she calls "symbolic form."

Go back to Frame 3 and choose another answer.

[*] *Philosophical Sketches*, p. 81.

---

*From Frame 4*                                                                    Frame 18

You said that Langer did *not* recommend art education in order to provide a vehicle or avenue for personal expression and creativity, and by these means to introduce order and control over the inner life.

This is true, for Langer actively dispelled false notions such as these. Though certain individuals may use art or develop certain expertise in the practice of an art "in order to provide a vehicle or avenue for personal expression and creativity," the role of arts education is neither specifically nor solely intended for these purposes. Indeed, it may be argued that personal expression in the sense of emotional catharsis is not a proper goal for art or artists. Also, expression and creativity have many vehicles in life, and the arts, though important, exemplify only one such category. Science and mathematics provide another.*

Not all individuals, in any case, are capable of or interested in the use of personal expression and creativity in the arts. They may seek these activities elsewhere, and may regard the arts only in terms of consumption or receptivity, rather than production or participation. Most important here is the implication that personal expression and creativity—such as experienced by some in artistic symbol making—"introduce order and control over the inner life." This point has already been analyzed at length, but we will emphasize it one last time.

Langer contends that the inner life has a logic and order of its own, vastly more complicated and of a different order than the symbolic logic of the language with which we speak and think. It is nonetheless rational and logical. Thus, any implication that "inner life" is in search or in need of order and control would be incorrect, except as it might apply to the relatively few people with demonstrable psychological disorders. Further, such contentions are open to challenge if one considers styles of art where order and control are not prized, or observes that the life styles of many artists across the centuries have been anything but ordered and controlled.

There was another correct answer. If you have not yet found it, go back to Frame 4 and choose again. If you have, go to page 166, below the line.

* See Brewster Ghiselin, ed., *The Creative Process* (New York: New American Library; Mentor Books, 1952), for several personal accounts of this kind of creativity.

---

From Frame 5

9. You are correct again. The use of behavioral objectives to enable the teacher to impose order and control over the activities and behaviors of the class, and by so doing, to guide each student to most effectively develop appropriate feeling responses was most definitely not recommended.

The issues of value ("appropriate feeling responses") and the imposition of value ("order and control") have been dealt with at length elsewhere (Frame 16, for example). Beyond this, it is extremely doubtful that a teacher can exert control over feeling responses in any way, except perhaps by fostering consistently poor attitudes or by adopting brainwashing techniques from totalitarian societies. At best, teachers can and should provide the opportunities and conditions for feeling responses and, thus, at least have some opportunity to guide these responses through various stages of refinement. But the exact nature and intensity of such responses will necessarily be unique for each person.

If you have followed directions and gone through the list in order, you have found all three choices that did *not* represent one of the six recommended applications of behavioral practice. If you didn't go back and identify the ones you missed. Go to Frame 6 after you have found all three choices.

Your answer was C:

Two levels of experience exist—psychical and physical. They are related or interdependent in that each experience in one realm has a correlate in the other.

This is a correct identification of a major position of strict behaviorism. Until relatively recently, an incredible number of thinkers have adhered steadfastly to this position as they found themselves unable to account for mental processes in any other way. Professor Langer, on the other hand, disagrees with this dichotomizing tendency and instead puts forth a biological view of mind dependent on intra-organic evolution, processes, and development; "feeling" rather than "knowing" so-called "objective" or scientific facts is seen as the prime characteristic of mind.

Langer maintains that just because the capacities and operation of the mind are not as susceptible as those of the body to scientific, "objective," and impersonal observation and measurement, they are not therefore illogical or unimportant. Indeed, she affirms that they are much more significant to the functioning of the "ultimate unit," the individual, who is not likely to demonstrate consistently observable behavior in his normal life.

If you haven't selected a second correct choice, go back to Frame 1 and choose again. If you have identified both correct answers, go ahead to Frame 2, page 184.

You said that Langer maintains that the mind, and the feelings it deals with, is continually in the process of thinking, remembering, recording, and dreaming, which results in the apprehension by the subject of the subjective state called self-awareness.

This is correct, and this statement is a paraphrase of Langer's direct thoughts quoted earlier. The essence of this affirmation is that mind is not an entity separate from the "physical" realm of existence but is itself intra-organic, self-perpetuating, and capable of inducing itself to action. Instead of affirming a purely "psychic" state, Mrs. Langer argues that "we continuously feel our own inward action as a texture of subjectivity, on which such objectively felt events as perceptions impinge, . . ." ° and from this substratum arise the many forms of human behavior that are articulated as "feelings." This perception of our own feelings forms the personal basis of all experience.

This question also had two correct answers; if you have not already identified both, go back to Frame 2 and make another choice. If you have, go to page 163, below the line.

° *Philosophical Sketches*, p. 27.

3. Your choice is inappropriate. The use of behavioral objectives to encourage an overt manifestation of a covert activity or behavior and the use of such overt behavior as a means of evaluating progress and as a basis for planning *was* recommended. Reread the appropriate discussion on page 169 before proceeding.

The attempt here is to bring overt responses to the level of consciousness of the student and thereby to make it possible for the teacher and student to observe them in some way. In both cases, the need has to do with selecting responses and behaviors: for the students, increased awareness of the process of "interpretation" (in the psychological, not the artistic sense) and the nature of selecting from among multiple choices can lead to a gradual refinement of the concept at hand; for the teacher, increased opportunity to observe overt indications of covert thought processes provides bases for selecting future experiences and for ordering them into a significant curriculum. Without such bases, neither the teacher nor the student has much to proceed with, and the teacher, especially, is left to assumption, guesswork, and other kinds of random planning.

Go back to Frame 5 and consider the next answer.

---

You felt that Langer defined the function of art as objectifying feeling so that we can contemplate and understand it, and formulating those inner experiences of life that elude expression by discursive language, our usual means of understanding and communicating.

This agrees perfectly with her expressed thought. The importance of this thought is found in the fact that language (discourse, discursive thought) has a logical structure that is different than the logical processes of inner life. Therefore, language is incapable of containing or conveying aspects of experience that are inner. Rather, in using feeling as its content, art makes an object (visual arts) or latent event (music, dance) of feeling, and by representing it as such to our minds, enables us to contemplate and understand its nature and processes.

There appears to be much wisdom in this vein of thought for teachers in the arts. It should be readily obvious that artistic "content" cannot be adequately conveyed in the terms or forms of our spoken language. Think of the possibility of explaining the essence of a composition to a deaf man, or the "feeling content" of a painting to a blind man.

Teaching the arts to young people and neophytes provides very similar problems. You cannot convey the significance of the feeling content through discourse (that is, explanation, description, or lecture). You must conceive of some means for allowing the individual to personally apprehend this content, to feel the embodied or objectified feeling content for himself at his own level of experience. This is why we spent so much time and effort earlier in this volume on conceptual learning, readiness, and so forth. Artistic concepts, or feelings derived from artistic contact, have no transportable substance and are nondiscursive; they follow a very personal course of development dependent upon the personal experiences of the subject. Fortunately, in music education you will not be faced with deaf people, but with people who *can hear* but do not know how to or have not had ample opportunity to *listen* in terms of "feeling" content.

There were two correct answers here. If you have not identified both, go back to Frame 3 and choose again. If you have both firmly in mind, go to Frame 4.

---

**From Frame 4**                                                      **Frame 24**

You said that Langer did *not* recommend arts education in order to educate individuals in feeling the objectification of subjective reality and the subjectification of the outward experiencing of nature.

But she did, and very much in those terms. Art objectifies, embodies, or formulates inner experience for our contemplation and understanding. Outward experience is subjectified through "the education of vision that we receive in seeing, hearing, reading works of art."* This vision is not one of eyesight or visual acuity in the literal sense, but, rather, "the development of the artist's eye, that assimilates ordinary sights (or sounds, motions, or events) to inward vision, and lends expressiveness and emotional import to the world".† Langer calls this "the subjectification of nature that makes reality itself a symbol of life and feeling,"†† and leaves little doubt that individuals who attain this state interpret reality in very much these terms. In a sense, reality functions for each of us as a kind of mirror that reflects certain vital essences of inner life. Viewed another way, "inner life" is like a flame that throws a certain light on aspects of life external to the individual. The light that is reflected back to the individual is therefore a reflection of his own subjective vision.

Even though the arts have often been praised for their nonutilitarian nature, and even though certain aestheticians have recommended a "disinterested" or nonpragmatic point of view for arts consumers, it seems as though the personal vision that art can develop may very well have a real function: enhancing or enriching many aspects of our daily lives. One must ask, in this sense, why every major culture in history has had a large artistic production, and why we can often best understand these cultures and our own heritage through contact with art.

Go back to Frame 4 and make another choice.

* Langer, *Philosophical Sketches,* p. 83.
† *Ibid.*
†† *Ibid.*

8. Your answer was inappropriate. The use of behavioral objectives to encourage creative responses and discovery learning by specifying and controlling the means, guiding principles, criteria, and general nature of the terminal behavior or product without in any way dictating the specific results, yet providing means for assessment by the student, class, and teacher *was* recommended. Reread the appropriate discussion on pages 171–172 before continuing.

Again, you are reminded that specific provisions need in no way limit creativity or discovery learning. In fact, in most instances we tend to identify both creativity and discovery in terms of the various limitations a person had to master in solving the problem, artistic or otherwise.

Certain specifications often enhance the efficiency and effectiveness of student efforts—especially those of beginners. Otherwise, the students may be cast unprepared into a totally free situation, where they are expected to deal with the elements of the art and to know how to judge their own efforts.

Go back to Frame 5 and consider choice 9.

---

Operant conditioning is the practice of strengthening (reinforcing) a desired behavior by providing a reward (reinforcement) if and when the desired response occurs. This condition may be present in a formal situation, as when teachers or parents induce a certain behavior by holding forth some form of extrinsic reward. It may also occur less formally, as when a student pursues actions that are motivated by his own view or insight into the possible rewards, and that sometimes result in desirable behavior or sometimes in undesirable behavior.

This practice should be avoided; otherwise, a student may join a performance organization for what *he* sees as the rewards of recognition, peer group approval, the desire to be with or near a friend, and so forth. This would not be entirely desirable for the teacher, who wishes to evoke musical behavior and musical feeling responses. On the other hand, a student may participate in a performance group out of a clear vision of the intrinsic musical rewards—the pleasures and satisfactions—held forth; this is a much more desirable aim of music education, but it requires special insight by the teacher, who must mix just the right amount of fun, recognition, and other such nonmusical rewards with opportunities for the kind of musical success that breeds musical satisfaction.

Go back to Frame 6 and attempt the last definition.

Your answer was D:

Mental operations (actions) are self-induced and often result in no observable or measurable overt physical behavior.

This is not a good choice. Until relatively recently, virtually all behaviorists have held that all mental activities have a physical correlate, and that as a result mental phenomena can be observed only as overt physical behavior. Some go even so far as to assert that only that which is observable in terms of overt physical behavior can be properly acknowledged; others affirm that no purely subjective realm exists at all since all important human functions eventually attain the level of overt physical behavior that can be "objectively" observed, measured, quantified, and qualified. Therefore, the above statement is not an accurate representation of the behaviorist position. In fact, the statement is part of one of Langer's proofs against behaviorism.

Langer especially rejects this particular behaviorist point of view; it is evident to her that the very active and essential nature of the subjective faculty she calls "mind" and its major operation—feeling—are being sacrificed to the demands of a "social science" attempting to reach the status of physical science by adopting the objectivity of physics and mathematics. Instead of the objective and impersonal sterility of the psychologist's testing laboratory, she affirms that life is a complex of felt experiences—felt intraorganically only by the feeling individual—which are not susceptible to the abstractions of science.

Science uses abstractions to arrive at conclusions; it does not, and should not, take the tangible or even intangible stuff of life, and force-fit it into an abstract methodology or system.

Go back to Frame 1 and make another choice that is more characteristic of behavioral thought.

You said that Langer maintains that behavior can be measured, observed, qualified, and quantified by means other and better than those currently employed by the behaviorists.

This is not so. She is indeed highly critical of their means and their desire for scientific methodology, but her criticism is definitely not in the terms suggested here. The life of "feelings" is presently and perhaps permanently unsusceptible to such *purely objective* measurement. There are too many subtle connections and interrelations among the various facets of "felt life" for a true picture to evolve. It is possible to objectively observe only very small portions of such a felt life. This, in scientific terms, is unsatisfactory since the many causal connections that exist should not be ignored or forsaken.

No, Langer is not interested in measuring, observing, qualifying, or quantifying behavior. She seems most interested in affirming that the complexities that confound the scientists who deal with human behavior are the very factors that should be exalted as most characteristic of mind. Nor does the system of behavioral objectives herein propose to so objectively measure musical behavior. The conditions under which behavioral objectives can be useful to the music teacher assume that certain kinds of musical behavior are susceptible to some kind of measurement, and that such a more tangible approach benefits both the student and the teacher in many ways. We must overcome the behavioral assumptions of countless generations of teachers that the psychic realm is mysterious or metaphysical and therefore unmanageable. Though no one should presume to deny the special qualities of music, it is possible to make the teaching of music a less random and more assertive skill. You will see that a highly qualified behavioral learning theory can be a major means to this end.

Go back to Frame 2 and try another answer.

---

*From Frame 5*                                                          Frame 29

4. Your response is inappropriate. The use of behavioral objectives as clear indications to the students of the goals at hand, the processes and criteria to be used, and the means of evaluating the eventual behavior *was* recommended. Reread the appropriate discussion on page 170 before proceeding.

The importance of this kind of thinking lies in the added efficiency it provides, for students are aware from the beginning of all that is expected of them. Where there is confusion of goals, means, criteria, and evaluation there will likely be confusion in the completion of the project or learning activity.

Such a clear statement of the project or learning activity in these terms also provides increased student self-monitoring of progress. The resulting behavior also gives the student more tangible evidence of progress, and can thus contribute to the development of attitudes favorable to learning or consuming music.

Go back to Frame 5 and consider the next choice.

---

*From Frame 3*                                                          Frame 30

You said that Langer defined the function of art as capturing the complex logic of human feelings as dynamic forms; embodying the structure of those feelings in a way that the logical structures of discourse cannot.

This is quite correct. The reasons for this seem almost simple upon examination. In contrast to emotions and feelings, language *appears to be* very logical and rational. Emotions and feelings *appear to be* irrational and illogical. Instead, emotions and feelings are a very logical and rational part of our human existence and experience. The problem is that they form an infinitely more complex system with a logic infinitely more complex and different than that of discourse.

As a means of coming to grips with inner experience, language does not sufficiently allow us to convey or handle the "feeling content" of "felt life." Like all media, language, as a raw material of art in poetry and prose, can be manipulated in such a way as to capture, objectify, or embody the complexities of "feeling content" and thereby to create of this content an art symbol. But language cannot in any way be used to explain or describe already existing feeling content; this must be felt by each feeling individual in terms of his own experience. Hence, the wise admonition by literary scholars against prose paraphrasing of poetry or literal interpretation of prose.

There were two correct answers to this question. If you have found both, go to Frame 4. If not, go back to Frame 3 and choose again.

---

*From Frame 4*                                                                                       Frame 31

You said that Langer did *not* recommend art education in order to prevent the corruption of feeling and the formless emotion represented in bad art.

But she most certainly did make such a recommendation. She noted that art successfully embodies or objectifies human feelings and that, therefore, bad art reflects a "corruption of feeling" or embodies "formless emotion." (See page 163.) Individuals who respond to or actively seek and consume bad art thereby indicate their own corruption of feeling or formless emotion and are denied, through the lack of significant contact and refinement, the "artistic import" and "felt life" of art, which has a truthful impact. Such art allows both contemplation and understanding of "inner life," and it is perhaps in these terms that we can understand best the spiritual essence of past cultures as we investigate their artistic production.

Go back to Frame 4 and make another choice.

---

*From Frame 5*                                                                                       Frame 32

7. Your response is not suitable. The use of behavioral objectives to encourage the teacher to consider goals in terms of practicality and with due regard for the readiness, interests, and needs of the individuals in the class was heartily recommended. Reread the appropriate discussion on pages 172–173 before continuing.

Here, behavioral processes assist the teacher to keep in touch with the realities of the situation. When actual behaviors are involved, frequently the readiness, interests, and needs of the class are most clearly indicated. If the students cannot or will not learn as expected, then the possibility is great that the activity or project lacks relevance to their abilities or concerns. Perhaps this is the greatest advantage of using behavioral objectives in planning: they tend to emphasize what the student will do or learn instead of what the teacher must do.

Traditional lesson plans often specified what the teacher would do, when he would do it; and so forth. Although this contributed a certain organization to the teacher's efforts, the results were not usually as commendable. The fact that the teacher *taught* a lesson on musical form, let us say, does not necessarily insure that everyone in the class understood all or even part of that lesson. Behavioral objectives, by specifying what the student will do in the way of overt behavior based on the learnings at hand, eliminate the worst aspects of this kind of "blind" teaching. Too often, the more traditional method of planning resulted in the exclamation by the teacher, "Well! I taught it to them; if they didn't learn it, it's their fault!" It is easy to see how this kind of attitude can spread into a general distrust or even dislike for the students. It assumes that students are lazy, stupid, or both, and that they somehow hinder the best efforts of a "good" teacher. It should be noted, too, that this kind of attitude generally results in a conformity-oriented style of teaching since everyone is supposed to learn the same thing at the same time —namely, at the time and in the way the teacher presented the lesson.

Behavioral objectives that are properly understood, well written, and sensibly employed can eliminate most if not all of these weaknesses, and in the bargain save the teacher much of the tedium of extensive lesson planning, well-organized lecture notes, and the like.

Go back to Frame 5 and consider choice 8.

---

*From Frame 4*                                                                    Frame 33

You answered that Langer did *not* recommend art education in order to appreciate art in terms of its programmatic suggestion of specific objects, stories, and ideas. You are correct.

This kind of notion has been hotly debated by artists and aestheticians for centuries. On one hand, those who might be called *purists* have held that art exists for its own sake and is an exercise in intellect. On the other hand, those who might be called *expressionists* assert that art *directly* "expresses" specific aspects of life. As with any extreme positions, the truth is likely to be found somewhere in between.

Langer, as well as many other contemporary aestheticians, holds that art arises from and within the *context of life,* but that it does not necessarily imitate, directly express, or suggest specific aspects of daily life. It *feels* like the experience of life in general feels.

Many teachers have gone far astray on this issue. Purists often end up dealing with music as though it was an abstraction like mathematics. They approach music in their classes as abstract sonorous patterns. Needless to say, personal meaning or relevance for young and developing intellects is difficult under these circumstances. Expressionists teach in such a way as to convince children that music always tells a story, paints a picture, or expresses a specific idea. Difficulty arises when the children do not "get" the intended message, picture, or story. The teacher is put in the embarrassing position of accusing the children of being dumb or inattentive, or of begrudgingly admitting that the composer's intent for the music has failed.

The contextualist position, on the other hand, dwells in broad terms on the *human content of music*. This content has a certain general relationship to life, and can therefore have tangibility and relevance for youngsters. It also has a cetrain pure or abstract character since the feelings embodied in the music are not the *actual* feelings of happiness, sorrow, grief, and so forth, that we encounter daily. They are the feelings *created* or *objectified* by the composer *to summarize an entire feeling domain*—feelings that we recognize as relevant to our life but distinct from actual emotions. They feel like life feels but are not directly attributable to any specific occasion in life. Thus, a funeral march need not remind us of a specific funeral. It sounds ("feels") like *all* those times in life when we have experienced a sense of sadness. And the patterns and forms of the musical art (repetition and contrast of various kinds) "feel" like these same aspects of unity and variety that give meaning to our daily affairs.

There is another correct choice. If you have not yet found it, go back to Frame 4 and choose again. Otherwise, go to page 166, below the line.

---

*From Frame 5*                                                                 Frame 34

5. Your answer is not correct. The use of behavioral objectives to develop situations where a feeling response is specifically called for and to make such responses overt in some way *was* recommended. Reread the appropriate material on pages 170–171, and then return to the discussion below.

If a feeling response is to be cultivated, behavioral objectives can be among the best means for creating the proper opportunities. The externalization of such feeling responses permits the student to contemplate his own feelings and to notice that the feeling responses of others are likely to be different and unique, yet understandable. When a "Why didn't I think of that?" thought goes fleetingly through the mind, the conditions of such learning are well established. In fact, the individual might be influenced by the "feeling responses" of the peer group.

It is often assumed that any kind of lesson that is designed to foster a feeling response must be unstructured and totally free. This is not necessarily so; behavioral objectives are most useful in this capacity since they create the proper atmosphere, define goals, and suggest guidelines and criteria that the student can use. Such lessons are not unstructured; they are structured differently. They have a focus, and they avoid the inefficient results of a totally permissive class. In other words, behavioral objectives create the atmosphere of permissipline, where a feeling response can be encouraged and guided without, on the other hand, being unduly confined. Many teachers will find that their attempts to create such a quasi-independent atmosphere may result in students finding such independence uncomfortable at first. With proper encouragement, though, they can readily make the adjustment. Remember, no matter how much the adolescent may indicate a desire for total freedom, he in fact finds this a very unstable condition, and covertly or unconsciously seeks the solace of minimal guidelines. Behavioral objectives help provide these.

Go back to Frame 5 and consider choice 6.

---

*From Frame 6*

Operant behavior is the result of the subtle but effective working of operant conditioning; where the student's behavior, when desirable, is reinforced by some form of reward. There is an inherent danger, then, in using behavior as the sole index of mental operations, for behavior that *appears* desirable may be occurring because of the wrong reasons or the wrong kind of reward. When behavior is motivated by external rewards or inducements rather than by the intrinsic qualities of the stimulus object or occasion, operant behavior is likely to result.

In musical performance groups, this is a very real danger. Directors often assume that the participation and co-operation of the group indicates a good *musical* attitude and considerable *musical* interest and learning, when in fact such participation and co-operation may be motivated by numerous extrinsic factors: the desire not to be in study hall, the desire to gain personal recognition, the desire to fulfill the wishes of parents, the desire to equal the achievements of an older sibling, and so on. In other words, the student is likely to regard the reward as the stimulus for a given behavior, instead of seeking the satisfaction and fulfillment of the musical performance and experiencing a "feeling response" to it.

As you can see, this condition should be avoided because it involves using *extrinsic* or imposed motivations instead of conditions that enhance the possibility of *intrinsic* self-motivation regarding musical involvement and achievement. Since there is little the teacher can do to control self-motivations that are not musical in origin and intent, he should then do all he can to properly emphasize such purely musical rewards. The task becomes one of using what is often a good set of circumstances to engender even better results. To do this, only musical goals and rewards should receive major emphasis.

Continually and unnecessarily posting the rewards of festival ratings, grades, or personal or group recognition—whether through positive means ("Let's work hard for our 'A' rating and carry on the school tradition!") or negative means ("We can't afford not to get an 'A' and break the school tradition!")—will most likely result in reinforcing nonmusical operant behavior.

Go to page 176, below the line.

# CHAPTER SIX

# *types of musical behavior*

One may say broadly that all the animals that have been carefully observed have behaved so as to confirm the philosophy in which the observer believed before his observations began. Nay, more, they have all displayed the national characteristics of the observer. Animals studied by Americans rush about frantically, with an incredible display of hustle and pep, and at last achieve the desired result by chance. Animals observed by Germans sit still and think, and at last evolve the situation out of their inner consciousness. To the plain man, such as the present writer, this situation is discouraging. I observe, however, that the type of problem which a man naturally sets to an animal depends upon his own philosophy, and that this probably accounts for the differences in the results.

Bertrand Russell, An Outline of Philosophy (London: Allen and Unwin, 1927), pp. 32–33.

Bertrand Russell was anything but a "plain man." His thoughts on the preceding page, though laced with some wit and not a little cynicism, represent another instance of a noted philosopher challenging the major premises of "laboratory" behaviorism. But just as behaviorists may unwittingly implement the "self-fulfilling prophecy" in their researches, so too may musicians confuse true musical literacy with the "wish fulfillment" of what they prefer to see. Performing musicians can be misled by their own rich experiences to believe that a musical education consists only of those aspects of performance that are apparent to the listener. Some nonmusicians might have us believe that performing music is merely a manual craft devoid of any creative insight.[1] Certain "cultured" musical critics imply that the noblest musical trait is manifested by the intelligent listener. And many music educators see their role as one of enlightening the otherwise "ignorant" masses to the "true" values of music. This they often do with an evangelical zeal that denigrates the values of those they intend to "reach." All such persons belie a natural bias. In each case there may be some truth, but in too many instances the individual may well succeed in demonstrating to himself that his path is the correct or only one.

The Russell quote contains several other insights. First, we as teachers are dealing with people and not animals. Thus, our job is infinitely more complex and more demanding, and thereby more rewarding and more satisfying. Second, we are not dealing with experimental subjects in the sterility of the laboratory. We are dealing with diverse and very real individuals in the microcosm known as the classroom. On both counts, the teacher's responsibility is great.

A personal aesthetic philosophy or point of view seems inescapable, but it is necessary, first, to avoid imposing such a viewpoint on the individuals who constitute the class. Second, it is absolutely imperative that you understand the *variables of musical behavior*—that is, behaviors that are essentially musical in origin and in application. All of these behaviors are essentially *covert* in their initial stages. Many, if left to themselves, would remain so. Some, such as those involved in performance, contribute to the overt behavior required for the execution of a musical score.

Learning activities intended to develop or refine musical literacy must therefore begin by considering the covert operations of the mind. None of these various functions are really distinguishable, for they operate with varying degrees of interaction or fusion. None are unique to music per se. They merely describe human functioning. We isolate them and interpret them in musical terms in order to show their relevance to and operation in musical situations, and to know what general musical behaviors—covert or overt—can be expected.

---

[1] See Abraham Maslow, *Toward a Psychology of Being,* 2nd ed. (New York: Van Nostrand Reinhold, 1968), p. 137.

There are several different categories of covert behavior. Each category involves different sets of *variables,* which may be acted upon, used, or limited in some way during a learning activity or situation, formal or informal. The first major category of covert behavior deals with *cognition*—that is, understanding, knowledge, conceptualization. Cognition is not really as cold and objective a behavior as you might think: it also involves *percepts*—knowledge gained through perceiving—which are invariably conditioned by factors unique to each individual, and even by certain *affects*—feelings, in the sense of moods and general emotions—which, too, are invariably personal and unique. Some of the variables in this category are indicated in the following list of covert cognitive behaviors.[2]

*Covert Cognitive Behaviors*

1. to perceive
2. to comprehend
3. to analyze
4. to identify
5. to differentiate or contrast
6. to compare or match
7. to synthesize
8. to apply abstractly
9. to evaluate or judge
10. to elaborate
11. to decide
12. to identify or empathize with; or to respond contemplatively to, in terms of concepts

All of these are variable *covert mental operations* that may never reach the stage of *overt behavior.* However, this is the purpose of identifying and distinguishing, however artificially, these cognitive operations of the mind: in order that means may be found to make them overtly observable in some way.

| *Cognitive Variables* | → involve → | *Covert Behaviors* |
|---|---|---|
| 1.  to perceive | | apprehends, recognizes |
| 2.  to comprehend | | forms conceptual patterns; transfers |

[2] Many of the ideas in this chapter have been influenced by the writings of Professor Ashael Woodruff, advisor and consultant to MENC and MMCP, and by my discussions with him. They have been, however, so colored and influenced by my own training, thought, and practice that it is difficult for me to give specific credit in each instance. I can but acknowledge my gratitude to Professor Woodruff and remove from his responsibility any attributions or interpretations that may not accord strictly with his own views.

| | | |
|---|---|---|
| 3. | to analyze | attends to subunits of a phenomenon |
| 4. | to identify | describes or labels |
| 5. | to differentiate or contrast | separates from like phenomena |
| 6. | to compare or match | establishes relationships and differences |
| 7. | to synthesize | combines phenomena into new relationships |
| 8. | to apply abstractly | interprets and acts deductively upon ideas |
| 9. | to evaluate or judge | weighs values and qualities |
| 10. | to elaborate | extends and develops |
| 11. | to decide | chooses between alternatives |
| 12. | to identify or empathize with; or to respond contemplatively to, in terms of concepts | how one "feels" in terms of what has been learned |

Some concrete examples of *overt equivalencies* might be helpful at this point.

1. The student demonstrates *perception* by locating a phenomenon by measure number in a score; by indicating its relative placement within the musical stimulus; by choosing one of the numbers the teacher points to as the music progresses.

2. The student shows *comprehension* when he can remember and reiterate information, as when he describes (in his own terms) the constituent parts of a three-part form; or when he uses such information in other behavioral ways, such as in successfully creating an original composition in three-part form.

3. The student demonstrates *analysis* when he is able to extract musical elements from a given context, as in isolating the factors that unify a given song and indicating the way in which they perform that function.

4. The student *identifies* by applying a descriptive or musical label to a musical element: he can refer to what he perceives.

5. The student *differentiates* or *contrasts* by indicating the differences between musical phenomena; for instance, he can differentiate among two-part, three-part, and rondo forms by description or in composition, by analysis, and so forth.

6. The student *compares or matches* by citing or using congruent but distinctive factors in analytically comparing two compositions in terms of "mood," or by creating two compositions with related though distinctive moods.

7. The student *synthesizes* by discovering new relevancies among combinations of concepts or elements, such as in creating a composition of his own or in discussing a composition in these terms.

8. The student *applies abstractly* by using reasoning based upon past learning to solve a musical problem. The reasoning is the abstract factor ap-

plied to the selection, elimination, or invention of alternative courses of action, and is observed by reading backwards from the student's response.

9. The student *evaluates and judges* when he discusses his own and other students' works, as well as those in the standard repertory, in terms of objective criteria.

10. The student *elaborates a musical idea* when he answers, by ear on his own instrument, a short musical statement made by the teacher, or when he composes a consequent phrase to a given antecedent phrase.

11. The student *decides* by interpreting alternatives and acting accordingly, as when he is asked to select those shapes in the room that are variations on a rectangle.

12. The student *identifies or empathizes with, or responds contemplatively* when what he has learned enhances his feeling response, as when a student indicates preference on the basis of his knowledge.

It is important to note that many of these covert cognitive variables are often falsely identified as *inherently overt* by many of us in ordinary discourse. For example, for many people, "to analyze" a musical score may have explicit connotations of written analysis. In the case of each of these cognitive variables, no such necessary overt application is necessary or implied. Such mental activity often remains purely covert, never reaching the level of overt behavior. Covert mental acts *may* have overt applications, as when a performer analyzes a composition so that he can play it better. It is important to note this kind of doublethink because many teachers today often assume that the covert behaviors they are working with will automatically have overt manifestations; but they never bother to check whether this is so. They may teach several lessons, yet have no clear idea whether or not the students are able to overtly apply these covert behaviors successfully, or whether the covert behaviors were in fact adequately learned in the first place.

Also, you have probably noted already that there is considerable overlap among these variables of cognitive behavior. Remember that we isolate them only to be able to discuss and focus on their individual relevancies. In fact, any one of these variables may be used in combination with or in the service of one of the others. The important thing to recognize, however, is that at any given time it is most usual (and most successful in teaching) to dwell on or emphasize one variable as being the most important at that time. After dwelling on the identification of a musical feature, the student may then employ "identification" as a means to the ends of differentiation or analysis.

Perception is necessary to analysis. Once a student can perceive elements, due emphasis can be given to processes of analysis. Similarly, analysis is essential to differentiation. But differentiation can be isolated, as in distinguishing between two or more phenomena. And differentiation is useful in comparing and contrasting; yet emphasis on contrasts will involve convergent as well as divergent aspects.

*GO TO FRAME 1, PAGE 230.*

As indicated earlier, the range of cognitive variables includes various kinds of perception and comprehension, but also some *affects*—that is, "feeling responses." But as with the behavioral objective you just completed, these are always related to some conceptual learning in progress or about to be undertaken. Thus, some more or less objective bases were provided for such an affective response. In the behavioral objective just completed, for example, the teacher might ask a student why his graphic design had five parts, when the composition listened to had a different number of parts.

The attempt to recognize and stimulate the feelings that accompany or result from learning emphasizes the simple fact that all cognitive learning involves feelings to some degree. The feeling components of concepts can be called *attensive,* in the sense that they catch our *atten*tion because of their in*tensive* character: in learning something, our feelings about it may become more *intense. Confluent education* attempts to merge the "feeling" components (affects) with the "knowing" components (cognitions) and thus to derive what is called "meaning" or "relevance." Thus, it is the affective aspects of a cognition that make it seem important or worth knowing.

## AFFECTIVE BEHAVIORS

In addition to the kinds of affects related to cognition, there is a second broad category of covert behavior that deals exclusively with *affective variables*. These entail mainly free, creative, "subjective" responses that are accompanied or determined by certain concomitant emotional tones or states.[3] Affective variables include the following:

1. to respond intuitively
2. to interpret freely
3. to prefer
4. to enjoy
5. to characterize in terms of "feeling"
6. to create or organize "subjectively"
7. to choose on the basis of "feel"

As you can readily see, these all entail various degrees or types of feeling response in which the student is enabled or encouraged to manifest some state of "inner life" or "felt life." We can say that these variables are pre-

[3] It is more than likely that all learning experiences, formal or informal, are always accompanied by some kind of affects in the form of satisfaction, pleasure, frustration, and so forth. However, these are not as intensive as the affects considered here, which are more akin to the affects experienced in works of art; artistic affects are somewhat more formal and less pragmatically related to the life situation.

conscious, and that classroom activities may have great bearing on making them more conscious.

These variables also exist first and foremost at the covert level. In life they most generally occur as purely mental states, though we may deduce that a student "likes" or "prefers" chocolate ice cream when he buys a chocolate ice cream cone. However, even this could be misleading since the student could be buying the cone for a friend; or he may just be trying the flavor, which he may end up disliking.

As with the cognitive domain, affective variables are also characterized by various types of covert behavior.

| *Affective Variables* → involve → | *Covert Behaviors* |
|---|---|
| 1. to respond intuitively | react without deliberate reasoning or "logic" |
| 2. to interpret freely | respond by the way something "feels" |
| 3. to prefer | liking or disliking according to subjective values |
| 4. to enjoy | derive pleasure according to the lack of unpleasant "feelings" |
| 5. to characterize in terms of "feelings" | subjective apprehending of the qualities or nature of a phenomenon |
| 6. to create or organize subjectively | formulation on the basis of personal criteria |
| 7. to choose on the basis of "feel" | decision made according to personal "feeling" |

Each of these *covert affective behaviors* has many possible forms of *overt equivalencies,* just as the cognitive behaviors did.

1. *Responding intuitively.* The student manifests behavior not based in conceptual reasoning or in logic consciously applied, as when a young child is asked to "move to the music," or to "do what the piano tells you."

2. *Interpreting freely.* Responses stemming from "feelings" are manifested in a response that is not stipulated by teacher preference, as when a young girl associated bright yellow with a funeral march because her pet canary had just died.

3. *Preferring.* Liking or disliking on the basis of subjective values is reflected in behavior where a pure and unarguable preference is indicated. Such behavior would result from questions such as these: Did you like that composition? Do you like this kind of music? What kind of music do you prefer? Observable musical preferences will also be indicated when the student is out of school, or after he has graduated.

4. *Enjoying.* The derivation of pleasure according to the lack of unpleasant feelings can result in many kinds of behavior: willingness to cooperate; evident satisfaction determined by physiognomy (outward appearance, smiling, foot-tapping, and the like); suggestions by the student of areas of study, music to be performed, and so forth.

5. *Characterizing in terms of feelings.* Subjective characterization of the qualities or nature of a thing can be seen when, for instance, a student describes the feeling content of a musical phenomenon in his own terms; when he makes an uncalled for value judgment, such as "That music stinks!" or conversely, "That's groovy!"; when he identifies according to subjective criteria the difference between what he considers to be "good" and "bad" music; or when he determines whether such a difference exists.

6. *Creating or organizing subjectively.* Formulation on the basis of subjective criteria has among its evidences the making of musical compositions on purely subjective bases (as in creating works that programmatically interprets a given title or mood); or the ranking of things in a hierarchy of importance or value to the individual (as in listing from "good" to "bad" the various styles of music known to the student; a side benefit results, to the degree that the teacher is advised of the various styles of music familiar to each student). This behavior is distinct from creation or organization according to teacher-specified criteria.

7. *Choosing on the basis of feel.* Decisions made according to personal rather than teacher criteria happen frequently, as in situations where a performer "chooses" a technique on the basis of feel rather than teacher direction; where classes are given opportunities to choose their own learnings, or to choose from several given possibilities; or where classes choose from several given responses according to feeling, as when a choice must be made between graphic representations of "moods."

It is not at all unusual to have quite divergent yet significant responses for instance, to different graphic symbols.

Some see in the straight line the tension of a taut string; others see undulating but continuous tension in the wavy line; and still others feel the "sawtooth" line conveys tension by its irregular and dramatic changes of visual motion and direction. Thus, any one of them could be a satisfactory choice made according to personal criteria.

It should be readily apparent that the subjective realm, the feeling realm, does not need to go unnoticed or untouched by the teacher: By providing ample opportunities for the exercise or application of the above covert affective variables that are manifested in overt behavior, the teacher can do much to expand awareness and to encourage and refine the affective response.

Since the affective response is so central in any kind of musical response, it deserves central attention in music education. Since the affective response is not subject to "objective" or teacher-specified criteria it is the one area where students can find a good measure of musical success, regardless of their academic or musical prowess or inclination. Since the affective realm is largely involved with feelings, values, and attitudes, it is the key to personal "motivation." In the long run, it is the factor that determines both the eventual success or failure of music education for each person and whether he seeks or avoids musical contacts outside of school and after graduation.

GO TO FRAME 3, PAGE 230.

## PSYCHOMOTOR BEHAVIOR

So far we have covered two categories of behavior and their variable manifestations: cognitive variables (see p. 207) and affective variables (see p. 210). There is one more basic category of behavior: *psychomotor* behavior. This behavior usually refers to the development of the muscular action and neuromuscular co-ordination necessary for skilled behavior such as musical performance. This category also has a distinct set of variables:

1. to attend to cues
2. to imitate and repeat
3. to monitor oneself
4. to follow instructions
5. to fixate through practice
6. to refine
7. to co-ordinate series of cues and acts
8. to acquire speed
9. to lessen time
10. to perfect
11. to hear inwardly

Each of these can be viewed as a separate step in the acquisition of the skilled behavior of musical performance. But as before, the boundaries among them are often obscured. They are not as separate as this list makes them seem. Furthermore, in order to eliminate the possibility of conditioned behavior (operant conditioning), the variables from the cognitive and affective domains of behaviors must be involved at all times. The psychomotor variables will at first be considered alone; then a consideration of the necessary synthesis of variables can be undertaken.

1. *To attend to cues.* Skilled acts are begun when the student responds to cues. Cues may be visual (the notated music, observing the teacher), aural, or *kinesthetic.*[4] Beginners should concentrate on only one at a time. Since

---

[4] Kinesthetic cues involve the "sense" or "feeling" of the muscles, tendons, and joints that yield information about the position and activities of the limbs.

the student should possess some aural abilities before instruction is started,[5] it is recommended that the teacher begin by directing the student's attention to kinesthetic cues dealing with embouchure, posture, fingering, and the like. Notation can be dealt with most profitably after the student has become sufficiently familiar with the aural and kinesthetic cues—as in the Suzuki Method of string pedagogy. Beginners can handle only the most relevant or obvious cues: too many or too subtle cues lead to confusion and possibly discouragement. The ability to attend to cues is closely entwined with the cognitive variable "to perceive."

2. *To imitate and repeat.* Copying the response of another person is often an essential part in the early stages of skill instruction. The teacher creates situations where the learner is expected to overtly imitate the demonstration of the teacher. This is related to "attending to cues" in that the student must sort out the relevant cues that he observes, interpret them, and make a trial attempt. So this too involves some cognition related to the variables of perception, analysis, and differentiation. If a trial act is successful, only *the ability to repeat it* will indicate whether the imitative behavior stemmed from understanding (cognition) or from chance. If the imitated behavior is to be capable of transfer and application to new and future performance situations, it must be cognitively assimilated into the student's conceptual framework. Thus, the teacher must not only (a) provide the model for imitation, he must also (b) help the student interpret the relevant cues and (c) insure that the student can transfer the skill to appropriate future situations.

3. *To monitor oneself.* The student must become increasingly able to make use of his own feedback. The assessment of skill development will in part be determined by his increasing ability to identify, locate, and eliminate his own errors. This self-diagnosis amounts to a conceptual understanding of the requirements of the skill—that is, knowing what to do, when, why, and under what conditions. To achieve this, the student must be gradually weaned of the teacher's diagnosis. As instruction progresses, in other words, the teacher should perform fewer direct corrections, relying instead on indirect questions and hints to lead the student to correct the most obvious aspects of his own performance. The teacher can always deal with refinements and subtleties, but each of these should also be assimilated in the student's understanding at each level.

4. *To follow instructions.* This involves following the verbal instructions of the teacher and decoding musical notation and performance directions (often in a foreign language). The notion that one is supposed to follow the conductor and the ability to follow the conductor is an added source of ongoing instruction to the student performer.

5. *To fixate through practice.* Skilled behavior requires repetition (practice) and leads to greater control and consistency. But not all practice is equally fruitful or efficient. Therefore, the teacher must teach the student

---

[5] See Edwin Gordon, *The Psychology of Music Teaching* (Englewood Cliffs, N.J.: Prentice Hall, 1971), pp. 120–21.

how to practice most efficiently and effectively. Without explicit directions, parents often force their children into futile and misguided "theories" of practice. Abstract periods are set aside, often "an hour a day." Although the earlier parts of such a period may be useful, the latter parts often involve merely going through the motions. Therefore, several short periods of practice should be recommended to parents and students.

Music educators often exacerbate the problems of practice by equating improvement with *quantity* of practice time in the form of "practice cards" signed by the parent. Aside from encouraging some parents to lie for their children, this practice fails to realize that the *quality* (effectiveness) of practice is more important than the quantity. Therefore, students should be taught how to eliminate certain kinds of errors. That is, they should know how to figure out rhythmic patterns and how to drill themselves on tricky passages: for the former, a conceptual ability to deal with rhythm and meter is called for; for the latter, the student must be directed to slow down and drill not only the error but a little bit of the music on either side of the error. If what practicing the student does is not productive, progress is not rapid and students become frustrated or lose interest. Teachers often conclude from this that the child was untalented, unmotivated, or "not cut out for this" when in fact the fault may be largely theirs. The quality of practice will be evident in lessons without practice cards. Motivation to practice should arise from a desire to improve and from some success at it, not from extrinsics such as practice cards.

6. *To refine*. This involves increasing accuracy in performance. Among other things, this means that the student is able to attend to more than one cue at a time: he attends not only to the most relevant cues, but also to more subtle ones.

Frequently, bursts of progress are followed by a seemingly latent period of slow or seemingly nonexistent progress. This is called a *plateau*. This leveling off can represent a period of refinement, where the performer makes small and subtle responses within the larger responses he has already acquired. This usually involves the integration of cues, mediating responses, and interpretations, into longer chains of responses. Thus, a plateau may involve significant covert refinement while the more overt aspects of performance seem to be stabilized.

Plateaus may also involve problems. They may represent fading interest, and the teacher must therefore "dangle the carrot" with new and potentially satisfying challenges. These may approach the limits of the student's present physical capacity. Fine muscle control is a matter of physical maturation, which the teacher can hasten by providing materials that help develop this control. Sometimes the learner may be confused, in which case he may require only clarification. Frequently, the student has exhausted a level of technique and requires new or advanced technical challenges. Overcoming one plateau should lead to a period of increasing gains, followed—if all goes well—by another plateau; and so on as the student progresses.

7. *To co-ordinate a series of cues and acts*. Any skilled behavior in-

volves many individual cues, mediating responses, interpretations, and acts. The more skilled the behavior, the longer the chains of effective sequences within it, and the more consistently they are applied. In other words, the individual components of a response link together in larger and larger patterns, or gestalts. These arise from fruitful practice of well-chosen musical materials.

8. *To acquire speed.* This involves the development of the fine muscle control necessary to physically execute passages in tempo and the increased ability to master and control the complex series of mental operations referred to in variable (7). Thus, this kind of speed in musical performance entails the dropping out of separate mediating responses in favor of larger patterns and the corresponding fine muscle control necessary to the execution of these larger patterns.

9. *To lessen time.* This involves mainly the amount of time necessary to learn a skilled action, and is closely related to variable (8). As a learner is able to increasingly drop individual mediating responses in favor of larger patterns, the time necessary to master the notation and techniques of a given composition will become shorter. Less practice will be needed. More music can be attempted, more progress can be made; and with each step, less time is used. So far, however, the description of skill development could have applied almost as well to typing or tennis. This stage, however, implies that the student is more easily able to master the notation and techniques, and, thus, lessons can be devoted to musical concerns. Music teachers should teach music as an art, not as a mere physical skill. The decoding of musical notation does not in itself constitute music as an art, only music as a storage and retrieval system. Matters of phrasing and interpretation should at this stage become the major emphases of instruction. Technique should be advanced to meet musical or expressive problems, and should not become an end in itself. As less time is devoted to the routine matters of notes (often the major or only concern some teachers display during lessons), the music lesson deals more with the expressive aspects of musical performance and the music performed. Thus, technique is learned in a musical or expressive context.

10. *To perfect or normalize.* This involves the ability to perform all music with the least amount of separate mediating responses, or put another way, with the longest patterns of execution. A good comparison is learning to read a foreign language. The neophyte usually has to translate it into English before it has meaning for him. The expert reads and derives meaning without the separate mediating responses: he reads and understands the foreign language itself. The process from cue to act becomes almost automatic or instant. These longer patterns of sequences are called *programs.* In expert performance, each aspect of the program of responses is perfectly timed and serves as the cue for the next response.

The term *program* has been applied to the patterns of cues and responses in the "programs" of learning machines. The reverse application should not be true. Music teachers should not "program" performance skills. Expert performers develop their own programs in terms of their own physical, mental, and musical uniqueness. Teachers who try to impose their own "programs" on students hinder the development of the students' full capacities. They should, rather, facilitate the development of each student's program.

11. *To hear inwardly.* This is a special cue or mediating response unique to musicians: the ability to form a mental (aural) image of the sound before the sound is actually produced. As such, it seems to be a kind of perception, and could thus be considered a cognition were it not for the fact that it is so inextricably a part of performance. This ability is also involved in feedback. A student compares the pitch actually played with the aural image that should have existed beforehand in the "inner ear." If this ability to formulate an aural image is deficient, so will be the student's ability to identify errors and, thus, his ability to make rapid progress will be diminished.

A good musician does not read music by "eye." He reads it "by ear." He sees the notes, that is true. But rather than a particular conscious interpretation of the *name* of the note, an aural image should arise. The player's technique responds to the aural image as the cue, not to a separate intellectual or verbal interpretation. The interpretation is musical and predicated on the aural image. This is why the "inner ear" must be cultivated in any instruction of skills involved in musical performance. Playing "by ear" and improvising make prime use of this capacity and also help develop it.

Thus, playing by ear does not contravene the intent of a musical education. It has practical benefits for both student and teacher, and can provide increased satisfaction for the learner. Additionally, musicians who can play "by ear" tend in greater numbers to keep playing. This is probably related to the fact that they can learn music from notes more efficiently and, hence, must practice the notation less. They can also enjoy playing alone or in "jam sessions" when music is not available or desired.

It should be repeated that the above departmentalization of variables is patently artificial. A skilled behavior cannot be broken down into such neat categories; in fact, all can be operative at any given time. Nonetheless, it is fruitful for the teacher to think in terms of such distinct categories. This is part of the teacher's role as a diagnostician. The teacher listens, observes, and identifies which of the psychomotor variables is weak or in need of specific attention. Then, new learning activities can be chosen or devised to begin a concentrated attack on the problem. The student's inability to sight-read well, for example, may not be related to his ability to attend visually to the notated cues or to perform the kinesthetic requisites. The teacher may decide that the problem is one of a poorly developed inner ear: The student cannot "hear" what his eyes see in advance of the notes he is playing. Thus, much work on "ear training" is called for: playing by ear, improvising, even sight singing (or whistling, if singing proves embarrassing) could provide the needed impetus.

Many teachers, recognizing that musical performance is a complex skill, often assume that all aspects of it must be attacked simultaneously— or as it works out in practice, randomly. Thus, they follow no specific course of action and each lesson is likely to be a carbon copy of previous lessons. This mode of attack thereby loses focus and direction. Complexity should not be an excuse for unambitious teaching

*GO TO FRAME 4, PAGE 231.*

---

It is necessary to remember that the development of psychomotor behavior is a process of growth. All growth is a more or less continuous activity. It has high points and low points, phases, and emphases. There are growth spurts and plateaus. As in biological growth, such musical growth is simultaneously a process of increased specialization of functions and a process of ever broadening their application. Only the teacher willing to devote time and attention to the details of psychomotor development will be able to effectively assist young performers in improving their performing ability.

It would seem that psychomotor behavior would be the most easily observed of the three types of behavior we have considered, since it always results in some sort of observable musical performance. It is precisely for this reason that evidences of such behavior must be treated with much care. As was pointed out in the last chapter, what appear to be desirable responses may in fact be inadequate references for surveying the operation of the mind. Performance without cognition and "feeling" seems incongruous to the musician, yet it is done every day by the students of some teachers.

Furthermore, expertise cannot be judged *only* by the performance. Whether it is a young student working for a year on music for festival, or a college senior who takes a year to prepare for a graduation recital, the inordinate amount of time needed indicates that this behavior is mainly due to time-consuming imitative learning. Many teachers are guilty of so "programming" their students. A piece practiced long enough without distraction from too many other concerns can be made to sound refined, finished, and polished, when in fact it has been learned by imitation and hence the student could not have put it together on his own.

Therefore, those involved in teaching performance skills are strongly cautioned against using behavior as the sole determinant of learning, or "programming" students through excessive repetition of performance actions. Instead, students involved in the acquisition of performance skills should be consistently confronted with cognitive and affective behaviors in an attempt to make them better able to "understand" the what, why, and how of their performance and to actually derive feeling or insight into feeling, as expressed by the "art symbol" conveyed in a musical composition. Without such cognitive and affective behavior, psychomotor behavior becomes meaningless, futile, unproductive, and often self-defeating. In the long run, it is the application of cognition and affection that is the contributing factor in the maturation of independent musicianship. This should be the goal of all instruction in musical performance rather than the development of performance technique in the abstract, as an end in itself. And all of this applies to performance groups as well as to private lessons.

## SUMMARY OF COVERT BEHAVIORS

So far, we have seen that there are three broad categories of musical behavior—cognitive, affective, and psychomotor—and that to varying degrees these categories are interrelated by the nature and complexity of the musical art. It is not possible to regard behavior in an art such as music in the same terms in which one might regard behavior in a typing class (which is the classic example used in basic texts on psychomotor skills) or even in many academic classes. For example, almost all musical behaviors depend, in one way or another, on perception: either perception of relevant cues in a performance situation or perception of the elements of music and their organization in a listening situation. Additionally, the exigencies of the arts in general, and music in particular, tend to put great importance on the affective category, recognizing that acts of cognition and acts of performance are all colored to some degree with feeling responses or emotional overtones (which are continually variable).

Musical behavior is not cut-and-dried. It cannot regard past experiences and learnings with detachment since the past forms an integral part of its living body. And any such thing that continues to live continues to embody life, and thereby involves "felt life." This is why arts education is so tricky. All learnings are susceptible to very personal feeling responses, some of which may be positive, some of which may be negative. Attitudes arise when feelings and emotions are associated with certain learnings, activities, or objects. These may be favorable or unfavorable to the concerns at hand. While it may be fascinating and interesting, it does not seem as likely that a student can be as personally "involved" in the dates of the Peloponnesian War or in how igloos are built as they can be in a musical experience.

Add to these factors the problems of adolescence already considered at length, and it can easily be seen that the lot of the music teacher is not an easy one. Yet this is all the more reason to work hard at it, for the satisfactions are correspondingly richer. Above all, however, the teacher must realize that his satisfaction should arise mainly from the act of teaching. Those who enter the profession to satisfy their own musical and personal needs inevitably sacrifice the interests and needs of their students and end up quite frustrated in both regards. The lack of attention to student needs most usually results in the teacher's inability to fulfill his own. In the long run, our profession and our art are poorer for each student who is not allowed to develop into an independently capable musician.

The various *covert* operations of the human mind that are involved in cognitive, affective, and psychomotor behavior can be brought to a more observable level by several general means. These too fall conveniently into three categories of *observable behavior:* to verbalize, to make, and to perform. Each will be considered in order, though they need not be regarded as self-contained.

### Verbal Forms: speaking; writing

*Speaking* can involve discussions, descriptions, anecdotes, explanations, and so on. The role of speech is to bring any of the cognitive, affective, or psychomotor covert behaviors to overt manifestation, however general. In the cognitive category, for example, comprehension, analysis, identification, differentiation, and judgment, can all be approached through speech. The same is true for the affective category, where preferences, interpretations, characterizations, and choices can all be spoken in some way. As for the psychomotor category, the teacher makes overt the covert thoughts of the student when he asks, "What mistakes did you make?" or "How do you think this passage should go?" or similar questions.

*Writing* can take the form of essays, written descriptions, selection of adjectives, the completion of answers on a directed listening sheet, and so on. Again, the three categories of cognitive, affective, and psychomotor behavior are equally susceptible to this manner of overt response. Analysis, identification, and differentiation, all cognitive variables, can be brought to the surface by having the student convey in writing the results of those mental operations. Similarly, preferences, choices, and characterizations, may be written as overt evidences of covert affective variables. Written work can perform a valuable service in the psychomotor domain too, as when a student is asked to describe or define, elements of musical notation or interpretive markings; or when a section or group is asked to indicate in writing their perception of the mistakes they made.

Thus, verbal behavior is one technique that can be used in making covert responses observable as overt behavior. This technique should be approached with great care, however, for students have varying degrees of ability and readiness with regard to verbal behaviors, which are not the same as musical behaviors. They are a means, not (as in the case of notebooks) ends of value in themselves. To consider them as ends is to confuse musical learning with verbal behavior.

Academic achievement can be, and has been, directly related to verbal behaviors. The student who, for example, reads well (that is, with efficient speed and effective comprehension) frequently does well in his various areas of study. On the other hand, those who do not read well are likely to experience difficulty in classes where verbal comprehension (manifested in the understanding of lectures, note taking, reading assignments, term papers, and so on) is at a premium.

Since musical behavior as a kind of capacity for a musical response has no direct or necessary relationship to verbal skill, overreliance on verbal skills in music classes can confuse and soon lose those students who are deficient in verbal skills. The trick, of course, is to conceive of activities that require verbal responses (written or spoken) in accordance with the youngster's abilities or feelings. This implies that no set standard for verbal responses is predetermined. The teacher must anticipate varying degrees of verbal refinement and verbal response, all or any of which may be relevant or significant for one individual yet not for others.

Above all, the teacher must avoid the lecture-demonstration-explanation format of teaching. This format includes no provision for students to verbalize cognitions, affections, and psychomotor behavior in their own terms at their own level of understanding. Even the so-called Socratic method, where the teacher employs "leading questions," can fail if the teacher has in mind a specific verbal answer to each of his questions.

Thus, speaking and writing as forms of verbal behavior should be viewed only as ancillary to the teacher's efforts, and should not be preponderant among the instructional means of making covert behavior overt. Of far more consequence is the frequent co-ordination of verbal behavior with one or both of the other two kinds of overt behavior.

*Making Something: composing (creating); arranging (or rearranging); organizing; notating*

This second manner of making covert mental operations observable as *overt behavior* is *to make* something as a result of these mental operations. The four types of overt behavior to be discussed under this heading seem quite obvious since they all result in some kind of *product,* which can be empirically studied by the students or the teacher.

*To compose or to create* involves not only the making of original musical or sound compositions, but also the creation of other nonmusical products that overtly display certain covert mental processes. Examples of the latter might be graphic designs created by students to show their understanding or interpretation of a given musical form (cognitive behavior) or their feelings about a given mood (affective behavior). Remember that improvisation, as part of the psychomotor category of behavior, is also a form of direct creation (that is, composition in a looser sense).

Original composition, however, usually embodies many if not at times all the variables in the cognitive and affective categories of covert behavior. This is its great value to the music teacher. The assumption, though not always an accurate one, is that if the student understands (in terms of all the cognitive variables), then he can put these cognitions and affections to work in creating something. There is also the added notion that we tend to

221

remember what we use, and tend to use what we remember. This in itself seems adequate justification for including much original creation in the music class.

It is not maintained that such creative efforts *necessarily* develop, sustain, or improve creativity or originality, though this may be a frequent and desirable by-product. Even for those who find creative expression in other areas (for instance, dance, visual arts, or creative problem solving in any area such as automotive mechanics), creation in music class provides them with a product identifiable as "theirs" and provides the teacher with great insight into the nature of their covert mental behaviors regarding music. Therefore, creation is viewed more as a *means* of instruction rather than as the *goal* of instruction.

*To arrange or rearrange* involves the manipulation of either given or freely derived elements into new configurations. Though choral or instrumental arrangements fit these conditions, they are most likely undertaken in theory classes. There are other kinds of arranging or rearranging available for less specific situations. Students can arrange a series of recordings or songs into a kind of suite or song cycle on the basis of predetermined criteria. The product would then indicate something about their understanding of the criteria. If, for example, they were to combine compositions on the basis of key, the successful completion of the activity would indicate far more about their knowledge of key and tonality than would a test on key signatures. Another kind of arrangement might result from the creation of artificial part forms by combining and performing extant and familiar compositions in various sequences. Arranging things in a hierarchy of some sort would also qualify, as when students are asked to rank forms according to numbers of typical sections.

*To organize* diverse or related elements or factors into something new is a process of synthesis. It conveys a much more unified product than does a mere arrangement of factors into rankings or artificial forms. Such organization into something new might involve the organization of two melodic phrases into a coherent melody, with appropriate changes made at cadence points. Thus, organization is a form of creation or composition where most if not all the elements or criteria are *predetermined* rather than, as in composing or creating, left to the free designs of the individual. *Organizing* a spoken fugue of sentences or sentence fragments given in advance is an example of such an activity. *Creating* a fugue form of sounds discovered in the room would be an example of the freer kind of creation.

Both can result in a variety of successful musical products, yet each has its own strengths as a learning activity. Organization gives the teacher considerable control and guidance over the progress of the activity. If all the prior experiences with fugue forms and fugal processes do not result in a successful "sound" fugue, then the teacher can judge the success of the teaching and the kind of progress being made by the class. On the other hand, activities dealing with organization can provide the prior means of developing an understanding of fugue forms and processes, or could be used "remedially" for those still unable to create freely.

*To notate* entails several diverse factors; among them the operation of the "inner ear" and the ability to render such aural images into some form of graphic representation. It should not be construed as the ability to take harmonic or rhythmic dictation using traditional notation. Depending on the kind of music class, this might be a part of the class activities. But notation can also be undertaken by less expert groups, who could invent their own notation to graphically convey the aural images they have. Melodic direction and relative size of intervals can be notated almost neumatically with invented symbols. Thus, a student might draw the following as he listens to or sings "Twinkle Twinkle Little Star":

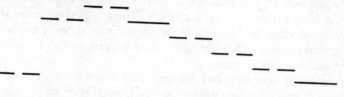

The following line diagram might designate the shape of the melody "Michael Row the Boat Ashore":

In all such instances, the student provides a graphic representation of his mental image, and in so doing provides the teacher with an overt manifestation of his covert mental activities. Students can also invent their own notations to organize or compose sound compositions. Many of their notation systems bear a striking resemblance to those invented by *avant-garde* composers. In encountering the problems of notation from this perspective, students can be led to an understanding of the purposes and functions of *any* notation system, and thus to a greater awareness of the musical elements controlled by notation.

In performance classes, a student who has learned a song of his own choosing by ear can be asked to notate it on staff paper. This provides a kind of reverse melodic dictation, which should, in any case, precede melodic dictation of an unknown melody heard only a few times. If the student cannot notate a melody he already knows (that is, a melody that he has an accurate mental image of), then he cannot notate a melody he does not know and hears played only a few times. All forms of ear training can be undertaken in this manner. In each case the teacher is able to observe some of the operations of the minds of the students.

Thus, *the act of making* serves a very important role in the teacher's plans. By having youngsters use what they are learning to make a product, the teacher is provided with many indications of learning, as are the students themselves. Keep in mind, though, that the product that is made, the outward behavior, is not really important as a creative end in itself. It will be so mainly for a few talented students, but with most other students it is important as a means for guiding and evaluating the learning that occurs at the covert level.

### Performing: playing; singing; conducting; moving to music

The third and last type of overt terminal behavior comes under the heading *to perform*. A performance is an overt act of some kind with respect to a musical stimulus or musical materials. Thus, a performance includes not only the quite obvious and common *playing* or *singing* of a musical composition in a group or as a solo, but also other overt musical behaviors such as *conducting* and *moving to music*.

Playing an instrument and singing also have uses in addition to the performance of musical compositions as such. *Singing* is used in sight singing to demonstrate the operations of the "inner ear." It may also be used in situations where students improvise harmony parts by ear or sing chord progressions as arpeggios (for instance, singing I–IV–V–I in C major as c–e–g–e–c; f–a–c–a–f; g–b–d–b–g; c–e–g–e–c; and so on). In either case, singing is an overt performance that manifests the variables of cognition and the functioning of the inner ear. *Playing* can be used in the same ways. For example, the student is asked to play back a passage played by the teacher; to "answer" a passage played by the teacher; to improvise a harmony part by ear; or to play chord progressions as arpeggios. The music lesson, too, is a performance; one that indicates the nature of the practicing carried out during the week, and whether or not the psychomotor, affective, or cognitive variables at hand are being learned.

*Conducting* has many applications as a performance. Through conducting, the student demonstrates certain cognitions regarding rhythm and meter and the ability to decode notation, to transpose, and to follow a multiple part score. Certain affective variables related to interpretation can also be made evident.

*Moving to music* includes not only the freely interpretive movements of young children, but also rhythmic responses such as tapping, clapping, or beating a rhythm or meter. Although it uses words as its vehicle and entails little actual movement, reciting metric and rhythmic chants also serves a similar performance function. (For instance: 2/4 *base*-ball; 3/4 *bas*-ket-ball; 4/4 *foot*-ball *play*-er; 5/4 *ten*-nis *tour*-na-ment, or *tour*-na-ment *play*-er; 7/4 *foot*-ball and *soc*-cer *play*-er; or *Eng*-lish *foot*-ball is *soc*-cer—these can be combined into poly- and changing-meter activities).

Performance should also be used to note what kind, if any, performance the student does outside of school, or after graduation. If a music teacher finds that his students—no matter how many perfect ratings they earned at festivals—no longer continue to play, then he should recognize that a problem exists somewhere and that it is not likely to be among his students. When performance for nonvocationally oriented students is understood as a *means* employed by the teacher to observe in some empirical way the cognitions, affections, and psychomotor skills of the learner, and not solely as a self-sufficient manifestation of musical skill, then many of the problems that arise in performance classes (and that have been explained above) can be eliminated.

The possibility of operant conditioning and operant behavior is lessened greatly when performance is used as demonstration of cognitions and affections. Students who are led to confuse their enjoyment of the act of playing with their enjoyment of music in all its forms are often lost to music when the opportunities for performance after graduation do not materialize. If, instead, performance is used as a means of teaching and of apprehending the cognitive and affective variables of behavior, then many more students will be able to improve their abilities to have feeling responses. Corollary to this is the likelihood that music will become an important ingredient for them in effective living.

When performance is used as evidence of psychomotor skill development in an expressive musical context, then the proper development of the student as an independent musician can take place. Here, the teacher uses the variables of psychomotor development as indexes of true skilled learning, not of rote learning, imitative learning, or apparent accomplishments that result only from excessive practice or repetition. When the cognitive and affective variables that inherently affect psychomotor development are likewise applied, the teacher is much more likely to encourage the kind of musical independence that causes youngsters to continue playing throughout life as an avocation, even if they have to create their own groups.

The choral director is in perhaps the most unenviable position to accomplish these goals, for most schools do not afford the choral teacher the luxury of private or group voice lessons. Therefore, vocal development as a psychomotor skill, and the attendant cognitive and affective variables, have to be worked into the choral class. Among other things, this means fewer performances so that time can be devoted to developing these abilities. It means, above all, that the teacher must conceive of ways to encourage overt group responses that manifest individual understandings of the skills or learnings at hand. Activities such as following a once-through performance with a project where each individual identifies in writing the faults of his section or part of the chorus serves these purposes well and without using an undue amount of time. Student conductors, many small vocal ensembles (trios and quartets, for instance) extracted from the larger group on an *evolving*, not a selective basis, listening assignments—these are all useful means of approaching this problem in the choral class.

*GO TO FRAME 5, PAGE 232.*

**SUMMARY**

So far you have learned that there are three categories of musical behavior, each of which is initially *covert:*

### Cognitive Variables

1. to perceive
2. to comprehend
3. to analyze
4. to identify
5. to differentiate or match
6. to compare or contrast
7. to synthesize
8. to apply abstractly
9. to evaluate or judge
10. to elaborate
11. to decide concepts
12. to identify with in terms of

### Affective Variables

1. to respond intuitively
2. to interpret freely
3. to prefer
4. to enjoy
5. to characterize in terms of feeling
6. to create or organize subjectively
7. to choose on the basis of feel

### Psychomotor Variables

1. to attend to cues
2. to imitate and repeat
3. to monitor oneself
4. to follow instructions
5. to fixate through practice
6. to refine
7. to co-ordinate series of cues and acts
8. to acquire speed
9. to lessen time
10. to perfect
11. to hear inwardly

You also learned that there are three kinds of overt behavior that render these covert behaviors observable to the students and the teacher:

*Overt Verbal Behavior*

1. to speak
2. to write

*Overt Making Behavior*

1. to compose or create
2. to arrange or rearrange
3. to organize into something new
4. to notate

*Overt Performance Behavior*

1. to play
2. to sing
3. to conduct
4. to move to music

Any of the various overt behaviors may be used individually or in combination with others to make the covert behaviors observable to the teacher and class. The teacher's job is to select the overt behaviors that seem best suited to the covert musical behaviors at hand, and to devise an activity or project where it is anticipated that the overt behaviors will reflect in some way the covert operations of each student's mind.

Remember, however, that beginners of any age have difficulty in directing their attention to more than one thing at a time. Therefore, your task is also to restrict the number of covert variables, according to the abilities and readiness of the class. This usually means that only one variable will be emphasized. Even though this might seem artificial, it is necessary in order for the teacher to be able to assess the results of the activity. If more than one variable is stressed, and the behavior is not as anticipated, it is difficult to tell which variable might have been at fault. So, starting with one variable and adding others later as competencies become known is a conservative but solid approach.

With older students who have the requisite readiness, more variables *may* be brought into operation. This can be done by specifying a variable such as "to analyze" which may depend for its realization on other variables—in this instance, such variables as "to perceive," "to identify," and "to differentiate," the major factors in analysis. By asking a student in a theory class, for example, to analyze something, you are testing many facets of his musical cognition. Therefore, if success is not total you must be prepared to diagnose or help the student diagnose which of the variables involved needs further attention. A student cannot analyze chord structure if he cannot yet perceive chords when they are not spelled vertically, if he cannot identify the chords he does perceive, or if he cannot differentiate between different inversions of chords.

For these reasons, even with advanced students it is best to proceed in a systematic way. In the example above doing so would involve experiences in identification, perception, and differentiation of chords and chord structures *before* the student is asked to make a harmonic analysis of a composition. Thus, even with advanced students it is wise to at least emphasize a given variable or two at a time. In this manner, the resulting overt behavior will clearly indicate the source of the difficulty or success. When too many variables are present, there are too many sources for error, and the behavior does not always clearly indicate which is at fault. Thus no new learning has occurred, nor has the difficulty been determined; and hence, planning for the future is difficult.

Most of the categories or covert behavior that we have covered are, of course, not unique to music. Nor, for that matter, are the corresponding types of overt behaviors unique to music. Some behaviors, such as the operation of the "inner ear" may be more highly developed in musicians, but even nonmusicians have tunes running through their minds from time to time. What is important about the foregoing exposition of behaviors is the manner in which they are applied to and derived from musical situations. So specified, they help to delineate musical behaviors, which, after all, are the major goals of teaching music. Different areas of musical instruction may emphasize certain kinds of behaviors: for instance, performance teachers are obliged to emphasize the psychomotor variables and the overt performance behaviors. But no area is exempt from due consideration of all these various kinds of musical behaviors. All musical roles—whether that of listener, performer, or composer—involve some synthesis of all musical behaviors.

The reason such strong emphasis has been put on musical behaviors is twofold. First, it tends to point up the importance of regarding musical behavior as a special, indeed unique kind of behavior. Truly understood, then, the ability to perform must also be co-ordinated with certain musical cognitions and affections. Otherwise, a true musical behavior will not result. How often it is said, "He played technically well, but unmusically." Implicit in such statements is the view that certain feelings and certain musical cognitions are necessary to a truly *musical* performance. The importance of wedding cognition and affection also holds for listening, where a purely emotive response—one without the slightest amount of conceptual bases or cognitive support—is suspect, and often for good reason. Similarly, the composer must have mastered certain aspects of the craft of composition. Assertions that the composer's feelings and personal expression are beyond criticism carry very little weight with musicians who realize, as Langer has, that such criteria might make the wailing of an infant the highest example of art.

The second reason for such a strong emphasis on musical behaviors is to encourage the teacher to think in terms of the students mastering musical behaviors. In the past, lesson planning has emphasized what the teacher did or was to do. Lesson plans consisted of step-by-step notes of what the teacher was to do. Often, by far too often, the teacher fulfilled the intent of

228

the lesson as far as his own actions were concerned, but payed very little attention to the effect of such instruction on the musical behaviors of the class. If no or little learning occurred, the last place the teacher looked for causes was his own teaching. He would assume, "Well, I taught them . . . if they didn't learn it was their fault."

Emphasis on musical behaviors puts the emphasis in teaching music back where it belongs: on the efficacy of instruction in developing musical behaviors in students. A beneficial by-product of such an attitude is the inevitable need to properly consider student interests, needs, and readiness. The long-range benefits of such an attitude can result in effectively meeting the long espoused but seldom realized ambitions of most sincere teachers of music.

Young performers can be led to a true state of *musical independence* that allows them to continue playing after graduation or outside of school. If need be, such capable and interested performers will create their own performance groups either on a formal or informal basis. Young performers can also, by such instruction, become intelligent, responding listeners in situations where they are the audience. Similarly, their taste can develop beyond the confines of the performance medium most familiar to them: orchestra and band students can find choral music rewarding, and vice versa.

Perhaps most important—because of the negligible impact music education has had so far on public taste—is the larger percentage of intelligent young people who are basically unaffected in any real behavioral sense by musical instruction in public schools and colleges. In most states, these people have musical instruction in elementary and junior high or middle schools. Because of no real concern for these people as intelligent listeners and, in many instances, because of an inordinate concern for teaching performance skills to everyone (even those not suited or interested), they are often lost permanently to music. Any change in their attitude is likely to be accidental or to result from factors unrelated to music education.

A program of music education that is based on the premises of accepted learning theory and that emphasizes the development of musical behaviors can do much to eliminate this unfortunate condition. There is absolutely no reason why otherwise intelligent young people cannot be led to an intelligent and feelingful regard for the musical art. With proper emphasis on the cognitions and affections involved in listening to music, and with proper application of the three types of overt behavior designed to control and guide such learnings, these students can be significantly led to realize that music is an important factor in effective living. If music education is ever to be a potent factor in general education, if music education is ever to contribute to the development of significant feeling responses among the general populace, if music education is ever to realize a revitalized musical taste and musical life in this country, then it must begin to apply teaching techniques designed to foster musical behaviors. Such teaching techniques begin with behavioral objectives: and that is where this book ends.

To check your own cognition of the variables of cognitive behavior, match each description of covert behavior in column B with the correct variable in Column A.

| A | B |
|---|---|
| 1. ___ to analyze | a. "feels" because of knowledge |
| 2. ___ to perceive | b. chooses between alternatives |
| 3. ___ to comprehend | c. extends and develops |
| 4. ___ to decide | d. weighs values and qualities |
| 5. ___ to elaborate | e. reasons using past learning |
| 6. ___ to identify or empathize with | f. combines into new relationships |
| 7. ___ to apply abstractly | g. conceives of relationships and differences |
| 8. ___ to compare or match | h. separates from like instances |
| 9. ___ to identify | i. describes or labels |
| 10. ___ to synthesize | j. attends to subunits |
| 11. ___ to differentiate or contrast | k. apprehends, recognizes |
| 12. ___ to evaluate or judge | l. forms conceptual patterns |

Now go to Frame 7 to check your answers.

Which of the cognitive variables below would be involved in the completion of the following behavioral objective?

Given hearings of "En Bateau" and "Stars and Stripes Forever," crayons and paper, and five minutes for each selection, each student will _____ by creating a graphic design that conveys his ideas about the general musical content of each piece.

A. Synthesize each. Go to Frame 8.
B. Evaluate and judge each. Go to Frame 16.
C. Match and compare each. Go to Frame 12.
D. Empathize with musical concepts. Go to Frame 20.

Identify each of the following situations in terms of the affective variables that best fit it.

1._____ The student in question is the leader and guiding force behind his own "rock" group.

2._____ The class is asked to identify which of a group of five reproductions of great paintings seems to "fit" the mood expressed by the music.

3._____ Each student is directed to think of and write down adjectives that they think describe the rhythmic motion, the "felt time" of a composition.

4._____ Each student is asked to directly reflect the metric pulse of the music with some kind of bodily movement; everyone does this simultaneously.

5._____ Given the opportunity, a student suggests that the class study the "rock operas" *Tommy* and *Jesus Christ Superstar*.

6._____ Each student is asked to arrange as many styles of music as he can think of in their order of importance to him.

7._____ Each student is given the opportunity to choose a recording and to explain the significance it has for him to the class.

8._____ Groups of three students create an original sound composition, the only restriction being to use either the title "Change" or the title "Feelings."

Go to Frame 25, where you will find a discussion of the answers.

---

*From page 218*

In order to check your understanding of the variables of psychomotor behavior, match the variables in column A with the recommended teaching activities in column B.

A

1.____ to attend to cues
2.____ to imitate and repeat
3.____ to monitor oneself
4.____ to follow instructions
5.____ to fixate through practice
6.____ to refine
7.____ to co-ordinate cues and acts in a series
8.____ to acquire speed
9.____ to lessen time
10.____ to perfect
11.____ to hear inwardly

B

a. The teacher provides an aural model or image by playing for the student.
b. The teacher says, "That was good; but can you identify some of the mistakes you made?"
c. The teacher assigns the student to choose a tune and to learn to play it "by ear."
d. The teacher helps the student sort out the important elements of the score.

e. Each student learns key signatures by learning to construct scales "by ear" and to derive key signatures from these performed (rather than notated) scales.
f. The teacher chooses materials to help develop fine muscle control.
g. The teacher directs the student's attention to the minimum major guidelines for creating a sound on the horn.
h. The teacher previews the next lesson with the student, and recommends means for practicing it during the week.
i. The teacher implements some sight reading in each lesson.
j. The teacher diagnostically aids the student to develop large patterns and effective, consistent sequences of performance behavior.
k. The teacher creates opportunities for the student to learn how expressive markings are interpreted.
l. The teacher initiates more advanced techniques for the student who has reached the limits of his present technical abilities.

Go to Frame 17 for a discussion of the answers.

---

From page 225

In order to review your understanding of these important points, fill in the blanks in each of the questions below by selecting one of the three alternatives that follow. Complete each question before attempting the next one.

1. The student will demonstrate his _____ by being able to blow and sustain a pitch on his trumpet.
   a. ability to attend to cues. Go to Frame 9.
   b. free interpretation. Go to Frame 15.
   c. elimination of mediating responses. Go to Frame 21.

2. The student will, given three varying graphic designs, _____ the one that he *feels* best represents the melodic form of the composition played, and will explain his choice to the class.
   a. decide on. Go to Frame 19.
   b. choose. Go to Frame 10.
   c. evaluate. Go to Frame 23.

3. Given their own choice of form and media, each group of three students will _____ a sound composition to be entitled "Night."
   a. organize. Go to Frame 18.
   b. arrange. Go to Frame 14.
   c. create. Go to Frame 27.

4. The student will display his ability to elaborate by _____ a phrase played by the teacher.
   a. imitating. Go to Frame 22.
   b. judging or evaluating. Go to Frame 13.
   c. improvising on. Go to Frame 26.

Your ability to recall and comprehend each variable or type of behavior and relate it to the proper category is an essential ingredient in making useful behavioral objectives. Therefore, test your own cognition by identifying each factor in the list below as:

| *Covert Behaviors* | *Overt Behaviors* |
|---|---|
| CV = cognitive variables | OV = overt verbal behavior |
| AV = affective variables | OM = overt making behavior |
| PV = psychomotor variables | OP = overt performing behavior |

1.____to arrange
2.____to discuss
3.____to elaborate
4.____to prefer
5.____to imitate or repeat
6.____to play
7.____to describe
8.____to notate
9.____to organize into
10.____to perceive
11.____to attend to cues
12.____to hear inwardly
13.____to create subjectively
14.____to synthesize
15.____to characterize by feeling
16.____to fixate by practice
17.____to evaluate
18.____to apply abstractly
19.____to compare
20.____to enjoy
21.____to interpret freely
22.____to monitor oneself

23.____to refine
24.____to compose
25.____to respond intuitively
26.____to sing
27.____to comprehend
28.____to decide
29.____to choose by feel
30.____to follow instructions
31.____to lessen time
32.____to analyze
33.____to select adjectives
34.____to identify
35.____to co-ordinate acts and cues into series
36.____to differentiate
37.____to perfect
38.____to conduct
39.____to acquire speed
40.____to identify with in terms of concepts
41.____to move to music
42.____to explain

Go to Frame 11 and check your answers.

---

1.  j  *Analysis* involves attention to individual subunits.
2.  k  *Perception* recognizes or apprehends phenomena.
3.  l  *Comprehension* indicates the presence of useful concepts.
4.  b  *Deciding* involves choosing between alternatives.
5.  c  *Elaborating* extends or develops given factors.

6. a  *Identification or empathy with* involves "feeling" in terms of past learning.
7. e  *Applying abstractly* uses reasoning based on past learning.
8. g  *Comparing or matching* takes into account similarities.
9. i  *Identifying* describes or labels phenomena.
10. f  *Synthesizing* combines elements into new relationships.
11. h  *Differentiating or contrasting* separates musical examples by emphasizing their differences (compare number 8 above).
12. d  *Evaluating or judging* weighs values and qualities.

If you are not satisfied with your performance on this exercise, or do not know why you missed the ones you did, review pages 207–208 and test yourself again. Then go to Frame 2.

---

*From Frame 2*

You said that each student would "synthesize each" of the compositions. Remember, these behaviors should be regarded as covert. You may have confused the aspect of this activity that calls upon the student to have impressions of the pieces (covert) and reflect them as a graphic representation (overt).

The purpose of this kind of activity is to encourage the student to focus aural attention on the handling of musical elements, and to reflect his impression in an overt way. In this case, the request for a graphic representation seeks to externalize the student's mental images. If a student is not entirely successful in completing the activity, this does not necessarily mean his impressions are faulty. It may mean that he is not very successful in capturing them in this particular overt form. Since graphic arts is not a musical skill or behavior, the student is not to be faulted. In this instance the graphic aspect was only a means, not an end. Subsequent activities along these same general lines, but requiring other kinds of overt manifestation, will surely allow the student some opportunity for fruitful conveyance of his impressions. Thus, the teacher must not regard such lessons as these as once-and-for-all matters. The more frequent and varied they are, the more some students will be able to successfully complete them, and the more others will be able to define or extend earlier successes.

Thus, there is a much more important musical behavior involved in this objective, so turn back to Frame 2 and make another choice.

---

*From Frame 5*

You said that the variable being demonstrated was that of *attending to cues*. Good; this is correct. When the teacher tells the student how to "buzz" in the mouthpiece, and he does, and then tells him how to hold the horn, and he does, the next step entails attending to these cues simultaneously: the kinesthetic "feel" of the embouchure and holding the horn, and the requisite pressure by the lips and the air column need to "buzz." These are the most important cues. If properly followed, they can lead to the musical behavior of blowing and sustaining a pitch on the trumpet. Go back to Frame 5 and answer question 2.

---

*From Frame 5*                                                    Frame 10

You said that the student would "choose" the graphic design he feels best represents the melodic form of the composition. Good; this is correct. The qualification "he feels" amounts to the affective variable "to choose on the basis of feel," and should be distinguished from "to decide" on the basis of cognition (that is, objective criteria). Thus, in this objective there is no one correct answer. But much can be observed concerning the students' learning by close attention to their verbal explanation. Thus, making the choice on the basis of feel provides the occasion for explaining (focusing attention on, or making overt) their subjective criteria in a general manner.

Go back to Frame 5 and answer question 3.

---

*From Frame 6*                                                    Frame 11

| 1.  | OM | 12. | PV | 23. | PV | 34. | CV |
|-----|----|-----|----|-----|----|-----|----|
| 2.  | OV | 13. | AV | 24. | OM | 35. | PV |
| 3.  | CV | 14. | CV | 25. | AV | 36. | CV |
| 4.  | AV | 15. | AV | 26. | OP | 37. | PV |
| 5.  | PV | 16. | PV | 27. | CV | 38. | OP |
| 6.  | OP | 17. | CV | 28. | CV | 39. | PV |
| 7.  | OV | 18. | CV | 29. | AV | 40. | CV |
| 8.  | OM | 19. | CV | 30. | PV | 41. | OP |
| 9.  | OM | 20. | AV | 31. | PV | 42. | OV |
| 10. | CV | 21. | AV | 32. | CV | Go to Frame 24. | |
| 11. | PV | 22. | PV | 33. | CV | | |

| *Covert Behaviors* | *Overt Behaviors* |
|---|---|
| CV = cognitive variables | OV = overt verbal behavior |
| AV = affective variables | OM = overt making behavior |
| PV = psychomotor variables | OP = overt performing behavior |

---

*From Frame 2*                                                    Frame 12

You said that each student would "match and compare each" composition. This mental operation is not necessary to completing the assignment as specified. Some students may make some such comparisons their way of completing the assignment, but this is not the value at hand. Actually, if only one of the two pieces were present, the activity would have much the same value. The advantage of having the two pieces is merely the increased opportunity for the class and increased evidence for the teacher. Go back to Frame 2 and try another choice.

---

*From Frame 5*                                                                          Frame 13

You said that the student would display the cognitive variable "to elaborate" by *another* cognitive variable "to judge or evaluate." Thus, no overt behavior is indicated, unless you assumed that the evaluation would necessarily be verbal. You should not make such assumptions for they often lead to confused aims. Too frequently, we do this kind of doublethink and automatically interpret covert references (choose, perceive, judge, and so forth) as overt acts. They are not. Choosing, perceiving, and judging, all occur first as covert phases of behavior. Overt manifestations *may* follow, as when you choose the kind of clothes you will wear, and then actually wear them. They also may not follow, as when you choose the kind of automobile or house you would buy *if* you had the money. Since you do not have the money, your choice may never become an overt behavioral fact. Go back to Frame 5, question 4, and make another choice.

---

*From Frame 5*                                                                          Frame 14

You said that the students would "arrange" a sound composition. No; arranging involves the ranking or reordering of given elements. In this example, the only given element is the title. Go back to Frame 5, question 3, and make another choice.

---

*From Frame 5*                                                                          Frame 15

You said that the variable being demonstrated was that of "free interpretation." That might be so if the student were allowed the opportunity to freely interpret the cues directed to his attention by the teacher. But this process of interpretation as a function of perception is quite different from interpretation in terms of feeling. "*Free* interpretation" is a variable of affective behavior and deals with the feeling response which is subjective. Neither the feeling response nor subjectivity in general is at stake here; the musical behavior is psychomotor in nature. Go back to Frame 5 and make a less problematic choice for question 1.

---

*From Frame 2*                                                                          Frame 16

You said that the student would "evaluate and judge each" composition. This variable usually involves value judgments: judgments of quality. Such is not really present in this behavioral objective. If this activity were followed by an activity in which the students discussed the "appropriateness" of one another's drawings, or the value or quality of the compositions they heard, then the factors of evaluation and judgment would be strongly present. Go back to Frame 2 and make another choice.

---

*From Frame 4*

Compare your choices in Frame 4 to these answers.

1. d, g   *To attend to cues.* The teacher helps the student perceive, and consequently learn, the most important cues in the score and in the creation of sound.

2. a   *To imitate and repeat.* When the teacher provides an aural model, he provides the opportunity for the student to imitate it and to repeat it. The model also provides a tonal goal that the student can seek.

3. b   *To monitor oneself.* When the teacher asks the student to identify or correct his own mistakes, he puts the student in the position of having to monitor his own performance. The more the teacher corrects mistakes for the student, the more unlikely it is that the student will develop requisite ability and musical independence.

4. k   *To follow instructions.* When the teacher aids the student in learning to interpret expressive markings, he is providing an opportunity for the student to learn to follow instructions (and the means to do so).

5. h   *To fixate through practice.* When a teacher previews a lesson with a student and recommends the means of practicing it during the upcoming week, he provides a much better chance for the student to fixate the desired responses through practice. The student is less likely to practice incorrectly and fixate incorrect responses that will have to be "unlearned."

6. l   *To refine.* When a teacher introduces the student to more advanced techniques, he enables refinement to occur. He may also allow the student to progress from the apparent stasis of a plateau.

7. j   *To co-ordinate cues and acts in series.* When a teacher aids the student to develop large patterns or effective and consistent sequences of performance behavior by his diagnostic help or by his selection of learning tasks, he provides the necessary experience for increased co-ordination of cues and acts.

8. f, j   *To acquire speed.* Speed is acquired both when cues and acts are co-ordinated in ever-longer sequences and when, as a necessary corollary, fine muscle control is developed.

9. i   *To lessen time.* Sight reading, done frequently, can provide the experience necessary to eliminate much of the time used in practice to master notation. Actually, though, the time factor is affected by almost all the psychomotor variables, particularly those related to the development of the "inner ear"—examples (c) and (e).

10. j     *To perfect.* The longer and more interrelated the patterns of performance behavior (cues and acts), the more expert the performance. Here too, the act of perfecting is to some degree dependent on whether or not all the other variables become spontaneous and naturalized in the act of performing.

11. c, e     *To hear inwardly.* Any practice in which the student is encouraged to play without notation can develop the ability to hear inwardly, the so-called "inner ear." This in turn aids significantly in the development and mastery of the other ten psychomotor variables. It is perhaps this well-developed and easily applied quality that most distinguishes a musician. It is not to be confused with "absolute" or "relative" pitch, however. Sometimes these help the operation of the inner ear; sometimes they hinder it: for instance, a person with perfect pitch is unduly bothered by slightly out-of-tune sounds.

Go to page 218, below the line.

---

*From Frame 5*        Frame 18

You said that the students would "organize" a sound composition. This is not correct. As indicated earlier, to organize involves considerable teacher control and thereby entails a corresponding limitation for each group. To organize usually means to synthesize given factors or qualities into a new entity. The only factor given in the example was the title. Everything else was left up to each group of students. Go back to Frame 5, question 3, and answer it again.

---

*From Frame 5*        Frame 19

You said the student would "decide on" the graphic design he feels best represents the melodic form of the composition. It may seem to be a semantic nit-pick, but it is useful to distinguish between decisions made according to objective criteria and choice made according to personal feelings. This objective clearly emphasizes that the response will be in terms of what the student feels, and thus has no objective criteria. Much will be learned, however, about the student's feelings and personal criteria by listening carefully to their explanations.

Go back to Frame 5, question 2, and try to find a more precise answer.

---

*From Frame 2*        Frame 20

You said that each student would "empathize with musical concepts." This is correct, as long as you understand that such mental operations as these must be done in terms of the concepts being learned. Thus, an objective such as this implies prior experience with either this kind of behavior, this kind of musical content, the elements that this music displays, or subsequent learnings that are to follow this initial activity.

Therefore, the behavioral objective should have clearly specified the covert behavior that was desired in the activity, as follows:

"Given . . . each student will *demonstrate his ability to empathize with musical concepts by . . .*"

Go to page 210, below the line.

---

*From Frame 5*                                                                                   Frame 21

You said that the variable being demonstrated was that of "eliminating mediating responses." You are confused. It is evident that the objective refers to a rank beginner and you should appreciate the fact that rank beginners invariably employ mediating responses and any other kinds of cues or stimuli they can find to help perform their tasks. Elimination of mediating responses occurs much further down the road to refinement and perfection. Go back to Frame 5 and make another choice for question 1.

---

*From Frame 5*                                                                                   Frame 22

You said that the student would display the cognitive variable "to elaborate" by imitating the aural example of the teacher. That is a contradiction in terms, which you should have noticed. Elaboration entails going on, extending, working out, not repeating something in the same manner. Such repetition would not manifest the ability to elaborate on musical ideas. Go back to Frame 5, question 4, and try another choice.

---

*From Frame 5*                                                                                   Frame 23

You said that the student would "evaluate" the graphic design he feels best represents the melodic form of the composition. In a loose sense of the term "to evaluate" you might be excused for making this response. As used here "evaluate" is a cognitive behavior and thus tied to objective criteria. This objective involves personal or subjective bases since it is predicated on which example the student "feels" is most appropriate. It is useful for the teacher to distinguish occasions using subjective criteria from those emphasizing objective criteria.

Go back to Frame 5, question 2, and answer the question again.

Now check and see how many variables or types of behavior you can recall from each category of covert and overt behavior. Number them consecutively under the appropriate column heading below. Then go back to page 226 to check your answers. If you fail to remember a considerable number, or, especially, if you put the variables under the wrong headings, you must review this material before you go on. The next chapter is predicated on your understanding and recall of this material.

When you are finished and satisfied with your results, go to page 226, below the line.

*Covert Cognitive Variables*                    *Covert Affective Variables*

*Covert Psychomotor Variables*

*Overt Verbal Behavior*                         *Overt Making Behavior*

*Overt Performing Behavior*

1. The student who started and now leads the rock group is manifesting *preference,* the act of liking or disliking according to subjective values. If the teacher is aware of this student's affective preferences, it would be wise for him to make use of them in the classroom. For example, this student could teach guitar chords to the others. His group could perform an original composition for class discussion. The teacher should assist this student to competently pursue his preference by showing the relevance of other musical learnings to his preferred music.

2. The class asked to identify the reproductions that seem to "fit" the mood of the music are exhibiting the variable of *choosing on the basis of feel.* They may or may not be able to discursively explain their choices, yet the teacher can often determine the nature of a student's "feeling response" by the kinds of choices he makes. By presenting such alternatives for students to choose on the basis of feel, a teacher encourages "feeling responses."

3. The class directed to think of and write down adjectives that they think describe the "felt time" of a composition will *characterize in terms of their own feeling.* Again, they may not be able to discursively substantiate their selections, but the nature of these selections can help the teacher better understand the kind of feelings or attitudes they hold. For example, some adolescents will characterize music without a strong metric pulse or rhythm as "weak," or "monotonous," and the like, and will prefer music with an emphatic rhythm. These characterizations can help the teacher plan future experiences by allowing for a better balance between what the class already responds to and experiences designed to lead to a better "feeling" about other kinds of music. Similarly, students learn about the diversity of characterization that is likely in any one group. They also learn that some of their peers, whom they respect, are not inclined to characterize the same kind of music in the same terms. This proves to be healthy.

4. Each student who directly reflects the metric pulse of the music with some kind of bodily movement will be *responding intuitively.* It would be important to carry out this activity at the piano or some other music source under the teacher's control, so that the meters and tempi could be varied rapidly and frequently, thereby preventing any conscious direction of their responses by the students. Having the class react simultaneously or with closed eyes will help eliminate imitation by unsure students.

5. The student who, when given the opportunity, suggests an area of study exemplifies *preference.* Though this is not a rule of thumb that invariably works, the preferences of one member of a peer group will frequently reflect, or determine, those of the remainder. If the suggestion had been *Lohengrin,* the teacher would have reason to be suspicious, but would nonetheless know the preference felt by the student who made the suggestion.

6. Students who arrange as many styles as they can think of according to their own judgment of importance manifest *subjective creation or organization.* Not only does such an activity allow for the operation of judgment, and especially "feeling," it is also likely to produce both a catalogue of the stu-

dent's knowledge of musical styles and his concept of style itself. Thus, the teacher can utilize subjective "feeling responses" in order to plan cognitive activities.

7. When each student is given the opportunity to choose a recording and to explain the significance it has for him to the class, each would be implementing two variables: *choosing on the basis of "feel"* and *free interpretation.* "Free interpretation" and "characterizing according to feelings" have significant differences. The former involves freely imaginative *mood responses,* such as associating colors with music, or moving to music in a way that reflects a student's feeling for the mood of the music. The latter involves students using their own non-technical vocabularies *to describe* a music composition as it affects them. "I think of bright red and yellow, like the sun at noon, when I hear this music" is free interpretation. "The brass section conveys a brightness and intensity that complements the soaring strings" is characterizing according to feelings.

8. When groups of students create original sound compositions in a situation where no restrictions other than titles are given, they would likely manifest *every variable* to some degree. They would choose the title, create or organize according to collective subjectivity, deal with the qualities suggested by the title according to their feelings about it, interpret freely the musical rendering of the title, react intuitively to many aspects in the situation, find meaning (of a musical sort) in their manipulation of the sound media, and even derive pleasure from the activity or the product. Even though specific concepts are involved in significant ways, the act of creation invariably deals with all of these affective variables. That is why it is an important tool in the public school music classroom: it uses specific prior learnings (cognitions) in enhancing the affective response.

Here, as with the cognitive variables, there is often a complex interaction between the variables. Here, as before, the teacher should *emphasize one variable,* even when others may be involved, in order to provide the necessary focus. In this way the teacher can systematically expand awareness without unduly shaping values. When the teacher attempts to shape values, social conformity rather than effective living inevitably results.

Go to page 213, below the line.

---

*From Frame 5*                                                                 Frame 26

You said that the student would display elaboration by "improvising on" the phrase played by the teacher. This is correct. It involves several variables from different categories. "Elaboration" is a cognitive variable. "Improvisation" is a type of performance behavior that involves the ability "to hear inwardly," which is a psychomotor variable. It also involves "performance," one of the types of overt behavior. Certain other cognitive behaviors may be involved, such as differentiation (of his answer from the teacher's statement) or synthesis (combining motifs from the statement).

Imitating is a bad answer since imitation—as used here—involves repetition of a behavior. This contradicts the intent of the objective, which was to elaborate a given musical idea.

Judging or evaluating is also a problematic answer because these do not always have overt phases. Thus, the way the objective involved read, the student's response could be purely covert (for instance, "That was good rhythmic development he used" may run through his mind) or overt in verbal form ("Those were really good rhythms you played," said aloud). The elaboration is intended to be a *musical behavior* (that is, playing) not a *verbal behavior* (talking at length about it). Go to Frame 6.

---

*From Frame 5*

You said that the student groups will "create" a composition. This is correct. They will create it since all the decisions except the title have been left to their free choice. This kind of freedom eliminates the other two choices (arranging and organizing), both of which entail a considerable amount of "given" factors. Creation is also likely to involve the operation of more cognitive and affective variables than are the other two choices, and it is most suitable as some kind of concluding activity. The other two choices are more valuable as activities that lead to concluding activities, for they help form the conceptual bases that make free creation possible. If the students have had experience in arranging and organizing only simple part forms, then when the teacher leaves the factor of form up to the class, their decision and implementation of a form will demonstrate their cognition in two ways: (1) they are likely to select the form they feel most comfortable with (if no one chooses a rondo form, the teacher should wonder if the class really understands it, and perhaps specify a rondo for the next composition to see whether or not they can handle such a form); and (2) their fulfillment of the activity is also likely to demonstrate how well they fit the form to the title. Go on to question 4 in Frame 5.

CHAPTER SEVEN

# the design of
# behavioral objectives
# for music learning

*Once an instructor or programmer decides he will
teach his students something, several kinds of activity
are necessary on his part if he is to succeed. He must
first decide upon the goals he intends to reach at the
end of his course or program. He must then select
procedures, content, and methods which are relevant
to the objectives, cause the student to interact with
appropriate subject matter in accordance with principles of learning, and finally measure or evaluate the
student's performance according to the objectives or
goals originally selected.*

*Robert F. Mager,* Preparing Instructional Objectives
*(Palo Alto, Calif.: Fearon Pub., 1962), p. 1.*

The design and use of behavioral objectives by the music teacher cannot be undertaken without considering and understanding learning theory as it applies to music instruction. Your aesthetic point of view regarding the worth of music and music instruction is also important. Unfortunately, it is quite possible to design and use behavioral objectives that are correct in form but serve poor educational objectives and aesthetic principles.

Given a list of twenty musical forms and fifteen minutes, the student will identify the definitions, descriptions, and diagrams of each by completing a test with ninety-five percent accuracy.

The form of this objective is acceptable: it meets the major provisions necessary to state instructional objectives in behavioral terms. Its problems stem from evident weaknesses in terms of learning theory and aesthetic principles. The memorization necessary to complete this task will result in poor learning because much information is quickly forgotten within a very short time. Such information is forgotten less quickly only when acquired through memorization. Using definitions, descriptions, and diagrams as musical learnings ignores the importance or existence of "felt life," the feeling response, and the nature of true musical behavior. That these are not ascendent in the mind of the teacher is indicated by the feature of a test and the unrealistic figure of ninety-five percent accuracy. In this objective, information about music has taken precedence over encouraging and cultivating musical behaviors and relevant "feeling responses" to music by involving the students with a musical stimulus of some kind.

One other caution should be mentioned before undertaking an analysis of the design of behavioral objectives. An objective that is well conceived in terms of learning theory and aesthetic considerations might still be poorly implemented by a given teacher. This is likely to happen when the teacher does not truly understand the implications of the learnings at hand or is just plain inefficient in implementing the activity. In the former instance, the teacher may become too involved in the activity and its progress: he may dictate responses, cheat the real aims of independent action by giving unnecessary help, and the like. In the latter instance, confusion and disorganization reign supreme.

With these cautions in mind, you should continually be aware that behavioral objectives in and by themselves are not the cure-all to the problems of music education. They are a means, and as such are not ends. As means they must be conceived and applied with significant musical ends firmly in mind. Even then, some may not work as anticipated; but their emphasis on overtly observable behavior clearly advises the teacher of such failures and gives the kind of evidence needed to overcome the difficulties at hand.

Unlike some of the recent "panaceas" in music education, whose proponents claim miracle-working effectiveness, the use of behavioral objectives still requires a good teacher. But a good teacher can become even more effective by applying behavioral objectives to learning situations in music. Such teachers will find that, to a large degree, this approach systematizes and gives them better control over what they have been doing, whether they have operated intuitively or "by the seat of their pants."

You should also remember at all times that behavioral objectives have as their most general purpose the function of making covert mental operations overt in terms of physical or verbal behavior. Such overt behavior is not a comprehensive indication of all learing, nor should it be regarded qualitatively. It is sought merely in order to observe, order, and emphasize certain mental operations, rather than assuming that they are unreachable and untouchable. Behavior in these terms provides the empirical data necessary to the systematic and relevant structuring of learning experiences in music.

Music teachers should also avoid regarding the need for encouraging overt behavior as the need for continual musical performance. This applies in both general music and performance classes. In general music classes, performance of music is only one kind of behavior that can be used. This is especially evident if you consider that most people are involved in music as listeners rather than performers. In performance classes, similarly, there is no good reason to assume that all activities must have performance as their means or end. There are many other instances where groups can be asked to decide, analyze, identify, or compare musical phenomena. Many such activities may then be applied to performance situations, but they also have considerable value in their own right because they help the performance student become more capable and also more aware of music as a listening experience. The incontrovertible fact is that most performing musicians in public schools will not have the opportunity to continue playing after graduation or as adults. But the attitudes and capacities that made them effective group members can be turned to fruitful ends if factors relating to feeling responses form a regular part of instruction in performance classes. With these preliminaries in mind you can now begin this final study.

## ELEMENTS OF AN OBJECTIVE

Behavioral objectives in music may be phrased in several ways. More or less information may be included depending on the nature of the covert behavior and the resulting overt behavior. But well-written behavioral objectives contain several basic elements.

1. *What* materials, media, and other limitations or guidelines *will be given?* This condition is applied only where appropriate; that is, only in situations where the teacher wishes to specify certain factors. It is usually indicated by the word "given" or by similar words such as

"using" or "employing." When nothing is to be specified in advance, no "given" factor is included; and if the teacher wishes to emphasize strongly that the activity has no prescribed factors or aids, the expression "without" may be included (for instance, "without referring to the text").

2. *Who will be affected* by the instruction? You should specify whether it is to be each individual student, small groups (specify the number of participants), large groups, or sections within large groups (for example, altos, sopranos, and so forth). Among other things, due consideration of who will be affected should help clarify the orientation of the learning.

3. *Covert behavior.* This segment identifies, from among the three categories of covert behavior, the specific variable that will be employed or observed. By providing for this element, the teacher avoids operant conditioning or operant behavior, and affirms that certain mental operations are anticipated. *This is really the major aim in a behavioral objective* since, as you have seen, not all covert learning reaches the level of overt behavior, nor does all overt behavior indicate the exact nature or degree of covert learning. Thus, even in instances where the overt behavior neither accurately reflects nor provides a basis for judging the covert responses, the provision of covert behavior guides the teacher in making plans to arouse such inner responses.

4. *Content.* What knowledge, skill, or feeling response will the covert and overt behavior deal with? Knowledge includes information and concepts; skill involves performance abilities; feeling responses (affects) involve mood and subjective responses. Consideration of this element enables the teacher to specify the content to be learned, and ensures that the class activity does not exist solely for its own sake but, rather, for real musical learnings.

5. *Overt behavior* (the major source of EVALUATION or, if done by the student, FEEDBACK). The specific kind of overt behavior will or should result from the covert processes already specified. This element specifies the kind of overt behavior you or the student will use to evaluate covert learning.

In addition to these five elements of well-written behavioral objectives, there are two more, which may or may not be needed.

6. *Level of proficiency* (if any is to be specified). What *criteria* will be used to indicate to the teacher or student the degree of success or what is or is not acceptable? This might be specified in terms of number or percentage of correct responses, or in terms of accuracy, consistency, or speed. In typing, for example, ninety-five words per

minute as a criterion indicates both speed and accuracy. In music one might specify "accurately and *a tempo.*" It would be difficult, indeed, to specify much more what constitutes accuracy unless you want to count the notes and keep track of the percentage of accuracy. Proficiency in musical situations, as in some others, can also be included by the use of such terms as "with consistency," and "with continual improvement." *A level of proficiency is usually eliminated for responses in the affective domain.* As personal responses, they should not be subject to external criteria.

7. *Time limitation* (if any is relevant). This provision indicates how much time is necessary or allotted for the completion of the activity and the acquisition or performance of the desired response (learning). This, like the first element (what will be given) is usually indicated in the form of a "given" factor, since it is a delimitation. If no time limit is specified, it is simply left out. If the time factor is related to encouraging *long-term* development, such statements as "throughout the year" or "in all such music" may be employed. Such time limitations thus provide for transfer of learning, or recognize the role of time in assessing skilled performance.

The organization or arranging of these elements into a well-expressed behavioral objective is not necessarily dependent on the numerical sequence in which they were presented. The major requisite is that each be considered, and included if appropriate. How they are eventually arranged into an expressive verbal statement can depend more on the laws of grammar and sentence construction than on any educational theory. But there are some guidelines that can be useful for combining these elements. These will be discussed after you have come to an understanding of the separate elements.

*GO TO FRAME 1, PAGE 265.*

---

**ANALYSES OF SAMPLE OBJECTIVES**

Given two hearings of "Ballet of the Chicks in Their Shells" from *Pictures at an Exhibition,* each student will, while listening, create a graphic diagram that represents their feelings about the rhythmic character of the composition and will explain it to the class.

The above behavioral objective contains most of the seven possible elements for musical instruction. Can you determine the missing one(s)? Take a moment, inspect the example, and try to identify the missing element(s).

| | |
|---|---|
| "Given the recording "Ballet of the Chicks in Their Shells" from *Pictures at an Exhibition*" | = *what means* are employed. |
| "each student will" | = *who* will be affected. |
| "while listening" | = a time limitation. |
| "create a graphic diagram" | = the *overt behavior*, "to make." |
| "that represents their feelings about" | = the covert cognitive variable, "to empathize with on the basis of concepts"; or the covert affective variable, "to characterize subjectively." |
| "the rhythmic character of the composition" | = *content;* concepts of rhythmic movement and its affects (feelings). |
| "and explain it to the class" | = the overt behavior, to verbalize. |

Thus, this objective makes no specification of proficiency: no criteria are provided for judging the success or failure of the resulting products. The key here is the covert response. If the teacher is interested in the covert *cognitive* variable "to empathize with on the basis of concepts," then perhaps some criteria should have been specified that indicate that the responses should have a visual character in accordance with the rhythmic character of the piece. If, on the other hand, the teacher is interested in the covert *affective* variable "to characterize subjectively," then no criteria is appropriate. From the resulting product, the teacher will be able to observe the nature of the student's response.

In either case, the second overt behavior, the student's explanation of his drawing, will provide the teacher in many cases with increased insights into the nature of the response. In turn, each student, in listening to each explanation and in seeing each drawing, is given some basis for comparing his response with those of his classmates (multiple feedback). It is to be expected that a great diversity of responses will be observed. Here the individual can learn in a concrete way that people are able to have different responses to the same musical stimulus, yet each in his own way can find significance in his own unique responses. Similarly, he may find certain likenesses among all responses and learn that though responses may differ, they often share many common features.

Another benefit of the second overt behavior in this objective is that it functions as a kind of cross-check to provide greater accuracy in the teacher's observations. A student's diagram may seem weird to the teacher or class until it is explained. After all, this is what is required of many people when it comes to abstract art, and this is no less true for the drawings of young children, which make perfectly obvious sense to them but may require a detailed explanation for parents or teachers. Conversely, the diagram may seem self-evident while the explanation seems misguided or weak. This suggests the possibility of further experience for the class.

Here is another example. Can you determine the missing element(s)? (Examine the example closely, then read on.)

Given his choice of popular or folk song and a week of practice, the student will be able to play the song by ear in at least two different keys, with accuracy and consistency.

| | |
|---|---|
| "Given his choice of popular or folk song and a week of practice" | = the *given* factors of both guidelines and a time limitation. |
| "the student" | = *who* will be affected: the individual student. |
| "will be able to play" | = the *overt* behavior "to play." |
| "the song" | = *content:* meter, rhythm, key, and so forth. |
| "by ear" | = the *covert* psychomotor variable, "to use the inner ear" |
| "in at least two different keys with accuracy and consistency" | = the criteria of *proficiency* specifying two keys ensures that it is really the ear that is operating, and that the behavior is not the result of a slow process of trial and error plus memorization. The teacher might even try to see whether the student can play it in more keys. This would be a convincing proof of mastery. |

In this objective, all the possible elements were included: the given factor, a time limitation, a covert behavior, the content, an overt response, the criteria, and who will be affected.

## EXAMPLE OF RELATING OBJECTIVES

Here is a more complex example. Analyze it and see if you can identify the missing element(s), if any.

The student will differentiate between the relative durations and meters of $\frac{2}{4}$ ♩. ♪ and $\frac{3}{8}$ ♩ ♪ by playing these patterns and their possible variants consistently and correctly at sight in his lesson and band material throughout the year.

| | |
|---|---|
| "The student will" | = *who* will be affected. |
| "differentiate between" | = a covert cognitive variable, "to differentiate." |
| "the relative duration and meters of $\frac{2}{4}$ ♩. ♪ and $\frac{3}{8}$ ♩ ♪ " | = *content*, clearly specified. |
| "by playing" | = the *overt* behavior, "to play." |
| "these patterns and their possible variants" | = another reference to *content*, this time emphasizing the need for transfer of learning to new yet similar musical situations. |

250

| | |
|---|---|
| "consistently and correctly at sight" | = criteria of *proficiency;* includes accuracy and time parameters. |
| "in his lesson and band material" | = what materials are *given.* |
| "throughout the year" | = time allottment; this too emphasizes the need for transfer of learning before the teacher will recognize the student's proficiency with these meters and derived rhythms. |

Again, all the possible elements of behavioral objectives for musical instruction were included; and in addition, they were overlapping or interrelated. If the student does not seem to be successfully completing the objective as anticipated, the teacher will, according to the provisions of the objective, have to check whether it is the student's ability to differentiate that is the source of the difficulty, or whether it is his inability to play at sight.

Thus, the following objective would be in order as a subsequent plan.

Given two minutes to preview the score, the student will differentiate between the relative duration and meters of $\frac{2}{4}$ ♩. ♪ and $\frac{3}{8}$ ♩ ♪ by playing these patterns and their possible variants consistently and correctly in the new music given at his next lesson.

| | |
|---|---|
| "Given two minutes to preview the score" | = a *time* limitation. |
| "the student will" | = *who* will be affected. |
| "differentiate between" | = a *covert* cognitive variable, "to differentiate" (the related cognitive variable, "to analyze" is implied, now that time for preanalyzing the score has been provided). |
| "the relative durations and meters of $\frac{2}{4}$ ♩. ♪ and $\frac{3}{8}$ ♩ ♪ " | = *content,* specified clearly. |
| "by playing" | = the *overt* behavior "to play." |
| "these patterns and their possible variants" | = another reference to *content,* this time with the specification of *transfer.* |
| "consistently and correctly" | = the criteria of *proficiency.* Hearing inwardly (that is, playing at sight) has been eliminated because there is time to preview (analyze) the score. Therefore the proficiency has only one aspect; the ability to differentiate. |
| "in the new music given at his next lesson" | = the materials serving as the basis for the learning experience. |

This new objective, derived as it is from the previous one, will permit the teacher to observe whether the source of difficulty with the first objective was the ability to analyze and differentiate, or whether it was playing at sight. If the student still does not do well with this objective, then it would seem that the purely cognitive factors involved in the differentiation of the patterns and the analysis of their possible variants is the source of the difficulty. The teacher would then be advised to construct an objective that has the aim of developing these abilities in the student on the purely conceptual or cognitive level. Even a Socratic leading-question–and–answer period with the proper behavioral outcomes specified would serve well in overcoming the difficulty. Clapping or counting aloud could serve here as the overt demonstrations, thus eliminating any possibility that the technical problems of the instrument were interfering with the student's interpretations.

If the student performs well on the objective immediately above, and does so consistently with a variety of music given at the next lesson, then the source of difficulty is not likely to reside in his abilities to differentiate and analyze: it is the ability to do this while playing at sight that needs attention. Thus:

Given five seconds to look at flash cards presenting variants of $\frac{2}{4}$ ♩. ♪

and $\frac{3}{8}$ ♩ ♪ , the student will immediately differentiate between the relative durations and meters of each by playing each pattern correctly. Each subsequent lesson will shorten the amount of viewing time allotted for preview.

*GO TO FRAME 2, PAGE 265.*

---

## EXAMPLE OF A COGNITIVE OBJECTIVE FOR GENERAL MUSIC CLASSES

Now study the following behavioral objective, which deals with a general music class.

Given twenty-five minutes, each group of three students will demonstrate their comprehension of the ABA principle by creating an original "sound composition" that successfully embodies a tripartite structure of statement–departure–return, and by performing it for the class.

| | |
|---|---|
| "Given twenty-five minutes" | = a *given* time limitation. |
| "each group of three students" | = *who* will be affected. |
| "will demonstrate their comprehension of" | = the *covert* cognitive variable, "to comprehend" (have a concept of). |
| "the ABA principle" | = *content*. |
| "by creating an original 'sound composition' " | = the *overt* behavior, "to make or create" plus the "given" factor of means or material (that is, "sound," |

"that successfully embodies a tripartite structure of statement–departure–return"

"and by performing it for the class"

whether musically traditional or not).

= the criteria of *proficiency*.

= another *overt* behavior, "to play." This can serve two functions. It shows whether what visually looks like an ABA form in score really sounds like one in practice. It can also serve as a springboard for discussion and analysis (aural), which can give the teacher further insights into class ideas.

Note that in this objective, "creating" is done in terms of concepts (cognition, comprehension) rather than as the covert affective variable of creating subjectively. These is no doubt that many subjective factors will enter into the creation of this work, but the teacher has clearly specified that this creation is subject to certain quite specific criteria. When such criteria are present, the activity becomes one that emphasizes cognition more than feeling. However, feeling need not go totally unnoticed. The teacher would do well to undertake a discussion of the feeling content of the various student compositions, once the issue of their form has been thoroughly treated. Among other things this technique, especially when applied consistently, can help insure that cognition and affection are not thought of by the students as two entirely separate mental phenomena. This is especially valuable when discussions center around how the cognition of musical techniques or principles contributed to the expressiveness of the composition in terms of its "feeling" content.

Even with the emphasis on cognition suggested by the specification of form and its criteria, this activity is not unduly structured or delimiting. Each group has the opportunity of deciding what "sounds" they will employ—found sounds, self-generated sounds, musical pitches generated by traditional musical instruments, electrically generated or manipulated sounds, or any combination thereof—as well as the means of notating their work (original, traditional, or a synthesis of both).

Additionally, by having each group perform their work for the class, the teacher can entertain the possibility of implementing a class discussion on each work as to whether, how, or how well the ABA principle was realized in each composition. This could add an entirely new domain. It would include analysis and perception, as well as verbal behavior. Therefore, the teacher would do well to write a separate objective for this activity or to include the behavioral objective for such an activity along with the former activity. This is one of the most significant advantages to this type of teaching: by continually having a definite product or behavior as evidence of musical learning, not only is the teacher enabled to plan more intelligently for future activities, but frequently an activity (or the student's enthusiasm for it) almost demands its own sequel. Spontaneity is not lost; it is encouraged. The idea is spontaneous for the teacher; but the plans for implementing the idea, as it arises from present activities, requires controlled planning.

*GO TO FRAME 3, PAGE 266.*

---

This objective, then, includes all the possible elements of a behavioral objective for musical instruction. By so structuring the activity, the teacher has managed to *individualize* instruction in a systematic way within a group lesson. Similarly, the feedback has been individualized so that each student can learn from his own participation in the activity. This would happen only if the teacher took the time to review the composition with the group, citing reasons and explanations for locating phrasings. Even better, perhaps, would be to draw such explanations from the group by Socratic questioning. In this way the students would be reviewing or reinforcing the material in their own terms. Whether or not a teacher would decide on this latter course would depend on the amount of time available to him or the importance he attaches to such an activity.

The general approach recommended here—posing a problem for the student, deriving observable answers (behaviors or responses), then providing the feedback necessary for the student to assess his own performance—is very much the same approach taken in the programmed and self-testing portions of this text. Depending on your answer to a multiple-choice question, you were given an explanation of why your answer was appropriate or inappropriate and some further hints, where possible, to get you back on the right track. Thus, the teacher is obliged to try to provide some means for student feedback. Yet even this is in vain if the teacher does not help the individual to interpret (or reinterpret) the feedback, and, hopefully, to adapt his behavior accordingly.

## EXAMPLE OF AN AFFECTIVE OBJECTIVE FOR PERFORMANCE CLASSES

The group objective given on page 252 dealt with the covert category of cognitive behavior. Similar objectives can be devised that deal with affective behaviors. For instance:

> Given several possible ways of interpreting measures ____ to ____ of _____, and the opportunity to try each possibility, the chorus will choose the one they feel is most appropriate by majority decision.

Here the means (majority decision, trials), the materials (the piece and the passage), the content (varying interpretations), the covert behavior (to choose on the basis of subjective criteria), are provided. Because this objective deals with affective behavior, no criteria are specified. The clever teacher might choose several valid ways of interpreting the passage. He could congratulate the chorus on their decision and cite the many advantages of the other interpretations as well. Obviously, the aim or value here is not in the decision made, but in the covert mental processes that the chorus is called on to use—that is, the *means* become the *goal*.

## EXAMPLES OF SKILL OBJECTIVES FOR PERFORMANCE GROUPS

Similar objectives can be devised that help individualize psychomotor skills. For example:

Each band member will demonstrate his ability to follow the conductor by correctly adjusting his performance as the conductor artificially changes tempo, dynamics, cutoffs, and interpretation.

"Each band member" = the specification of individualization in terms of *who* will be affected. Literally everyone would have to be on his toes for this activity (especially if its application is unpredictable).

"will demonstrate his ability to follow the conductor" = the covert psychomotor variable, "to follow directions." This in turn entails the ability to comprehend the gestures of the conductor, which is a covert cognitive variable.

"by adjusting his performance" = an overt behavior, "to play" (that is, through playing, the student demonstrates his ability to adjust to the conductor's directions in conducting).

"correctly" = the *proficiency* criterion. One hundred percent is implied, but realistically, the conductor must be sure that his conducting is not partially to blame for any failure to attain this level.

"as the conductor artificially" = *given* means. The conductor will introduce conducting gestures in unusual places, in unusual ways, or with the reverse implication of what the band is used to (reversing dynamic markings, for example; *ff* becomes *pp*).

"changes tempo, dynamics, cutoffs and interpretation" = the *content*, the knowledge being dealt with covertly and which is reflected overtly in their performance of these musical elements.

Even the factor of time is considered here since this objective is eminently suitable at any time during the year, and especially at those times when the teacher feels the group needs to be reminded of the need to watch the conductor. Therefore, any specific time reference is omitted. If the teacher has planned his tricky conducting well, he will also devise ways of ensuring the accuracy of his observations, such as by making his alterations during times when only one or two sections or individuals are playing. Thus, by directing his attention to this smaller group, he can spot offenders as they linger after unexpected cutoffs, as they continue to blast away when *ppp* is suddenly indicated, and so forth. Even more likely is the possibility that he will find the members of an entire section blindly following one another instead of the conductor. Of special value here is the possibility that the conductor may learn something about his own conducting technique.

## A RECOMMENDED FORM FOR OBJECTIVES

Earlier it was pointed out (a) that the organization of the elements of behavioral objectives do not follow any necessary sequence (as the foregoing samples have demonstrated); (b) that the only strict rule is that each element be duly considered and that all be used as a kind of check list to make sure that everything has been properly provided; and (c) that the construction of behavioral objectives can often depend more on the laws of grammar and sentence construction than on any education theory.

However, experience has shown that music education students, student teachers, and even experienced music teachers who are unfamiliar with thinking in terms of behavioral objectives often profit from, and have their task initially simplified, when a more or less standard formula is used as a starting technique. Once this formula is understood (normalized), and the individual can write successful objectives—even if they are sometimes grammatically awkward—then it is relatively easy to rearrange the elements of the objective into the most logical or expressive presentation. The recommended sequence of this formula, remember, should only be used as a guide, a check list. Not all of the seven elements *need* to be included at all times, but items 2–5 should always be present. With these conditions in mind, you can make sensible use of this formula.

1. "Given"—then specify:
    a. what *materials, media,* and *guidelines* are to be employed (if any)
    b. *time limitation* (if any)

2. "Who" will be affected:
    a. "the student will"; "each student will"
    b. "each group of ____ students will"
    c. "the group (band, chorus, etc.) will"

3. "Covert behavior"—specify preferably one cognitive, affective, or psychomotor variable in whatever grammatical terms seem appropriate.

4. "Content"—specify the knowledge, skill, or feeling content being considered.

5. "By"—specify at least one overt behavior:
   a. verbalizing
   b. making
   c. playing

6. "With"—specify criteria (if any): "with accuracy," "with a successful tripartite structure," "with ____ percent accuracy," etc.

7. "And" (optional):
   a. can add another overt behavior
   b. can add further means used by the teacher to implement the activity or the evaluation.

Using the foregoing formula as a reference and guide, study the following example, which was derived from the use of that formula:

| | |
|---|---|
| 1. "Given" . . . . . . . . . . . . . . . . . . . . . | Given a copy of the text, and a reading of the little poem, "I've Never Seen a Purple Cow" and ten minutes, |
| 2. "Who" . . . . . . . . . . . . . . . . . . . . . | each fourth grade student will |
| 3. "Covert behavior" . . . . . . . . . . . . | identify [or "demonstrate his ability to identify"] |
| 4. "Content" . . . . . . . . . . . . . . . . . . | its meter and rhythm |
| 5. "By" . . . . . . . . . . . . . . . . . . . . . . | by: a. underlining the accented syllables, |
| |     b. placing bar lines in the text before each accented syllable, and |
| |     c. numbering the counts each syllable gets (one number = one count; numbers joined by a "–" are added, e.g., 1–2 = two beats; 1–2–3 = three beats), |
| 6. "With" . . . . . . . . . . . . . . . . . . . . | with not more than three errors, |
| 7. "And" . . . . . . . . . . . . . . . . . . . . . | and handing these in to the teacher [or, correcting his own after class discussion]. |

The items included in brackets are other possibilities. They would not appear in a finished objective. The information in item 5c would probably not be specified by the teacher who uses this system. It is included here so that you can understand how this activity would be implemented with a consistency designed to aid both the teacher and the class.

In this objective all elements have been derived, in order, from the formula given previously. Note the following explanations by referring to the objective.

1. Here the *given* factors include: (a) what *materials* and *media* are included, and (b) a *time limitation.*

2. *Who* is indicated as "each fourth grade student will." This expression can be distinguished from "the student will" by using the former to refer to individualized instruction in large or small groups, and the latter to refer to the instruction of only one student, as in a private lesson. The use of the word "will" is purely a matter of personal disposition. It indicates an affirmative or positive apprehension. Those who feel uncomfortable with what has been called "the future militaristic imperative tense" may use the expression "the student should."

3. The *covert behavior* here specified is "to identify." In some instances you may or may not have to write "demonstrate his ability to," "indicate a knowledge of," and so on. This merely provides for the bias of our grammar or of our particular mode of thought, which in some instances infers automatic overt manifestation as an inevitable consequence of covert behavior.

4. *Content:* In this objective, *concepts* of meter and rhythm are considered. What is ideal here is that the material and the means being used are all conceptually familiar to the students: words, underlining accented words, and numbers. Thus, the students can concentrate on the concepts at hand without undue interference from the other aspects of the situation.

5. *By:* The *overt* behavior indicated here falls in the category "to arrange" (that is, to arrange the underscorings and the numbers in their proper places). Other possibilities that could have been used here, or might be in the future, are to recite the poem, tapping or clapping on the accented syllables ("to perform"), or to count aloud while the poem is read ("to verbalize").

6. *With:* The level of proficiency specified here is three errors or less. If the poem is regarded as being in 3/4 time, having sixteen measures of three beats each—one of which is accented—and having each measure bounded by bar lines, there are about eighty possible responses in this activity. Thus, three errors represents considerable accuracy. It is not necessary to go to the trouble to figure out the total number of responses. It is pointed out here in order to emphasize how many responses are possible in as simple an exercise as this. The teacher should have some clear idea of the number of responses—large or small in number?—in order to set the criteria. Clearly, twenty-five errors here is too many, and one hundred percent seems unrealistic.

7. *And:* "Handing these in to the teacher" allows the teacher to observe and evaluate the number of errors made by each individual. It also allows the teacher to observe whether or not there is any particular error or particular concept that prevails for most of the class. In either or both cases, the teacher is advised of the source of the difficulty, and possible "remedial" action may even be indicated.

The second possibility suggested was to have a class disscussion on the completed project. It would be necessary to avoid letting the class make any changes during the discussion. As individual issues are identified and cleared up, or upon completion of the entire discussion, the teacher can *then* direct the class to make whatever corrections are necessary. After these are done (and a time would probably be specified here), the teacher may present the definitive version to the class and ask how many had it entirely correct; or how many had all but a few places correct. Or the teacher may end up collecting the papers to check completely who was and who was not able to reinterpret the situation and act adaptively.

There is no reason to think that these two possibilities are mutually exclusive. There is every reason to expect that the wise teacher would use both approaches frequently with this and other kinds of lessons. The advantage of the second approach, of course, is that it encourages the student to reinterpret his mistakes in light of new or clarifying information, and to adapt his behavior accordingly. The other activity would seem more suited for those situations or classes where many such opportunities for reinterpretation and adaptation have been provided, and where the teacher wants to assess the readiness of the class to go on to another step, such as setting the poem with rhythmic notation. If student independence is necessary for a subsequent step, the teacher must be assured that most students can perform step one by themselves before going on confidently to step two. Thus, both of these suggested activities can work together.

As you can see—in the example above at least—the proposed formula provides very successfully for each of the seven elements in a behavioral objective for music instruction, and even results in a sensibly constructed presentation. Anyone used to working with such objectives is accustomed to the way in which the consideration of all seven elements often suggests many alternative courses of action. The problem is to decide on one potentially successful course.

## EXCEPTIONS

The use of this formula does not always work so simply. Take, for instance an example analyzed earlier:

Each band member will demonstrate his ability to follow the conductor by correctly adjusting his performance as the conductor artificially changes tempo, dryamics, cutoffs, and interpretation.

1. *Given:* it is safely assumed that the band members will have their instruments and music. But "artificial" conducting changes is a given means here.

2. *Who:* "each band member will"; this works out fine. It is included and is in a sensible location.

3. *Covert behavior:* "demonstrate his ability to follow the conductor" (the psychomotor variable, "to follow directions"). This step of the formula also works out well. It is included (as it must be) and it is in the location recommended by the formula.

4. *Content:* according to the formula this should have been specified next. Including the content at this point would have suggested a changed meaning. The objective would have read:

   demonstrate his ability to follow the conductor's artificial changes of tempo, dynamics, cutoffs, and interpretation.

   This may not at first glance seem too objectionable, but on deeper inspection you should note that this arrangement suggests that the student should follow the conductor *only* during instances of artificial conducting changes. Thus, the content seems best located elsewhere in the objective.

5. *By:* "adjusting his performance" is included, but again it is out of order. It has been preceded by the criterion "correctly," which, according to the formula, should follow the indication of overt behavior. Thus, as with *content,* above, all you need do is indicate the overt behavior and rearrange it into a sensible sentence after you have considered all the elements as a check list.

6. *With:* the criterion "correctly" should go at this place. It is possible to say "with correctness," but that seems quite weak.

7. *And:* is not applicable here, so it is left out. Something like "and doing so throughout the year" could have been included to make this objective an ongoing process.

So if you had followed the formula in putting together this objective, you would have ended up with this statement:

1. *Given:* artificial conducting, or artificial changes of conducting,

2. *Who:* each band member will

3. *Covert behavior:* demonstrate his ability to follow the conductor's

4. *Content:* changes of tempo, dynamics, cutoffs, and interpretation.

5. *By:* by adjusting his performance

260

6. *With:* correctly. (The expression "with" is left out.)

7. *And:* (not applicable)

After using this statement as a check list, the remaining step is to rearrange the various specifications into a more logical sentence structure.

"Each band member will" "demonstrate his ability to follow the conductor" by "correctly" "adjusting his performance" *as the conductor artificially* "changes tempo, dynamics, cutoffs, and interpretation."

The italicized portion dictates some rewording of the "given" factor and the "content." Another version might go like this:

"Each band member will" "demonstrate his ability to follow the conductor" by "correctly" "adjusting his performance" *to the conductor's artificial* "changes of tempo, dynamics, cutoffs, and interpretation."

Either way would seem fine for purposes of instruction (if not as exercises in syntax).

Writing behavioral objectives requires some practice. After you have handled a few of your own, "mediating responses" (such as the need to think of each of the seven elements) soon drop out, and writing objectives then becomes second nature for you. In the long run they are far simpler and far more efficient in terms of your time than the traditional long-winded lesson plan.

*GO TO FRAME 4, PAGE 267.*

---

## SUMMARY AND CONCLUSION

To this point, you have had the opportunity to write five behavioral objectives according to prespecified ideas. It is hoped that you have availed yourself of this opportunity, for only through practice will you develop this ability. As you increasingly refine your ability to write objectives, the process will become more and more natural. Soon you will be able to automatically translate your general ideas, goals, and class descriptions into viable behavioral objectives.

Even though the attainment of such proficiency seems desirable, it is not without certain dangers. Many teachers who reach this stage of competence in planning are likely to imagine that it is no longer necessary to work out objectives in advance. This is usually a mistake. Such a totally casual approach to the design of instructional goals and processes invariably neglects both many of the finer points of objective writing (such as the distinction between identification and differentiation; or the fact that a given way of phrasing a behavioral objective can change its entire meaning, even when the elements remain the same) and the planning necessary for efficient and effective implementation of the objective. Though classroom teachers (of theory, general music, and so on) are often at fault in this regard, performance teachers (private and group lessons, performance ensembles) are perhaps more so.

To affirm that performance teachers should have planned their teaching in advance and should have these plans in the form of written behavioral objectives might seem the height of idealistic folly to many. The idealistic folly, however, is found not in these requisites but in the false self-esteem that allows some teachers to imagine they have skills and capabilities that allow them to teach without any deliberate planning, "off the top of their head," so to speak. These kinds of teachers walk into a rehearsal with no clear prior notion of what music will be worked on, what musical learnings aside from pure performance skills will be introduced or worked out, how much time will be devoted to given aspects of the lesson, how this rehearsal relates to past and future lessons, whether or not the students are motivated by the music and the musical experience or by some form of "operant conditioning," what long-range effect this lesson and all lessons are to have on each student, how the rehearsal allows for feeling responses—all of which have been discussed at length. It is no wonder that these classes can often lapse into drilled learning sessions where the music being studied is rehearsed and rehearsed, with the teacher noting all errors, correcting all mistakes, and so on. Nor is it any wonder that this kind of teacher has had negligible impact on the taste, preferences, or lifelong desire to perform or be involved with music, on the part of the group membership.

If "idealistic" is understood as "unrealistic," and "folly" as "deficient in understanding," then it is not the course of action recommended here that should be labeled "idealistic folly," but, rather, that followed by those who unrealistically imagine or even hope that they have had a significant musical impact on their students. It is they who are "deficient in understanding" through their lack of willingness to even consider, let alone understand, the psychological and philosophical contingencies of truly effective teaching in music, or even the general obligations of the teaching profession.

Perhaps the most unrealistic deficiency in understanding manifested by the music teacher who ignores or decries teacher planning is that musical instruction, which has no generally agreed upon syllabus, therefore has less structure and organization. This is a gross fallacy, for the very lack of strictly prescribed guidelines in music should not indicate more freedom or latitude, but instead cries out and demands more planning and structure by the teacher. The choice of *what* to study and in *what order* is not a simple matter of teacher preference. It is a matter of student needs and interests, and of adherence to and an understanding of learning theory and of the musical experience as an artistic phenomenon. Once the teacher recognizes the need for planning and the advantages of using behavioral objectives as the vehicle for such planning, teaching becomes not more difficult, but essentially less demanding in its execution and more rewarding in its results.

Such planning, as has been emphasized at length already, can prevent most of the common forms of problem behavior, thus freeing the teacher, in a sense, to teach rather than restricting him to disciplining the students all the time. The rewards and satisfactions that result from being able to teach rather than control (or survive, as many teachers would put it) far outweigh the seeming inconvenience of having to plan teaching in advance, using behavioral objectives. The rewards and satisfactions of being able to empirically observe student progress, student learning, increased student insights or feelings regarding music, far outweigh whatever personal musical needs the teacher may imagine are being sacrificed.

Just as the student is able to revel and take pride in the demonstrable indications of his successes, so the teacher is able to take pride in those same successes. The pride of influencing young people in ways designed to foster the role of music in effective living seems far more important and desirable than whatever pride accrues from the immediate but misleading gratifications of local reputations or ratings. And there is no reason to doubt, and every reason to expect, that teachers who achieve success through their ability to plan and execute lessons in accordance with learning theory, an aesthetic point of view, and behavioral objectives that reflect such understandings—such teachers will in fact be given recognition in their localities or regions. It will not be immediate, but it will not be falsely awarded. And it will lend needed credence to the profession of music education.

It would seem to be far more important that such teacher recognition arise from student reactions and successes than from outside sources. A successful teacher will never adequately know the limits of his influence over his students, but his success as demonstrated empirically through student behavior in learning situations will indicate that his influence has been significant and positive. Teachers who ignore behavior in learning situations dream about and imagine all sorts of things about their ability and effect as teachers, but there will always be the nagging doubts and suspicions about the large number of students who misbehave, who are not interested, or who do not perform after graduation. And the teachers whose conscience does not permit such introspection are indeed dangerously likely to inculcate in students an active dislike—and other poor attitudes—toward musical instruction, musical learning, and the musical art in general. Ask any teacher of college music appreciation classes about the attitudes toward music held by otherwise intelligent and open-minded students. Or merely observe the musical behavior of the general public if you need more evidence.

There is no doubt that those who find the writing and planning of behavioral objectives to be an odious chore are in some way unwilling or unable to understand the obligations of teaching. There is also no doubt that those who learn to write behavioral objectives will find them easier and easier to write, and therefore less and less demanding of their time. This latter group, too, will find their teaching immeasurably improved (or should we say, the learning of their students immeasurably improved?). This brings greater rewards in the satisfaction derived from teaching and the increasingly less obvious problem of student misbehavior.

Teachers are prone to bemoaning inadequacies in their local school systems or communities. Music teachers often complain about the "cultural level" of the area and use this as an excuse for either the ineffectiveness of their teaching or the lack of what they consider any real need for planning (since, they assume, no one can benefit from such planning). Though it must be admitted that there are many problems in American schools and American society today—and, thus, that all such problems cannot be overcome by any one teacher using any special teaching approach—the means recommended here can serve to immeasurably lighten the burden on the teacher, and will have *some* impact on the students taught. Where administrative or other factors preclude the most desirable teaching practice (which is probably everywhere), the use of the means and methods outlined thus far can go a long way toward meeting the goals of the teacher and the profession.

In the long run, this kind of teaching, if carried out by more and more teachers, could work wonders for the accountability of musical instruction in public schools. When music teachers can begin to show, and do so in empirical terms, the effects of their instruction on the young people who pass through the schools, it seems ever more likely that better conditions and attitudes can be fostered. It is a question of whether music educators wish to be part of the problem or part of the solution. We have contributed to the problem in the past; we can also contribute to the solution in the future.

To check your understanding, answer the following question. When you are finished with it, answer the second question.

Of the seven elements of behavioral objectives for musical learning that were given, identify the *four that should always be present* in some form.

   A. Who will be affected; content; covert behavior; overt behavior. Go to Frame 16.
   B. Who will be affected; content; what means; covert behavior. Go to Frame 9.
   C. Content; covert behavior; overt behavior; level of proficiency. Go to Frame 13.

Of the seven elements of behavioral objectives for musical learning that were given, identify the *three* that are *optional* or *variable*, depending on the intent of the teacher.

   A. Content; what means; time limitation. Go to Frame 7.
   B. What means; time limitation; level of proficiency. Go to Frame 11.
   C. Who will be affected; what means; level of proficiency. Go to Frame 18.

---

See if you can distinguish the elements of this behavioral objective by filling in the right-hand column.

"Given five seconds" =

"to look at flashcards" =

"presenting variants of

$\frac{2}{4}$ ♩. ♪ and $\frac{3}{8}$ ♩ ♪ " =

"the student" =

"will differentiate between" =

"immediately" =

"the relative durations and meters of each" =

"by playing each pattern" =

"correctly" =

"Each subsequent lesson will shorten the amount of viewing time allotted for preview" =

Go to Frame 14 and check your answers. They need not be word for word to be correct; they should just convey the same general sense.

---

*From page 254*                                                                    Frame 3

Here is a behavioral objective dealing with large-group instruction in a performance setting. See how well you can do this time in again identifying the elements of this objective by completing the right-hand column.

Given a new motet by Palestrina and five minutes, each member of the chorus will, using a pencil, indicate their comprehension of phrasing in the Palestrina style by lightly marking in their scores the places where they *should* and *should not breathe* ( ∕ = breathe;  ⌢ = no breath), and handing these to the teacher with their names on the cover.

"Given a new motet by Palestrina" =

"and five minutes" =

"each member of the chorus" =

"will indicate their comprehension" =

"of phrasing in the Palestrina style" =

"by lightly marking in their scores" =

"the places where they *should* and *should not breathe*" =

"( ∕ = breathe;  ⌢ = no breath)"; "using a pencil" =

"and handing these to the teacher with their names on the cover." =

Go to Frame 8 to check your answers. Again, you need not have the exact wording; just make sure your answers conveys the same sense as those given.

---

*From page 261*                                                                    Frame 4

Here is an opportunity for you to practice. See if you can write a behavioral objective by completing the right-hand column in accordance with the formula guideline on the left (you may refer back to page 256 if the guidelines are not entirely clear as yet) and the general description of the class that you will hypothetically teach, which is given below.

You want to undertake an activity that shows whether or not students working in small groups understand some of the major functions of traditional notation (relative factors of pitch, duration, silence, and dynamics). To do so, you have them compose original "sound compositions" of sounds found in the room, using original notation that conveys the same four qualities as traditional notation. You also want them to be able to perform and explain their notation.

1. *Given:*


2. *Who:*


3. *Covert behavior:*


4. *Content:*


5. *By:*


6. *With:*


7. *And:*


When you are through, go to Frame 10 and check your objective against the one given there, and see if the two bear any significant relationship. They need not be the same, so use the given version only as a model for comparison.

Following is a description of a hypothetical idea that you are to develop into a behavioral objective. Use the space provided.

After working for some while with the qualities of major and minor modes and how they sound, you want to evaluate whether each of the students can recognize the two modes aurally. Therefore, you plan to play a mixture of unfamiliar songs in different modes for the class, and have them indicate by using colored paper (one color for major, another color for minor) which examples are major and which are minor. You anticipate that a consistent score of eight or nine out of ten examples would be a satisfactory indication that the class is ready to use this learning in other contexts.

If you completed this exercise without referring back, you could profit now from checking your solution against the formula on page 256. Make changes if you like. Then go to Frame 12 and check your results against the objective suggested there.

---

Here are several more descriptions of ideas that a teacher or different teachers might want to implement. Write behavioral objectives for each as though the idea was yours. Compare your objective with the answers given, each of which, remember, represents only *one* possible way of proceeding. You should look for improvement in your ability as you move down this list of exercises.

1. The choral teacher, having started the year with fifteen freshman tenors, wishes to determine whether they are equally adept at reading the treble and bass clefs, in order to provide experience in this skill for those who cannot. To find this information, she plans to notate two chorales in the two

different clefs for the tenors, and to sing through each several times while she walks among the class listening to and evaluating each tenor. After you have written your objective, go to Frame 17.

2. The eighth grade general music teacher, after many activities dealing with the concepts of *texture, polyphony,* and *imitative counterpoint,* decides to evaluate the success of these studies by having small groups of students compose short three-part compositions based on (word) sentences or sentence fragments chosen by the group. These compositions should satisfactorily reflect a polyphonic texture and the principle of free imitation; each group will perform their work for the class, who will listen and affirm or deny in discussion whether a polyphonic texture and "free" imitation were in fact used, explaining why or why not. After you have written your objective, go to Frame 15.

3. The band instructor, having introduced and worked for several weeks with the technique of using the register key on the clarinet, has had Bertha Bump practicing this skilled behavior for several weeks. Each week, new technique exercises and compositions featuring this skill were used. Now he decides to use all of the music she has been working with, to evaluate her progress thus far and to plan for subsequent lessons. He feels that in playing all the works, she should probably be able to correctly bridge the registers without squeaking, hesitating, or stumbling. After you have written your objective, go to Frame 19.

---

*From Frame 1*

Frame 7

You said that the three elements of behavioral objectives for musical learning that are optional or variable are: content; what means; time limitation.

These are not all correct. The means and the time limitation *are* variable or optional. Whether or not they are included depends on the degree to which the teacher wishes to structure or control the activity. If the activity is to be the free exercise of cognition, affection, or psychomotor behavior, these two variables may be omitted. Content, on the other hand, should always be included because it indicates what will be included in the instruction: what information, skill, or aspect of "felt life" is being considered or emphasized. Put another way, what is being learned, or what material is learning to arise from? Go back to Frame 1 and make another choice for the second question.

---

*From Frame 3*

Frame 8

"Given a new motet by Palestrina"

= what materials are *given.* It also implies previous experiences with Palestrina's motets and motet style by specifying a "new" motet. Furthermore, if it is new, then this is the first contact with this particular composition. This in turn assures comprehension rather than rote learning or memorization through previous rehearsing of the work.

"and five minutes" = a *time* limitation, evidently one predicated on the belief that the chorus has had enough experience with the style in question (that is, enough readiness) to be able to perform the task in this amount of time. One can see, in any case, whether or not this is possible. If at the end of five minutes the class complains that they need more time, then comprehension is evidently not all the teacher expected it would be. The product will indicate comprehension by showing how many were able to complete the task correctly and how many were correct in what they did but needed more time to finish.

"each member of the chorus" = *who* will be affected. In this case instruction has been individualized for a large group. Similarly, the feedback will be individualized as the teacher returns the corrected score to each student. Work? Yes! Worth it? Yes!!

"will indicate their comprehension" = the *covert* cognitive variable, "to comprehend" (that is, to have a concept of) the stylistic practice in question.

"of phrasing in the Palestrina style" = *content:* the learning under consideration.

"by lightly marking in their scores" = the *overt* behavior, "to organize" the breath or phrase markings.

"the places where they should and should not breathe" = the criteria of *proficiency.* Such places should be correctly marked, and other places should not be marked.

"( / = breathe; ⌒ = no breath)"; "using a pencil" = the *given* means of implementing the overt behavior. It is decidedly a good idea to use (and therefore have available for those who forget to bring one) pencils rather than ink.

"and handing these to the teacher = *given* means by which the teacher

270

with their names on the cover"

Go to page 254, below the line.

will be able to evaluate the learning progress of each.

---

From Frame 1

You said that the four elements that should always be present in behavioral objectives for musical learning are: who will be affected, content; what means; covert behavior.

No, these are not all correct. The means—that is, the materials, media, and prescribed guidelines—may be left to the individual or the group on many occasions. Therefore, they would not usually be included in the behavioral objective for such an activity (unless, of course, the teacher wished to emphasize this fact by saying, "Given their free choice of . . ." or "With no restrictions as to . . ."). Go back to Frame 1 and answer the first question again.

---

From Frame 4

Here is a model of a behavioral objective that conveys the intent and means suggested in the description you were given.

1. *Given*—"Given a choice of sounds found in the room." These are the materials or media to be used. The opportunity to choose somewhat frees the situation for feeling, even though that is not specifically at stake here. No time was specified in the description you were given, but you might have included what you thought would be a reasonable amount for completing this activity.
2. *Who*—"each group of three students." Remember here that *small* groups should consist of no more than three or four persons.
3. *Covert behavior*—"will demonstrate their comprehension of." The covert cognitive variable, "to comprehend," most accurately conveys the "understanding" described in the hypothetical class you were given to work with, though you could also use "understanding" itself in the objective. It would seem necessary that this activity should have been preceded by others that had isolated and studied the four functions of notation in question. If this is the first such activity and is supposed to explore rather than demonstrate conceptual knowledge, the covert cognitive variable might have been "to analyze"—for instance, "will demonstrate his ability to analyze." "To differentiate" or "to identify" might also work here, but like analysis, they would each imply something other than understanding, comprehension, conceptualization. From experiences in analysis, differentiation, and identification, the inductive bases for "comprehension" might be developed.
4. *Content:* "the four major functions of traditional musical notation (pitch, duration, silence, and dynamics)." This is the material that is being offered

for comprehension; the material that is to be comprehended. It should be specified.

5. *By:* "composing original sound compositions that use original notation"— the overt behavior, "to make" (create).

6. *With:* "the same four functions as traditional notation"—criteria of proficiency. The original notation must indicate pitch, duration, silence, and dynamics with some success. The degree of success indicates the student's comprehension of these factors.

7. *And:* "explaining to the class how their notation works and then demonstrating the notation by performing the composition"—two additional overt behaviors, "to verbalize" and "to perform."

Thus, your behavioral objective should have some resemblance to this example:

> Given sounds found in the room, each group of three students will demonstrate their comprehension of the four major functions of traditional musical notation (pitch, duration, silence, and dynamics) by composing original sound compositions that use original notation having the same four functions as traditional notation; and will then explain to the class how their notation works, and will demonstrate the notation by performing the composition.

With the exception of a time limitation, which you may have chosen to include, all the elements recommended for behavioral objectives in musical instruction are included here. Additionally, this objective (which only reflects a very general idea in the mind of the teacher) provides for all three kinds of overt terminal behavior as evidence of the covert cognitive variable, "to comprehend." This avoids the possibility that a group might conceive of seemingly successful means of notation by accident or luck. If they cannot explain how their notation works, or if they cannot perform their own work, then the teacher should realize that comprehension is not complete.

If this objective were applied as intended—that is, as a kind of culminating activity after a period of concentration on the functions and factors of traditional notation—the teacher could well observe whether or not the instruction had been successful. If this were an exploratory activity (and if the objective were changed accordingly, to specify "identification" or "differentiation"), whatever kind of notation the class invented could then be analyzed or discussed by the teacher and class as to its strengths and shortcomings, eventually "discovering" the four major functions that traditional notation has performed. In either case, this activity, which is essentially cognitive in intent, also encourages—or at least permits—a degree of feeling response since no specification about form or content has been made. Thus, the activity has the dual advantage of developing cognitions about musical processes and encouraging the feeling response.

Although no general rule of thumb can be given, you are advised to question and doubt any proposed activity where cognition or psychomotor skill seems emphasized *for its own sake;* where cognition or psychomotor skills are divorced from feeling responses or musical expression. In large part, whether the teacher in public schools is teaching vocationally or avocationally oriented students, it is music as an *art,* not as a discipline which is important and which will have an impact on effective living. And if the cognitions or skills that are taught have no immediate feeling component, but will eventually lead to such a condition, the process should be as speedy (efficient) as possible. The teacher can also anticipate certain motivation problems until such time as the feeling component is achieved.

That was a difficult exercise for you to undertake: the idea and resulting objective were complex, and did not stem initially from your own thoughts. Under the circumstances, you must be the best judge of how well your version agreed with the solution given. If you are not satisfied with your performance, or in any case would like more practice, another opportunity to interpret the problem and act accordingly follows. If you think you can, this time see if you can complete the objectives without having to refer to the formula. If you are not ready for this yet, you may have to refer back to page 256. Eventually, however, you should be able to write your own objectives without having to refer to the seven elements in the formula. When you can do this, writing objectives will have become much easier for you.

Go to Frame 5, page 268.

---

*From Frame 1*                                                    Frame 11

You said that the three elements of behavioral objectives for musical learning that are optional or variable are: what means; time limitation; level of proficiency.

This is correct. These three elements may or may not be included, depending on how much control the teacher wishes to exert over the activity or how much latitude the class is to have in completing the project. If the means, the time, and the proficiency are left unspecified, the activity will likely be quite free and diverse in its results. In many teaching situations this is a desirable condition. No means may be specified in situations where the class should be left with a freely subjective choice or where the teacher seeks to discover what kind of choices the student will make. Time limitations may be deleted when the activity is not based on skilled learning and where, therefore, the time necessary to master a given skill is not a parameter of the lesson. Time may also be deleted in situations where completing the project or activity is unpredictable or worth however much time is necessary. Level of proficiency is usually not stipulated for covert variables from the affective category. To do otherwise is to imply or apply value judgments to feeling responses.

Go to page 248, below the line.

---

*From Frame 5*                                                    Frame 12

1. *Given:* "Given a series of ten mixed aural examples in major and minor, and slips of black and white paper." This specifies the materials and media.
2. *Who:* "each student will." The teacher will observe the learning of each student in the class.
3. *Covert Behavior:* "identify." This specifies explicit recognition of major

and minor. Differentiation involves only the ability to tell one from an-other, but identification is proper in an objective that involves somehow labeling or categorizing phenomena. Thus, "to identify" includes "to differentiate," but differentiation need not always include identification.

4. *Content:* "the major and minor mode." This specifies what knowledge will be acted upon in identification.

5. *By:* "holding up a black slip for minor or white slip for major immediately after the example is played." This is a place where learning theory can support a variety of techniques. The manner of eliciting overt responses (to verbalize—that is, to label—but using the slips of paper as silent symbols) used here is superior to having individuals raise their hands. Raising hands (a) would not include all members of the class, and (b) would lead to imitative responses by weaker or unsure students. Thus, by having each student flash a slip on command "immediately after the example is played," the teacher sees at an instant who is responding correctly and who is not.

6. *With:* "a consistent score of at least eight when the examples are replayed in scrambled order." If, while going through the examples the first time, the teacher discusses the responses with the class and provides a basis for reinterpretation for those who might have missed or guessed, then a second scrambled playing of the examples will insure that the responses are consistent and not a matter of luck. This will also help reinforce the correct responses.

7. *And:* not applicable.

Thus, your objective might look something like this:

Given a series of ten aural examples in major and minor, and slips of black and white paper, each student will identify the major and minor mode by holding up a black slip for minor or white slip for major immediately after the example is played, with a consistent score of at least eight when the examples are replayed in scrambled order.

Go to Frame 6, Page 268.

---

*From Frame 1*                                                    Frame 13

You said that the four elements that should always be present in behavioral objectives for musical learning are: content; covert behavior, overt behavior; level of proficiency.

No, you have one of these wrong. The level of proficiency need not be specified in every case. This element is most usually eliminated in objectives that deal with affective variables. Because they are affective (that is, because they deal with feeling responses, "felt life," and subjective values), it is often difficult and always dangerous to provide external criteria. Doing so amounts to the imposition of value by the teacher. Even in cases where a title is used for interpretation in an original composition, the results are likely to be so diverse and personal that it is not really possible to consider this a criteria. It is, in fact, a guideline, a delimitation, and as such is included as *means*—the "given" factors. Go back to Frame 1 and answer the first question again.

"Given five seconds"

= a *time* limitation; this is a crucial factor here since the amount of time necessary to respond is a prime factor in the mastery of this skill.

"to look at flash cards"

= the *given* materials to be perceived.

"presenting variants of $\frac{2}{4}$ ♩. ♪

and $\frac{3}{8}$ ♩  ♪ "

"the student"

= *content*, specified clearly.

"will differentiate between"

= *who* will be affected.

= the *covert* cognitive variable, to differentiate."

"immediately"

= the *criterion* of time as a factor in the mastery of this skill; thus, it is not a "given" time limitation, but a criteria of proficiency.

"the relative durations and meters of each"

= *content* reference.

"by playing each pattern"

= the *overt* behavior, "to play."

"correctly"

= performance *proficiency;* coupled with the reference to "each pattern," this implies total accuracy.

"Each subsequent lesson will shorten the amount of viewing time allotted for preview"

= a further use of time or speed as a criteria of performance. If the student, at his next lesson, is not able to reduce the viewing time to four seconds, then more work is needed with the current five-second format until the preview time can be shortened with success for the student. This is more than just transfer of learning; it also involves the psychomotor variable, "to lessen time." As was mentioned earlier, this variable, as with so many others in the psychomotor category, is inextricably wed to cognitions as well as to kinesthetic factors. Here, what is at stake is the cognitive aspects of "differentiation." Increased mastery here will, in fact, lessen the time necessary for the student to respond correctly in playing.

If the student could not perform this objective successfully, the time factor of five seconds could be extended to the point where the student *could* perform the objective. Subsequent attempts could then gradually shorten the time until the desired condition was reached. It would be wise to vary the flash cards to avoid the possibility that such extended practice might result in conditioned behavior, or mere rote learning. The real test of this learning would be the application of these new skills in a new musical context: this would require another behavioral objective with its own criteria and behaviors.

Go to page 252, below the line.

---

*From Frame 6*                                                                                      Frame 15

2. Given their choice of sentences or sentence fragments, and twenty minutes, each group of three students will demonstrate their comprehension of *texture, polyphony,* and *free imitation* by composing a short three-"voice" composition with a polyphonic texture and free imitation successfully employed; and by performing their work for the class, who in turn will indicate in discussion whether the two elements were present, and will give some reasons for their opinion.

Some special factors here: "Choice" is a means in this objective, not a cognitive or affective variable, because the choice itself will not show any relevant learning. "Twenty minutes" time limit insures short compositions yet recognizes that at least five minutes may be spent in choosing the word material. "Successfully employed" is a kind of criteria hedge that implies that these musical techniques are too difficult and varied to pin down to absolute criteria and that, in any case, various degrees of success are possible. The concluding performance and discussion, which doubtless would be carried into the next class, insures that this objective uses all three overt behaviors— to make, to play, and to verbalize. Not only does this serve as a cross-checking feature of the activity, it also provides the added benefit of a directed listening situation for the nonperformers. This in itself can lead to valuable learnings, not to mention the fact that a class so busily engaged (even mentally) is less apt to misbehave.

Go back to Frame 6 and write an objective for the third example.

---

*From Frame 1*                                                                                      Frame 16

You said that the four elements that should always be present in behavioral objectives for musical learning are: who will be affected; content; covert behavior; overt behavior.

That is correct. These four must always be included as a minimum, for they specify who the instruction is intended for, what is includes, and what covert and overt behaviors are anticipated as a result of the learning activity. The other three elements depend on the intent of the teacher and the degree to which the teacher wants to control the activities of the class. The four required provisions help ensure that several very important aspects of learning are duly considered in each lesson. Thus, the individual or group (and their readiness), the subject matter to be learned, the mental involvement of the class, and the overt results are all properly identified for the attention of the teacher or class. Go back to Frame 1 and answer the second question.

---

*From Frame 6*                                                                   Frame 17

1. Given two similar SATB chorales, one with the tenor part notated in the treble clef, the other in the bass clef, each of the fifteen freshman tenors, after two times through, will demonstrate his ability to read in each clef by singing each example with conviction and considerable accuracy of pitch as the teacher walks among the group.

Some special factors in this objective: "Ability to read" in specific clefs represents the *covert* psychomotor variable "to attend to cues," for the cues are varied according to the clef sign, which is also a cue. "With conviction and considerable accuracy of pitch" are criteria of *proficiency*. Pitch needs to be specified so that the mere ability to read the clef signs is not the only factor being evaluated. Going through the music too often would involve the danger that the group would learn their part by ear, and, thus, not be "reading" at all. Therefore, it is advisable to limit the performance to two times. If this isn't enough time to complete your observation, do another example the same way. Whether or not the chorales were accompanied by a piano would depend on past practice of the choral teacher with this kind of music. Go back to Frame 6 and write an objective for the second example.

---

*From Frame 1*                                                                   Frame 18

You said that the three elements of behavioral objectives for musical learning that are optional or variable are: who will be affected; what means; level of proficiency.

You have two of the three correct. The means and the proficiency may or may not be given or specified, such as in a freely subjective composition. But the factor of "who will be affected" should always be included, for it specifies who the instruction is to reach. This is an important ingredient in any teaching situation. Responses from individual students, small groups, and large groups can vary considerably. Thus, the teacher should specify which kind of response would be best in a given learning situation. Go back to Frame 1 and choose another answer for the second question.

---

*From Frame 6*                                                                   Frame 19

3. Given the music studied by Bertha Bump over the last several weeks, she will demonstrate her ability to fixate through practice the tech-

nique of using the register key on the clarinet by correctly bridging the registers in that music with no squeaking, hesitating, or stumbling, and with accuracy and consistency.

Some factors of importance in this objective: The *given* factor here is very specific since "fixation through practice" is the aim. Therefore, only the music that has been practiced in this regard would be appropriate. The *who* is represented by the individual student. The *content* is the correct use of the bridge key. This involves not only the kinesthetic operations of the fine muscles, but also the cognitions necessary to perform the operation. The proficiency has three criteria: no squeaking, no hesitating, and no stumbling, plus the further needs for accuracy and consistency. These are all necessary since the three "thou shalt not" provisions could be fulfilled, but in the wrong register or with the wrong pitches; or the register key could be used inconsistently.

Go to page 261, below the line.

CHAPTER EIGHT

# the use of
# behavioral objectives

*If it is asked, "What is the content of speech?", it is
necessary to say, "It is an actual process of thought,
which is in itself nonverbal," . . . What we are considering here, however, are the psychic and social
consequences of the designs or patterns as they am-
plify or accelerate existing processes. For the "message" of any medium or technology is the change of
scale or pace or pattern that it introduces into human
affairs.*

Marshall McLuhan, Understanding Media: The Extension of Man (*New York: New American Library,
1964), p. 24.*

Teaching can be regarded as a *medium* both in the sense of "an intermediate means or agency,"[1] and in Marshall McLuhan's sense of "any extension of ourselves."[2] Music teachers are one of the means or agencies by which the musical art is propagated. As an "extension of ourselves," music teachers seek to share their high regard for music with others.

If, as McLuhan believes, "the 'content' of any medium is always another medium,"[3] then it would seem that the content of the medium of music education is the medium of music. The content of music at its most basic level is sound reflecting the various functions and actions of *mind* that Langer calls "feeling." Thus, the content of the medium of music education would seem to be mind or feeling. It is not mere overt behavior or the acquisition of information *about* music that are the self-sufficient goals of musical instruction.

Behavioral objectives, too, are a medium. Since "the 'message' of any medium . . . is the change of scale or pace or pattern that it introduces into human affairs,"[4] then behavioral objectives can be seen as the means by which music educators effect changes in the scale or pace or pattern of musical behavior in human life. In another more specific sense, behavioral objectives are the means by which *covert mental behaviors* are selectively evoked and developed. Operating under the principle that "it is the medium that shapes and controls the scale and form of human association and action,"[5] behavioral objectives are the medium of an effective musical education. First and foremost, they are used to elicit the covert affective behaviors that serve as the pivot and *raison d'être* for both cognitive and psychomotor responses.

It is true, as critics of behavioral learning theory have pointed out, that behavioral objectives when applied to arts education can be instrumental in leading to *conditioned* and therefore mindless behavior. The special use of behavioral objectives recommended here takes into consideration factors not given proper emphasis in the past. Using behavioral objectives that properly evoke and emphasize *covert behaviors* in the student, and that are devised according to the aesthetic understanding held by the teacher of the musical art —these factors dispel the possibility of the kind of learning that has been criticized in the past. Do not regard the resulting overt behavior as the goal of instruction for the student. It is the goal of instruction, in one sense, for the teacher, who will use this overt behavior to evaluate the success of teaching and learning and as a basis for future planning. What is important for the student is the fact that his *overt* behavior presupposes *covert* musical behaviors and thus is an important tool in the development of these faculties and capacities. Additionally, there are practical benefits for the students: they are better able to assess their own learning; they are better motivated when learn-

---

[1] *Funk and Wagnalls Standard Dictionary: International Edition,* p. 791.
[2] McLuhan, *Understanding Media,* p. 23.
[3] *Ibid.*
[4] *Ibid.,* p. 24.
[5] *Ibid.*

ing is made more tangible; and in terms of accountability, they serve as better examples, to peers, parents, administrators, and other teachers, of the efficacy—the power to produce an effect (affect??)—of music education.

Remember that a seemingly well-written behavioral objective can serve unworthy educational or philosophical goals. Consider, for example, the following behavioral objective, and imagine the effect such teaching would have over a long period of time, and its consequences for the teacher.

> Given twenty names of famous composers, each student will identify each composer according to the recognized facts of music history by indicating the dates of each, by listing five important compositions of each, and by achieving a grade of at least ninety-five.

All the elements of a behavioral objective, except perhaps a time limit.(which, in any event, is implied in the duration necessary for testing), are included, and in the order recommended by the formula given earlier. Yet philosophically, would such learnings, even if attained, contribute in any way to feeling responses, "felt life," or effective living? What "artistic import," or whatever you choose to call it, does such learning serve? Or consider the educational merits of this objective. What provision has been made for conceptual development, transfer, reinforcement, motivation, and the like? In what possible ways can rote memorization or sheer recall of unrelated objective facts be construed as fulfilling the conditions of effective teaching? And what are the chances of any given class meeting the criteria specified? Furthermore, what about the attitudes of those who are not inclined to be interested in the "activity" or who perform poorly? What kind of classroom atmosphere would you expect to find here, and what kind of behavior or misbehavior problems could you anticipate? Finally, what effect would such teaching, and whatever "discipline problems" arise, have on the administrative regard for the teacher?

As you can see, it is not really the formal adherence to the structure of a behavioral objective that is most important. It is your ability to use the structure, the formula, or the check list as a *means* of making due consideration of learning theory and aesthetic philosophy as they apply to music. If each element of the formula or check list is considered in terms of all the educational and philosophical issues covered earlier, then the resulting behavioral objective can be valid; that is, if those educational and philosophical issues were understood. This is why those issues were treated at length first, and why ample opportunity was afforded you for checking, clarifying, and reinforcing your understanding through frequent self-tests and branching program segments.

## INTERPRETING THE RESULTS OF BEHAVIORAL OBJECTIVES

1. The first rule for the proper use of behavioral objectives is to make sure that each of the seven elements that may be included in an objective are

used to stimulate a consideration of the applicable educational or aesthetic requisites of music instruction.

2. The second rule is to use properly the information you gain through observing the student behavior generated by the behavioral objective.

In order to fulfill this second condition, it is necessary to consider several more elements that are implied by the written instructional statement you have been learning how to devise. That statement of instructional goals in terms of overt behavior has, as you should recall by now, seven possible elements:

1. *Given:* includes materials, media, guidelines (or restrictions), and time limitation.

2. *Who:* includes a specification of who would be affected by the instruction.

3. *Covert behavior:* this clearly specifies or emphasizes the covert cognitive, affective, or psychomotor variable that you wish to selectively evoke.

4. *Content:* here, the knowledge, skill, or feeling response being used as the agent for the covert behavior is manifested. It is the learning that you seek.

5. *By:* this includes the specification of one or more overt terminal behaviors (to verbalize, make, or perform) as demonstrable evidence of the covert behavior at hand and the learning it represents.

6. *With:* this specifies the criteria of proficiency that you view as a desirable indication of significant learning or progress.

7. *And:* here you have the option of including any further means or any further overt behaviors to be included as a kind of cross-check.

Now, to these seven possible elements of the actual written behavioral objectives are added three more, which should be used in conjunction with the objective:

8. *Evaluation*
9. *Revision*
10. *Reapplication*

These three new conditions help assure a systematic approach to the use of behavioral objectives, and in so doing, avoid the abuse of behavioral objectives. To refer to this systematic control, the term "systems approach" is often used. It describes a process of "quality control" involving three basic steps:

Pre-test ⟶ Instruction ⟶ Post-test

*Pre-test.* This entails an evaluative activity that determines how much the student knows about something (cognitive), how well he can do something (psychomotor), or how he feels about something (affective). The word "test" should not be misconstrued: in most situations an evaluative application of a behavioral objective can perform this function very well.

*Instruction.* This entails various degrees or amounts of learning activities or projects designed to improve or encourage knowledge (cognitive) or skill (psychomotor), or to refine or cultivate feelings (affective). Such instruction should not be misconstrued as lectures by the teacher: an exploratory venture designed as a behavioral objective performs this function very well. In fact, such activities perform this function better than any lecture.

*Post-test.* This is the activity that concludes a sequence of instruction. It is used to evaluate how much the student has learned as a result of the instruction; how much he has improved his skill; or how much refinement or development of feeling has taken place. This post-test, furthermore, serves as a kind of new pre-test. Depending on the results of the post-test, new instruction, new activities or projects can be planned to overcome difficulties, to review previous learning or skills, to provide a new approach to feeling, or to reinforce any of these factors.

The results of such post-testing activities should not be construed as either graded tests or as value judgments (which is what graded tests are). The results—good or bad—may stem from the nature or quality of the instruction (that is, from your teaching or from administrative or physical plant factors that affect your teaching); they may stem from the efforts or capabilities of the learner; from chance; from maturation (of you or your students); or from a number of other possibilities or any combination of possibilities. This is the main reason why these activities should not be graded. What would a grade reflect: your success as a teacher, the amount of work applied by the student, the amount of learning actually acquired by the learner, the effect of the administrative attitude toward music, the effect of the physical conditions in which learning must occur, or luck (good or bad, yours or your students')?

These post-testing activities, instead, should be regarded merely as means for evaluating current instruction and for planning subsequent instruction in terms of current readiness. The sequence of

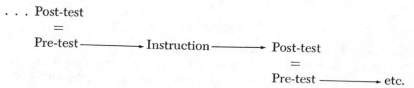

provides the systems approach rationale used in the last three elements that follow the design of a behavioral objective. Thus, in addition to the seven elements actually contained in the written statement of an objective, each objective or activity that arises from an objective should also be subject to these last three considerations.

## EVALUATION

8. Evaluation is directly comparable to, and should be understood in terms of,

> . . . Post-test (of the present activity)
> Pre-test (for readiness for future activities).

The teacher evaluates by assessing the relationship between attainment (demonstrated behavior) in the activity and the behavior that the objective specified or predicted. Thus, if the objective specified that a student would indicate a certain (covert) learning by manifesting a certain (overt) behavior, and if this observed behavior did not meet the criteria specified, then the evaluation of the post-test advises the teacher that some new or different course of action is neded. On the other hand, if the resulting behavior did meet the criteria, or depending on the degree to which it did, the teacher can plan whatever review, clarification, or reinforcement may seem desirable.

*GO TO FRAME 1, PAGE 307.*

---

## REVISION

9. Revision is directly comparable to, and should be understood in terms of *instruction*. The teacher, in this regard, uses the results of the evaluation activity (the post-test and pre-test) as the bases for deciding on and planning subsequent instruction (learning activities). This instruction may involve only one such activity or it may involve several. In any case, on the basis of the evaluation derived from the post-test and pre-test, the teacher plans to

| A. augment | B. review | C. replace |
|:---:|:---:|:---:|
| or | or | or |
| reinforce, | restructure, | retain |

the current activity, and/or to structure new ones.

A. *To augment* involves additional emphasis or refinement. *To reinforce* involves more experience and opportunity to implement a certain behavior. Success in deriving satisfaction improves the likelihood that the behavior will be retained.

B. *To review* involves a re-presentation, in much the same form, of the learning. *To restructure* involves approaching the learning from another, new, and different angle; it is the same learning, but a different activity is designed to accomplish it.

C. *To replace* implies the recognition of a totally unsuccessful objective and the design of a new one to serve the same aims. *To retain* involves recognition of a successful objective and the intent to use it again with other materials or content, or other classes, or at another time.

Considerations such as these, which follow on the heels of any given activity, give the teacher considerable latitude in planning for the future. Therefore, it is imperative that you realize that the systems approach should not be regarded as purely linear or directly sequential as the diagram on page 283 seems to imply. In fact, depending on the results of a given objective, the teacher has many alternatives. Three examples among the unlimited possibilities are illustrated below.

1: . . . post-test
          =
     (a) pre-test⟶ instruction⟶ post-test⟶ (b) pre-test . . .

2: ⟶ pre-test⟶ instruction⟶ post-test ⟶ pre-test . . .

3: . . . post-test
          =
                                              1
     (a) pre-test⟶ instruction⟶ post-test ⌐⟶ (b) pre-test . . .
                                           |
                                          2|
                                           ↓
              (c) pre-test . . .

*Example one.* The first activity (a) is undertaken on the basis of the prior post-test, and is completed successfully. Then an entirely new sequence is started (b). The two sequences may be related (in fact, they probably *should* be related) but are not necessarily mutually dependent. Thus, the post-test of sequence (a) does not become the pre-test for sequence (b).

*Example two.* Here, the first sequence begins in the same way that sequence (b) in the first example began: as a self-contained sequence that is not necessarily predicated on, but is probably related to, the activity that preceded it. It is followed by another such activity. This is very much like the traditional "unit" approach, with unit following unit in a more or less self-contained manner and with each related in some way. There is, however, no need for complete mastery or success in the first sequence in order for the second sequence to be undertaken. If success were not complete in sequence one, the teacher might return to these learnings, this content, at a time in the near future.

*Example three.* In this example a somewhat more complex relationship evolves. The first sequence (a) is based on the results of the prior activity. At the conclusion of the first sequence, the teacher goes on to a new sequence (b), which is *not directly based* on sequence (a). At some time in the future, perhaps directly after the second sequence, another sequence (c) is started, which *is* directly based on sequence one. Here is a closer look at example three:

$$
\ldots \text{ post-test}
$$
$$
=
$$
$$
\text{(a) pre-test} \longrightarrow \text{instruction} \longrightarrow \text{post-test} \overset{1}{\underset{2}{\rightthreetimes}} \text{(b) pre-test} \ldots
$$
$$
\text{(c) pre-test} \ldots
$$

For example, an activity (a) dealing with the recognition of instruments is completed with success. Then a second activity (b), in no way related to instruments, which deals with the concept of "form in music" is successfully completed. Then the teacher returns to the first sequence and uses the recognition of instruments (a) as the basis for the third activity (c), which might deal with the role of instrumentation in delineating or expanding musical form.

All of this explanation has been included to warn you against thinking that behavioral objectives must follow a single, continuous, unbroken line, like a herd of circus elephants. Rather, depending on the results, some will be immediately followed by others that are directly related; others will be left to various times in the future. The two major requirements under the category of *revision* (or if you prefer to think in terms of the systems approach, "instruction") are that (1) some conclusion about the result of instruction be made on the basis of the observable results of an objective; and (2) each objective relate to and depend on the results of *some* (but not necessarily the immediate) past objective.

Using these guidelines, you will see that if an objective is unsuccessfully fulfilled, it need not always be reviewed or restructured immediately. The reason for failure, you may find, was that the class or individual did not have adequate *readiness* for the task. Thus, you could return to the same objective at a time in the future when you thought that the necessary readiness had been attained. Of course, in the meanwhile you should be including activities designed to develop the readiness to the necessary level.

*GO TO FRAME 2, PAGE 307.*

---

**REAPPLICATION**

10. Reapplication is directly comparable to, and should be understood in terms of,

$$
\longrightarrow \text{post-test}
$$
$$
=
$$
$$
\textit{pre-test} \text{ of the next or some future activity}
$$

Thus, reapplication is essentially the creating of another activity that will eventually culminate in new evaluation. As such, reapplication can take one or more of several general forms:

a. Direct reapplication of a previous instructional activity in the form of an evaluative activity.

b. Reapplication to similar but new particular learning experiences or conditions, resulting in transfer of learning.

c. Reapplication to totally new experiences, contexts, or conditions.

In the first form (a), an activity would be repeated with only minor changes as review for some, reinforcement for others, and clarification for still others. Thus, it is a means of insuring that the success of the first activity was total and not haphazard.

In the second form (b), an activity would be repeated in essence, but with the conditions or emphases altered. When finding variations of shapes in the room is reapplied as finding variations of color in the room, the conditions have been changed. Success in the second activity would help insure that the concept of variation is sound. On the other hand, if the change is from finding variations visually in the room to aurally in music, then the emphasis is altered from visual perception and cognition to aural perception and cognition.

In the third form (c), an activity would be repeated in a highly varied manner. Using the example of variation again, this might entail creating an original sound composition that manifests the variation concept.

Thus, reapplication may take several forms. In order to systematically develop the learnings at hand, it is probably most effective to reapply an activity that manifests learning, in all three ways and perhaps several times. Some teachers seem determined to cover all the material during any given lesson, semester, or year. But it is more important to deal thoroughly with the concepts taught than to merely "cover all the material." This latter expression conveys its own essential weakness: it puts an emphasis on what the teacher does, not on what the students are learning. "Material," here, seems to definitely include musical information and materials because it is really never possible to "cover" all the potential concepts in the musical experience.

*GO TO FRAME 3, PAGE 307.*

---

### SYSTEMATIC EVALUATION: SUMMARY

The addition of the three further requirements of evaluation, revision, and reapplication, or

. . . post-test/pre-test ⟶ instruction ⟶ post-test/pre-test . . .

to the previous seven elements included in a behavioral objective promotes instruction that is cohesive, coherent, and systematically controlled by the teacher in terms of students needs, interests, and abilities. Additionally, the essential unity of music—its unity with the feelings and "Mind" of man and its unity as a phenomenological experience—is emphasized and kept intact by the cohesiveness of such instruction.

This is the eventual value of approaching instruction in music through behavioral objectives. The teacher who (1) devises behavioral objectives according to educational theory and aesthetic philosophy, (2) who efficiently implements these objectives, (3) who follows each objective with an application of the systems approach, and (4) who makes subsequent plans on the basis of observed behavior—such a teacher is very likely to have unity and focus of instruction, that perhaps the aspect of current music education practice that is most sadly lacking. The concepts to be learned, the materials to be used, the exact nature of the activities created, invented, or devised are still matters for the individual teacher to decide. After all, the teacher too must work from within the framework of a well-established conceptual understanding of music. But this kind of individuality must not be confused with complete freedom or license. The individual teacher is still required to make these decisions on the basis of learning theory, a philosophical point of view about the aesthetics of music, and adolescent or child psychology.

Applied in this manner, behavioral objectives are, in effect, learning activities with informal and ungraded evaluation built-in. Some of these activities involve exploratory ventures: free experiential contact and investigations of concepts or skills to be learned. Some are strictly "instructional": participation in the activity promotes discovery learning. Some, though comparatively few, are strictly evaluative: cumulative or culminating activities designed to judge progress and to plan for future activities. Though behavioral objectives can be used for purposes of grading (more about this later in this chapter), they should not be regarded by either the teacher or the class as "tests" in the usual sense. They are no more tests than are the finished artifacts of an art class. They are for teacher and student evaluation, and grades are not the necessary results of such evaluation.

## BEHAVIORAL OBJECTIVES AS AIDS IN IMPLEMENTING ACTIVITIES

The use of behavioral objectives enables the teacher not only to organize a course of study that is logical and orderly in its progression and relevant in its applicability, but also to implement learning activities and projects most effectively. In the broadest sense, behavioral objectives by their nature require a clarity and conciseness of thought that encourages the teacher to think through each activity most carefully. In considering covert variables, overt behavior, content, means, time, and proficiency guidelines, the teacher will necessarily cover most of the crucial factors in planning the implementation of activities.

For example, in selecting the covert variable the teacher avoids confusion of goals: if the covert variable is "to differentiate," then it should be obvious that two or more factors must be present so that differentiation can take place. Similarly, if the covert variable "to identify" is employed, then some means for labeling or referring to the identified factors must be either a part of the student's present abilities or provided in the activities.

Continuing this line of thought, the very fact that many activities will have the *means* specified as given factors in the behavioral objective promotes the organization of the activity, in regard to the materials needed. Usually, the only other step needed at this point is to take a moment to locate the materials to be used. In books or music this would involve noting page numbers; thus, last minute thumbing and hunting through pages is avoided. When records are used, the albums should be located and the side and band numbers noted. A further aid, where possible, is to prepare the selection on tape. This is especially helpful when only a portion of a composition will be used or when certain sections must be repeated several times. Playing "drop the needle" can not only ruin a recording, but perhaps more serious, it can interfere with the natural and unbroken flow of a lesson as the teacher stumbles about embarrassingly trying to find the proper place on the record. If other materials such as paper and pencil, crayons, color chips, visual illustrations, and reproductions or photographs of artworks are needed, these too will have been specified in the objective, which then will serve to remind the teacher to secure and arrange such teaching aids in advance.

The necessity that behavioral objectives impose upon the teacher to think in terms of time limits, proficiency levels, and other restrictions serves, in addition to their learning purposes, the benefit of providing a useful guide for both teacher and student as to the dimensions of the project. Similarly, due consideration of overt behavior helps initially to determine the means and materials that are necessary, and, eventually, the kind of activity the class must undertake. If the eventual behavior is to be verbalized in writing, then, obviously, the class must have something to write with and on. Furthermore, both the class and teacher should realize that writing—not moving about the room, talking, or playing—is the required behavior.

The relationship between the overt and covert phases on an activity is frequently misconstrued or mishandled by many teachers in implementing learning activities. The behavior resulting from a learning activity is often regarded as an *end* in itself rather than as a *means* for determining covert behavior (learning.) Thus, sight singing and "dictation" in theory classes have tended to become self-sustaining activities seemingly of value in themselves, when in fact their real value is to help assess the student's ability to hear inwardly.

Behavioral objectives help to overcome misapplication of learning activities by emphasizing the covert behavior that is at stake. When an objective is not realized, one of the recommended alternatives is to revise it. In terms of sight singing, the student who performs poorly may profit from some other form of overt behavior by which he can manifest his ability to hear inwardly, and, thus, a new objective can be constructed. All the while the teacher is reminded that it is the ability to hear inwardly that is the learning at stake, not the rather mechanical practices of sight singing and dictation.

A behavioral objective also specifies *who* will be affected by the activity. This aids the teacher in implementing the activity. If it is to be small-group work, then small groups will have to be assembled by some means. If it is to be individuals or large groups, then some means of conveying the directions to the individual or class must be clearly devised before the activity can fruitfully begin.

By these processes, behavioral objectives allow the teacher to efficiently institute an activity with the least amount of predictable confusion on the part of the class. Occasional confusion, clarification, redirection of effort is inevitable. Such instances, however, are the exception and not the rule, and, thus, classes can progress more smoothly and learning can be more efficient and more effective.

*GO TO FRAME 5, PAGE 307.*

---

## BEHAVIORAL OBJECTIVES AS LONG-RANGE CURRICULAR GOALS

Behavioral objectives should also be used in planning a course of study for a year, or even longer periods of time. Such behavioral objectives are not less specific in the covert and overt behaviors involved, but, rather, are more general with regard to materials, limitations, and so forth. Thus, in writing such long-term behavioral objectives the specific "given" factors can be omitted; instead, the many kinds of overt behavior to be elicited are clearly specified.

By the end of the year each student will demonstrate his comprehension of simple part forms (binary, ternary, rondo, song form and trio, variation) by:

1. composing original compositions that successfully manifest these forms;
2. identifying these forms in aural examples;
3. analyzing these forms from the musical score without aural examples;
4. finding and choosing, from the music they listen to outside of class, examples of each, and explaining these to the class;
5. applying these forms abstractly to visual examples, diagrams, graphic representations, and vice versa; and
6. characterizing specific examples in terms of how the student feels about the ways these forms contribute to the musical expression of the selection.

Similar objectives should be devised for all kinds and phases of instrumental instruction. Factors related to assembling the instrument (and keeping it clean), posture, embouchure, tone, theory rudiments (notation, meters, and so on), the anticipated number of pitches the student can play, and other relevant factors should all be devised. Where more than one teacher is responsible for any instruction, co-operative development and agreement upon objectives should prevail.

With objectives such as the one above planned well in advance for each area of instruction, each learning to be undertaken, the teacher has only to refer to the combined total before planning more specific objectives. In other words, the teacher uses the long-term objectives relevant to a specific area of instruction as the basis for deriving specific teaching objectives. Thus, these long-term objectives contribute both *focus* and *systematic development* to the activities of a year by serving as the composite goal toward which any single activity is aimed.

A prime advantage of long-term objectives is their uncanny propensity for forcing the teacher to think clearly about *what* should be taught. Organizing a curriculum in terms of what should be taught, and what can be overtly evaluated as evidence of the success of such teaching, can do much to overcome many of the major problems in the profession. Consider, for example, the following factors, which are implicit in the long-range objective given above. The teacher is virtually obliged to think in these terms:

1. Comprehension of the forms in question is the important goal, not the passing of tests or the recording or recalling of information.

2. The year of study will emphasize the five simple part forms indicated in the objective, and not a historical survey of all forms or some other such diverse undertaking.

3. The forms in question must be approached in at least six different ways, and activities that emphasize the six relevant variables must be included with regularity:

    a. creation of original works

    b. aural identification

    c. visual identification

    d. identifying, choosing, and explaining from among music the students prefer (that is, transfer to a personal listening repertory)

    e. abstract application of concepts between the visual and aural realms (as these concepts are traditionally characteristic of all art forms)

    f. characterizing in terms of feeling (in order that *concept* may serve *affect*).

When a comprehensive list of such long-range behavioral objectives is made, it constitutes a curriculum. A curriculum may cover a varying time span, according to the requirements of the situation or the scope of the teacher's responsibility. If a curriculum is devised by the collective effort of all music teachers, each contributing their own special relevancies, and with their complete collective agreement, then all teaching efforts are more likely to have the relevance and effectiveness that is so missing in most music teaching today.

In school systems whose musical instruction is headed by a supervisor of music, the temptation is great for a curriculum to be produced full-blown by the individual in charge. This can produce sorry results. It is often difficult to teach from such an impersonally derived document: seldom will all teachers in the system have the same understanding of the objectives as the person who formulated them. For this reason, among others (not the least of which is *esprit de corps*), the supervisor should act as a stimulator, facilitator, and co-ordinator of the collective efforts of the music staff in drawing up a comprehensive curriculum. In this way, the singularity of purpose that results is collective, not dogmatic.

Each teacher, in surveying the comprehensive list of long-range behavioral objectives that apply to his specific grade level or situation, is on one hand beneficially limited, and on the other hand free. The teacher is limited to the degree that such a curriculum of long-term objectives prevents unproductive or unrelated tangents, aimless wandering, and dead ends, and at the same time helps to provide focus and ensuring transfer of all learnings. Freedom results from the opportunity each teacher has to employ the specific materials, activities, and sequences that best suit the needs, interests, and abilities of both the class and the teacher (in terms of instructional goals). Thus, due consideration of the long-term objective given as an example on page 290, might evolve into the following specific teaching objective:

> Given twenty minutes of preparation and the use of only self-generated vocal sounds, each group of three students will demonstrate their comprehension of second rondo form by creating an original composition in that form using original notation, performing it for the class, and characterizing their feelings about the expressive contribution of the form for their contribution.

In turn, this specific objective may also serve another long-range behavioral objective that deals with the recognition and understanding of the role and operation of musical notation; or an objective dealing with the concepts of unity and variety or unity *in* variety as the broad determinants of form in traditional music.

Conceivably, various groups will complete this activity in various ways: some groups may create purely linear compositions in which the sounds are organized in succession, much as melodies, in determining the form; others may organize their sounds into vertical sound-mass combinations. In either case, other long-range behavioral objectives dealing with melody, rhythm, timbre, textures, and so forth, may be found relatable to the present activity.

Thus, this one objective, specific as it seems, is derived from a much more general and broader goal. Also, it will be necessarily related to several other long-range objectives. Through the use of both long-range and specific teaching objectives, transfer of learning, opportunities for continued and refined application of learnings, and skills and concepts are provided. Without the use of behavioral objectives in these two ways, relationships among lessons become much more tenuous and less evident. These objectives virtually force you to recognize the inherent relationships among activities, and, thus, the essential unity of music. The students in your classes will increasingly observe this as well.

It is much better for the class to go as far as it can in terms of their readiness and progress, and to do so at the rate of speed that is most appropriate, than for the teacher to regard long-term objectives as "the material that must be covered." Some classes may go farther, faster. The result may be that after several years, the long-range objectives should be redrawn along more realistic lines for the age group or community involved. This may not, on the other hand, be necessary if it is possible for the teacher to devise specific objectives that are in line with the requirements of the long-range objectives, but which are well suited to the abilities of the various classes. If such activities, with multiple outcomes for multiple levels of ability, are possible, then such long-range objectives can usually serve diverse needs.

The objective on page 292 (please refer to it now to refresh your memory) is well suited for a competent, fairly well-prepared group. A less prepared or less able group might have the following objective instead:

> Given one full period and the use of any "found songs" of their own choosing, each group of three students will demonstrate their comprehension of three-part form by arranging the individual songs into at least two separate three-part forms, and by explaining to the class how three parts obtain from the use of only two contrasting musical segments.

This objective serves the same basic goals as the one before it, but recognizes that the abilities of the class are *presently* (not inevitably or necessarily) limited to the rearrangement of extant musical segments, rather than the original creation of larger compositions. In both cases, however, an understanding of "three-partedness" would be evident in those who successfully completed the objective. These understandings might differ in degree or level of refinement, but this is inevitable even within homogeneously grouped classes.

Thus, the use of long-range objectives in this manner also requires that the teacher consider the readiness of each separate class, and that different results be possible within the same specified context. In an extremely heterogeneous class the wise teacher might selectively assign the more refined objective to the students who were ready for it, and the less demanding one, presented before, to the students who were more suited for that project. With this in mind, remember that neither long-range nor specific teaching objectives are inviolable. Both can and should be adapted, or even sacrificed, depending on the contingencies of the situation.

It would be a good idea at this point to derive several more specific teaching objectives from the long-range objective given on page 290. Of course, the number and kind of specific objectives that can be obtained from a long-range objective of this kind are almost infinite, depending on the situations, and the individuals, so it is not possible to indicate any correct answers here. However, if you are to profit from this discussion, you should be able to create at least several specific objectives according to your own situation, interests, or abilities, and to check their accuracy by comparing them to the formula for writing behavioral objectives given earlier and the three further recommendations given on page 282.

## BEHAVIORAL OBJECTIVES AND SHORT-TERM PLANNING

When long-range behavioral objectives are used to protect and insure the sequential and developmental arrangement of activities necessary for transfer of learning, then it is not necessary for a teacher to plan specifically too far in advance; in fact, this should probably be avoided in most situations. Planning several months or weeks of *specific* behavioral objectives can have several inherent disadvantages:

1. Planning too far ahead does not allow for new contingencies as they arise. If an objective fails, or even if it succeeds, the teacher is obliged to plan remedial activities, revise the lesson, or perhaps repeat the lesson. If a new topic or area of interest is generated by the class, it is often wise to follow it up when it arises rather than at the time in the distant future that was allotted for it.

2. Planning too far ahead does not take the readiness, needs, or interests of the class into proper consideration. To plan too far in advance in specific terms assumes total control by the teacher. There is little room for group decisions or for "permissipline."

3. Planning too far ahead inevitably leads to the diminished effect of the three steps of "evaluation-revision-reapplication." Many teachers become too eager to move on to the next planned activity, rather than basing future plans on the information acquired as a result of present activities. To such teachers, moving on implies moving forward, when, in fact, repeating an activity or reapplying the same activity in a different context may be more of a step forward than undertaking the next planned activity.

Thus, the teacher should at all times have several activities specifically planned in advance. Beyond this, however, it is most useful to wait until the results of the present activity have been evaluated. Then the teacher can plan for future activities and their sequence and arrangement, in terms of observed needs. Even when you plan several activities in advance, you should feel no compulsion about dropping those plans and inserting something new in light of new contingencies.

The thread of continuity and transfer is provided for daily planning by relating all such plans to the long-term objectives specified by the teacher at the beginning of the year or term. And even these are not inviolable. At best, they represent an anticipation or an intent. Some may not be realized fully; others may be surpassed. You are obliged to move on only when and if the class is ready. To move on because of the compulsion of year-end goals may be to move too fast for student readiness. This usually involves problems in attitudes, co-operation, and discipline.

At the end of each year or term, the teacher should reevaluate the long-term objectives specified for that period of time. Several factors should be observed:

1. How many students reached these objectives?
2. How many students surpassed these objectives?
3. How many students fell short, and how far short?
4. Did the work on these objectives contribute in developing real musical behaviors, feeling responses, or other such goals?
5. Is it your observation that the objective was unrealistically set in terms of criteria, or that the specific teaching strategies used to meet the objective were poorly conceived?
6. On the basis of your answers to these questions, what revisions can you make to improve each objective for future use?

It is quite necessary to apply this evaluation procedure to all long-term objectives, even those that work consistently. Such evaluation allows the teacher to keep up with the times in several ways:

1. The nature of the subject matter or content may be changing. Thus, the teacher must be aware of the need for altering the long-term objectives in order to reflect new developments in the living musical art.

2. The nature of teaching materials or the physical plant involved may permit new or revised objectives to be designed and applied. Using new materials as they are developed allows the teacher to continually improve teaching effectiveness.

3. The nature of the student may change. From year to year, changes may seem slight. But over several years, the abilities and capacities of the student population may undergo a change that should be properly reflected in teaching goals.

## BEHAVIORAL OBJECTIVES AS PERSONAL RESEARCH

It is the responsibility of every dedicated teacher to update and improve their teaching skills continually by keeping informed of developments in the profession. Some, desperately clutching for ideas that "work," regard this task as only an avenue for getting through the school day with a minimum of complications. Others more properly regard it as a necessary step in improving instruction, which has as a beneficial by-product the greater rewards that make teaching more pleasant.

Though research in music education is not something to be taken lightly, many teachers, on the other hand, are unnecessarily apprehensive about undertaking personal research relevant to their teaching. With some minimal safeguards, every teacher can carry out small research experiments and derive some degree of usable information. The kind of research referred to here is related mostly to determining the relative or comparative success of varying teaching methods or materials. The profession is beset with a plethora of new "methods" and related teaching materials. Far too often, it seems, teachers adopt these methods and materials as a result of an uncritical "bandwagon" mentality, as if being up to date was simply a matter of employing the latest ideas. In such situations, the use of behavioral objectives, coupled with a few other safeguards, can give more reliable information than is possible from only casual observation. More important, perhaps, is the fact that the use of behavioral objectives encourages the teacher to evaluate the results of new or different methods or materials, and enables a more objective and reliable evaluation than would be possible without the criteria and behavioral evidences provided by behavioral objectives.

In addition to well-written and well-conceived behavioral objectives, there are a few other factors that the teacher should consider in planning such personal research.

### 1. Reducing Variables

If a testing situation is to give up useful information, you must be sure that the results observed are due to the methods or materials under consideration. If a new teaching technique is applied experimentally with two classes of widely varied ability, it becomes difficult to judge whether success or failure is due to the method or the abilities of the students. Thus, some attempt must be made to reduce the number of variables that can affect the situation. For the purposes outlined here, this should involve the following:

a. Using relatively homogeneous groups for comparison. In music classes, grouping on the basis of relatively equal musical abilities is more important than grouping along socioeconomic lines, IQ, or sex.

b. Reducing or controlling the number of variables in the behavioral objective being used. If too many covert variables are involved, success or failure will be difficult to judge since it will not be evident which variable has caused the result.

c. Precautions designed to eliminate outside influences or effects. This involves making sure that whatever changes are observed are a result of the new techniques or materials, and not of factors outside of the music class and, thus, beyond the teacher's control. Therefore, care must be taken to avoid situations where parents, other peers, other materials, can effect the results of the experiment.

d. Considering the effects of time. Very often, if too much time is allowed, the ongoing conceptual development of the learner that accompanies maturation may unduly influence the results of the experiment. Thus, the ability of the student to accomplish a task may be due to his increased mental or psychophysical maturation and not to the new methods or materials being used.

## 2. Validity

Validity is determined by how accurate an evaluation procedure is in describing (making evident) the sample of behavior that is the goal of the instruction or materials involved. Thus, to test musical understanding by having a student reiterate the names of composers and their dates would not constitute a valid measure of their comprehension.

Sight singing and melodic, harmonic, and rhythmic dictation are "testing" activities that, under certain conditions, purport to evaluate an individual ability to effectively use his inner ear. Far too often, they provide an inaccurate description of the operation of the inner ear because of confusing variables in the situation (such as the inability to sing comfortably or confusion of the symbols used for chords), and because even successful performance in the activities is not necessarily relevant (valid) for the purposes of musicianship. If the inner ear is important to a musician, it is mainly through its use in musical contexts, such as playing and conducting. As evaluation procedures of the operation of the inner ear, sight singing and dictation activities are *not valid* when a student who performs well in all of them is unable to identify errors in his own performance or the performance of others.

In the kind of basically informal research outlined here, the teacher's task is to insure that the proposed procedure for evaluation truly and accurately measures or makes observable the results of the new teaching technique or materials. The safest way to accomplish this is to be sure that the overt behavior specified in the objective is an indication of the covert operations that are at stake. In essence, *each behavioral objective should have this kind of internal validity anyway,* so that the ability to conceive of and write significant objectives will frequently overcome problems of validity.

## 3. Accuracy

Accuracy is ensured by a sample of behavior that is large enough to protect against the operations of chance. Thus, a one-time occurrence of success with a given task does not usually fulfill the conditions of accuracy. Such a singular success could very well result from chance, or even from a misconception by the student (for instance, the correct response could be given for the wrong reason or by incorrect means). Accuracy is also related to the number of individuals evaluated. Thus, success of new methods or materials with only one, or a small number of students would not adequately insure the attribution of success to the materials or methods involved. This is the basic principle behind standardized tests.

Though very large samples are impractical for the teacher who is eager to carry out personal campaigns to assess the relative merits of various teaching techniques and materials, it is important that the teacher try to involve as large a number of students as is practical and reasonable. Thus, in experimenting with a new instruction book for beginning trumpet students, all such students might be divided into two relatively equal groups, with each group using a different book. Similarly, with general music classes, two groups constituting a large numerical sample will make whatever feedback accrues a much more accurate and reliable basis for decision making by the teacher.

In the absences of the formal processes and controls of the professional researcher, the music teacher will likely benefit most from working with the kinds of comparison groups recommended here. One group serves as the *control* group, and the other is treated to the *experimental* methods or materials. Then, the achievements of one are measured against the achievements of the other. If reasonable care has been taken to properly consider (1) the reduction of variables, (2) validity, and (3) accuracy, the teacher will in most cases have reliable grounds for making decisions on the relative merits of the methods or materials being tested. In any case, this decision will be far more accurate than if only casually undertaken without some controls.

In general, if behavioral objectives are well conceived and well written, they all should:

1. have reduced the variables in the situation to manageable limits;
2. have overt behaviors that are valid manifestations of covert learnings (behaviors);
3. protect the accuracy of the overt behaviors (as manifestations of covert behaviors) by specifying criteria and providing or allowing for transfer or reapplication.

Thus, the essential conditions of personal research by the music teacher are provided by the existence and use of good behavioral objectives. In this sense, the use of behavioral objectives provides the means for evaluating teaching success. This process is quite different from the traditional evaluation procedures that assess student success for the purposes of giving grades.

It should be obvious that such small-scale, personal research is a well-recommended activity for every music teacher. Evaluation of a variety of teaching approaches prevents a teacher from getting in a rut. Similarly, it provides a firm basis for the teacher to improve teaching skills, and it enhances the continual improvement that is necessary in vital teaching. A beneficial by-product is the continued satisfaction that the teacher can derive from the act of teaching. Getting in a rut or being in a "rat race," whatever you call it, results from a kind of teaching boredom. Such boredom in turn results from the lack of a continual challenge, a significant goal (other than mere survival, that is.). If the teacher's only goal is to get through each day, each week, or each year, and to draw pay in doing so, the rut or "rat race track" is well established. If, on the other hand, the teacher's goals are drawn in terms of teaching effectiveness and its rewards, then the kind of personal research outlined here can serve as a very useful if not indispensable aid in continually updating and improving teaching effectiveness.

*GO TO FRAME 6, PAGE 308.*

## BEHAVIORAL OBJECTIVES AS STUDENT "CONTRACTS"

Of the many uses of behavioral objectives, and of the many reasons for including them when planning learning experiences, one that is frequently overlooked is their relevance when made known to the class. Though this is obviously neither possible nor practical in literal terms for very young students, it becomes a much more realistic possibility with adolescents.

In musical learning situations, it is possible to advise younger children of the goals at hand, the criteria, and the other aspects of the behavioral objective, by means of a paraphrase in terms they will understand.

Given contrasting examples of improvised music of a distinct rhythmic and mood character, each student will demonstrate his ability to freely interpret the music by moving to the music, changing the character of these movements as the character of the music changes.[6]

Paraphrased, the children might be advised to:

"Listen to Mr. Piano. Its music is going to tell us several different things to do. See if you can tell what Mr. Piano is saying, then do what it has told you to do."[6]

As children approach and reach adolescence, the behavioral objective, in a sense, becomes something of a *contract* between students and teacher. It signifies what is expected of everyone, what the criteria are, and what the expected results will be. It provides a kind of agreement (if, that is, the class accepts the objective as a goal worthy of their efforts) as to minimal expectations and what is open to their free choice. It provides a tangible or observable end-product for the students to use in assessing their own progress. This end-product, when given in the form of a behavioral objective, also becomes its own reward: the attainment of the goal. No further rewards are necessary, though they may be employed on occasion.

For these reasons, it is especially necessary that the behavioral objective hold forth some goal that meets student interests or needs in terms of effective living. To adolescents, "effective living" generally means the present or the near future since the distant future is still rather indefinite to them. The behavioral objective that meets present needs successfully will invariably have its natural, more long-range consequences as well.

By the junior high school years, behavioral objectives, either presented

---

[6] Since very young children often learn initially by imitation, by rote, it is not as crucial here that the teacher avoid conditions that would permit imitation. If situations such as these are combined with situations where the children are able to independently interpret music freely in terms of feeling (such as choosing stories, verbal descriptions, creating visual designs to music), the chances of totally imitative behavior being encouraged are thereby limited.

directly and literally to the class or paraphrased in less technical language, become the guiding force of all class meetings. These objectives direct all efforts, including those of the teacher, and serve as the main basis of evaluation. Everyone comes to know and respect the operation of these objectives.

Making the student aware of the behavioral objectives involved has advantages other than these for the teacher. Among many other things, when students are advised of the objectives at hand, they are less likely to confuse the purposes of these objectives.

Many teachers at all levels frequently employ activities and behavioral objectives that deal with mood responses, subjective characterizations of one kind or another, and "programmatic" references. In fact, many activities of this kind have been described behaviorally throughout this book. When students are *unaware* of the covert variables and the content (if any) involved, they are likely to derive many mistaken notions. The result of poor teaching and a history of poor critic-poets who insist on verbal or visual imagery for all music is that many people think that all music presents a picture or conveys some kind of story. When they can identify neither the picture nor the story, they feel unfulfilled. In contrast with this, when classes are informed that these activities are means—not ends—designed to encourage free subjective responses, they are advised of an aesthetic principle that they can both grasp and use.

Similarly, many classes spend endless hours participating in musical activities that, to them, have no apparent purpose other than to serve the teacher's will. They have no idea of the relevance of most of what the teacher has them do. When, instead, they know that they are creating sound forms in class in order "to understand musical form," they then have a clearer perception of what relevance the activity has. When their learnings that deal with musical form are applied to listening examples of their own choosing, or to rock, folk or pop pieces, it becomes increasingly clear.

Behavioral objectives shared with the class in whatever language make clear to the class not only the purposes of all learning activities, but also the many possible applications of the learnings. If the understanding of musical form is approached on many different occasions—from the point of view of creative activity, aural activity, performance activity, pure contemplation— young people soon learn to regard music in proper perspective. They soon learn it is not something "gifted" people do or make, but something all people can approach and involve themselves in at many different levels. Even the so-called gifted or talented youngsters can (and should) learn that music can be a keen source of avocational interest. Perhaps what the musical world needs now is fewer professionals and teachers competing for too few jobs; what it may need is more talented amateurs.

Perhaps the most significant benefit of sharing behavioral objectives with your classes is rather subtle in its effect. Children in America seem to grow up with a rather strange notion about teachers. Instead of looking upon teachers as partners in learning, many children are led to regard teachers as "the enemy," a worthy though not unbeatable opponent. This attitude often derives from the all too frequent situations in all teaching where the teacher seems to be tricking the students by homework assignments, tests, and the like, the merits of which are unknown to the class, and the results of which are used to label and categorize them in often unfair ways. Many children regard homework assignments and tests in just this vein. They view these things as a guessing match between them and the teacher (who undoubtedly has something up his sleeve). The game gets more and more involved as the youngster matures and reaches secondary school and finally college. Here, the student, now fully realizing the implications of the game and the lack of true relevance in its rules and regulations, perfects his own repertoire of tricks. All sorts of means are used to find the easiest and most effective ways of completing assignments and scoring well on tests. Often the time saved by these means is applied to pursuits that the student deems more worthy. This often amounts to "discipline problems."

When classes know of the full criteria involved at any given time, when they can see the relevance and eventual application of the learnings, then a chance of a co-operative educational effort is greatly improved. In situations like these, the teacher is not an enemy and the class is not involved in gamesmanship (beyond the typical behavior of the age group, that is). Students can then view the teacher as an instrument for learning, rather than a fountainhead of knowledge. Respect is personal rather than abstract.

Involved in all of this is the issue of grades. Behavioral objectives are a very useful and reliable means of assigning grades without unduly affecting subjective judgment, and their appropriate use all year can help overcome many of the problems inherent in the grading situation.

## BEHAVIORAL OBJECTIVES AS BASES FOR GRADING

The many weaknesses of grading and grading systems were discussed in Chapter Four. There, we discussed the weaknesses of grades that are used as motivating forces, rewards, or punishment or even as incentives. Here, the problem is this: When grades are a necessary administrative function required of the teacher, how are they to be fairly and accurately awarded? What are the bases for grading in a content area that stresses the feeling response and personal involvement with the content, and where the objective aspects present are minimal and often unimportant?

Now that the design, use, and advantages of behavioral objectives have been fully explored, some ideas about their application to grading can be suggested.

### Relations with Administrators

Every effort must be made to educate administrators about the unique problems of instruction in music, especially general music classes. They must be presented with a rationale that argues that musical instruction involves the development of concepts that have varying personal applications and varying personal levels of mastery. These considerations indicate that musical instruction should not be forced into unnatural strictures such as periodic examinations on information. Administrators must be presented with the idea that musical instruction, indeed all arts education, has no generally agreed upon body of knowledge or realm of skill that is as invariably applicable as are most of the other areas of public school instruction, such as the sciences, mathematics, the languages, and the social studies. The "facts" of music are generally the least important aspects of *musical* instruction in the public schools. Thus, no such *a priori* determination of results in terms of student conformity or mastery is either possible or desirable, and, hence, no single measure (such as tests) of such learnings is adequate. Above all, you must present administrators with a clear and logical alternative by which you intend to arrive at viable grades for the students in your charge. The conditions by which you can arrive at such alternatives can now be considered.

### Relations with Students

Seldom should short-range, specific teaching objectives be used as bases for grades. To implement a policy, no matter how infrequent, where the everyday variety of behavioral objectives are utilized to derive grades can have a severe inhibiting effect on the willingness of the class to take part freely in class activities. Rather, long-range objectives are the bases for evaluating student progress. While always keeping clearly in mind that your objectives are not absolutes, you can evaluate students by your judgment of how far they have progressed *from where they were* toward the anticipated goals.

On the occasions when grades are due, "testing" activities in the same form as the ongoing activities of the class should be used as empirical evidence of student progress. Among other things, this insures that the students will be evaluated in terms and contexts familiar to them. To adopt the activity approach recommended thus far, but then to evaluate by means of a written test on facts and information would do severe disservice to the cause. Another advantage is that even the testing activities are done within the context of student behavior and their ability to use or demonstrate learning. This avoids the possibility of classes conceiving of musical instruction as an accumulation of abstract, irrelevant knowledge, learned for its own sake. Thus, "tests" should be structured in the form of behavioral, but individual, class activities.

By sharing behavioral objectives with the class throughout the year, you can lead the class to understand these objectives as minimal standards to be reached by all at their own level of accomplishment. In conjunction with this, you must also lead the class to understand that these objectives in no way pretend to enforce conformity, stunt independence, stifle creativity, or inhibit excellence beyond these minimal standards.

302

Attainment of the aforementioned minimal standards pre-specified in the behavioral objectives, or continual behavioral change towards such attainment (hence, the need for regarding learning as changes in the frequency of a desired behavior), should be regarded as an "A" or its numerical equivalent.[7] The grade thus reflects the concrete achievements of the individual student, rather than an abstract factor of excellence pronounced by an omniscient and omnipotent teacher. Learning or progress that falls short of the minimal standards specified in the long-range behavioral objectives may then be ranked accordingly. Some soul-searching should be done first by the teacher, to make sure that the objectives and criteria as specified are realistic for the group or individual.

Students must at all times be advised of the minimal role and small importance of grades in musical instruction. Grades in general should be very much de-emphasized. The teacher must be consistent and fair in all dealings with grades, and students must at all times know what the grade means—what it reflects and how it was determined.

Grades should reflect learning (in terms of behavior) and not how seemingly well or poorly an individual may behave (in terms of discipline). Though one might expect that learning and self-discipline go hand in hand, there are many instances where a student's behavior may seem problematic and where learning is still ongoing. Exceptionally bright youngsters may be very "experimental" from time to time, and may seem to flout proposed criteria or limitations. This is to be expected, and should be neither rewarded nor punished with grades. Some youngsters manage to delicately balance learning with a certain degree of growth-typical behavior that is often misconstrued as poor discipline. Teachers are often surprised to receive a good answer when they throw a quick, unexpected question at a student who is apparently paying little attention.

If a student is not learning and not behaving, even then the nagging question of "Why?" should prevent a teacher from readily punishing the student with a poor grade (negative reinforcement!). The misconception involved in the notion of using poor grades as punishment or motivation is revealed when you consider the effect of such a grade on the student who has neither cared nor been apparently motivated during all the previous instruction. What in the grade will magically transform "D" work into "A" work?

Obviously, lower grades will be awarded; it is the conscious and purposeful act of using or regarding these grades as punishment that the teacher must avoid. Grades should be regarded as just one more means, an annoying one at that, of providing the student with information concerning relative

---

[7] There are some who will claim or wonder why, if the criteria are minimal standards, a "D" or its numerical equivalent is not awarded. This misconception arises from the archaic notion of rewarding (positively reinforcing) excellence with the highest grade, instead of rewarding concrete achievement with the highest grade. In this latter capacity, the grade may still be regarded by the student as a reward, but his attitudes in this instance are less likely to cause him to look at grades as a form of legalized blackmail. And in any case, the student's greatest reward comes from a sense of accomplishment and the satisfaction of learning.

progress and success. Any inordinate concern they may have for grades belies ill-conceived goals on their part, resulting from either parental pressures or the tradition of grading itself. Grades are abstractions: mere symbols that attempt to summarize in a supremely singular form the many complexities of learning over many weeks or months of classes. It should be evident to anyone that they do not, indeed cannot, do this with any degree of reliability or even significance.

## GRADING SKILLED LEARNING

There is one particular area of music instruction where grading is a special problem: the area of skill instruction in musical performance. Directors of various ensembles are notorious among their colleagues in other areas of the school for their overly generous and generally unrealistic grading practices. Grades are often given "off the top of the head" or "by the seat of the pants." They have no necessary basis in fact, and most often the only basis is the wish fulfillment existing in the mind of the director.

Music schools at the level of higher education are notorious for ignoring a prospective applicant's grades in high school music classes. This brings to light one specific aspect of grading in performance organizations: the use of grades in realistically advising students of their ability and "talent." Far too many students who have certain advanced degrees of musical ability and who find genuine satisfaction in music and musical participation are unduly encouraged to consider music as a vocation by the unwarranted awarding of unrealistic grades or competition ratings. When they go on to a music school they find far too often that they like music and musical participation, but that *studying* music as a serious and lifelong vocation is difficult, often beyond their capacities, or is not personally satisfying. Many, often less independent souls, continue to think undoubtedly of the pot of gold at the end of the rainbow. Some manage to find it; far too many do not. Even those who do reach the end may, after encountering the competition in the many musical vocations, experience second thoughts, however late.

Grading performance groups is indeed a difficult proposal. It is no wonder that the teachers who have no long-range behavioral goals in mind must resort to magic to call up grades at the end of each marking period. When long-range objectives are set for the group as a whole, according to individual readiness, some viable and relatively objective measure of student progress and attainment can be observed and used as a basis for grading. Thus, students in the ensemble for their first year are judged in accordance with their development relative to objectives that are perhaps three years away in eventual applicability. Seniors, on the other hand, are judged according to their continued progress toward and mastery of the terminal goals of the course. Private or group lessons should provide the major bases for judgment, and in all cases student progress relative to the readiness level with which the individual began the course is an important factor. Thus, a fourth-chair player might, in fact, receive a grade equal to or higher than the first chair player if his progress and effort has been more notable.

Here, all the previous considerations of grading apply. And most important among all considerations is to de-emphasize the role and importance of grades. Musical performance and the desire to improve musical performance should have as its major reward and goal the satisfaction derived from the act of performance and from the learnings acquired in performance situations that allow the individual to be an effective consumer of music in all styles and media.

In general, teachers will gain much from a soul-searching consideration of the role and importance of grades in their own education, and the relevance of those grades in terms of actual learning. Furthermore, much insight will be gained if every teacher would consider the fact that grades, whether used as mere symbolic evidences of student attainment or as motivating forces, must be respected by the students in order to have any impact or influence on them. In order for students to respect the grades given them, these grades must be realistic. If everyone gets an "A," if everyone gets a 95, then no one will take grades seriously, one way or another. If, in their understanding, no fair or firm bases for grades can be seen, then grades will lose all significance. If, on the other hand, students can see a direct relationship between their grade and their achievement or effort, they can at least regard such grades as realistic and find some meaning in them.

These, then, are the considerations that each teacher should at least consider before undertaking the relatively serious task of grading in musical instruction. It would certainly be too idealistic to hope or even anticipate that grades will cease to have importance. Unfortunately, the importance attached to grades by educational institutions in this country almost dictates some level of concern by the students. Woe to the student who is independent enough to regard learning as more important than earning grades.

The use of behavioral objectives does hold out some promise for the upgrading of our currently archaic systems and overregard for grades. They provide the criteria and bases for pass/fail systems, avoiding any overly permissive application of that formula. They also provide empirical bases for systems that employ bargraphs or other kinds of scales. And for really progressive systems that use various forms of anecdotal accounts and descriptions of student progress and attainment, behavioral objectives provide both the language, the content and the criteria for formulating such records. They may even serve as a kind of check list of student abilities.

## CODETTA

There are undoubtedly many more advantages that could be sung in praise of behavioral objectives; perhaps the area has been overdone already. But one last observation seems warranted. The approach recommended here is intended to make the act of teaching a more controlled process. The use of behavioral objectives and the behavioral learning theory upon which they are based stem from the social science of psychology. While Langer has already sufficiently pointed out the weaknesses of this field in terms of scientific precepts and practice, she has done so mainly in criticism of behaviorism's claims to have found certain human truths.

This still leaves considerable advantage to be made of behavioral learning theory. Science (and its stepchild, psychology) can often tell us what is False. It can perform this function well in terms of teaching. It can guide us in our effort by enabling us to avoid false applications of teaching strategies and false evaluations of learning.

Truth, however, is a much more difficult proposition. The approach recommended here has attempted not to pronounce any dogma of what, specifically or "scientifically," true teaching is. This can be left to the resources of the musician-teachers who make up the profession. The ultimate Truth will be found, of course, in the musical art and its sister arts. The very essence of art is found in its objectification and reification of Human Truths. They deal with the human condition in all its great variety.

This, of course, is why art is so important to each of us individually, and why collectively the arts are so necessary to mankind. This is also why the responsibilities of music educators, and arts educators in general, are so varied and so great. And this is why this book was written: in order to give those teachers who wish to prepare themselves to handle these responsibilities some ideas and means for reasserting the prominence of music in personal education. Until music education can have a significant impact on society in terms of human insights and the development of feeling individuals, then our job is not yet done.

From page 284                                                      Frame 1

Evaluation, used in conjunction with a behavioral objective, should result in:

    A. grading. Go to Frame 25.
    B. planning. Go to Frame 12.
    C. student motivation. Go to Frame 20.

---

From page 286                                                      Frame 2

Revision, as an element in the correct use of behavioral objectives, involves:

    A. changing the behavioral objective to a more realistic level. Go to Frame 18.
    B. retaining the objective but changing instruction. Go to Frame 10.
    C. planning all subsequent instruction on the basis of the evaluation phases. Go to Frame 24.

---

From page 287                                                      Frame 3

Reapplication, when used in conjunction with behavioral objectives, should result in:

    A. refinement, development, and transfer. Go to Frame 27.
    B. repetition, revision, re-evaluation. Go to Frame 14.
    C. alteration, re-evaluation, revision. Go to Frame 22.

---

From Frame 27                                                      Frame 4

Evaluation, revision, and reapplication are three factors in the use of behavioral objectives that are:

    A. considered when and where applicable. Go to Frame 8.
    B. always considered and in sequential order. Go to Frame 16.
    C. considered at all times for grading of the student. Go to Frame 26.

---

From page 290                                                      Frame 5

After studying the following behavioral objective carefully, write down all the major factors that the teacher should consider and prepare in advance of the lesson, in order that it can be implemented effectively.

Given ten aural examples of songs in duple and triple meters, each student will correctly identify each meter by writing a 2 or a 3 on his answer sheet with at least eighty percent success after three sessions, and will do so consistently in subsequent lessons throughout the year.

Use the space below for your answers. When you have all your observations down in writing, turn to Frame 28 and check your answers against the factors suggested there.

*From page 298*

Do each question in order before going on to the next.

1. Identify the behavioral objective below that *best reduces variables*.

A. Go to Frame 7.
B. Go to Frame 23.
C. Go to Frame 15.

2. Identify the one that is *least valid*.

A. Go to Frame 21.
B. Go to Frame 11.
C. Go to Frame 17.

3. Identify the one that is *most accurate*.

A. Go to Frame 19.
B. Go to Frame 13.
C. Go to Frame 9.

A. Given a recording of the Bach Little Fugue in G minor, each student will identify the various entrances of the fugue subject by immediately raising his hand, and by the second listening will be able to do so with consistency and accuracy.

B. Given ten selected examples of songs from the song series, each student will demonstrate his comprehension of musical form by identifying each as AB, ABA, or AABA form, with ninety percent accuracy.

C. Given the use of only self-generated sounds and twenty minutes, each student will demonstrate his understanding of unity and variety by creating a rondo form, performing it for the class, and explaining how his composition uses unity and variety in the delineation of the form.

---

*From Frame 6*                                                                              Frame 7

You said that the behavioral objective that best reduces variables is A:

Given a recording of the Bach Little Fugue in G minor, each student will identify the various entrances of the fugue subject by immediately raising his hand, and by the second listening will be able to do so with consistency and accuracy.

Sorry, there is a very significant variable banging around in this objective: the psychomotor variable, "to imitate." This objective has the unfortunate weakness of permitting this unspecified variable to be substituted for the main variable, "to identify." How? By the very fact that the overt behavior being used—raising hands—will not necessarily or accurately reflect the student's ability to identify the fugue subject. It may, instead, reflect only his ability to quickly imitate the response of the person in front of him or the person recognized as "smart" in these matters.

If the teacher really wants to assess the student's ability to perceive entrances of a fugue, some other overt behavior will have to be devised that will eliminate such impingements of other variables. Various teachers have devised many different successful means for doing this. One way is for the teacher to point at numbers on the chalkboard, which identify measure numbers. The student then selects the number the teacher is pointing to at the moment when the subject is heard. If students are doing the listening activity individually, and are using a cassette tape recorder, identification can be done by using the footage counter. Go back to Frame 6 and choose another answer for question 1.

---

*From Frame 4*                                                                              Frame 8

You said that the elements of evaluation, revision, and reapplication are considered "when and where applicable," with regard to behavioral objectives. No! These elements should be added to the four other elements of behavioral objectives, which must always be considered and used. Without properly considering these factors, and doing so in the order given, most if not all of the benefits of using behavioral objectives would be lost. Go back to Frame 4 and try another choice.

You chose objective C to be most accurate in its measurement:

Given the use of only self-generated sounds and twenty minutes, each student will demonstrate his understanding of unity and variety by creating a rondo form, performing it for the class, and explaining how his composition uses unity and variety in the delineation of the form.

Correct. It is possible to create in the specified form an original score that appears accurate yet has a performance that is at odds with the facts, or an explanation that is weak or misinformed. But it is less likely that a student who fully completes all three overt behaviors successfully will have done so by chance. The repeated measures of behavior here serve to guarantee not only the *validity* of this musical understanding, but also the *accuracy* of the evaluation.

It is not always possible or practical, of course, to have more than one measure of learning for a given behavioral objective. There are many instances where this would be inordinately time consuming. In some instances it is best to repeat the entire objective several times in both the immediate and distant future, perhaps slightly varying the context, materials, or some other factor. Some activities are more self-sufficient and need no such evaluation: these would include most of the affective variables. Activities such as these must mainly guarantee validity; that is, the overt behavior must clearly reflect some affective state of mind. Whatever this state of mind may be, it is seldom evaluated in terms of accuracy. In fact, even if the same activity were repeated many times, it might be expected or even hoped that the student's response would be somewhat different each time. This would give added impetus to the idea that feeling responses are variable, according to the individual, his moods, and ever-evolving conceptual understanding.

By now you must have noticed that objective C was the strongest in all regards. A well-conceived, well-written behavioral objective will usually have this uncanny ability to resolve complex issues. On the other hand, the other two choices displayed varying degrees of problems. This, too, is to be expected, since a single weakness in a behavioral objective is like a weak link in a chain or an imperfect element in an architectural structure. Such weakness always manages to have significant effects on other elements in the complex.

Go to Page 299, below the line.

You said that revision, as used in conjunction with behavioral objectives, involves "retaining the objective but changing instruction." This is only one of several possibilities. To follow it steadfastly would eliminate many of the other advantages of revision. Thus, your answer is not the most suitable one of those offered. Go back to Frame 2 and try another answer.

*From Frame 6*

You said that the least valid objective was B:

Given ten selected examples of songs from the song series, each student will demonstrate his comprehension of musical form by identifying each as AB, ABA, or AABA form, with ninety percent accuracy.

There is probably a better choice you could have made for the least valid objective. Objective B has problems but they are not insurmountable. Whether or not comprehension is indicated by identification is the main question, but at least this objective specifies a large enough sampling of behavior. If a student is able to correctly identify nine or ten examples, this would tend to indicate his ability to identify these forms. At least the teacher would have this firm basis of information. Whether the student hears simple songs in "parts" and is able to identify these by letters without really "understanding" the principle of musical form involved, is still unresolved in this objective, however.

There is a more logical winner of the prize for being least valid. Go back to Frame 6 and try to find it.

---

*From Frame 1*

You said that the element of evaluation results in "planning" when used in conjunction with behavioral objectives. This is correct. On the basis of success, failure, or the degree of either, the teacher uses evaluation to plan subsequent activities. In fact, evaluation is the main reason for even working with behavioral objectives: the entire rationale is predicated on the need to specify and structure some firm bases for evaluation so that the teacher has some information, some observations, some realistic basis for understanding what is being learned and how well, and for planning accordingly.

Go to page 284, below the line.

---

*From Frame 6*

You chose objective B to be most accurate in its measurement.

Given ten selected examples of songs from the song series, each student will demonstrate his comprehension of musical form by identifying each as AB, ABA, or AABA form, with ninety percent accuracy.

Even though this objective has ten samples of behavior (that is, responses to ten examples) and the criterion of ninety percent accuracy, it is not necessarily the most accurate. In fact, in this particular instance, one of the other choices presents a much greater degree of assuredness.

The difficulty of this objective regarding variables and validity has already been discussed (see Frames 11 and 23). The same weaknesses it had in those areas affect it here. The identification of form according to the specifications of the objective would present a degree of accuracy only with regard to the variable, "to identify." The accuracy of these responses in assessing the much more broad specification, "comprehension of musical form," is subject to serious doubt.

If the objective had specified the main aspect of musical form that is involved—melodic unity and variety—then it would be more accurate in its measurement. Even then, it would be accurate only with regard to the three small part forms covered in the activity. These understandings would not necessarily be present when larger or more complex forms were confronted.

Go back to Frame 6 and make another choice for question 3.

---

*From Frame 3*                                                                  Frame 14

Your answer was that reapplication, when used in conjunction with behavioral objectives, results in "repetition, revision, and re-evaluation." Not necessarily so. First, repetition is only one possible form of reapplication. By choosing this answer, you have limited yourself considerably. Second, even in situations where repetition is used, it would naturally be followed by a new evaluation before a new revision was made. Go back to Frame 3 and choose another answer.

---

*From Frame 6*                                                                  Frame 15

You said that the behavioral objective that best reduces variables is C:

Given the use of only self-generated sounds and twenty minutes, each student will demonstrate his understanding of unity and variety by creating a rondo form, performing it for the class, and explaining how his composition uses unity and variety in the delineation of the form.

Indeed it does. The variable in question is "to understand" (or "to comprehend"). Not only is this variable given adequate focus by the objective, but multiple means are used to guarantee that "understanding" is truly manifested. If the student's creation, performance, and explanation are all satisfactory, the teacher can be assured that the student "understands" the principle of unity and variety at the level manifested in the project; but, this understanding is not necessarily comprehensive. It applies only to his understanding of unity and variety as applied to or derived from the rondo principle involving successive sounds. It does not demonstrate understanding of, say, the role of harmony (combined sounds) or the operation of unity and variety in other or longer forms.

It is possible that some of these understandings are present. This is not the question. The teacher is obliged to regard the present objective as demonstrating only an understanding in the simple rondo context. If other understandings are to be taught and evaluated, then other objectives specifying other contexts must be devised.

Go back to Frame 6 and answer question 2.

---

*From Frame 4* Frame 16

Your answer was that evaluation, revision, and reapplication are three factors that are "always considered and in sequential order," in the use of behavioral objectives. This is correct. These three elements should be added to the other four elements in behavioral objectives, which should always be operative. Furthermore, they should be considered in the order given so that the systems approach can be most fruitfully applied. The planning that results from due consideration of these elements in order does not necessarily have to follow a linear course, but the systems approach breaks down when the system is not followed in order.

Go to page 287, below the line.

---

*From Frame 6* Frame 17

You said that the least valid objective was C:

Given the use of only self-generated sounds and twenty minutes, each student will demonstrate his understanding of unity and variety by creating a rondo form, performing it for the class, and explaining how his composition uses unity and variety in the delineation of the form.

Assuredly not. It is the most valid of the three because it takes three measures of behavior (create, perform, explain; to make, to perform, to verbalize) to guarantee that the behavior validly measures the covert variable of understanding. Thus, a student must do well in all three areas for this objective to be fulfilled. Students whose creations may appear to be logical, but whose performances or explanations indicate a weakness of conception, would not adequately fulfill the specifications of this objective.

Successful completion of all three tasks shows not only conceptual understanding of the content involved, but also the ability to implement and reason verbally with the concept. Thus, the learned behavior is a valid measurement of understanding in this context.

Go back to Frame 6 and choose another answer for question 2.

---

*From Frame 2* Frame 18

Your answer was that revision, as an element in the correct use of behavioral objectives, involves "changing the behavioral objective to a more realistic level." This is a distinct possibility, but not the invariable result of revision. There are other possible results of using revision, to ignore them would severely diminish the effectiveness of behavioral objectives and the "systems approach." Thus, you should go back to Frame 2 and choose a more appropriate answer.

---

*From Frame 6*                                    Frame 19

You chose objective A to be most accurate in its measurement:

Given a recording of the Bach Little Fugue in G minor, each student will identify the various entrances of the fugue subject by immediately raising his hand, and by the second listening will be able to do so with consistency and accuracy.

Aside from the fact that the overt behavior specified may in fact measure the wrong kind of behavior (it may measure the student's ability "to imitate" other students rather than his ability "to identify"), only two hearings are specified, and only one example is heard. It is quite possible and even likely that among the various responses made by each individual are some made by chance. Since only two hearings of only one example are provided, there is little opportunity for the teacher or the students to discuss or analyze the variety of possible responses made by the class.

The individuals who made a substantial number of tentative responses, those who made a number of incorrect responses, those who made some apparently correct responses by chance or for the wrong reasons, will have little opportunity to reinterpret the situation, reapply their interpretations and act again. Only by the continued application of such correct responses could this objective be considered accurate, and even then the difficulty of what is being measured (and this is a question of validity)—"imitation" or "identification"—is still unresolved.

This objective could be improved immeasurably by providing for discussion between the minimal two hearings. Even then, it would help if at least one other fugue were included. This would allow a more reliable measure of the student's ability to hear the fugue texture and process.

Go back to Frame 6 and choose another answer for question 3.

---

*From Frame 1*                                    Frame 20

Your answer was that evaluation, used in conjunction with a behavioral objective, results in "student motivation." This is possible, especially if the results of the evaluation are favorable. While such evaluation *can* benefit the student, properly applied evaluation insures the integrity of the instructional process from the teacher's point of view. Of the choices you were given, one is far more appropriate, so go back to Frame 1 and try again.

You said that the least valid objective was A:

Given a recording of the Bach Little Fugue in G minor, each student will identify the various entrances of the fugue subject by immediately raising his hand, and by the second listening will be able to do so with consistency and accuracy.

This is correct. It is least valid because it does not necessarily measure the covert variable, "to identify." Many students may imitate the behavior of others in the class, thereby proving only their ability "to imitate." This is a psychophysical behavior, not a cognitive behavior.

This kind of confusion of aims and means is common. You must draw upon your own musicianship to devise overt behaviors that are valid in making covert behaviors observable. Teachers who evaluate a student's "understanding" of notation by tests on the names of the lines and spaces, for example, have given little thought to the process. It is necessary to know the names; but it is a musical behavior to correctly play the notes that fall on the lines and spaces of a given clef. Teachers who think they are testing comprehension of musical form, or who wish to evaluate a feeling response by having a student play a composition, may find themselves observing only the kinesthetic abilities of the student, and not the cognitions or affections present in a psychomotor response.

Go back to Frame 6 and answer question 3.

---

You said that reapplication, when used in conjunction with behavioral objectives, results in "alteration, re-evaluation and revision." This is a good possibility, but it is only one possibility of many. Reapplication need not alter the activity at all. It may directly implement the activity again with the same or ever-changing conditions and contexts. If something works well, stay with it; make very minor improvements in the implementation of the activity, but feel no obligation to necessarily alter, re-evaluate, and revise everything. You must always evaluate an activity, or re-evaluate it when you reapply it, but in such circumstances you are interested mainly in student progress and not in the efficacy of instruction. Go back to Frame 3 and find a more appropriate answer.

---

You said that the behavioral objective that best reduces variables is B:

Given ten selected examples of songs from the song series, each student will demonstrate his comprehension of musical form by identifying each as AB, ABA, or AABA form, with ninety percent accuracy.

Sorry, this objective includes multiple variables. Though more than one variable need not constitute a weakness (as with behaviors such as analysis, which involve several different behaviors), this particular example has made an unnecessary confusion of behaviors. "To comprehend" is not necessarily dependent on "to identify," nor does the latter necessarily manifest the former. It is quite possible for students to correctly "identify" something without truly "comprehending" it. In any case, comprehension of musical form is a broad and multifaceted quality. The mere identification of, or even comprehension of, the three small part forms herein specified does not constitute "comprehension of musical form." At best, it could constitute a comprehension of only the three forms specified.

It would be a far safer undertaking to insure that the identification of the forms did in fact reflect comprehension. To do this, an additional overt response may be warranted. This might involve a verbal description or explanation of the forms in question. It might involve dealing with the factors that cause the three forms in question to have "form." Some additional overt behavior, or many future behaviors, would be necessary to be sure that this objective successfully attained its goal.

Go back to Frame 6 and make another choice for question 1.

---

*From Frame 2*                                                          Frame 24

You answered that revision, as an element in the correct use of behavioral objectives, involves "planning all subsequent instruction on the basis of the evaluation phase." This is correct. Revision involves six possible courses of action based on the results of the evaluation: (A) augmenting or reinforcing, (B) reviewing or restructuring, and (C) replacing or retaining. Remember, the planning does not need to result in a purely linear sequence, with each activity serving as the basis for the next. Frequently, an activity is undertaken and evaluated and revisions are made for reapplication at some time in the future, with intervening activities (perhaps serving to improve readiness) separating the revision from its reapplication. Go to page 286, below the line.

---

*From Frame 1*                                                          Frame 25

Your answer that evaluation, used in conjunction with a behavioral objective, results in "grading" is definitely incorrect. Grading all lessons can cause youngsters many problems. They may become apprehensive about failure and, thus, their response is not freely given. This is especially true where affective responses are at stake. Grades also place a premium on extrinsic reward rather than the intrinsic values of the achievement itself. Finally, grades add nothing to a student's self-evaluation. Projects accepted or returned with comments, corrections, and suggestions are very useful and require no additional value judgment in the form of an arbitrary symbol.

Go back to Frame 1 and choose another answer.

You said that evaluation, revision, and reapplication are three factors in the use of behavioral objectives that are "considered at all times for student grading." No so. In fact, these steps most usually are not undertaken as a basis for a grade, but as a basis for future planning. The application of grades as a result of considering these three elements would severely diminish the effectiveness of behavioral objectives since students would become increasingly "uptight" about their participation. Go back to Frame 4 and choose another answer for question 1.

You said that reapplication, when used in conjunction with behavioral objectives, results in "refinement, development, and transfer." This is correct. By continually reapplying learnings based on prior behavior in any of the three ways given (reapplying with *minor changes,* reapplying in *similar but different circumstances,* and reapplying in *vastly different contexts*), the opportunity, at least, for the learning to be refined, developed, and transferred is provided. The idea is to reapply learnings first undertaken in quite simple terms in continually more sophisticated situations created especially for that purpose.

Go to Frame 4.

The lesson was:

Given ten aural examples of songs in duple and triple meters, each student will correctly identify each meter by writing a 2 or a 3 on his answer sheet with at least eighty percent success after three sessions, and will do so consistently in subsequent lessons throughout the year.

You should have listed at least these five planning considerations:

1. The teacher must prepare at least ten examples of duple and triple meters, and arrange them in a mixed order of presentation. If the second and third sessions are to be truly effective, it would be wise to have at least one other set of songs in order to avoid the possibility that the class might come to recognize the songs and not the meters. In all cases the songs should clearly manifest the meters in question.

2. Since each student will covertly identify the meters by the overt behavior of writing on paper, both paper and pencil should be available in the (almost predictable) event that not everyone will come to class adequately supplied. If this activity is used with younger children, it would help to have a prenumbered place on the paper for each example.

3. Since the answer sheets will eventually be collected by the teacher after the third session (this would seem to be the most efficient way to evaluate the lesson), it would seem necessary to instruct each youngster to write his or her name on the paper.

4. Since three sessions of listening (identifying) are planned, provision must be made for discussion, explanation, and clarification of errors made during the first two sessions. Thus, during the first and second listening, each answer will be reviewed by the teacher in whatever way or terms seem appropriate (verbally; by having class move to the meter; and so forth) to enable those who made mistakes to understand and overcome the sources of their errors. Whether this process is to be done by considering each example one at a time or by considering the answers after the complete group of ten has been heard will be decided by the teacher as well.

5. Last, and not least, the provision "to do so consistently throughout the year" should serve as a reminder to the teacher to reapply these learnings at various relevant times throughout the year, and to use each such instance as evidence of learning or the need for review or more experience.

Go to page 290, below the line.

# a bibliography
# for teachers

BENNER, CHARLES H., *Teaching Performing Groups*. Washington, D.C.: Music Educators National Conference, 1972.

BERLEANT, ARNOLD, *The Aesthetic Field: A Phenomenology of Aesthetic Experience*. Springfield, Ill.: Charles C. Thomas, Publisher, 1970.

BIEHLER, ROBERT F., *Psychology Applied to Teaching*. Boston: Houghton Mifflin Co., 1971.

BROWN, GEORGE ISAAC, *Human Teaching for Human Learning: An Introduction to Confluent Education*. New York: The Viking Press, Inc., Esalen Books, 1971.

BRUNER, JEROME S., *The Process of Education*. New York: Random House, Vintage Books, 1963.

CATHER, WILLA, "Paul's Case," in *Youth and the Bright Medusa*. New York: Alfred A. Knopf, Inc., 1920; or, in Speare, Edmund M., ed., *A Pocket Book of Short Stories*. New York: Simon & Schuster, Inc., Washington Square Press, 1969.

CRONBACH, LEE J., *Educational Psychology*. New York: Harcourt Brace Jovanovich, Inc., 1963.

DEBONO, EDWARD, *New Think*. New York: Avon Books, 1971.

———, *Lateral Thinking: Creativity Step by Step*. New York: Harper & Row, 1970.

DEWEY, JOHN, *Experience and Education*. New York: Collier Books, 1971.

———, *Art as Experience*. New York: Putnam's and Coward McCann, 1959.

DUEKSEN, GEORGE L., *Teaching Instrumental Music*. Washington, D.C.: Music Educators National Conference, 1972.

FOWLER, CHARLES B., "Discovery: One of the Best Ways to Teach a Musical Concept," *Music Educators Journal*, 57, No. 2 (October 1970), 25.

FOWLER, CHARLES B., ed., et al., "Technology in Music Teaching," *Music Educators Journal*, 57, No. 5 (January 1971), entire issue.

FRIEDENBERG, EDGAR Z., *Coming of Age in America: Growth and Acquiescence.* New York: Random House, Vintage Books, 1965.

———, *The Dignity of Youth and Other Atavisms.* Boston: Beacon Press, 1966.

———, *The Vanishing Adolescent.* New York: Dell Publishing Co., Inc., Delta Books, 1968.

GARDNER, HOWARD, *The Arts and Human Development.* New York: John Wiley & Sons, 1973.

GARDNER, JOHN W., *Excellence: Can We Be Equal and Excellent Too?* New York: Harper & Row, Harper Colophon, 1962.

———, *Self-Renewal: The Individual and The Innovative Society.* New York: Harper & Row, Harper Colophon, 1965.

GAUDRY, ERIC, and CHARLES D. SPIELBERGER. *Anxiety and Educational Achievement.* Sydney, Australia: John Wiley & Sons Australasia Pty. Ltd., 1971.

GERHARD, MURIEL, *Effective Teaching Strategies With the Behavioral Outcomes Approach.* West Nyack, N.Y.: Parker Publishing Co., Inc., 1971.

GHISELIN, BREWSTER, ed., *The Creative Process.* New York: The New American Library, Mentor Books, n.d.

GOODMAN, PAUL, *Growing Up Absurd.* New York: Randon House, Vintage Books, 1960.

GORDON, EDWIN, *The Psychology of Music Teaching.* Englewood Cliffs, N.J.: Prentice-Hall, Inc., 1971.

HOLT, JOHN, *The Underachieving School.* New York: Dell Publishing Co., Inc., Laurel Ed., 1972.

ILLICH, IVAN, *Deschooling Society.* New York: Harper & Row, Harrow Books, 1972.

JONES, RICHARD M., ed., *Contemporary Educational Psychology: Selected Essays.* New York: Harper & Row, Harper Torchbooks, 1967.

KAGAN, JEROME, ed., *Creativity and Learning.* Boston: Beacon Press, 1970.

KELLEY, EARL C., *In Defense of Youth.* Englewood Cliffs, N.J.: Prentice-Hall, Inc., Spectrum Books, 1962.

KIRSCHENBAUM, HOWARD, SIDNEY B. SIMON, and RODNEY W. NAPIER, *Wadja-get? The Grading Game in American Education.* New York: Hart Publishing Co., Inc., 1971.

KNELLER, GEORGE F., *Existentialism and Education.* New York: John Wiley and Sons, Inc., 1967.

KOHL, HERBERT, *The Open Classroom.* New York: The New York Review, distributed by Random House, Inc., Vintage Books, 1969.

KRATHWOHL, DAVID R., BENJAMIN S. BLOOM, and BERTRAM B. MASIA, *Taxonomy of Educational Objectives. The Classification of Educational Goals. Handbook II: Affective Domain.* New York: David McKay Company, Inc., 1971.

LABUTA, JOSEPH A., "Accent on the Output," *Music Educators Journal,* 59, No. 1 (September 1972), 53.

LANGER, SUSANNE K., *Philosophical Sketches.* Baltimore: The John Hopkins University Press, 1962.

———, *Problems of Art.* New York: Charles Scribner's Sons, 1957.

LARSEN, EARNEST, *You Try Love and I'll Try Ajax.* Liquori, Mo.: Liquorian Books, 1969.

LARSON, RICHARD, "Behaviors and Values: Creating a Synthesis," *Music Educators Journal*, 60, No. 2 (October 1973), 40.

LATHROP, ROBERT L., "The Psychology of Music and Music Education," *Music Educators Journal*, 56, No. 6 (February 1970), 47.

LEONARD, GEORGE B., *Education and Ecstasy*. New York: Dell Publishing Co., Inc., Delta Books, 1968.

LIVESLEY, W. J., and D. B. BROMLEY. *Person Perception in Childhood and Adolescence*. London: John Wiley & Sons Ltd., 1973.

MALPASS, LESLIE F., ed., et al., *Human Behavior*. New York: McGraw-Hill Book Co., 1965.

————, *Social Behavior*. New York: McGraw-Hill Book Co., 1967.

MARTIN, J. H., and CHARLES H. HARRISON, *Free to Learn: Unlocking and Ungrading American Education*. Englewood Cliffs, N.J.: Prentice-Hall, Inc., Spectrum Books, 1972.

MASLOW, ABRAHAM H., *Toward a Psychology of Being*. New York: Van Nostrand Reinhold Co., Insight Books, 1968.

MERCER, R. JACK, "Is the Curriculum the Score—or More?" *Music Educators Journal*, 58, No. 6 (February 1972), 51.

MUUS, ROLF E., *Theories of Adolescence*, 2nd ed. New York: Random House, 1968.

NAPLES, JOHN T., "Existentialism and Aesthetic Education," *Music Educators Journal*, 58, No. 3 (November 1971), 26.

O'BRIEN, JAMES P., "Stop the Conveyor Belt—the Kids Want to Get Off," *Music Educators Journal*, 58, No. 9 (May 1972) 25.

POSTMAN, NIEL, and CHARLES WEINGARTNER, *Teaching as a Subversive Activity*. New York: Dell Publishing Co., Inc., Delta Books, 1969.

REGELSKI, THOMAS A., "Self-Actualization in Creating and Responding to Art," *Journal of Humanistic Psychology*, 13, No. 4 (Fall 1973), 57.

————, "Towards Musical Independence," *Music Educators Journal*, 55, No. 7 (March 1969), 77.

REIMER, BENNETT, *A Philosophy of Music Education*. Englewood Cliffs, N.J.: Prentice-Hall, Inc., 1970.

ROSENBERG, MILTON J., et al., *Attitude Organization and Change*. New Haven: Yale University Press, 1966.

SCHWADRON, ABRAHAM A., *Aesthetics: Dimensions for Music Education*. Washington, D.C.: Music Educators National Conference, 1967.

SHERMAN, ROBERT W., "Creativity and the Condition of Knowing in Music," *Music Educators Journal*, 58, No. 2 (October 1971) 18 (Part I); 58, No. 3 (November 1971), 59 (Part II); 58, No. 4 (December 1971), 48 (Part III).

SHOSTROM, EVERETT L., *Man, The Manipulator: The Inner Journey from Manipulation to Actualization*. New York: Bantam Books, Inc., 1968.

SILBERMAN, CHARLES E., *Crisis In the Classroom: The Remaking of American Education*. New York: Random House, Vintage Books, 1970.

SMITH, RALPH A., ed., *Aesthetics and Criticism in Art Education. Problems in Defining, Explaining, and Evaluating Art*. Chicago: Rand McNally & Co., 1966.

THOMAS, RONALD B., *M.M.C.P. Synthesis*. Media Materials, Inc. (Box 533, Bardonia, N.Y., 10954), n.d.

THOMSON, ROBERT, *The Psychology of Thinking*. Baltimore: Penguin Books, Inc., 1959.

TOMAS, VINCENT, ed., *Creativity in the Arts*. Englewood Cliffs, N.J.: Prentice-Hall, Inc., 1964.

WEINSTEIN, GERALD, and MARIO D. FANTANI, eds., *Towards Humanistic Education—A Curriculum of Affect*. A Ford Foundation Report. New York: Praeger Publishers, 1970.

WOODRUFF, ASAHEL D., "How Music Concepts Are Developed," *Music Educators Journal*, 56, No. 6 (February 1970), 51.

———, "Open Up the Well of Feelings," *Music Educators Journal*, 58, No. 1 (September 1971), 21.

WRIGHT, CHARLES R., *Mass Communication: A Sociological Perspective*. New York: Random House, 1962.

ZIMMERMAN, MARILYN PFLEDERER, "Percept and Concept: Implications of Piaget," *Music Educators Journal*, 56, No. 6 (February 1970), 49.

# index

*Page numbers for programming frames are in italics.*

Accountability, 174
Activity for learning, 65–67
Acts. *See also* Reinforcement; Response, overt
  coordinated with cues, 215–16
  mental, 175–76
  physical, 175–76
Adolescence, 99–101
  conformity, 104–6
  conscientious, 104–6, 139
  feelings, 180–83
  independence, 104, 106
  individualism, 99–101
  learning "contracts," 299–301
  musical values, 180–83
  peer group, 100, 105, 148, 153
  problems:
    attention, 124
    girls', 123–24
    listening, 124–25
    seating, 124
    singing, 121–22
  self-image, 103, 107
  stable/rational, 104–6, *135, 153, 155*
  syndromes, 104–6
  traits, 103–7, *129–30, 142–43*
  unstable/irrational, 104–6, *139, 144, 148, 153*
Affection. *See also* Feeling response; Feelings; Response, affective
  in cognition, 207–8
  in meaning, 8
Art:
  and behaviorism, 163–64

Art (*cont.*)
  functions, *189, 193,* 196–97
  purposes, 163–64
  symbols, 165–66, 179
Arts education:
  and facts, 165, 167–68, 178–79, *192–93*
  for "life," 163–65
  music, 164–66
  philosophy, 2
  problem solving, 164
  purposes, 163–65, *189–90, 193–94, 197, 201, 202, 203*
Atomism, 167, *190–91*
  defined, 174, *186, 190–91*
Attention span, listening, 124–27
Attitudes:
  administrator's, 126–27
  community, 126–27
  and concepts, 111
  in meaning, 8
  and mistakes, 74–76
  and motivation, 67–70, 111
  musical, 63, 64, 167, *204*
  values, 111–12 (*see also* Values)
Aural skills, 124–25. *See also* Ear; Listening
Avocation, 101
  musical, 47–48, 95

Band instruction, examples, 48, *51, 52–53, 53–54, 54, 56, 57–58, 58, 80, 81, 83, 87, 131, 133, 139,* 167, *250–52, 255–56, 259–61, 269.*

Band instruction, examples (*cont.*)
>    *See also* Instrumental lessons;
>    Musical performance
Behavior. *See also* Response
>    adaptive, 46, 74–77, *81–82, 85,* 87,
>         *89, 90, 91–92,* 95
>    affective:
>         covert, 210–13, 226, *230–31, 233,*
>              253
>         variables, 210–13, 226, *230, 233,*
>              *249,* 253
>    change in, 159–60
>    cognitive:
>         covert, 207–10, 226, *230, 233,* 249
>         variables, 207–10, 226, *230, 233*
>    conditioned, 111, 280
>    covert, 169–72, 175–76, 219–20, 280
>         in objectives, 247
>         student awareness, 299–301
>    evidence of learning, 4
>    growth-typical, 99–101, *128, 134,*
>         *138–39, 142–43*
>    increasing frequency, 4–5, 11
>    mental, 184
>    musical, 38–39, 49, *84,* 176, *198,* 206,
>         219–20, 221, 228–29
>         self-rewarding, 112
>    nonadaptive, 74–77, 96
>    observable, 72–74
>    operant, 174–76, *187, 190–91,* 204
>    overt, 94–96, 100, 159, *159–60,* 162,
>         169, 175–76, *195,* 207–8, 280
>         and covert compared, 73
>         making forms, 221–24, 227, *233,*
>              249
>         in objectives, 247
>         performing forms, 224–25, 227, *233*
>         second in objectives, 249, 253
>         student awareness, 299–310
>         verbal forms, 220–21, 227, *233,* 249
>    problems, 69, 94, 96–98, 111, 113
>         administrators, 126–27
>         attention, 124
>         girls', 123–24
>         listening, 124–25
>         physical, 121
>         seating, 124
>         singing, 121–22
>    psychomotor:
>         covert, 213–18, *231–32, 233,* 237–
>              38
>         variables, *231–32, 233, 237–38*

Behavior (*cont.*)
>    reading backwards, 174
>    thwarted, 74–76, 87
>    uniform, 64–65
Behaviorism, 159–63, *184–88, 187, 191,*
>    *195, 199*
>    and art, 163–64
>    and arts education, 164–65
>    criticism, 161–62, 206
>         by Langer, 160–62
>    feeling response, 160–68

Choice. *See* Decision making
Chorus instruction, examples: 5, *24, 28–*
>    *29, 30, 35,* 48, *56, 85,* 121–23,
>    *133,* 155–56, 167, 225, 254, *266–*
>    *67, 268–69, 269–71,* 277
Cognition, 7. *See also* Behavior, cogni-
>    tive
Combs, Arthur E., quoted, 161, 169, 174
Concepts:
>    artistic, 197
>    and attitudes, 111
>    developing, 10–15, *21–22, 22,* 27–28,
>         *28–29, 33–34, 38–39, 138–39,*
>         164–65, 167, 169
>    empathy with, 207, 209, 226, *230,*
>         *238–39*
>    in meaning, 8
>    musical, 41, 95
>    as tendencies, 15
>    verbalized, 14–15, *27–28,* 138–39
Conditioning, operant, 164, 174–76, *187,*
>    *190–91, 198*
>    and performance, 176–77
Confirmation of an act, 42, 44, 74–76,
>    *81–82,* 96
Conformity, 99, 100, 112, *131, 136, 137,*
>    *140–41, 143, 145, 148*
>    curriculum for, 102
Consequences of an act. *See* Confirma-
>    tion of an act; Contradiction of
>    an act; Reinforcement
Conservation, 7, *19, 24, 25, 30–32, 36,*
>    *36–37,* 95. *See also* Transfer of
>    learning
Contradiction of an act, 42, 44, 74–76,
>    *81–82,* 96
Creativity, 113–14
Cronbach, Lee J., quoted, 6, 9, 65

Cues:
  aural, 44–46, *52, 60–61,* 95
  coordinating with acts, 213, 215–16
  decision making, 71, 75
  kinesthetic, 213
  perceptual, 42
  performance, 45
  relevant, 42
  visual, 44–46, *52, 60–61,* 95
Curriculum:
  activity-oriented, 111
  for conformity, 102, 111, *140–41, 143, 145, 148, 150*
  developmental, 66, 71
  facilitating transfer, 294
  implementing, 292–94
  for "life," 102–3, *143, 147–48, 151*
  organization, 102–3
  permissipline, 115–18
  permissiveness, 145–46
  planning, 65, 66–67, *79–80,* 88, 95, *128–29, 134–35, 139, 143,* 168, 169–74
    collective, 291–92
    long-term objectives, 290–94
    systematic development, 291
  sequential, 66, 71
  spiral, 71

Decision making, 70–71, *81, 86–87,* 95, 116
  conceptual basis, 14
  as interpretation, 70–71
Delacroix, Eugène, quoted, 158
Discipline. *See also* Behavior, problems
  censure, 109
  control devices, 98, 107–12
  control problems, 96–97, 104–7, 111
  defined, 97–98
  punishment, 108–10
    scolding, 108–10
    singing, 122
  self-, 97, 112
  symptoms, 98
  teacher patience, 98
  variables, 127–28

Ear, inner, 44–45, 118, 217–18
Education, confluent, 175
Experience:
  "felt," 162, 164, *188*

Experience (*cont.*)
  indirect vicarious, 9
  inductive, 9, 15, *21, 26–27, 32–33, 37–38*
  inner, 163, 200–201
  personal, 8, 65–67, 71, 94–95
  physical, 160
  psychical, 160

Feedback, 45, *52, 57,* 73–74, 87, 118, 172, 213–14, 247, 254
Feeling response, 3, 164, 165, 168, 175–76, 179, *184–85, 203*
  and behaviorism, 160–68
  eliciting, 170–71
  overt, 170–71
Feelings:
  actual, 203
  and art, 10, 163–65, 177–80, *196–97*
  behavioral objectives, 175
  behaviorist objection, 159
  covert, 175–76
  "created," 203
  educating, 163–64, 182–83
  "felt life," 3, *88,* 94, 166–67, *189, 201,* 210
  Langer's definition, 161–62
  as Mind, 162, *184, 188, 191–92*
  musical, 178
  objectified in art, *203*
  overt, 180
  quality, 178
  reading backwards, 180
  teaching, *143,* 167–68
  in various musics, 180–83
Form, expressive, 3
Friedenberg, Edgar, cited, 101

General music classes, examples: 7–9, 16, *18, 19, 20, 21, 22, 24, 26, 27–28, 28, 30–31, 32, 33, 34, 34–35, 36, 37, 38, 39,* 43, 55–56, 58, 69, 75, 76, *79, 80, 81, 82, 83, 85, 86, 87–88, 89–90,* 94–96, 113, 116, 117, 121–23, *124–27, 128–29, 131, 132–33, 134–35, 138–39, 141–42, 143, 145, 146–48, 151,* 170–71, 172, *230–31, 234, 235, 235–36, 238–39, 241–42, 243,* 249, 253, 257, *268, 269, 271–72, 273–74, 276,* 290–91, 292, 293,

General music classes, examples (*cont.*) 299, *308–9, 310, 311, 312, 314–16, 317–18*

Goals:
  as behavioral objectives, 170
  and creativity, 113–14, 171
  extrinsic, 174–75
  instructional, 69–70, 261
  open systems, 169
Gordon, Edwin, cited, 214
Grading:
  and administrators, 301–2
  dangers, 70, 73–74
  deemphasizing, 303, 305
  and discipline, 303
  and motivation, 68, 70, 119–20, 303–4
  musical performance, 120, 304–5
  as negative reinforcement, 120, 303
  practicality, 172
  precautions, *283*
  problems, 119–20
  and student relations, 303–4
  tests, 75
  using behavioral objectives, 301–5, 316

Harris, Sydney J., quoted, 93, 109
Heterogeneous classes, 100
Homogeneous classes, 64, *88,* 100

Illich, Ivan, quoted, 40, 62
Individual:
  differences, 106
  feelings, 178
  instruction, 71–72, 75–76, 79–80, 89–90, 254
  maladjustment, 103
  progress (grading), 120
  "the ultimate unit," 143, 170
Instrumental lessons, examples, *19–20, 47, 56, 58, 59, 81, 82,* 87, *91–92,* 95, 118, 120, *132, 149–50,* 169, 213–18, 223, *224–25, 231–32, 234–35, 237–38, 239, 242–43, 250–52, 265–66, 275–76, 277–78,* 290–91, 297–98
Interpretation. *See* Decision making; Reinterpretation
Invariant qualities. *See* Conservation; Transfer of learning

Junior High School, 101, 299–300
  singing, 123

Langer, Susanne K., cited, *143,* 167, *184–85, 188, 189, 191–92, 193, 196–97, 199, 201, 202–3;* quoted, 1, 3, 157–58, 161, 163, 164, 165, 168, 173, 178, 179, *192, 193, 195, 197*
  on feeling, 1–3, 10
  *Mind,* reviewed, 2
Lasker, Henry, cited, 123
Learning:
  and attitudes, 111
  behavioral, 169–74
  conceptual, 169
  discovery, 113–14, 171, 179, 190
    basis for meaning, 9
  musical, 204
  philosophy, 2
  skilled (*see* Musical performance)
  theory, 15–16
    behavioral, 159–60
  verbal, 166
Lecture, 9, *18,* 22–23, 43, 56, 98, 110
Listening, *19, 22, 24, 25, 28–29, 29–30, 30–31, 31–32, 33–34, 36, 36–37, 38–39, 42–43, 51, 53, 55–56,* 58
  active and passive, 124–25
  developing via performance, 48–49
  directed, 43, 79, 125–26
  visual aids, 42–43, *51, 55–56*

McLuhan, Marshall, quoted, 182, 279
Mager, Robert F., quoted, 244
Maslow, Abraham, cited, 206
Meaning:
  basis in experience, 8–10
  personal, 8–10, 174
  teaching for, 8–10
Media, hot and cool, 182–83
Middle school, 101
Mind:
  and art, 163
  and body, 160
  as feelings, 162, *195, 199–200*
  theory of, 2
Motivation, 95
  extrinsic, 68–70, *80, 83–85,* 174–75, *204*
  imposed, 68–70, *80, 83–85*
  intrinsic, 68–70, *80, 83–85,* 204
  self-, 68–70, *80, 83–85,* 103, 105, 111, 116

Multiple outcomes, 64–66, 100, 117, 170, 212–13
Music:
  human content, *203* (*see also* Feelings)
  listening, 125–26 (*see also* Listening)
  notation, 3
  programmatic, 300
  supervisor, 291–92
  symbolism, 3
  "youth," 180–83
Musical independence, 87, 229
  in performance, 6, 46, 47–48, 58–59, 76–77, 95, *149*, 176
Musical performance:
  affective objectives, 254–55
  "by ear," 44–45
  and cognition, 228–29
  confirmation, 44
  contradiction, 44
  covert behaviors, 213–18
  cues, 44, 45, 46, 52, 60–61, 213–14
  ear training, 217–18
  ensembles, examples, *21, 25, 26–27, 29, 31, 32–33, 37, 37–38, 43, 46, 47, 49, 51, 53–54, 56, 58–59, 60, 75, 81, 85,* 95, 113, 117, 120, 121–23, *128–29, 140–41, 145, 149–50, 151, 155–56,* 166–67, 172, 174–76, 179–80, *186–87, 204, 230,* 250–52, 254–55, 262
    motivation, 198
    objectives, 255–56
  and feelings, 166–67
  in general music, 76–77
  goals, 46–50, 52–53, 55, 57–58, *60*
  grading, 210, 304–5
  improvisation, 118
  mediating responses, 44
  from notation, 43–46
  and operant conditioning, 176–77
  and perception, 44
  practicing, 214–15
  problem solving, 26–27, 32–33, 37–38
  recreation piece, 118
  skills, 176 (*see also* Behavior, psycho-motor)
  small ensembles, 118, *155*
  solo, 118
  stimuli, 42, 44
  and taste development, 76–77
  teaching, *21, 26–27, 32–33, 37–38, 47–49, 51–59, 60*

Musical performance (*cont.*)
  technique, 180
  time factors, 45–46, *52, 54, 57, 59, 61*
Music Appreciation class, examples *22, 24, 28, 30–31, 33, 34, 34–35, 36, 37, 38, 39, 51, 53,* 116, 117, *124–27, 128–29, 132–33, 134–35, 141–42, 143, 146–48, 151,* 169, 170–71, *230, 234, 241–42, 243, 253, 271–72, 276,* 290–91, 292, 293, *308–9, 310, 317–18. See also* General music classes
  in performance classes, 95
Music education profession, 16, 50, 177
Musicianship, 45
  independent (*see* Musical independence)
Music learning:
  activities (situations), 65–67
  conceptual, *20, 26, 32, 37*
  described, 4
  experiential, 8–10
  identifying, 4–8, *18–19, 24, 30, 35, 36,* 49
  misconceptions, 41
  negative, 4, *30*
  structuring, 41–42
Music teacher:
  competencies, 16–17
  contextualists, 203
  expressionists, 202–3
  as facilitator, 41
  patience, 98
  pitfalls, 6–7, 9–10, 13–15, 47–49, 96–97, 166–68, 289–90, 300–305 (*see also* Grading)
  planning, 261–64, 292–95
  purists, 202
  responsibilities, 7, 8–9, 11–12, 46–50, 65–66, 75–76, 79–80, 83, 87–89, 91–92, 94–96, 228–29, 301–5
    discipline, 97–99, 103–12
    roles, 114–15
    success, 177
Music teaching:
  autocratic, 111, 113, 115, *132–33, 133–34, 137–38, 146, 150–51, 155*
  democratic, 114–15, 116, *132–33, 133–34, 146–47, 152, 154*
  to educate, 41
  as a medium, 280

Music teaching (*cont.*)
  misconceptions, 41
  to nurture, 41
  permissive, 113–14, *132–33, 133–34, 136, 141–42, 150, 152–53, 155–56* (*see also* Permissiveness)
  as a science, 306
  styles, 113–19
Music theory classes, examples 15, *21, 27–28, 28, 30–31, 33, 34, 34–35, 36, 37, 38, 39, 80, 81, 82, 83, 86,* 94–96, 116, 117, *124–27, 128–29, 131, 132–33, 134–35, 141–42, 143, 146–48, 151,* 169, *170–71, 231, 234, 238, 241–42, 243, 253, 271–72, 276,* 290–91, *292, 293, 297, 308–9, 310, 317–18.* See *also* General music class
Muus, Rolf E., ed., cited, 101

Objectives:
  arts oriented, 161
  behavioral, 4
    accuracy, 297–98, *308–9, 310, 311–12, 314*
    affective, 169–74, 254–55
    augmenting, 284–86
    conditions, 169–74, *185–86, 188–89, 190, 192–93, 194, 198, 201–2, 203*
    as "contracts," 299–301
    covert variables, 288–89
    designing, 15–16
    elements, 5, 246–48
    as evaluation, 282, 284, *307, 314, 316*
    feeling, 174
    for grades, *316*
    as implementation aids, 289–90, *307–8, 317–18*
    as instruction, 282–88
    interpreting results, 282–88
    long-range (curricular), 290–94
    as a medium, 280
    misconceived, 281
    need for, 261–64
    as personal research, 295, 298
    planning, *186, 202,* 288–90
    planning format, 256–61
    as post-test, 282–88
    precautions, 245–47

Objectives (*cont.*)
  behavioral (*cont.*)
    as pre-test, 282–88
    psychomotor, 255–56
    as reapplication, 286–87, *307, 312, 317*
    reducing variables, 296–98, *308–9, 312–13, 315–16*
    reinforcing, 282–86
    relating, 250–52
    replacing, 282–86
    restructuring, 282–86
    retaining, 284–86
    reviewing, 284–86
    as revision, 284–86, *307, 310, 313–14, 316*
    short-term (daily), 294–95
    systems approach, 282–88, *307, 309–10, 313, 315, 317*
    validity, 297–98, *308–9, 311, 315*
    writing models, *265–78*
  humanistic, 160–61
Orchestral instruction, examples, 48, *56, 129, 151,* 167. See *also* Musical performance

Patience, 98
Peer group. See Adolescence, peer group
Perception:
  and cognition, 207–9
  of cues, 42
  in meaning, 8
  musical, 10–15, *22, 22–34, 28–29, 38–39, 41*
Percepts, 95
  and cognition, 207–8
  mental product, 10–11
Permissipline, 115–18, *131, 132–33, 133, 136–37, 141, 145, 149–50, 150, 153–54, 155, 168, 203*
  defined, 112
  in performance ensembles, 117–18
Permissiveness, 112, 115, 116, 131. See *also* Music teaching
Piaget, Jean, cited, 7
Planning. See Curriculum; Objectives, behavioral
Pratt, Carrol C., quoted, *18*
Preparatory set, 11
Problem solving, 70–71, *81, 86–87,* 95, 116

Problem solving (*cont.*)
  and arts education, 164
  in performance, *26–27, 32–33, 37–38*
Proficiency criteria, 5, 247–48
Puberty, 99–101
Pubescence, 99, *124, 138–39, 142–43*
  traits, *128*
Punishment. *see* Discipline; Reinforcement, negative

Readiness, 11, 12, 64–65, 67, *79–80, 82, 85, 87–88, 89–90,* 95
  for listening, 125–26
  planning for, 283, 294–95
  restricting variables, 227
Reinforcement, 72
  confirmed act, 74–75, 82, *91*
  negative, 74–76, 96, 107–9, *130–31, 135–36, 140, 144, 149*
    grading, 120
  non, 107, *130–31, 135–36, 140, 144, 149*
    "evil eye," 109
    ignore behavior, 110
    remove causes, 110
    verbal, 109–10
  operant, 174–76 (*see also* Conditioning)
  positive, 107–8, 111–12, *130–31, 135–36, 140, 144–45, 149,* 198
Reinterpretation, *90,* 92
  adaptive behavior, 74–76
Response. *See also* Behavior
  affective, 79, 82, 116, 160–68, 168
    as motivation, 212–13
  cognitive, 79, 82
  confirmation, 42
  contradiction, 42
  covert, 5, 10, 65, 168, 173
  creative, 171
  feeling (*see* Feeling response)
  imaginative, 79, 82
  incorrect, 74–77
  individual, 98
  listening, 125–26
  mediating, 42, 44, 45, 46, 52, 54, 95
  multiple, 64–66 (*see also* Multiple outcomes)
  musical, 66
  normalized, 44

Response (*cont.*)
  overt, 5, 10, 65, 66, 72–74, 75, *79–80, 81–82, 85, 87, 89, 90, 91, 91–92,* 169–72, 173, 250
    and covert compared, 73
  physical, *79, 82*
  provisional, 73
    grading, 73
  to stimuli, 10–15
  subjective, 10
  tentative, 73
  variety, 41
  verbal, 66
Rothschild, Lincoln, quoted, 173
Russell, Bertrand, quoted, 205

Sachs, Curt, quoted, 157
Sexual growth, 99–100
Singing activities, 121–22
  and feeling, 166–67
  recommendations for, 121–22
Situation, 65–67. *See also* Learning
Skills. *See* Behavior, psychomotor; Musical performance
Socratic method, 76, 252–54
Stimulus:
  changes of, 7
  defined, 10
  musical, 41, 95
  in performance, 42
Symbol:
  art, 3
  notational, 3, 45

Tendencies:
  from concepts, 15
  transfer of learning, 11 (*see also* Transfer of learning; Conservation)
Time:
  element in objectives, 5, 248
  in teaching performance, 45–46, 52, 54, 57, 59, 61, 213, 215
Transfer of learning, 6–7, 11, 12, *19, 24, 25, 30–31, 31–32, 36, 36–37,* 66, 71, 95, 170. *See also* Conservation
  curriculum for, 290–95

Ungraded schools, 101

Values. *See also* Attitudes
   and behaviorism, 161
   grading judgments, 120, 170
   indicators, 168
   judgment, 116, 283
   musical, of adolescents, 180–83
   personal, 170
   system, 125–26
   teaching, *143, 194*
Variables. *See* Behavior, covert; Behavior, overt
Venture activities, *85*

Verbal behavior. *See* Behavior, overt
Verbalizing. *See also* Behavior, overt; Response, verbal
   concepts, 14–15
Vocation, 47
Voice change in boys, 121–22

Woodruff, Asahel D., cited, 207; quoted, 12, 14
Words and learning, 9–10

Zimmerman, Marilyn P., quoted, 7